DESERT

Jan 21, 1960

To Bob Mc Fadden

with best wishes

George Bauchop (signature)

Congo R.

NAIROBI

MOMBASA

TANGA

ZANZIBAR

DAR-ES-SALAAM

asai R.

EOPOLD-
VILLE

(KA...
ELIS...

N'...
(CO...

Zambesi R.

SELUKWE
(CHROME)

BEIRA

Madagascar

JOHANNES-
BURG

LOURENCO
MARQUES

KIMBERLEY

DURBAN

CAPE
TOWN

EAST LONDON
PORT ELIZABETH

SEAPORTS
SOUTH of SAHARA

The *Eastern Glen* approaching Cape Town

SEAPORTS
SOUTH of SAHARA

The Achievements of an American Steamship Service

by ROBERT GREENHALGH ALBION

*Gardiner Professor of Oceanic History
and Affairs, Harvard University*

With the Collaboration of
JENNIE B. POPE

APPLETON-CENTURY-CROFTS, Inc.
New York

Foreword

To those who thrill to the excitement of salt water and particularly to those whose imaginations tingle at the thought of strange harbors in foreign lands and climates—and what American's imagination does not?—*Seaports South of Sahara* by Robert Greenhalgh Albion is a treat. "Down East" (in New England) the traditions and lore of the sea are deep-rooted and still strong, although a hundred years have passed since the era of the China trade, the clipper ships and the whaling industry. It was in shipping that the economic foundations of this part of the country were laid. The glamor of the windjammer is still bright in the nation.

In this book, however, is the story of nautical enterprise and excitement now in the making; but instead of wooden ships and sail, we read of the evolving steamship of our own times. We read of living men of today who are engaged in stiff international competition to assure the supply of strategic materials for our current industrial-military economy, and of a business struggle equally severe between competing American steamship lines. There is no more exciting area in the world than Africa "South of Sahara," fabulously rich in minerals, starkly savage in its life.

Farrell Lines is making American maritime history. It is demonstrating clearly and emphatically that ships wearing the flag of a nation do in fact stimulate the commerce of that nation. It is demonstrating the cultural exchange which follows in the wake of enlightened trade, thus demonstrating the value of American-flag ocean commerce as an asset to the health and wealth of the United States.

We are indebted to the Farrell family for its wisdom and determination in establishing the South African service, and to

v

Mr. Albion for a bit of current history which has the delightful flavor almost of fiction and which points lessons of importance to those who look upon ships as mere vehicles for the transport of goods, and fail to recognize them as animate bits of our country showing our flag and demonstrating our way of life to the world.

Vice Admiral E. L. Cochrane, USN (Ret.)

Cambridge, Massachusetts
April 1959

Contents

Illustrations

SEAPORTS
SOUTH of SAHARA

Introduction

THREE separate threads run through this book. It is, at one and the same time, a summary account of American maritime policy since 1914; an area study of the coasts and commerce of South, East, and West Africa; and, third, an account of the American-flag steamship service to those regions, initiated by the Shipping Board and continued under the private ownership of the Farrell family. The common denominator, which accounts for that tripartite arrangement, is the "essential trade route" pattern which has been the prime feature of the nation's merchant marine policy and performance since World War I.

The study had its inception in the efforts to find suitable readings on the subject for a course in maritime history. The available material tended to fall into two extremes. On one side were two academic studies, one by a political scientist in 1937 and the other by an economist in 1956; both were strongly critical of the government policy and of the private operators. The alternative lay in a varied array of publications produced under government or shipping industry auspices, much of which was apt to be quite the reverse. There appeared to be a need for an objective study which would give a picture of just how things worked.

It seemed that this could be most effectively achieved if the story centered in intimate detail around the performance of a single fairly typical shipping company. The choice fell upon the Farrell Lines story after Vice Admiral Edward L. Cochrane, wartime Chief of the Bureau of Ships, first Maritime Administrator, and Dean of Engineering and vice president at M.I.T., pointed out that the line had probably done as much as any to promote commerce at both ends of its runs.

The company responded generously and wholeheartedly to the suggestion of using it for a case study of American maritime policy. It was mutually agreed that this was not to be simply a conventional "line history" of the type so common in Britain and so rare in America. Opportunity was given to visit the line's African ports of call from Cape Town up to Zanzibar and from the Canaries down to the Congo, along with their inland outposts at Johannesburg and Nairobi. There was a chance to ask all sorts of questions of everyone from directors to deck hands, and free access was given to the company's archives, even the most confidential. In authorizing this co-operation, the directors had voted that "Farrell Lines as such would have no direct control of the contents of the book." They have fully lived up to that indispensable decision. As a corollary of that, the company is naturally not responsible for opinions which may be expressed in these pages.

The choice of Trade Routes 15-A and 14-1 for the case study was made primarily because of the Farrell performance rather than because of Africa. But, even in the three years of preparing this study, the steadily increasing significance of Africa, not to mention its fascination, has led to a more expanded treatment of the African aspects.

Finally, this study has confirmed my opinion, already held, that the nation's "essential trade route" policy is a most valuable one, producing rich results far beyond its modest cost.

It is out of the question to acknowledge individually here the helpful co-operation received from so many, both inside and outside the Farrell establishment, except to say that I am deeply grateful. But one of those who helped most is not here to receive those thanks; Walter B. McCormick, assistant to the president of Farrell Lines, gave most generously of his time and advice until his death in mid-1957. In this collaboration, my part has once again been the research and the preparation of the first drafts; that of my wife, Jennie Pope Albion, has been the presentation of that material.

R. G. A.

Harvard University

Chapter I

WITHDRAWAL FROM THE SEA

B ETWEEN the Civil War and World War I, the shipping of
the United States gradually relinquished its former commanding position on the longer sea routes. Liners and tramps
under other flags took over the carrying of most of the nation's
exports and imports. By the turn of the century, less than one
tenth of them were being transported in American vessels; the
rest were reaping profits for foreign flags.

Those fifty years of "time out" were all the more surprising in
view of what American vessels had earlier achieved and what
they would accomplish again. From the very first, the colonists
had taken to the sea vigorously and successfully, particularly in
New England where rocks were the only sure and generous crop
of its farms. The colonists wanted goods from England, which
had scant use for what they had to offer in return; so Yankee in-
genuity developed "triangular trades." Codfish and lumber,
for instance, were taken where such products were wanted, usually the West Indies, and where they were exchanged for such
things as sugar and molasses. Then, swapping and reswapping,
the colonists persisted until at last they had the goods that they
themselves needed. By 1700, they had more than a thousand vessels and were laying the foundations of many a seaboard fortune.

The valuable maritime asset of virgin forests of pine and oak
growing close to the water's edge enabled the Americans down
to about 1830 to build vessels 25 to 50 per cent cheaper than the
British could. By the Revolution, British shipowners had bought
large numbers of these bargains; altogether American-built ves-

1

sels were estimated to make up one-third of British tonnage. [1]

Independence changed the maritime picture for the colonies, for the new nation was now outside the rigid British mercantile system. No longer able to function under the Navigation Acts, they were cut off from selling their vessels to the British. American mariners of modest means, shut out of the sugar islands, lost a market for their schooner-loads of salt cod or pine boards, but those with enough resources to sail farther afield could now seek cargoes in regions no longer forbidden them in Eastern and European waters.

Scarcely was that expansion under way, when the United States had its first chance at the rich opportunities in neutral trade during 20-odd years of war between the British and the French. Its merchant marine doubled and redoubled during that "Heroic Age," and its flag was carried into ports all around the world, with high profits at the occasional risk of seizure, until the War of 1812. Many of those distant contacts were to be maintained, however, in the general peace thereafter.

The sailing of the first Black Ball square-rigged packets from New York and Liverpool in January 1818 marked an American achievement, particularly bound up with the central theme of this book, and one that would leave a lasting impression on the world of shipping. This innovation of scheduled line sailings was a combination of two earlier approaches to such service. Official British mail brigs had fairly regular schedules on some important routes from Falmouth, but carried only mail and passengers. Many shipowners of various nations operated vessels as "regular traders" between specific ports, taking cargo for others as well as their own, but instead of fixed sailing dates, they usually waited around until fully laden. The new packets, carrying mail, passengers, and cargo, sailed on definite routes and on fixed days, "full or not full." This was a calculated risk that any loss from leaving on schedule would be more than compensated by the preference of shippers for dependability in place of the uncertainties of "regular traders" and "transient" tramps. With the liners, a shipper, at his convenience, could send his goods to a particular pier—hence the term "berth service"—knowing that the line would take them at its next sailing.

It proved to be a successful gamble; not only did the Black Ball prosper, but so, too, did several rival lines from New York to Liverpool, London, and Le Havre. [2]

The principle of regular line service became more highly developed with the advent of steamships on the longer runs. The "square-riggers on schedule," at the mercy of the winds, could not predict their arrival time; and so their heyday ended with the arrival at New York of the British steamships *Sirius* and *Great Western* from England in 1838. Thereafter, steam became a permanent feature of the North Atlantic shuttle.

With these "mail liners," the subsidy came into world shipping. The early marine engines were so coal-hungry that little space could be left for sufficient cargo to meet expenses. Around 1840, the British government granted mail subsidies on three major routes to companies that have since become outstanding: the Peninsular & Oriental (P & O) to the East; the Royal Mail to the West Indies and later South America; and the Cunard to North America. This was an official realization of the public's interest in mail and passenger service on certain "essential routes" that were vital for communication purposes. During the next few years, further subsidies were granted for line service to South Africa among other regions. These grants were charged usually to the Postmaster General, but sometimes to the Navy on the ground that the vessels could be used in war.

Before long, the United States followed suit during its remarkable decade, 1845–1855, which came to be called the "Golden Age" of its merchant marine. Various different influences served as stimuli, with American shipping responding in magnificent manner. For a few exhilarating years even the time-honored primacy of Britain's Red Ensign was threatened. The ending of Britain's Corn Laws in 1846 opened a market for American grain, while its abolition of the Navigation Acts in 1849 admitted American ships to the China-London trade and to British registry. Also, with the fashion for full skirts, the cotton trade boomed as never before. There was a tremendous influx of Irish and German immigrants. The acquisition of California, followed by the Gold Rush, led to the brilliant development of the big, beautiful California clippers, in which carrying capacity was sacrificed for speed. By the mid-1840's, Congress was voting subsidies for steamship lines to Le Havre, to Bremen, to the American west coast by way of Panama, and to the New York-Liverpool run. This last produced the spectacular performance of the Collins liners, which established a better speed record than the Cunarders for a few years. [3]

For a while, the American merchant marine almost equaled the British in size and exceeded it in quality; the British themselves bore testimony to the prestige of American shipbuilders and shipmasters. [4] Altogether, one would have to go back to the days of the Elizabethan Sea Dogs or of Holland's subsequent maritime supremacy to match the pride and enthusiasm that pervaded American seaports in the thrill-packed early 1850's—the high-water mark of the old merchant marine.

Before the decade was out, the ebb tide would be beginning to run strongly. The American flag gradually disappeared from the distant sea routes. Between 1860 and 1910, the tonnage registered for foreign trade fell from 2,546,000 to 782,000, and the percentage of cargo carried in American bottoms from 66.5 to 8.7. Yet the import and export totals increased in value from $762 million to $2,983 million, a rate even sharper than the shipping decline. [5]

Numerous factors were involved in the decline, which was to last for a full half century. The California market no longer called for costly clipper speed. The Collins subsidy was canceled, after two spectacular disasters. The flood of immigrants began to fall off. The Panic of 1857 played its part. Then came the Civil War, which may be blamed only for accelerating the trend. The Confederate cruisers caught the imagination by leaving flaming wrecks of Yankee square-riggers all the way from the Straits of Sunda to the Bering Sea—even today the Malays of Cape Town sing about the *Alabama*. Actually the raiders caught only one per cent, but fear, clearly reflected in the increased war risk insurance rates, caused some 400,000 tons of those vessels to "flee the flag" into foreign registry. The influence of the ship-building industry in Congress was to prevent their readmission.

More fundamental causes of the "Dark Age" began to appear after the war. Some would explain it in very general terms: the diversion of considerable capital from shipping to industry and railroads; the shift in national interest from the sea to the rapidly opening West; or the conservatism that clung to wooden hulls and paddle wheels and sail when other nations had discarded them for iron and propellers and steam. But one must look across the Atlantic at British and German shipbuilding and shipping for a more direct reason.

Decade after decade, as those maritime systems expanded in size and power, the American flag appeared less and less on the distant seas. The United States still kept a respectable total tonnage, protected from that foreign competition, in the coastal trade and on inland rivers and lakes, in steam as well as sail. For a while, too, in foreign trade, the tramp Down East square-riggers still carried on their losing struggle; but in steam, the handful of subsidized lines were woefully few. The government subsidy policy was too spasmodic and inadequate to accomplish much. Occasional acts from 1864 onward produced a temporary line to Brazil, the more important and longer-lived Pacific Mail service to the Far East, and the fairly successful American Line route on the transatlantic main line, already well served by foreign-flag liners. Some shorter lines to the Caribbean completed the meager list. Even the comprehensive mail subsidy act of 1891 had rates too low for substantial results. [6] When the nation eventually returned to the distant sea lanes in World War I, it had to start from scratch, but had valuable precedents in the network of foreign cargo liners already serving the essential trade routes.

A major factor in that successful foreign competition was the complete reversal of comparative costs in shipbuilding. Now the cost across the Atlantic often was a third less than in American yards, partly because iron or steel sources for steamship hulls were closer at hand, and greater technological advances were being made in Europe in the rapid development of steam. The new compound engine enabled a ship to go much further on a ton of coal; and this left more space for carrying heavy bulk cargoes. The Suez Canal, opened in 1869, boosted steam traffic, being unfitted for sail. Moderate-sized steam freighters began to be built in such large numbers by the mid-1870's that the shipyards were said to be making them by the mile and cutting them off to the owner's order. These began to crowd the sailing vessels out of the most important trades except on the extremely long routes.

If American shipowners could have had their way, they would have bought those cheaper foreign ships, but they were blocked until the eve of World War I by the stronger influence in Congress of the shipbuilders of Pennsylvania and Maine. Instead, because of the high cost of operating under the American flag, on top of the higher initial building costs in American yards, various investors in the United States began to operate under foreign flags. As late as the turn of the century, a freighter of 8,000 gross tons cost about $450,000 in the United States and only $350,000 in Britain; it cost $860 a month to operate a small American freighter as against $491 for a British. [7]

The most ambitious venture was J. P. Morgan's International Mercantile Marine, created in 1902 to dominate the North Atlantic. It included the White Star and other lines under British registry, the Belgian Red Star, and an American-flag line. The "Great White Fleet" of United Fruit, many Standard Oil tankers, W. R. Grace's service to Chile and Peru, and the nucleus of the United States Steel's Isthmian Line were all under British registry. It has been estimated that in 1901 "the 672,000 gross-ton American-controlled foreign-flag fleet nearly equaled in size the 880,000 gross-ton American-flag fleet in the foreign carrying trade." [8] It might be said that the United States was using Britain's Red Ensign as a "flag of convenience" just as later, it would use the flags of Panama and Liberia for similar reasons.

Those efficient, economical freighters of the 1870's contributed much to the immediate British and German success by making possible the development of cargo lines. In later years, American policy would long seek to emulate this significant step. Yet for all its importance, the cargo liner has seldom been appreciated by the public, to whom an ocean-going steamship is apt to mean either a crack passenger liner or a tramp. But a cargo liner is as different from a tramp as a bus from a taxi; the first is a common carrier that comes along at a scheduled time to pick up whatever is going its particular way, while the second is "chartered" by a person to go wherever he sees fit.

Before long British and German cargo lines were operating on most of the important world routes. Manufacturers in industrialized centers could now count on keeping their customers regularly supplied in all distant areas, and could also rely on dependable delivery of raw material imports from those sources. If a whole shipload of sugar from Cuba, cotton from New Orleans, or iron ore from Sweden were needed by such a manufacturer, he might charter a tramp steamer for the purpose, but normally, for "less than shipload" lots, he relied upon the cargo liner, which would probably sail on its outward passage with scores of different commodities for hundreds of different consignees. In every seaport of importance in the whole world, these cargo liners became regular visitors.

Many such lines served United States ports, connecting them with various regions beyond the seas, though not as adequately as Britain and Germany were linked by their own lines to distant markets. Naturally, foreign-flag shipping did not exert itself to develop American export of commodities, which would compete with their own. Many distant cargoes, moreover, such as Australian and South African wool, Ceylon and Indian tea, and Malayan rubber, reached the United States only after being carried hundreds of miles out of their way for transshipment at the so-called "London entrepôt" or some other British or German port. Dating back to medieval Venice and Genoa, such re-export systems were among the most profitable roles in commercial history, being interposed between the producer and the consumer to collect tribute.

American imports of South African wool illustrate the workings of the "London entrepôt." In 1858, the direct imports came to $550,000; in 1913, they were only $35,000; and in 1920 had risen to $12,700,000. [9] The low 1913 figure meant that America's substantial purchases of that wool were coming by way of England, presumably in British cargo liners—some 2,400 miles out of the way. [10]

Other far-reaching activities in the maritime-commercial-financial field, by Britain and also Germany, were the financing of imports and exports for many nations, particularly in the London money market, while much of the marine insurance underwriting came through the the services of Lloyd's which itself was in a position to exert pressure in the shipping field. Heavy overseas investments long had meant remote control by those maritime giants—such as Britain's in South African gold mines, Malayan tin and rubber, South American cattle, and railroads all about the world. The choice of ships to carry the equipment for such varied interests and their products could depend on such control, implemented overseas by colonies of British and German businessmen and officials, including the agents or representatives of the steamship lines. [11]

The extent to which foreign-flag ships were taking over American contacts with distant lands is shown by the sailings from New York to other continents in 1913. Out of the total 1,855 sailings, American-flag ships accounted for only 119. Britain had a long lead at 850, followed by Germany at 348, France at 174, Italy at 94, and Holland at 87, with lesser totals for eight other flags. The most popular destination was western Europe from Hamburg down to Bordeaux at 470, followed by the British Isles at 375, the Mediterranean at 304, and the east coast of South America at 262; the African total was only 39, composed of 31 British and eight German ships. The leading lines were Hamburg-American at 152, North German Lloyd at 112, White Star at 106 and Cunard at 91. [12]

Fairly typical of what was happening on most of those distant sea lanes on the eve of World War I was the line service of the British and Germans from New York to South Africa. Since this study is primarily concerned with the later impact of American-flag service on that same run, those earlier foreign-flag lines are pertinent background.

Regular steamship service from New York to Cape Town and ports beyond went back two decades to 1893. Before that, American-flag sailing vessels in considerable numbers had made their way to and from South, East, and West Africa. But when the discovery of gold in the Johannesburg area in 1886 stimulated the South African demand for mining equipment and certain other American products, exporters at New York and other ports found the sailing vessels unable to meet the needs for regular scheduled services. Six years later, several New York concerns joined in exploring the possibilities of starting steamship service, but nothing came of it.

The following year, 1893, four of the British-flag lines well established in the United Kingdom-South African trade combined almost simultaneously into two services which would continue on that run for more than half a century. Senior, in point of time, the Union Line had maintained subsidized mail service since 1853 between Southampton and South African ports; and since 1873, had encountered strenuous competition from the Castle Line. The latter was headed by Sir Donald Currie, the most dynamic figure in the whole story of shipping to South Africa. In 1900, he would absorb the older Union Line to form the Union-Castle Line, whose big mail steamers have been the most impressive regular visitors to Cape Town and other ports ever since. [13] Also in the new movement were the Clan Line, owned and operated by Cayzer, Irvine & Company, who would ultimately secure control of Union-Castle in 1956; and Bucknall Brothers' British and Colonial Line. The latter would be absorbed in Sir John Ellerman's huge shipping combine and would be known as the Ellerman-Bucknall Line.

The first of those new services from New York to South Africa bore the trade name of the "American and African Line" and was a joint enterprise of Currie's Castle Line and the Bucknall Brothers' British and Colonial Line. Its first voyage was in May 1893; the chartered freighter *Worcester* sailed from New York for Cape Town and beyond with a general cargo of some 2,000 tons. A few weeks later, in June, the other two of that competitive quartet went into action under their own names as the Union and Clan Line, and despatched the *Arroyo*, also chartered, on the same run, with 18,000 cases of oil as the principal part of her cargo. [14] After Union and Castle merged in 1900, the Union-Castle Line participated in both combined services from New York.

Some of the initiative for drawing these services to New York came from that city. Two decades later, the senior partner of Norton & Sons (later Norton, Lilly & Company), shipping agents, told how this had come about in "1892 or 1893," when his firm, which "operated sailing vessels to South Africa . . . thought it was time to change" to steamers. They had been about to go "into the market to charter," when a cable from London asked them to await the arrival of "a representative of Donald Currie." As a result, the firm became the agents for the American and African Line, receiving a commission for securing and loading its cargo. [15]

The competition between the original lines was orderly and not too strong since this new service was merely a sideshow to their main routes from Britain to the Cape. It was undertaken primarily to provide the growing South African market with American products not easily available in Britain. [16] Another distinctive feature of the early setup was that it was a strictly one-way affair. There was no dependable flow of return cargo at that time. Since a two-way shuttle service did not seem feasible, many vessels copied the *Worcester's* first voyage on which she went from South Africa to India, where ample cargoes for Britain were usually obtainable. Many later voyages would return from Britain to the United States in ballast, an unprofitable procedure.

These pioneer lines were charter members of what would become the U.S.A.-South African Outward Conference. This system, which had started on the run to India in 1875, was primarily a British development, but it had spread rapidly to other routes and the other nations often saw fit to co-operate in it. It was a device by which steamship operators sought to avoid unprofitable competition, and, in particular, to keep out interlopers who might seek to skim the cream in profitable periods. At its fullest extent, it involved uniform rates, rotation of sailing, pooling, and deferred rebates. [17]

The last, which belonged only to the early days of the New York-South African run, was the most potent as well as the most controversial weapon in the conference armory. The purpose of the deferred rebate was to keep shippers from giving their business to other than conference ships, that might offer more tempting rates. Those loyal to the conference would receive a rebate, often ten per cent, on their freight payments at the end of six months or so. The shippers were thus kept "absolutely in hand. Cargo cannot get away whenever some tramp steamship owner thinks that it is a good market . . . and puts on a steamer for a single voyage." [18] Such rebates were particularly unacceptable to some of the export commission houses in New York; Thompson & Company sued the conference for treble damages under the Sherman antitrust law. After fourteen years in the federal courts, the Supreme Court in 1917 found in the firm's favor. [19] By then, the rebates had long been abandoned by the conference, and the year before had been prohibited for the United States in the Shipping Act of 1916. [20]

In the interim, the German Hansa Line of Bremen in 1901, Britain's Prince Line in 1902, and R. P. Houston & Company in 1904, all fought their way into the conference through rate wars. [21] The two British newcomers differed from the other conference lines, as their main service was between United States ports and South America. These seven lines were still operating on the New York-South African run in 1913, although the conference had reorganized from time to time. All signals were called from London, with the New York agents meeting weekly.

Their system of uniform rates was established at the same rate from New York as from Britain or Germany. The actual cost was considerably more on the American run since it was a longer nonstop haul, which meant more coal bunkers at the expense of cargo space. [22]

By their rotation system, one liner at a time took its turn "loading on the berth." As soon as she was "about completed" London was cabled "for the next steamer's name." [23] A complication was that different agents had different piers, so that shippers at a distance from New York had to keep close track of successive ships on the berths, instead of being able always to ship to a single pier. Union-Castle, being in both the original services, had twice as many sailings as any of the other lines. [24]

Linked with this rotation method was the practice of conference-wide contracts with particular shippers. Such contracts all contained the same *quid pro quo;* the conference promised frequent and adequate cargo space, and the shipper, to use only conference ships.

The absence of strenuous competition was accentuated by the practice of pooling the combined earnings on the run after certain allowances had been deducted to cover the expenses of the ships that actually carried the cargo. Then the profits or losses were divided among the member lines, none of which, of course, were dependent on this route alone. [25]

A few months before the outbreak of World War I, the House Committee on Merchant Marine and Fisheries made an extensive investigation of charges that the foreign lines, through their conferences, were discriminating against American shippers. The manager of a conference line, defending the setup as the most satisfactory way for all concerned, stated that he knew "the word 'pool' sounds wicked . . ." but "our English principals have apparently found it to be the only way to insure stable and regular service. I do not think that any shippers from New York have a complaint of any consequence." [26] The latter do not, on the whole, seem to have been particularly discontented with their dependence on foreign lines. Characteristic of various reports was this comment: "All the witnesses who have appeared . . . in the interest of the South and East African trade have testified that the rates . . . are maintained at the same level as from Europe; that there is no discrimination against American shippers . . ." [27]

Such remarks led the author of a consistently antisubsidy study of shipping policy to declare, in italics, "The evidence of the committee demolished completely one of the stock arguments of the shipping lobbyists—the charge that foreign steamship companies discriminated against American exports." [28]

The full text of the committee recommendations, however, gives a much less positive picture. While almost all of those who publicly testified gave favorable accounts, the committee also received "a considerable number of complaints . . . objecting to excessive rates, discrimination between shippers in rates and cargo space, indifference to the landing of freight in proper condition," and other details along that line, including "the unfairness of certain methods"—these being specified. The committee was further informed that "It seemed to be the general impression among shippers who filed complaints that the conference lines so completely dominate the shippers . . ." that they "cannot afford, for fear of retaliation, to place themselves in a position of active antagonism to the lines by openly giving particulars of their grievances." [29]

The senior partner of the export commission or "indent" house of Arkell & Douglas did, however, dare to speak. His firm, along with some others, had a long record of seeking independence from conference domination. He stated that the "American carrying trade, as we all know, is monopolized by foreign steamship owners. . . . The control of the ocean today is a stronger and more pronounced and determined monopoly" than "railroad or water transportation" is in the United States. He called conditions so bad that "you lose 25 to 30 per cent of the export trade of the world" because steamers or sailing vessels are not available. [30]

Other evidence pointed to its not being the best of worlds from the shippers' viewpoint. Even with rates equal to those from Europe, the routes and services did not always meet American needs for adequate space and there was that natural lack of interest in promoting overseas markets for American goods. James A. Farrell, Sr., for instance, while president of the United States Steel Export Company, would acquire ships to meet his concern's heavy export requirements. [31]

The American public as a whole, however, showed no particular concern about their merchant marine shortcomings as long as the foreign liners came and went frequently and efficiently. Aside from the shipping interests, American consuls in foreign ports most often urged improvement, as they saw the relationship of shipping to shipments. Year after year, reports came from all over the world, such as this one from South Africa in 1907: "There is a general agreement on the part of consuls that deficient shipping facilities largely account for the backward condition of American trade." [32] The Navy, too, had appreciated the need for American-flag shipping not only in the Spanish-American War, but in its world cruise of 1907–1909, when it had had to acquire foreign-flag vessels as auxiliaries.

In the meantime, as World War I grew nearer, the British and also the German flags flew more frequently and more aggressively than ever before or since on the sea lanes of the world. In later days, those nations would be looking backward to 1914 with a similar mixture of wistfulness and resentment that the Americans had felt for a half century in nostalgic retrospect to the early 1850's. In 1914, the four chief maritime nations presented three patterns. Britain had maximum size in commerce, merchant shipping, and naval strength. Germany was likewise strong in all three aspects, on a somewhat smaller scale. Norway had scant commerce and a tiny navy, but it had a large and efficient tramp fleet. The United States, on the other hand, was exactly the reverse of Norway in respect to those three aspects. Its exports, totaling $2.4 billion in 1913, were close behind Germany's 2.5 and Britain's 3.1; the imports stood at 2.2, 2.6 and 3.8 respectively.[33] The United States Navy had only recently been crowded out of second place by Germany's fleet. Yet the American seagoing shipping on distant runs consisted only of a few lines with aging ships, the products of a spasmodic and inadequate shipping policy. The First World War would deserve full credit for terminating those negative years.

Chapter II

CARGOES AND AFRICA

UNTIL World War I, the United States had very little direct trade with Africa. Nor did it have much knowledge of, or interest in, that continent. The diamonds, gold, ostrich feathers, and other African products that were imported had usually made the roundabout passage by way of London. From the days of sail, Americans had traded with Asia, with the South Seas, and above all, with South America. Now Africa would round out the picture.

The resemblances between Africa and South America have always seemed striking, ever since the days of fourth-grade geography. Both continents bulge out into the South Atlantic; both stretch downward toward the Antarctic; both have vast areas of wasteland either in desert or impassable jungle. Their climates have a wide range, from the steaming heat of Guinea and the Guianas to the salubrious "white man's regions" of the Plata, Chile, and South Africa. Both are rich in minerals, but, until well into the twentieth century, they have had little industrial development. Both have European and native elements in their population, though in one case they have blended gradually and in the other have remained fairly rigidly separated.

Back in the fifteenth century, when Europe began its overseas expansion, Africa was the first object of interest, only because the Portuguese mariners were pushing very slowly down its west coast to find a way around it to India. As soon as Vasco da Gama had rounded the Cape of Good Hope in 1497 and proceeded on to India, Europe pretty much forgot Africa. Only the Barbary

15

pirates and the sorry slave trade made them remember its existence.

European interest had shifted across the Atlantic to the New
World discovered by Columbus. There the treasures unearthed
by the Spaniards became a center of attraction and cupidity. By
1562, when John Hawkins began peddling slaves at the cannon's
mouth along the Spanish Main, outside nations were commenc-
ing their long efforts to "sell Latin America" in order to fill the
commercial vacuum left by Spain in its neglect of almost everything save the silver of Mexico and Peru. Those commercial designs on Latin-American lands lasted for centuries while Eng-
lishmen, Dutchmen, Frenchmen, and, in later days, Germans
and Americans competed for those markets.

Much as these two vast continents seemed alike, there was an
important difference that would affect outside contacts. South
America, after three centuries of European colonialism, had
thrown it off almost completely by 1825. This was a good half
century before European colonialism would take over most of
Africa. This "scramble for Africa" and increased European interest therein made scant impact upon the United States. Not until the mid-twentieth century did it begin to appreciate to any
extent the rich potentialities of that continent, where by that
time, colonial ties were loosening.

By the eve of World War I, Africa was growing faster, as far
as commerce was concerned, than South America, which was
nonetheless appearing in steamship advertisements as the "Fastest-Growing Continent." [34] The contrast is particularly pertinent if one omits North Africa, which really belongs to the Mediterranean world, and northern South America—Colombia,
Venezuela, and the Guianas, which really belong to the Caribbean. That leaves Africa "South of Sahara" against east coast
and west coast South America. The most tangible source of comparison lies in the combined imports and exports to and from
Britain and the United States. On that basis, South America led
Africa $277 to $94 million in 1873. Forty years later, they stood
respectively at 884 to 513—Africa's increase had been 445 per
cent to South America's 383. By 1938, Africa had actually pushed

ahead, at $916 to $885 million; and in 1953 that lead was continued with 3,145 to 2,839 millions.[35]

In the course of those eighty years, South, East, and West Africa showed a rate of increase five times as fast as the east and west coasts of South America. By the nature of things, the United States had the lead in South America and Britain in Africa. The American gains "South of Sahara," however, were phenomenal. Between 1913 and 1948, their exports and imports rose from $28 million to 1,012 millions—a full billion! This 3,600 per cent gain was very much higher than with any other continent.

The term "South Africa" naturally first suggests the Union of South Africa, a dominion formed in 1910 out of the former Cape Colony and Natal, predominantly British, and the two former Boer republics, Transvaal and Orange Free State. The phrase "British South Africa" in the commercial records includes not only the Union but also Northern and Southern Rhodesia, the former German colony of South West Africa, and the protectorates. The steamship lines in their "South African" conferences take in Mozambique (formerly called Portuguese East Africa), which lies across the routes of Transvaal and the Rhodesias to the sea. Sometimes the whole region is called Southern Africa.

East Africa, in the steamship parlance, extends from the northern boundary of Mozambique to Cape Guardafui, the sandy eastern "horn" of Italian Somaliland. Its principal maritime elements are Tanganyika, the former German East Africa; Kenya, with Uganda in its hinterland; and the colorful island protectorate of Zanzibar. These are all collectively known as British East Africa, a term once limited to Kenya. East Africa also includes the big French island of Madagascar, along with Mauritius and other British islands far out in the Indian Ocean. For the American steamship lines, at least, the East African service was regarded as an extension of the South African run.

West Africa, in the maritime definition, extends from just above Cape Verde at the western tip of the bulge, down along the Guinea Coast and then southward through Portuguese Angola to the South West African border. It includes also the Canaries and other islands off the coast. One region normally included in West Africa but often attributed to Central Africa is the rich, enormous, and almost landlocked Belgian Congo, which has a scant 25 miles of seacoast.

The trade with South Africa, and to some extent East Africa as well, has followed a pattern quite different from the West African. In the former, the difficulty has lain in securing return cargoes for the homeward passage, but in West Africa, it has been just the reverse. Between 1913 and 1957, American cargoes to South and East Africa totaled $5.9 billion, but the returning African shipments came to only 3.3 billions. On the West African run, on the other hand, the 2.4 billion outward cargoes were overshadowed by the $3.9 billion worth of cocoa and other homeward ladings. [36]

Of all the principal commodities of import or export in the trade of the United States with the regions South of Sahara, gold from the mines of South Africa's Witwatersrand ("Ridge of the White Waters") has played the most distinctive role ever since its discovery in 1886. The gold ingots from the "Rand" have overshadowed all other South African offerings to the outside world, much as the silver from Potosi and other mines dominated the trade of Spanish America years before.

That gold did much to enable the South Africans to buy what they wanted from outside, for their other more normal offerings were seldom, if ever, enough in themselves. Between 1913 and 1950, for instance, the Union of South Africa received imports worth £3.6 billion. Its normal exports, at £1.9 billion, would pay for little more than half of that, but the £2.3 billion worth of gold bullion not only made up the difference but left a modest balance as well. [37] Its gold, like its diamonds, however, did not do much to fill ships seeking return cargoes to the United States.

South Africa's rise to first place in gold production was rapid. It exported £23,000 worth in 1886, the year of the Rand discovery; £15.3 million by 1898; and nearly 40 per cent of the world's supply, £37.5 million, in 1913. [38] In later days, South Africa's output was stabilized at about one-third of the world output. Its exports reached a peak of £242.0 million in 1948 and stood at £193.1 in 1957. [39]

Until World War II, most of the gold was carried by sea to

Southampton, whence it went overland to London. There, in the custody of the Bank of England, it was normally sold to the highest bidder. Much of it continued on quickly to the United States. In 1921, for instance, 96 per cent of it went to New York. The following two years, however, 58 per cent went to the United States and 37 per cent to India. Occasionally, additional modest sums went direct from Durban to India. [40]

By 1940, some of the gold had begun to go directly to New York, some of it in the American-flag liners. The first shipment by the American South African Line is still a Farrell tradition. The gold—packed as usual in boxes each containing two ingots weighing 27 pounds, with a million dollars' worth weighing about a ton—was put aboard at Cape Town with a minimum of formality. There was no strong room prepared, so the precious cargo was locked in the cabin of the stewardess. The general casual attitude lasted as far as the pier in Brooklyn where the incoming ship was met by a formidable collection of security elements—police, F.B.I., armored trucks, and all the rest. After that, security conditions aboard ship were vastly improved; the door of the gold room was welded shut as soon as the treasure was deposited. Such shipments lasted well through the 1940's and were regarded most favorably by the company as desirable business. A usual "double shipment" of two millions paid $25,-000 freight, the equivalent of thousands of tons of ore. During World War II, most of the shipments were on private account, but after that the principal ones were made by the South African Reserve Bank. [41]

As it developed, the so-called Witwatersrand stretched into a "golden arc" sixty miles long and several miles wide on a plateau in southern Transvaal with an elevation of almost 6,000 feet. Its whole length is dotted with the continuous high mine dumps—striking white hills supposed to be waste until they were found to contain uranium. Some of these dumps crowd in on the suburbs of Johannesburg itself.

This center of the Rand suddenly came into being with the discovery year and rapidly became South Africa's largest city. Although several hundred miles from the sea, Johannesburg has always been a focal point in South African shipping considerations. The combined demands of the mines themselves, of the white and native workers with their huge payrolls, and of all the financial and general business activity generated by the mines have made it the ultimate destination of much of the cargo from beyond the seas, with various seaports competing for its business. [42] The Farrell Lines have long maintained a representative there to look out for the wants and needs of the many actual and potential customers. In 1955, for instance, its ships brought cargo to some 1,430 different consignees in Johannesburg and to 350 others in smaller communities in the Rand, with only 22 exporters handling the return cargo. [43]

The most obvious objects in this gold-inspired trade have been mining machinery. England has naturally had a strong advantage in competing for such orders because British capital long predominated in the mining companies. These amounted in 1923 to some £6 million, or 11 per cent of the total South African import trade. [44] There were some forms of mining machinery in which the Americans excelled, and these led to modest but fairly steady exports worth one to two million dollars a year. [45] Along with that went much more for the department stores and other distributors for the general Johannesburg market. Altogether, the city of skyscrapers and hectic frontier atmosphere was able to attract imports of every sort from overseas.

Senior to gold in point of time was the diamond, even more precious and with its own effect upon the general commercial situation. Its discovery in 1870–71 in huge volcanic deposits around Kimberley brought a rush of outsiders—and rather brawling ones—into the deep back country where the Boers had "trekked" to get away from the English. Now the two peoples mixed again, and by the end of the century would be fighting.

Though the United States was always a large purchaser, the diamonds before World War II did not go there directly, but normally first to Britain and then to Holland or Belgium for cutting. [46] The output was rigidly restricted to keep prices up. In later days, other parts of Africa, the Belgian Congo in particular, sent huge amounts of industrial diamonds to the United States.

It was the bulky and less precious ores and metals that really

Painting by Stubbs

The schooner *Susan Scranton* of New Haven; commanded and partly owned
by Captain John Guy Farrell, 1872-78

Terence J. McNally

Aerial view of Cape Town and Table Mountain

made possible an adequate two-way service between the United States and South Africa. The industrial nations came to need more and more of certain "critical" or strategic minerals. The United States was still relatively self-sufficient, compared with Europe, but its growing steel industry had a particular need for chrome, manganese, and other alloys in more adequate quantity and quality.

As early as 1907, rich deposits of chromite ore, running to 60 per cent content, were being developed in Southern Rhodesia, while ore running around 40 per cent content was soon being mined in the Transvaal. Once the homeward run from South Africa was under way, around 1920, chrome became its mainstay. Some of the ore came in the form of blackish powder, some in lumps. Between 1921 and 1940, for instance, the 10.1 million tons of chromite comprised 75 per cent of the total cargo tonnage, although only 4 per cent of the value from that area, [47] for the freight earnings were low, sometimes only a quarter of the rate for outward general cargo. They at least helped to fill the ship. The ideal cargo is one which leaves her "full and down" —loaded to the Plimsoll marks and with her holds chockablock. That calls for a mixture of heavy and bulky cargo. When wool could be secured in addition to chrome, everything was fine.

Africa came into the manganese picture more slowly. The principal supply came first from the Gold Coast's Nouta Mine, with its high-grade ore cropping out on a ridge more than two miles long. This has been called the world's largest single deposit. South Africa had supplied only a few driblets before 1925 when a huge new deposit was opened at Postmasburg; the quality was not quite as good as the Gold Coast's. Manganese is shipped in the form of a dry powder, as anyone who has walked under the loading galleries at Takoradi will well recall. Its value per ton has been even less than chrome with freight rates consequently very low.

Although the United States has needed to import a still larger supply of manganese than chrome, it has had more overseas deposits to draw upon and so Africa's role has been less. It is a "must" in steel manufacture; some 14 pounds are needed in making every ton, and still more where specially tough steel is desired. Its importation from West Africa started off with 1,100 tons in 1919; it had already jumped to 66,000 tons by 1923. Not until World War II did the United States use South African manganese to any extent; thereafter those shipments gradually gained momentum. From 1940 to 1957 they were valued at $83 million as compared with $157 million for West Africa, where the Belgian Congo and Angola added to the Gold Coast supply.

Copper gradually became one of Africa's most valuable offerings to the outside world, but most of it went to Europe, as the United States had been fairly self-sufficient. South Africa had mined and exported a modest amount of copper since 1862. [48] The real impetus came around the turn of the century, when tremendous deposits were discovered on both sides of the boundary between Northern Rhodesia and the Belgian Congo. Together, they have been producing almost a quarter of the world's supply. About two-thirds has come from the Rhodesian "Copperbelt's" half dozen mines, owned by an intricate combination of British and American capital. The other third comes from the mines of the Belgian Union Minière du Haut Katanga, [49] which also produce rich quantities of tin, lead, zinc, and other minerals including uranium. The regions are close together with their capitals barely a hundred miles apart. Later an additional copper supply was developed in South West Africa.

With the coming of World War II, it suddenly became expedient to ship Katanga minerals to the United States for refining instead of to Belgium. [50] This included not only copper but also tin, cobalt and numerous other minerals, in huge quantities. As technology has grown more complex, so, too, have Africa's offerings, which cover much of the range of America's critical needs.

Developing in secret at the start, uranium became one of Africa's leading mineral offerings. When the extremely "hush-hush" project for the atomic bomb first got under way, the Katanga produced the original ore for it. Then an Amherst geology professor discovered a huge amount of accessible uranium in the gold mine dumps in South Africa's Rand. The Union has become the world's third largest uranium producer, ranking after the United States and Canada. Its sales of uranium and other fissionable materials jumped from £3.9 million in 1953 to 50.0 in 1957. It was reported in 1958, "its reserves are enough to make it the leading producer if greater markets for uranium should materialize." [51]

Down through the years South Africa has produced a considerable supply of nonmetallic minerals. Particularly rich deposits of asbestos have furnished for a long time some three-quarters of the American crude imports of that mineral. Corundum, a valuable abrasive, has come in modest quantities; and for a while in the 1920's, various forms of mica and fluorspar were also brought to the United States.

South Africa's oldest and, next to gold, its most valuable export commodity has been wool. The fleece of the Cape's fat-tailed sheep was too coarse for export, and the sheep were used mainly as mutton for the passing Dutch Indiamen. Then, in 1789, the King of Spain gave two rams and four ewes from his jealously guarded flock of merino sheep to the Dutch government, which sent them down to the Cape. Although those particular sheep were only on loan for two years, their progeny remained as the nucleus of a great wool-raising industry. Incidentally, Australia's still larger flocks came from some of those same merinos. These sheep produced the softest of wool and "could live on land where most sheep would starve"—a description which fits a huge semi-arid area known as the Karroo or High Veld in the northern part of Cape Province. By the eve of World War I, South Africa had some 25 million wool-bearing sheep, each producing an average of five pounds of wool a year. Most of it went to England, which kept about a third and re-exported the rest in its entrepôt trade, but a fair amount went directly to Germany. In the mid-nineteenth century, American ships had carried some of the wool direct to Boston, then and ever since the nation's wool-importing port. Those direct shipments dwindled away; what Americans still bought came chiefly through the London entrepôt until World War I.

Less extensive projects involved other African flocks. Sometime during the past century, so the story runs, an adventurous soul risked his life to smuggle out of Turkey some angora goats. This led to a substantial output of mohair from South Africa, all of which went to Bradford in England until World War I, when some began to cross the Atlantic. A dozen Karakul sheep from Bokhara were imported in 1907 by the governor of South West Africa, then a German colony. Their very valuable "Persian lamb" furs—2,574,000 pelts—were valued in 1951 as $15 million as exports; four-fifths went to the United States. Less valuable but fairly constant export income from South African flocks were the sheep, goat, and kid skins that could be counted upon as a fragrant part of most American-bound cargoes. "Capes" became the stock name for the gloves from these skins.

Of all South Africa's export commodities, the most locally distinctive and most highly speculative were ostrich feathers—"the flimsiest, craziest, and in some ways, most hazardous industry that even South Africa has ever known."[52] Its feathers were even more vulnerable than its diamonds to economic conditions; a change in style could wreck the ostrich market overnight. As early as 1826, Cape Colony was exporting 1,209 pounds of feathers, valued at £2,805. The first real boom came in the 1880's, attended by wild speculation in the purchase of ostriches; another was caused by Edwardian styles in the early 1900's.[53] The number of birds climbed from 746,000 in 1911 to 776,000 in 1913, a peak not again approached.[54] That was the year of maximum exports, especially to the United States. Then the market began to break—new styles and driving in the early windy open automobiles were blamed—even before World War I shut down on the trade. By 1916, the ostrich flocks had been cut almost in half; by the 1950's, only some 40,000 birds were left, with a modest export of feathers continuing to America.[55] South Africa began to make even more money, however, from products requiring special refrigeration service, as will be seen in that connection.[56]

A continuing offering in fairly constant cargoes has been tanning materials, notably wattle bark and extract, used to give weight and strength to sole leather. After trying Australian wattle around 1880, Natal planters found the black wattle tree better. The bark is chipped and ground on the plantations and sent out in bags or bales. An increasingly larger portion has been sent in concentrated extract, since some producers began this method to save freight during the high rates of World War I.

In 1913, an experimental lot had been sent to American tanners, who soon began to import it. British East Africa, as time went on, began to ship an even heavier amount, along with considerable mangrove bark for the same purpose. [57]

Rich offerings of vegetable products came from British East Africa: cloves, coffee, pyrethrum, and particularly sisal. This last is one of the "hard fibers," especially useful for binder twine. In 1893, the German East Africa Company brought a thousand sisal plants from Florida; by 1900, from the few that survived the journey, 150,000 plants had been developed. The output rose from 1,000 to 20,000 tons between 1904 and 1913. British East Africa, too, had started sisal cultivation in 1903, and it spread on a lesser scale to Mozambique, South Africa, Belgian Congo, Angola, and Madagascar.

An earlier and more colorful instance of transplanting initiative provided another export staple for East Africa. This was the work of Sultan Said, of whom more will be heard; he introduced cloves into Zanzibar around 1840, as one of the first as well as the chief of his successful efforts to provide the island with export offerings and make it a trade center. The great bins down along the Zanzibar waterfront send out a sweetish aroma that extends even out to sea. American sailing vessels were soon carrying cloves in quantity to Salem, which had developed into an active center for spice imports. For a while, in the 1920's, cloves held their own with sisal in American imports, but the fiber soon drew well ahead. Up to 1930, sisal and clove imports stood at $15 and 10 millions, but by 1955, the score was 172 to 24. The ships, which always put in at Tanga, now anchor only occasionally off the Sultan's palace at Zanzibar. Part of the decline came from the fact that the United States had developed synthetic substitutes for flavoring. Closer at hand was the more serious competition from Madagascar, where the French during the 1930's had begun the production not only of cloves but also of the vanilla bean as a rival product. In later days, a generous portion of the Zanzibar cloves have been shipped to Indonesia to flavor its cigarettes.

Probably the smallest single units in Africa's exports have been the tiny white blossoms of the pyrethrum—"insect flowers" as they are called because of their use in a nonpoisonous insecticide. The original African plantations were in Kenya in the heart of the Mau Mau country. The blossoms, patiently hand-picked, are even smaller than the tea leaves grown still further inland in Kenya, near the headwaters of the Nile. The United States received most of its early pyrethrum from Japan. The Kenya imports, beginning modestly in 1935 with 9,535 pounds, worth $66,000, had jumped by 1955 to $1,421,000. By then, the Belgian Congo was sending an almost identical amount. In the intervening years, the rival Japanese supply had disappeared, but the new insecticide D.D.T. had become a competitor. Much of the supply came to be shipped in extract to save freight.

Few African commodities could duplicate coffee's sudden and substantial boom since World War II. In the decade before the war, the American imports from all parts of Africa averaged $830,000 a year; in the first postwar decade that jumped almost fifty fold to $40 million. Some of that gain was at the expense of the traditional Brazilian and other Latin-American sources. In 1930, the latter shipped 11,560,000 bags to the United States, and Africa, only 44,000; and by 1957, it was estimated that, along with Latin America's diminished 17,100,000 bag total, would come some three million bags from Africa. It happened that that African share, at all three dates, coincided almost exactly with the increase of "instant" or soluble coffee in the United States at the expense of the usual ground bean. Virtually no instant coffee was drunk in 1930 except for the "G. Washington" pioneer output; the consumption increased to around two per cent in 1949, and to 17 per cent in 1956. [58]

Until the soluble opportunity arose, American coffee drinkers had not been enthusiastic about the strong "robusta" coffees that made up most of the African output. Some mild "arabica" beans from Africa, to be sure, could hold their own with the best Latin American, but the rest could not command a respectable price. Coupled with instant coffee, in producing the African boom, was some well-timed promotional initiative in bringing the African coffee possibilities to the attention of a wealthy firm which had decided to spread its commitments.

Some of the best African coffee has come from Kenya and

other parts of British East Africa, not far from Ethiopia where coffee is supposed to have originated centuries ago, before spreading to Mocha, Java, and Rio. More good coffee has come nearby from the eastern part of the Belgian Congo and the former German regions of Ruanda-Urundi, given to Belgium after World War I. The shipments from those two regions have been excellent cargo, paying nearly $40 a ton for the 10,000 mile trip to New York. This is almost twice as much as for the sisal from East Africa, and four times as much as for the chrome and manganese from down the coast. The rest of the coffee had not so far to travel, coming as most of it has from the Guinea Coast or from Portuguese Angola, which has experienced the most rapid coffee boom. In millions of pounds of United States imports, Angola and British East Africa were virtually tied for first place in 1957, followed, in order, by the Belgian Congo, French West Africa, and Madagascar, with smaller amounts from several other regions in East, South, and West Africa. Ethiopia, close behind the Congo, is not rated as "South of Sahara."

Even more remarkable than the story of coffee has been the fantastic record of cocoa, more localized in area but stretched over a longer period of years. Of all the African imports into the United States from 1913 to 1957, cocoa stands an easy first. Its $1,361 million total, more than a billion and a third, equals, with the sole exceptions of gold and diamonds, any two of the other African offerings.

The cocoa exports, more than any of the other top commodities, have been primarily a native African achievement, whereas most of the other exports have resulted from European or American capital, initiative, and direction. Tete Quashire, a Gold Coast "boy," furnished the original initiative that has made his country the leading cocoa producer in the world. The Spaniards had brought cocoa from its original starting place in Latin America to their colony, Fernando Po, a lush and lazy island within sight of towering Mount Cameroon. Lacking workers for their plantations there, they imported natives from the mainland on contract. One of these was Quashire; in 1879, when his time was up, he defied rigid prohibitions to smuggle home some cocoa seeds, from which he raised a few trees. From them, plantings began to spread over the eastern part of the Gold Coast, now Ghana. The first exports were 80 pounds in 1891; and within the decade, the trees were already numbered by the millions.

Most of the present huge crop is raised on little holdings of a few acres each, belonging to natives. Many of them have become prosperous, and some, wealthy. One may see them in the department stores of Ghana, dressed in their brown, togalike costumes, shopping for a wide variety of up-to-date goods. Ghana, and Nigeria which produces nearly half as much, have marketing boards, which buy up the offerings at a fixed price. The sales are arranged in London. Cocoa raising has spread to other parts of West Africa, especially the French areas. In 1957, of the $134 million worth of cocoa imported by the United States, 46 per cent came from West Africa as compared with 51 per cent from Latin America, which formerly almost monopolized the market. Ghana at 27.9 millions ranked just behind Brazil for first place among nations. While the United States imports of Africa's coffee that year were worth twice as much as its cocoa, they represented only nine per cent of the American total. [59]

One of Africa's most deliberately planned offerings has been the Firestone rubber from Liberia. African rubber had gained grim world-wide notice in connection with the forced collection of wild rubber in King Leopold's Congo "Free State." As a result, Belgium in 1908 took the rich region from its king and made it a national colony.

The second rubber episode was of an entirely different nature. With seeds smuggled out of the Amazon rubber jungles, Britain had developed new plants at home, and then began cultivated rubber plantings in Ceylon, Malaya, and other parts of Southeast Asia. Coming into production around the start of World War I, these soon crowded out the old wild rubber supply from Brazil. The sharp drop in rubber prices at the end of that war led the British to set up their Stevenson Rubber Restriction Act in 1922; it soon pushed the price up from 14 cents to $1.24 a pound. This aroused the American tire and automobile manufacturers, the major consumers of rubber, and led to a quest for

alternate sources. Ford set up plantations in Brazil and Goodyear in Panama and Costa Rica, but the greatest continuing
supply has come from the plantation which Harvey Firestone
started in Liberia in 1926, of which much more later.[60] The
first modest shipments to the United States came in 1935 and
rose quite steadily until they reached a $51 million peak in 1951,
falling back to $37 million in 1957.

The bulkiest products to come regularly from West Africa to
the United States have been huge logs of mahogany and other
cabinet woods, a trade of long standing, and one more field of
competition with the Caribbean and Latin America. The Gold
Coast and Ivory Coast have been leaders in this business, which
is fairly evenly divided between British and French West Africa.

The oldest of the West African offerings, and the one that
lies behind some of the earliest commercial efforts in the area,
has been the product of the oil palm tree. Some of this, known
commercially as palm oil, has already been pressed out before
shipment; much of the rest comes in the form of palm kernels.
These palm products are useful in the manufacture of soap and
margarine, and have various other industrial uses. Palms grow
in the same general region as cocoa, and, since the seasons of
the two products alternate, it makes a convenient arrangement
for workers and shippers. The palm products are gathered to a
large extent at trading posts where they are exchanged for imported products wanted by the natives. Outstanding in this field
is the United Africa Company, a descendant of the Royal Niger
Company, and now, appropriately, a subsidiary of Lever
Brothers, with their soap interests.

Relatively little of the palm oil and kernels from the British
and French West African sources has come to the United States,
which has been taking most of its supply from the Belgian Congo.
There the ubiquitous Lever interests have their "Huilever"
to handle the palm products.

In addition to all those conventional African products, variety
and sometimes adventure has come to the shipping world in
the occasional shipments of wild animals of every sort, chiefly
for zoos in America. The Farrell Lines lost some of their enthusiasm in this field after an episode which occurred aboard

the *African Star* in 1951. At Mombasa, a hippopotamus was
taken aboard for New York and a seaman who had been a circus
roustabout was assigned to attend to it. A few hours out, his
right hand was badly chewed. The captain put back to Mombasa, put off the hippo for some other ship to carry, and sent
the seaman to the hospital. Complications set in and he was
flown to New York, but eventually he lost the lower part of his
arm. In the Federal Court, he won a $65,000 suit against the
line. The hippo wound up in a New York zoo under the
name of Falstaff. [61] Animals, to be sure, could also create problems traveling in the opposite direction. South African racing
rules in some cases do not allow a horse to race in South Africa
unless it has been born there. On one occasion, the *African Pilgrim* was heading for Cape Town with four pregnant South
African mares returning from Kentucky where they had been
sent to be bred. One mare foaled at sea; much to the consterna-
tion of the owners. [62]

The American exports to Africa have been an infinitely more
complicated affair. As has been the case for many generations
on many sea lanes, the cargoes outward bound from an industrial country to a less developed region have been widely diversified in contrast to the relatively few commodities brought
home in return. In 1930, for instance, the American commercial
statistics listed 48 different articles of importation from the
Union of South Africa, but it listed 286 separate export categories. Aside from major commodities such as automobiles,
lubricating oil, and agricultural implements, there were substantial quantities of chewing gum, canned asparagus, corn
breakfast foods, wool bathing suits, paper envelopes, flashlight
cases, water meters, face powder, manicuring preparations,
pianos, soda fountain equipment, and so on, ad infinitum. [63]

In the last century, on the eve of the Civil War, things had
been much simpler. The United States was still only partly
industrialized and was still getting a large part of its own manu-
factured needs from Britain. Consequently, the list of major
American exports to Africa in 1858 was little longer than the
list of imports from there. Three of the eleven leading exports—

rum, gunpowder, and firearms—smacked of the old slaving era. Higher than any of them ranked tobacco, which would still be a West African standby a century later. Other items, in descending order of value, were flour and wheat; lumber, iron, copper and brass manufactures; ship's bread; and vehicles.

Overshadowing all else at $694,000, were cotton manufactures, a real American achievement. This was the result of Salem's early and continued close contact with Zanzibar and its famous Sultan, who had introduced cloves.[64] He made a commercial treaty with the United States before any other western nation, and American consuls, often from Salem, enjoyed an influence there shared only by the British consul. For years, the inhabitants of the region wore white cotton cloth brought out in the Salem vessels, making such an impression that it was known as "Mericani" in every bazaar. As late as 1878, Zanzibar took £95,000 worth, which was ahead of Manchester's ubiquitous cotton goods at £86,000 or the cheap cloth brought over from British India, at £67,000.[65] The Naumkeag (later Pequot) Mills at Salem are said to have been established to meet that demand. Even down to 1913, British East Africa was still a good market for unbleached cotton cloth from the United States.

In view of the tight European colonial controls, it was unique for an American product to get such a strong lead.[66] American goods ordinarily were "competitive" only when they represented something that was not easily available in Europe. With the high American wage scale and the influence of those European economic controls, it was very difficult to compete simply on a price basis, not to mention the complications arising from those European economic controls.

The nature of American exports to South Africa in 1913 may be judged from what the holds of the conference freighter *York Castle* carried from New York in September. The principal items in her $584,000 cargo, in order of value in thousands of dollars, were iron and steel manufactures at 98; plows, windmills, and other agricultural machinery and implements at 88; "case oil" and other petroleum products at 62; mining machinery at 48; canned goods, lard and other foodstuffs at 44; wax at 37; and automobiles and parts at 28. So it went, down to heterogeneous minor items such as sheepdip, organs, and flypaper. [67] Naturally, the exact relative values of various items would vary from ship to ship. The automobile figures, for instance, were higher in some of the spring sailings. Despite the prominence of various industrial products in such lists, the British were comforting themselves with the thought that the increase in America's share of Africa's imports, though at almost the same rate as Germany's, did not seriously compete with their own manufactures. Oil, flour, and lumber, they pointed out, made up a considerable part of the American total. [68]

At the end of four decades, the total 1913–1957 figures for all United States exports to South and East Africa show that automobiles and parts, as might be expected, led all the rest at $775 million. Then, in order by millions of dollars, came iron and steel manufactures at 545, petroleum products at 405, cotton manufactures at 396, agricultural implements and machinery at 384, earth-moving machinery, etc. at 154, lumber, etc. at 141, and mining machinery at 96. [69] Most of those commodities had traveled by line freighters, but much of the lumber went by chartered tramps. Tankers, as time went on, carried most of the petroleum products, but lubricating oil remained good line cargo. On the West African run, the 1913–1957 totals ran, in millions: automobiles and parts 331, petroleum products 225, tobacco 170, cotton manufactures 163, iron and steel manufactures 125, flour 114, and agricultural implements and machinery 76. More than half of that high cotton goods total was run up in three years, 1945–47; normally the British and other colonial powers looked out for such needs of their distant subjects.

The automobile shot into first place among American exports to South Africa in World War I and has maintained secure primacy since. A British source credited this to clever salesmanship by the Americans who "score heavily on propaganda as well as on price." [70] The British had sent out surplus cars, not needed for European consumption, and had not bothered to consider the circumstances peculiar to Africa. The American consul at Port Elizabeth explained what these were: the towns and homesteads were far apart; the South Africans were sportsmen to the core and wanted to get to their golf, cricket, and football matches; the automobile was supplanting the horse for pleasure riding; and motor taxis were coming into vogue. [71] In addition, the Afrikaner farmers were beginning to appreciate the possibilities of motorized equipment on their farms.

When the dislocations of war gave the American cars a special entry into South African markets, they had the chance to demonstrate certain advantages over the British. The strong and light American models proved far more adaptable to the African excuse for roads. Also, they were considerably cheaper in Africa at that time than the British makes of the same class, although their price in Africa was double or more what the American buyer paid. [72] Then, the American manufacturers, mindful of the value of service to car owners, kept their agents amply supplied with spare parts. [73]

American cars by 1918 had almost a fourteen fold lead over the British and, what was more significant, a sevenfold lead in 1920 after things had returned to relative peacetime normality. Even in 1913, South Africa had stood fifth among all foreign purchasers of United States cars. In 1927, South Africa at $12.9 million ranked third as a customer. By 1937, at 21.0 (37,000 passenger cars), it stood first of all. [74]

The automobile trade in South Africa centered in and around Port Elizabeth, partly on account of its central geographical position, but more particularly because of its own initiative. Situated more or less midway between Cape Town and Durban, it could distribute cars easily in either direction by sea, and it also had good rail connections with the interior. East London had an equally good location for coastwise traffic and a somewhat nearer one to the major inland centers, but it did not have Port Elizabeth's energetic and resourceful Chamber of Commerce. It was that which exercised the decisive influence at the particularly crucial moment in 1922, when Ford of Canada's representatives arrived to find the best place for an assembly plant. The next year saw the first Fords being assembled at Port Elizabeth. When General Motors learned of that, they sent out representatives in 1925. Their first car was assembled in 1926. Both firms at first rented premises, but later constructed extensive plants of their own. Next, came the tire manufacturers, with

Firestone building a factory and going into production in the fall of 1936. Goodyear began production early in 1947, after finding a location nearby. General Tire Company was next in completing its first tire, in 1949. [75]

Some of the other American automobile manufacturers sent their cars out already assembled. Originally, these were shipped in crates, but the Farrells were pioneers in shipping them un-crated. This involved more risk of a dent or worse, but the cost of crating was saved. As it proved, the total overall cost was much the same. In 1938, the freight on a crated car was $9 a measure-ment ton of 40 cubic feet; for the unboxed it was $12; in 1957, the rates were $26.50 and $30.50 respectively. A medium-sized car cost around $250 to transport. So far as General Motors and Ford went, most of the material was shipped out in knocked-down form. Eventually, South African products were utilized in the assembling to such an extent that in 1956 it was claimed that 40 per cent of the value of the finished car was of South African origin. Altogether, automobiles represented about one-third of the steamship lines' outward freight earnings.

The automobile exports to South Africa were highly sensitive to economic fluctuations. The number of cars that it imported has been called a true gauge of its prosperity. [76] And the record for passenger cars, the most sensitive of all, bears this out. In the postwar boom of 1920, 6,643 American cars were exported to South Africa; a year later they fell to 579; by 1928 they had risen to 21,815 and almost duplicated that in 1929. In the deep depression of 1932 they dropped to 3,783, but then, with the increased buying power of South African gold, climbed to 25,616 in 1934, 36,418 in 1936, and an all-time high of 37,513 (valued at $21 million) in 1937, from which they fell off gradually. [77]

The export of cars to West Africa developed far more slowly, mainly because so few roads were passable for motoring. When the trade eventually did prosper in the 1950's, it would be pri-marily with the Belgian Congo.

The export of petroleum naturally came to be linked with those automobiles as time went on, but kerosene for the lamps of Africa was being shipped in large quantities for many years before the automobile era. Kerosene, gasoline, and other "white" petroleum products were usually transported as "case oil." For easy handling, two five-gallon cans were packed in a wooden case, a good head load for a native porter. These symbols of American enterprise are said to have penetrated into the jungles, far beyond where any white man had ever gone. For years, that case oil would be one of the chief sources of revenue for steamships on the United States-African run. It was not until 1921 that gasoline overtook kerosene in shipments to South Africa; two years later, the first tanker reached Durban. At that same time, the Union was getting half its gasoline from the Dutch East Indies. [78] Eventually, South Africa met a good share of its oil needs by extraction from coal. Lubricating oils, on the other hand, remained one of the major stand-bys of the export trade from America. It was later carried more cheaply and efficiently than the packaged methods in tanks installed on the Farrell freighters. In West Africa, case oil maintained its popularity until World War II; in 1938, for example, it constituted two-thirds of all outward tonnage.

The United States had already achieved a modest lead in what the commercial records listed as "Agricultural implements and machinery," before its automobiles overtook the British. That was the only major area of South African imports in which it was ahead in 1913. Its prairie wheatfields and other broad farming areas gave more occasion for developing good farm equipment than did Britain's small-scale agriculture. This was another field where American manufacturers took the initiative in finding out just what African conditions required. They sent representatives to demonstrate the equipment to the farmers; incorporated their suggestions into particularly designed implements; and developed, as one consul said in 1921, "a product that is really saleable in this market." [79]

Plows that could be used "in dry, baked soil, in new and rough lands, with unskilled native labor and oxen" were the most popular of the American implements at the start. Another perennial favorite was the steel windmill in that generally very arid region. Cultivators, mowers, reapers, planters, seeders, hayrakes, and tedders rounded out the list. Finally, tractors overtook all the rest. It took patient demonstration to persuade the conservative Afrikaner farmer that this newfangled machinery would serve him better than the native and the ox. In 1927, International Harvester set up an assembly plant at Durban. By 1948, tractor exports at $22.0 million was both double the amount for other farm equipment and was even ahead of the 21.4 for automobiles and parts.

Two favorite American specialties in the wide category of "iron and steel manufactures," that ranged from structural steel and railway rails to wire and nails, were from the outset barbed fence wire and galvanized sheets, the favorite roofing material. Tin plate was another speciality exported in more modest amounts.

South Africa's nascent industrialization probably made itself felt in this field of iron and steel more than in any other. Altogether, the gross output of South African industry jumped from £40 million in 1915 to £675 in 1948, having received a marked stimulus from both World Wars. The big government-controlled South African Iron and Steel Corporation (ISCOR) was helping the Union to meet a fifth or more of its basic forms of those metals. At first glance, it would look as though industrialization might spoil some previously good markets, but experience here and elsewhere showed that it simply shifted the national purchases from simpler commodities to more complicated ones, which the country was all the more able to afford.

There was still room for plenty of American machinery in various forms. For years, a moderate demand for mining machinery for the Rand, the Copperbelt, and elsewhere was always less than the amount taken from England. The Americans led, however, in a related type of machinery which gradually overtook the mining apparatus. Frequently called "earth-moving" or "road-making" machinery, it was the sort of contractor's equipment that one sees on American highways under construction, and often runs to mammoth size. It included some of the heaviest objects, except perhaps the occasional steam or diesel locomotive, ever transported by sea to Africa. In the post-World War II decade, exports of earth-moving and related equipment topped mining machinery at $98.8 to 94.4 million, a reverse from the 1930's. This reflected, of course, the sorely needed boom in road construction in South Africa. Heavy sales were made likewise in British West Africa and the Belgian Congo, where need of better roads was still more imperative.

Promising development of hydroelectric power is taking place in various parts of Africa. South Africa lacks large rivers for this. Nearly completed in 1958 is the Kariba dam in a gorge on the Zambesi, 300 miles below Victoria Falls in Rhodesia. Another major development will be on the Volta River in Ghana, with bauxite production as one of its aims. Finally, overshadowing all others, is the proposal to dam the mighty Congo at Inga, 25 miles above Matadi. Aluminum companies from the United States and six other nations are examining the potentialities of the proposed power-generating station. [80] The material for these projects naturally means many heavy cargo lifts from the United States.

The original American export speciality, cotton manufactures, especially wearing apparel, has retained a high place. In the early postwar years, from 1946–55, exports of cotton goods to the war-starved markets were so heavy that they almost equaled the automobiles, at $311.7 million to 316.6, but later they fell off. In their old Zanzibar stronghold the "Mericani" had lost heavily. In West Africa, outside of Liberia and the Belgian Congo, cotton goods seem never to have gained a foothold. The Gold Coast and Nigeria took practically none, except for the abnormal postwar year, 1946. British firms kept them well supplied, while the striking prints of Dakar presumably came from French looms.

West Africa used large quantities of tobacco from the United States. Its quality may be deduced from its listing in the commerce statistics under "Blackfat, Waterbaler, and Dark African." West Africa likewise took a great deal more of American flour than did South and East Africa, while the big flour mills at Dakar used considerable American wheat. The rum and gunpowder shipments of 1858 had pretty much ceased.

Such then were the major elements in the cargoes that shuttled back and forth across the sea between the United States and the seaports South of the Sahara. Aided by the American inauguration of two-way steamship traffic, this amounted to $8 billion worth of American offerings between 1913 and 1957.

Chapter III

CAPE TOWN TO ZANZIBAR

REALLY good natural harbors along the long stretches of the Atlantic and Indian Ocean coasts of Africa may almost be counted on the fingers of one hand. Mariners have known from the earliest days that these shores offer almost no safe havens. Even in fairly recent times, most of the ports below Sahara have had to send and receive cargoes by means of lighters or surfboats; the ships seeking or delivering those cargoes had to anchor off-shore, well beyond the line of breakers. Africa has been said to have the shortest coastline of any continent, and that, translated into maritime terms, means a minimum of shelter.

The harbor, however, is only one element of a port's success. Its hinterland and its well-timed initiative can do even more to attract ships and cargoes. Dredging and artificial breakwaters can create a fairly good harbor if the other considerations make it worth while. The potential cargoes in the back country can build up an outlet on the coast if nature has not provided one. Without such help Beira might still be a nameless sandspit, and Zanzibar just another island. The six major ports in Southern Africa in recent times have been: Cape Town (Table Bay), Port Elizabeth (Algoa Bay), East London and Durban (Port Natal) in the Union of South Africa, and Lourenco Marques (Delagoa Bay) and Beira in Mozambique, also known as Portuguese East Africa, but more properly a part of Southern Africa. British East Africa has four major ports: Mombasa in Kenya, Dar-es-Salaam and Tanga in Tanganyika; and the island protectorate of Zanzibar. Various other ports took less active parts in the commerce of those regions.

The South African ports had one thing in common with those of the Rio Plata—trade with them meant really "long hauls" from the United States or Britain. By the shortest regular shipping routes, Buenos Aires is 6,360 miles from London and 5,871 from New York, while Cape Town is 6,068 miles from London and 6,786 from New York. In fact, that route from New York to Cape Town is said to be the longest nonstop steamship run in the world. [81]

The South Atlantic is vast and empty; sometimes no other vessel is sighted during a whole voyage. One location on that great circle route between New York and Cape Town is said to be farther from land than any other place in the seven seas. The voyage from New York took about a month in the old ten-knot freighters but in recent years its length has been cut almost in half. Sunshine and quiet seas are usually to be counted upon, with comfortable temperatures, except at certain seasons for two days out of New York or out of Cape Town.

At the end of that fair weather route, as it came to be advertised, lay one of the world's most beautiful seaports. Thousands have thrilled to the experience of a dawn landfall at Cape Town. Other first glimpses of Africa have their own charm, but none compare with Table Mountain and its surrounding peaks gradually taking form in the first pink-gray flush of dawn. As the day grows brighter, the buildings of Cape Town itself appear, crowded between the harbor and the mountain, that huge mass of sandstone with a long, flat, level top.

In most other African ports, the hinterland has been more important than the harbor. At Cape Town, it has been the reverse. For centuries, its sheltered harbor, only 30 miles from the Cape of Good Hope, has made it the "Tavern of the Seas" for vessels rounding the tip of Africa.

It was first settled by the Dutch East India Company in 1652. [82] Its purpose was to have fresh crops raised for the relief of scurvy, ravaging crews from their ship fare of hardtack and salt meat. Before the end of the century, other Calvinists—Huguenot refugees from France—joined the original Dutch and Walloon settlers. For another hundred years those "Boers" or farmers went their placid way, furnishing vitamins to the Dutch East India-men and other ships. That comfortable period ended when the French invaded Holland during the French Revolutionary and Napoleonic wars. England, realizing the danger of letting such a strategic naval base fall into enemy hands, seized the Cape in 1795, returned it during the lull in the fighting, and then took it for keeps in 1806. Cape Town lost much of its original raison d'être in 1869 when bypassed by the opening of the Suez Canal.

Until the twentieth century, Cape Town alone of the ports enjoyed the unusual African luxury of sheltered access to the shore for the loading and discharging of vessels. Its Alfred Docks were constructed in 1870. Conspicuous features in its harbor are the exceptionally powerful tugboats. The government owns sixteen of these, which are distributed between the five major ports. They are essential because of the strong South Atlantic and Indian Ocean winds that often reach gale and sometimes hurricane force. [83]

These are part of the effective port equipment developed by the South African Railways and Harbours Administration. All the South African ports have been furnished with extensive quays, mounting cranes to lift cargo into and out of ships. By 1950, there were some 64,000 feet, or 12 miles of such quays in these ports, with 273 cranes. [84] When port congestion did result, it was more the fault of the Administration's railroads than its harbors.

The "main line" of the South African steamship service stretched on around the Cape of Good Hope, involving an extra 1,600 miles in addition to the 6,786 from New York. The phrase "fair weather route" definitely does not apply to the voyage be-yond Cape Town. For some thirty miles as the ship heads toward Cape Point, rugged peaks close to the shore are extraordinarily beautiful above the long "cape rollers" piling in from the South Atlantic. And particularly at the tip where the winds are ever howling over its twin hills, one can only agree with Sir Francis Drake, who called it "a most stately thing and the fairest Cape we saw in the whole circumference of the earth." At the same time, the wild scenery and the wind-driven ocean seem to support Bartholomeu Diaz, the first European to see it, in reputedly christening it the Cape of Storms. Certainly the voyage around Good Hope and up the east coast puts a mariner on his mettle. It has always been an inhospitable shore with harbors of refuge few and far between, and the strong Mozambique current to combat.

There have been some tragic disasters on that harsh coast. The Portuguese carrack *São João,* homeward bound from Goa to Lisbon, piled up there in 1544; of the 500 men, women, and children who struggled ashore, only a handful reached safety. [85] Three other shipwrecks there have lived on in maritime tradition—the East Indiaman *Grosvenor* in 1782; the transport *Birkenhead* in 1852; and the liner *Waratah* which "went missing" in 1909. [86]

For all that, vessels pushed regularly up the coast to deposit and pick up cargo. Once in a while, if special cargo offered, a ship might put in at Mossel Bay's open roadstead, but usually the next port of call after Cape Town was Port Elizabeth, or Algoa Bay, 425 miles away. Algoa Bay lacked the outer range of islands which gave such excellent shelter at Delagoa Bay, and was a rather rugged place. An old port manual of the 1880's reads: "Port Elizabeth is only an open roadstead . . . A heavy surf constantly breaks on the beach and surf- or whaleboats are generally the only boats which can effect a landing through it." [87] Not until 1933, would it be equipped to receive large vessels within its harbor.

Its history dates back to 1820, when thirteen shiploads of men, women, and children were deposited at Algoa Bay as a counterweight to the Boers and troublesome native Kaffirs. Normally the British government left the inauguration and support of colonies to private initiative, whether it be at Boston, Barbados, or Bombay. Only on the rarest of occasions did official initiative and financing occur—at Halifax in 1749 to offset the French in the Maritimes; at Sydney in 1787 to get rid of prison inmates; and now at Algoa Bay. Port Elizabeth, named by the governor for his wife, was to be successively associated with ostrich feathers, wool, and automobiles. [88]

East London, 131 miles up the coast, became the marginal port of call on the Cape Town-Beira "main line." It usually ran second to Port Elizabeth as a wool port, and had its own auctions, but it shared very little of the automobile trade. It was the most convenient port of entry for the diamond center, Kimberley, and also for Bloemfontein and much of the Orange Free State. Its rise has been a fairly gradual affair; for some time its principal raison d'être was the Kaffir trade with the Transkei hinterland, one of South Africa's richest native agricultural regions.

Until the later days of dredging and docks, East London's "conditions were worst of all. The winds, which blew continually, and the terrific swell combined to make its roadstead the most disliked of all on the Cape Coast." [89] The big surfboats, for loading and unloading, had to be hauled in by hawsers, which ran through rollers in the bow. Some of the most vivid recollections there center around the unusual method of unloading passengers, which lasted down into the Farrell period. It was so rough that passengers were lowered in big wicker baskets onto the deck of a tug. One steamship man recalls with particular gusto the day in his East London boyhood when a very self-important Union-Castle agent was caught in the line of fire of a seasick woman passenger in a descending basket. Even as late as 1936, the Sailing Directions declared, "The surf at the entrance is often dangerous and sometimes impassable." [90]

By that time, however, things had generally improved, with sheltered quays, cranes, and all the rest, in the most informally pastoral setting of any of the South African ports. East London alone among them is on a river—the Buffalo—whose banks rise some 200 feet on either side.

East London's jealousy of Port Elizabeth was understandable. Back in 1918, the editor of the British and South African Export Gazette, reporting that the East London Chamber of Commerce was complaining that they did not have the shipping facilities to England and the United States to which they felt they were entitled, remarked, "I cannot, however, recall a time at which E. London ever believed that she had received, over no matter how short a period, proper consideration in shipping arrangements." [91]

Leaving Cape Province for Natal, a liner next heads for the

one accessible spot on the inhospitable coast of that province—
Durban or Port Natal, 265 miles from East London. Nature had
provided an ample and sheltered landlocked harbor, six square
miles in extent, but a bar with only 12 to 14 feet of water at low
tide forced all the larger vessels to remain outside. Finally, just
after the turn of the century, millions of feet of sand were
dredged away, and it was a proud day in Durban's history when
the big 13,000-ton Union-Castle liner, *Armadale Castle,* drawing
22½ feet, safely crossed the bar and docked inside on June 26,
1904. [92] From that time on, Durban's role as the foremost port
of South Africa was secure.

Founded in 1842 at a period of dangerous native attacks, it
had had a steady growth as a trading center. It had the advantage
of being closer to the Rand than any other Union of South Africa
(but not Portuguese) port. It was named for Sir Benjamin D'Ur-
ban, then governor of Cape Colony. In the initial settlement of
Durban, the British barely beat out the Boers who were advanc-
ing into the area; ever since, Durban and Natal have been more
strongly British than most other parts of the Union.

The area of "Port Natal," as it is often called, falls into several
distinct parts. On the south side of the entrance is the Bluff, a
striking wooded ridge 200 feet high; down at its foot are the coal
piers, which have provided Natal coal both for export and for
bunkerage. At Island View nearby are oil tanks and bunker facilities. On the north side of the entrance is the low and sandy
"Point." Beyond it to the northward, good beaches extend,
backed by the broad Marine Parade with its resort hotels, reminiscent of the Atlantic City boardwalk. But, following the channel into the port, one appreciates that the Point contains the
principal docks for general cargo, with more than a dozen well-
equipped berths. Up beyond the city proper, are the so-called
Maydon Docks, for the discharge of timber and heavy cargo,
along with an electric conveyor plant that can load 500 tons of
manganese ore an hour. [93]

Often a vessel is moved more than once from one part of the
port to another to complete her cargo requirements. Altogether,
Durban has some 27,000 feet of quayage and 143 cranes, including one of 80 tons capacity, to 24,600 feet and 49 cranes at

Cape Town. [94] Durban needs all that for its docks handle more cargo than any of the others—7.2 million tons in 1955 to 4.5 for Cape Town, 2.1 for Port Elizabeth, and 1.1 for East London. [95]

After Durban, a ship enters the waters of Mozambique, one of the most prosperous remnants of Portugal's once-great pioneer empire. Brazil has gone its own way; India is threatening to close in on Goa and Communist China on Macao; but Mozambique and, over on the west coast, Angola, are flourishing. Neglected and asleep until the imperialistic surge of the late nineteenth century, they now have commercial value. This is not so much for what they produce, though Angola is beginning to go heavily into coffee, but because they lie between the rich hinterlands— the Transvaal, Rhodesia, and the Belgian Congo—and the sea. Passive exploitation of geography has been paying off very well.

Both of the Mozambique ports—Lourenco Marques 307 miles north of Durban, and Beira 476 miles still further to the north-ward, have been made by their hinterlands. Lourenco Marques could claim, however, at least until the Durban bar was pierced in 1904, that it had the finest setting north of Cape Town. Even a quick glance at the map of Africa shows it as one of the few major indentations on the coast. Unlike Algoa Bay, which is merely a shallow affair, open to a boisterous sea, Delagoa Bay receives excellent protection from an island and adjacent prom-ontory, almost twenty miles away and barely visible from the port. It is the one port in the region where the *Sailing Directions* has no warning remarks to make about gales or sand bars.

The bay was originally sighted in 1502 by Antonio de Campo, who had been on Da Gama's famous first voyage. It was investi-gated more thoroughly in 1544 by two second-string Portuguese explorers, Lourenco Marques and Antonio Caldeira. Its exist-ence as an outpost of empire was extremely sketchy down through the next three centuries, with no indication of more than spasmodic residence by the Portuguese. [96]

The Dutch, appreciating the sheltered bay, maintained a fort there from 1721 to 1730. One British naval captain, while chart-ing the coast and trying to check the slave trade, hoisted the flag there in 1823, and another did likewise in 1860. The Portuguese protested loudly, citing their long history there. Some of the

British sneered at such claims as "archaeological," and pointed out how little the Portuguese had to show for their three centuries of opportunity. Finally, Britain and Portugal submitted the question to Marshal MacMahon, the President of France, for arbitration. He gave Portugal even more than it claimed, which further convinced the British that the old soldier was not quite bright.

In a stubborn contest it became a matter of British pride to keep the name "Delagoa Bay," the name inscribed upon the Admiralty chart in 1827. It was equally a matter of Portuguese honor to call it Lourenco Marques. [97] Until well into the twentieth century, steamship advertisements, and the official South African yearbook called it Delagoa Bay. Portuguese irritation finally produced a postal edict that any mail addressed "Delagoa Bay" was to be returned to the sender with the notation that it was improperly addressed.

The discovery of gold in the Rand in 1886 suddenly transformed Lourenco Marques from a scrubby little town into a flourishing seaport. By the rail connections which quickly developed, Johannesburg is only 349 miles from Lourenco Marques, as compared with 482 from Durban, 665 from East London, 712 from Port Elizabeth, and 956 from Cape Town. That situation has led to competition among the ports for that rich hinterland trade similar to that between Boston, New York, Philadelphia, and Baltimore in their efforts to reach the West by rail around 1850.

The railroads from the five rival ports all reached the Rand between 1892 and 1895. Some of them had been under construction for a long time, for the railroad movement had started very slowly in South Africa, because of two serious problems. On almost every route there had to be a sudden steep climb up to the high central plateau. This was a unique feature of most of South and Central Africa, with altitudes of 5,000 or more feet in many places. Second, the long, sparsely inhabited stretches would furnish scant, if any, passenger or freight business. The first line completed was a two-mile one, from the Point to the city at Durban in 1860. A year earlier, a road was begun from

Cape Town up to Wellington, 54 miles away, but it was to take years to finish.

The discovery of diamonds gave a boost to the lagging movement; in the 1870's, Port Elizabeth, East London, and Durban all began roads to the interior. In 1873, the Cape Colony government took over its railways from private management and made, for better or worse, the decision to cut the gauge from the standard European and American 4' 8½" of its earlier lines to 3' 6". It justified this because of the steep climbs and the need for economy with the long unprofitable stretches. H. F. Varian, a British engineer, who helped build more African railroad mileage than almost any other man, calls this gauge "a great handicap in the trade and development of a country of great distances, as the speed on a 3' 6"-gauge is half of what it is on a 4' 8½"-gauge. All efforts to change this . . . have been ineffectual. . . ." It was pointed out that the extra cost of 4' 8½" as against 3' 6", as shown by alternative tenders, was very small. [98]

That decision has probably cost the owners of ships serving South African ports many millions of dollars because of seaport congestion and delays by the railroads' inability to bring up and carry off cargo rapidly enough. Even the crack "Blue Train" between Cape Town and Johannesburg averages little more than 40 miles an hour. Freight cars, or "goods vans" are so small that one man can easily push one along the piers. Many of the routes are single track. The whole setup is pretty primitive, contrasted with a long American freight train of a hundred forty-ton cars, more or less, rolling along on schedule at 50 or 60 miles an hour. To make matters worse, as time went on, the railway administration, with its official authority, would prevent any extensive truck competition with its overworked rail lines.

The port rivalry for hinterland contacts intensified with the Rand gold discoveries in 1886, just after the three Cape Colony ports pushed rail connections through to the diamond fields at Kimberley. Five separate governments complicated the final stage —Cape Colony, Natal, Orange Free State, Portuguese East Africa, and, above all, Transvaal, which controlled the final approaches. Kruger, its tough old Boer president, was suspicious of British advances, and determined upon an outlet to the sea at

Lourenco Marques, not only because it was closer but also because it was not under British control. A Dutch company, apparently with some American capital, undertook the line from Delagoa Bay to Pretoria, the Transvaal capital near Johannesburg. Its first rails were landed at "L.M." in 1887. In the meantime, Kruger held off the approaches from the other ports until 1892, when Cape Town, Port Elizabeth, and East London all gained rail contact with the Rand. The "Dutch" line from Delagoa Bay was opened in 1894. Durban, which would ultimately do the most valuable business of all, was still dependent upon oxcarts for part of its Rand contact until 1895.

Lourenco Marques immediately boomed; it brought in materials for the Boer republics, which would be at war with the British within five years. In 1903 it was the only port north of Cape Town where a large liner could come alongside a dock.

Then, in 1909, the Portuguese took shrewd advantage of their geographical position. Knowing that the Rand mines needed more native labor, they agreed to furnish a large number of native "boys" on contract, provided that Transvaal (which was not absorbed into the Union until the following year) agreed to bring in half its imports "to what are known as the competitive areas" through Lourenco Marques. This so-called Mozambique Convention, renewed from time to time during the following decades, is still in force in the late 1950's with the same general terms. The Portuguese percentage has been applied to tonnage rather than to value, so the South Africans have filled the stipulated quota largely with bulky items such as timber and oil. They are, incidentally, usually brought by tramp or tanker rather than by line freighter. The valuable general cargo, automobiles, machinery, and so on, generally pass through the Union ports. In 1926, for instance, the South African imports through Lourenco Marques amounted to 53.2 per cent of the tonnage, but only 7.4 per cent of the value.[99] To offset the greater distances from the Union ports, the South African Railways have attempted to make them competitive by reducing freight rates.

Another major aspect of the railroad situation in South and Central Africa has been the race for copper and other mineral cargo from the Rhodesian Copperbelt and the Belgian Congo

Katanga. Since 1955, Lourenco Marques has joined in that pattern also with its new Limpopo rail connection. It thus taps both rich hinterlands, the Rand and the Copperbelt-Katanga.

The Portuguese have made the most of their transit advantages. They have also decreed that at least three out of four in every office and business be Portuguese. With their prosperity they have built a beautiful white city with considerable Latin-European charm. Crowds come down from the Rand each year to relax in this "Transvaal Riviera" on the Indian Ocean. [100]

Whereas Lourenco Marques has been regarded as one of the best of African ports in providing quick turnaround, the reverse has been decidedly true of Mozambique's other major port, Beira, which is the sea gateway to Rhodesia. Its very name became synonymous with delay. Lourenco Marques had not been much of a town before the Rand discoveries, but Beira was nothing at all, not even a name, when Cecil Rhodes in 1890 pushed his "Pioneer Force" into Matabeleland and Mashonaland, which would later be named Rhodesia in his honor. With his dream of an all-red British strip up through Africa from "the Cape to Cairo," he moved rapidly in that period of flux to prevent the Germans, Portuguese, or Belgians from blocking such a movement.

No ready-made seaport was available for this new region north of Transvaal. [101] There was, to be sure, a magnificent natural harbor, one of the best in all Africa, at Nacala, near the old Portuguese capital at Mozambique, but it lay almost five hundred miles too far north to serve the new Rhodesian hinterland. [102] The choice fell on a desolate sandspit at the mouth of the muddy Pungue (or Pungwe) River, as the one spot where steamers could find relative shelter, combined with a potential short route to the hinterland. As the interior activity grew, steamers began to make regular runs up from the south. Rhodes himself came up from Durban in the Union liner *Norseman* in 1891 and journeyed inland by river and horseback. The Portuguese kept a gunboat on hand, apparently suspicious of British designs to grab this outlet to the sea.

The sandspit, soon named for the province of Beira in Portugal, was still a sorry place several years later. The town was simply "a long straggling street," with ill-fame from the health point of view. This was confirmed "by the fever-stricken look of most of the inhabitants." With mangrove swamps reaching almost to the backs of the houses, "mosquitoes were a constant plague by day and by night." [103]

Then, and until well into the twentieth century, Beira and its Rhodesian hinterland were among the last examples of governmental and economic control by chartered companies. Two of the most celebrated and long-lived were the English East India Company, chartered in 1600, and, two years later, the Dutch East India Company, which founded Cape Town. The "scramble for Africa" led to a revival of the pattern, with the German East Africa Company set up in 1885, the Royal Niger Company in 1886, and the British East Africa Company in 1888. Those three soon relinquished their political powers, but here the company rule lasted longer.

In 1889, before undertaking the settlement of what would become Rhodesia, Cecil Rhodes secured a 25-year charter for the British South Africa Company, which agreed to extend the railroad northward and encourage trade and commerce. In return, it was to govern the new region and to have all its mineral rights. The contract, expiring in 1914, was extended ten years. The company rule ended in 1923, when Southern Rhodesia, rejecting the idea of joining the Union of South Africa, became a British protectorate. The company received £3,750,000 as recompense for its past expenditures; it had never paid a dividend, but retained rich land and mineral rights.

The latest and longest-lasting of these chartered companies was the Companhia de Moçambique or Mozambique Company, chartered for 50 years by the Portuguese government in 1891. Much of its £1,500,000 capital was British and some was Belgian. It received sovereign rights over two territories of Portuguese East Africa, including Beira as the most important feature. The company charter was not renewed in 1941; and the Portuguese government took over direct administration in 1942. During its last years, this Mozambique Company was the sole survivor of the chartered companies ruling in Africa; over on the west coast, the Royal Niger Company had yielded its political rights in 1900. Not until the late 1940's, however, did the port of Beira and the railroads serving it come under governmental control in Rhodesia, as well as in the Portuguese area. [104]

The inadequacy of the port facilities both outside in the approaches and inside in the so-called harbor, as well as the rail setup combined for a while to give Beira a bad name in shipping circles. [105] Shoals, sandbanks, and sand bars still offer problems to the incoming and outgoing shipmaster, with a five-knot current to boot. There are times each month when the neap tides leave a controlling depth of only 23 feet—too shallow for a loaded freighter—over the main sand bar. And, in addition to all the other serious causes of delay, a ship can be "bar bound" if she becomes ready for sea at those particular times. Durban, by energetic dredging, long ago overcame an even worse handicap but Beira has not yet reached that stage.

Inside the port, matters were complicated by the lack of adequate anchorages that could be trusted; normally only eight ships at a time could lie at anchor. In times of congestion, all the rest had to wait outside the bar. Originally, cargo had to be landed by lighter alongside the muddy shore of Chiveve Creek, where the 18- to 25-foot rise and fall of tide seriously complicated such operations. By 1938, a 2,712-foot marginal deepwater quay, capable of accommodating five or six good-sized freighters at a time, had been constructed along the Pungue River. Most conspicuous among the gradual improvements in cargo methods, and the one with which American ships have been the most concerned, has been a conveyor belt for loading chrome. Even in that, however, there have been international recriminations as to just who miscalculated—it cannot carry heavy chunks, but only powdered chrome.

The burden of traffic at Beira more than outstripped these very slow improvements. The total tonnage handled rose from 1.2 million tons in 1938 to almost 1.6 in 1948 and to 2.9 by 1954, about evenly divided between exports and imports. [106] The copper exports, which contributed much to the congestion, rose from 232,000 to 409,000 tons during those years, and chrome ore from 225,000 to 456,000. [107] The bulk of Beira's traffic, nearly 72 per cent in 1948, and 62 per cent in 1954, has been with the

Rhodesias, North and South; the Belgian Congo's share ranged between five and ten per cent; and Nyasaland got some of the remainder. [108]

With those shipments of copper and chrome almost doubling in six years, it is small wonder that the facilities of Beira were not equal to the occasion. Even before World War II, it had been a little slower than the other Southern African ports in shipping turnaround. Except for the few ships for East Africa, it was, of course, the outermost port on the "main line." Ships' officers under various flags had very ample opportunity to become acquainted with it. Some went hunting; some learned to fly; and one Farrell captain was able to build himself a large motor launch during a wait there. Perhaps the most popular of Beira's somewhat restricted social diversions, an 18-hole golf course "with grass all the way," was quite unusual in that part of the world.

Such opportunities increased in the postwar years. The average Farrell turnaround in 1938 was 5.7 days, with the longest at 16 days. [109] In 1947, 16 days, instead of being the lone maximum, had become the average, and in 1948 that had risen to 24 days. [110] The *Selma Victory*, a Farrell-chartered Victory ship, was in port 66 days, from Christmas 1947 to the beginning of March, in addition to a few preliminary days of waiting outside the bar. One British ship, the Harrison Line freighter *Defender*, according to well-established local tradition, had a 102-day wait at Beira, with a Clan liner as runner-up at more than 90 days. [111]

There were frequent occasions between 1947 and 1950 when 20 to 30 ships at a time would be waiting. Only about a dozen at a time could be handled inside the port, the luckiest ones alongside the quay and the others at buoys where they could be served by lighters. The rest usually chose to remain outside the bar rather than anchor in the treacherous mud inside. Access to the port facilities was a matter of first come, first served, which was applied without favor to particular flags or lines; only mail steamers did not have to wait their turn.

This whole question of port delays has been a very real problem to shipping lines. One great trading company with its own line of freighters has expressed the problem well: "Ships are paid for the . . . carriage of goods from one seaport to another. A ship earns money only when it is on the move. All the time it is idle it is denied the opportunity to secure extra income. . . . A ship is neither designed nor paid for acting as a floating warehouse. . . . Port capacity depends to a large extent on the rate at which the inland communications can handle goods passing through the port." [112]

The shipping conferences often met serious cases of congestion and delay by the imposition of a heavy "surcharge" on the freight rates to or from such a port. In the case of Beira the Farrell Lines went even further. In the last days of 1948, its directors voted to suspend service there until conditions improved. This seemed the only way to maintain schedules, although the loss on freight earnings involved would be around 1,750 tons of cargo into Beira and 15,000 tons out each month. [113] Altogether, the line made only four visits to Beira in 1949 out of 22 to Southern Africa, but that did not end the trouble. [114] Whatever the shortcomings of Beira's harbor facilities may have been, there was a general feeling that here, as elsewhere in such cases, the real fault lay with the rail connections to the hinterland. [115]

Beira's main rail line to the interior was a single-track, 3' 6"-gauge affair. What was more, the configuration of the Zambesi valley forced it into a circuitous route several times the direct distance. The original route, completed in 1897, had run 374 miles to Salisbury. Then it dipped south to Bulawayo, near which it united with the main north-south line from Kimberley, a part of Cecil Rhodes' dream of a Cape to Cairo railway. By 1905, this joint line was crossing the Zambesi by a bridge at Victoria Falls. Thence it pushed northward to the Rhodesian Copperbelt, and on over the Belgian Congo frontier, reaching Elisabethville, center of the rich Katanga region, in 1910. Those two rich mineral regions now had rail contact either with Beira or with Port Elizabeth and other ports in the Union. Because of the roundabout route, the Copperbelt, some 700 miles from Beira in a beeline, was about double that distance by the railroad. The principal chrome mines at Selukwe, near Bulawayo, only 250 miles from Beira in a direct line, were 650 miles away by rail via Salisbury.

That chrome, which was the principal Beira export to the

Painting by C. G. Evers

The *African Patriot* unloading into surfboats at Accra

The *African Endeavor* passing the Bluff at Durban

United States, suffered from a rail priority policy, which gave copper an overriding preference even in times of severe congestion, while the coal traffic absorbed much rolling stock. As a result, in 1957, "chrome producers have been plagued with an almost continuous shortage of freight cars, resulting in accumulation of large stockpiles in the mining areas (at present an estimated year's production) and periodical failure to meet export commitments, or inability to accept orders from overseas." [116]

The physical condition of the railroad was bad. The postwar rush of traffic had caught the rail authorities unprepared; the directors of those private lines, moreover, anticipating the government acquisition both in Mozambique and in Rhodesia, were not inclined to incur heavy expenses. So Beira's main rail artery retained its handicaps. On the tortuous route, with its inadequate roadbed, sharp curves, and steep grades, trainloads were limited to 800 tons instead of a possible 1,500. With only nine such trains a day in each direction, the total 7,200-ton daily arrivals at Beira would scarcely fill a single freighter. [117]

In the late 1940's, with the respective governments taking over the roads, conditions improved somewhat. In the course of a decade, the traffic increased to 15 trains a day, thanks to better rolling stock, sidings, and signal systems in particular. Some of this was aided by American loans or grants, in view of the essential minerals involved.

Also, two other rail lines, the so-called Benguela and the Limpopo, had in the meantime begun to divert some of these minerals through Lobito and Lourenco Marques. It had taken almost 30 years to complete the Benguela line to the Atlantic coast port of Lobito. [118] Originally projected in 1902 by Robert Williams, a lieutenant of Cecil Rhodes, the first through trains to the Katanga did not run until 1931. The economic advantages of such a road are obvious. Beira and Lobito are almost equidistant by rail from the Copperbelt. When the copper or other cargo reaches Lobito, however, it is only 5,900 miles from New York, instead of the 8,250 from Beira, with naturally a corresponding saving on the trip to Europe. Economic nationalism, however, not only complicated the project while it was taking form but continued to do so later in traffic and rate questions.

Rhodesia, not wanting to lose revenue for its own railroad, only reluctantly agreed to admit a minor percentage of its imports through Lobito 20-odd years after the road was opened. Also the Belgian Congo and South Africa had their own negative attitudes. The terrific pressure and congestion at Beira finally forced concessions toward the Benguela route to Lobito on the west coast. [119]

The "Limpopo line," the second project, was purely an east coast affair. Since Lourenco Marques had a potential port capacity of more than it really needed, a rail line of 300 miles or so was run up to Rhodesia, joining the old Beira line near Bulawayo. This meant that shipments from the Copperbelt and Katanga could move easily to Lourenco Marques, and leave the final stretch of the old road free for the chrome shipments closer at hand. The line, completed in 1955, follows in part the stream which Kipling described as "the great grey-green, greasy Limpopo River."

In 1935, the American-flag steamships would move a thousand miles up the coast beyond Beira to the ports of British East Africa with their old Arab background and their sticky, humid heat. [120] It was a long jump beyond the "main line," but once there, the four major ports are closer together than any of those down the coast. It is only 69 miles from Mombasa to Tanga, 75 miles from Tanga to Zanzibar, and 45 miles from Zanzibar to Dar-es-Salaam. In shipping matters, these four ports of the "B.E.A. range" are more closely linked than any in Southern Africa. Headquarters in New York hopefully predict the probable dates of arrival and departure at each port from Cape Town up to Beira. For British East Africa, however, they simply assign two weeks for the range and let nature take its course. The general agent at Mombasa has been given authority to move a ship around from port to port as he sees fit, depending upon the amount of cargo offering at each.

Zanzibar, an exotic island twenty miles off the coast, has an Arabian Nights atmosphere, which ranks it with Cape Town as one of the most delightful ports of call South of Sahara. It was the only real point of contact between the western world and the upper half of East Africa during most of the nineteenth century. This was the case of a port with neither a harbor nor hinterland. Its success came from the initiative of Said, its Sultan, whose cloves and imports of cotton and commercial treaties have twice been mentioned. [121] Around 1830, he had expanded out from Muscat and Oman over near the Persian Gulf to seize Zanzibar and the adjacent African east coast. He moved his seat of government to Zanzibar where he could better regulate the flourishing slave trade, East Africa's "big business" until the British put a stop to it. But along with that traffic in human flesh, he gave legitimate commerce a succession of stimuli, so that Zanzibar would have something to offer in exchange for the outside goods it wanted. This was a commerce that involved more than Zanzibar itself, with its adjacent island of Pemba. Zanzibar (the name of both the island and its port-capital) became the entrepôt for traffic with the mainland throughout that region—traffic involving "black ivory" as well as white. What was more, the Sultan of Zanzibar claimed political sovereignity over the mainland, an authority which was stronger along the coast than inland. Because of its leading position, Zanzibar became the jumping-off place for most of the important explorations of central Africa in the third quarter of the nineteenth century—Livingstone, Speke, Baker, Stanley and the other explorers were frequent visitors at the British consulate, now occupied by the trading company which acts as agents for the Farrell ships.

The very activity of those explorers ultimately undermined Zanzibar's commercial pre-eminence. After Stanley, in particular, had made the outside world "Africa-conscious," the international scramble soon shifted the center of interest and influence to the nominal possessions of the Sultan on the mainland. By the mid-1880's a lively scramble was on, the German, Karl Peters, and the Scot, Sir William Mackinnon, taking the lead in developing what today are known as Tanganyika and Kenya respectively. By a deal in 1890, Britain gave Germany the strategic island of Heligoland in the North Sea in exchange for the present Kenya and its hinterland, Uganda, plus a protectorate over Zanzibar. Today its Sultan still exercises nominal rule even over the mainland coastal strip; his red flag flies over Mombasa along with the Union Jack. As time went on, Mombasa, Tanga, and Dar-es-Salaam, with their rail connections into deep hinterlands, would gradually draw trade away from Zanzibar, which had only its cloves for outside appeal.

Some of the foreign lines still make Zanzibar a regular port of call, with their liners anchoring off the Sultan's palace and the clove-scented waterfront, while cruise ships give their tourists a special treat with a few hours ashore. The American freighters, however, are less regular—it was said to be a standing rule that they would put in only when sure of $1,500 worth of freight earnings.

Mombasa, the outlet for Kenya and Uganda, was only a sleepy Arab village when Zanzibar was at its peak, but it had been much more important than the clove island centuries earlier, and would be again, with its modern docks and its railroad. Likewise an island, it has, however, instead of twenty miles, only a tidal strait between it and the mainland. That narrow strait, by providing an excellent harbor situation and a certain amount of security from invasion by land, was one reason for Mombasa's centuries-old significance. The Arabs were well entrenched when the Portuguese began to come out, around 1500. The two contested over it for more than two centuries—old Fort Jesus, built by Portugal in 1593, is the source of some grim legends— but Portugal eventually lost out in that whole region.

In Mombasa there is a statue to Sir William Mackinnon, the head of the very successful British India Steam Navigation Company ("B.I."), who was a pioneer in appreciating the possibilities of East Africa and in checking the sweeping imperialist ambitions of Peters and the other Germans. He was a prime mover and heavy investor in the Imperial British East Africa Company, which the British government took over in 1895 after he and others had lost heavily on their initial investments.

One particular project of those early imperialists was a railroad to the interior, to beat the Germans out to the lakes. The project won final grudging approval in London, but the widespread skepticism was reflected in a quatrain in a London newspaper in 1896:

> The use of it, no one can conjecture,
> What it will carry there's none can define,
> An' in spite of George Curzon's superior lecture,
> It's clearly naught but a lunatic line. [122]

It was this railroad project that "made" Mombasa. R. A. Preston, a British engineer who had been in charge of the improvements of Madras harbor, came over in 1896 to build the road. He brought with him 300 laborers from India. He found that "the place was still an Arab seaport village, totally unequipped to receive the cargoes of . . . bulky materials due to arrive there. When the men unloaded a small two-wheeled refuse cart, the inhabitants asked curiously 'Is that the railway?' There was no dock. The ships came in as close to the shore as they dared at high tide, dumped their cargoes into the bay, and left the coolies to retrieve the goods when the tide went out . . . The only hotel was a native hut. Food was almost impossible to secure . . . All the water was contaminated; everyone drank coconut milk to avoid dysentery." [123]

Probably no other African railway presented quite so many difficulties in construction. There were plenty, even from the purely engineering standpoint. Like many of the other roads, it had the sharp climb from tidewater up onto the African plateau, often a mile or so above sea level. But this line had an added hurdle in the Rift Valley. Not far beyond Nairobi there was a precipitous drop of some 1,500 feet down a steep escarpment, eventually rising again on the far side, so that the high point on the road had an elevation of more than 9,000 feet. But that was not all; wild beasts along the line did not appreciate the advances of civilization. On one occasion, despite all precautions, lions ate up thirty of the Indian laborers, which had a depressing influence on morale. Even after the road was completed, lions would sometimes besiege station agents who would telegraph out frantic appeals for help.

One important by-product of the railroad construction was Nairobi, which ultimately became the most sophisticated city South of Sahara and a center of British business in the area. No one had ever planned it, but the road construction bogged down there in 1899 for a while. Later, traders moved into the abandoned shacks of the railway workers, and the city just grew. Eventually, Farrell Lines would establish one of its five African representatives there. To make matters the more fantastic, within view of the city's tall buildings, giraffes, hartebeeste, baboons and lions roam about in their native habitat.

In 1904, the road reached its initial objective, Kisumu, on Lake Victoria near the headwaters of the Nile. Although almost on the equator, the altitude makes it so cool that wood fires and blankets are the rule at night. Later, it pushed on ever farther to Kampala in the Uganda hinterland. Even though some accidental decision at the outset fixed the gauge at one meter, almost three inches narrower than the already too-narrow South African, the "Lunatic Line" has served an indispensable role in carrying the coffee, tea, and pyrethrum to tidewater at Mombasa. At the same time, however, the line has been largely responsible for Mombasa's gaining a reputation second only to Beira's for port congestion and delays. Of the four main ports in British East Africa, Mombasa was the only one to have modern dockage facilities until 1956, when Dar-es-Salaam got its new dock. At Zanzibar, at Tanga, and at Dar until recently, lighters have been necessary for the removal and loading of cargo. The insular position of Mombasa has given it two harbors. The old one, with its old custom house, is now used for the Arab dhows. Once a year, with the monsoon, Arab traders sail these ancient-type vessels laden with rugs, dates, and other commodities from across the Indian Ocean, as their ancestors have done for centuries, waiting until the monsoon shifts its direction so they can sail home again with what Mombasa has had to offer. The other port, called Kilindini, has been developing its modern facilities since World War I. These have been most effective, but the single-track, meter-gauge railway was long unable to carry from the docks the variegated incoming cargo, which is always more of a problem than the more uniform outgoing.

In early 1952, when Beira conditions were again deteriorating, Mombasa began to have its troubles. The *African Star*, arriving on February 3, was delayed 49 days to March 24 before even berthing; and finally sailed April 6, after 62 days in port. Some other vessels spent up to 60 days at that same time. It is true that two other Farrell ships saved time because their Mombasa cargoes had been transferred to the *African Star* at Lourenco Marques and Beira. Because of these delays, the Mombasa Imports Cargo Phasing Committee was formed early in 1952 to control the handling of incoming cargo. Each ship was allowed a certain maximum time for getting its cargo out. [124]

Dar-es-Salaam ("Haven of Peace") was a relative newcomer in maritime circles. Established in the 1880's by the Sultan of Zanzibar, as an alternative to an older slaving port just up the coast, it was to become the capital and commercial outlet of German East Africa. A 780-mile railway goes to Kigoma on Lake Tanganyika, close to the site of the "Dr. Livingstone, I presume" episode. It was completed in 1914, just before World War I transferred Tanganyika to Britain, despite the brilliant operations by German forces still unconquered at the end of the war.

Beyond its fairly narrow entrance it has a good-sized sheltered anchorage. Many of the buildings were substantially built by the Germans. Until 1956, this was a lighterage port, like Zanzibar and Tanga; that is, the vessels anchored in the stream and unloaded by lighter. Such a port is in an intermediate position between the wholly unprotected surf ports and those ports with modern docking equipment. Dar-es-Salaam in 1956 opened the modernly equipped Princess Margaret Quay, dedicated by the Princess on her visit there that year. [125] A novel part of the quay is knows as "Belbase." That was an outgrowth of an arrangement made several years previously whereby Belgium would retain an extraterritorial claim to an outlet for the products from the eastern Belgian Congo and from the Ruanda-Urundi region taken over from the Germans. They also established another "Belbase" at the head of the rail line at Kigoma.

Tanga is perhaps commercially the steadiest of the major East African ports, albeit the least glamorous. It has been a well-protected lighterage port, specializing most impressively in the exportation of sisal.

Aside from those ten ports on the "main line" to South and East Africa, American liners drop in occasionally at numerous others to leave or pick up cargo. South of Dar-es-Salaam, there are Mtwara, which received all sorts of modern equipment in connection with the fantastic peanut program of the British Laborites; Lindi; Mozambique, original capital of the Portuguese on the coast; and its nearby entry port of Nacala with its rail contacts to the interior. Off the eastern coast of Africa, the great French island of Madagascar suddenly began large-scale production of cloves and vanilla in the late 1930's. At one time, Farrell ships had visited there, but in later days that was not generally considered worth while. Likewise, the line did not continue its occasional early time-consuming runs still further out to the island of Mauritius.

The most permanent later Farrell contact outside of the "big ten" was Walvis Bay. Although over on the western coast, South West Africa has been served by ships of the South and East Africa run. Karakul skins have long been a valuable offering, and much ore has recently been shipped from there in large quantities, but the atmosphere of Walvis has been most strongly affected by fish products. One Farrell captain wrote some vigorous verses about its fishy odors. [126] Sometimes the Farrell ships would also stop at the old German port of Luderitz Bay, once Angra Pequena, to the south of Walvis. None of those extra ports, however, could compare with those from Cape Town up to East Africa, either in cargo or in interest.

Chapter IV

RETURN TO THE SEA

AMERICAN complacency with its dependence upon foreign shipping came to an abrupt end with World War I. The dislocations caused by that conflict showed the nation all too clearly what it meant to lack cargo liners of one's own. Later in the war, the heavy inroads by German submarines caused the United States to construct a huge fleet of freighters. The combined effect of all this was to lead the United States to create and support regular line service, after the war, on what it came to consider were the "essential trade routes" to all important ports of the world.

The last week of July 1914 at New York saw the summer rush of crack liners in full swing, along with the usual coming and going of freighters. In all this port activity, there were only two American-flag liners leaving for other continents: the old American Line *St. Louis* for Southampton and the even more aged little "Red D" Line's *Philadelphia* for Venezuela. [127]

With the next Saturday, August 1, came the news of war, with Germany and Russia already engaged, and with Britain and France expected to join the conflict momentarily. The German ships that had sailed that week were ordered back to New York. One, the *Kronprinzessin Cecelie,* barely eluded the British and French cruisers bent on her capture in a mad race back, but found refuge at Bar Harbor. [128]

The United States faced a tantalizing outlook: new shortages and trade openings but not enough ships. German shipping and German exports were about to be suddenly eliminated from the world of commerce where their role had been a substantial one. Analine dyes were about all that the United States really needed from Germany, and the loss of direct contact between Hamburg, Bremen, and New York was not too serious. The real impact would be in the distant nonindustrial regions, where German shipping services and cargoes had served a vital need—South America, Africa, Australia, and New Zealand in particular. It seemed probable that Britain would not be able to fill that vacuum. Despite what seemed a pretty secure control of the seas, it would need so many of its own merchantmen as transports or armed cruisers that its elaborate network of line services would probably have to be contracted, not expanded. The need for munitions, moreover, and for other war materials would undoubtedly reduce, rather than increase, its potential industrial offerings.

Once again, as in 1793–1812, American commerce and shipping had the chance to take advantage of Europe's belligerent preoccupation. As one official expressed it: "The United States at this moment has a grave duty and responsibility as well as a great opportunity. . . ." [129] This time, however, was different when it came to exploiting the chances for neutral profits. The United States saw that its neglected seagoing tonnage would prevent its taking full advantage of the waiting markets in those rich and distant nonindustrial regions, even if its factories might be able to supply those needs. Besides, there was no established American commercial foothold left in those far-off places.

The crying lack, after a half century of inadequate maritime policy, was in seagoing steel freighters, capable of regular service on distant runs. The existing established lines in overseas service provided only a drop in the bucket. The protected "coastal" trades had produced rather more potential tonnage. The intercoastal steel freighters of American-Hawaiian and Luckenbach, and the West Indian liners of Ward and Bull, as well as the long-range coastal steamships of Morgan (Southern Pacific), Mallory, and Clyde could be of some limited service. Much of the large total tonnage of the nation, however, was of no use on the high seas.

For about a half century, Congress had denied the "free ships"

argument for admitting cheap foreign ships to American registry. [130] After a partial relaxation in 1912, it finally let down the
bars during the first few weeks of war. [131] By mid-1915, some
523,000 tons of shipping, much of it already American-owned,
had been transferred to American registry; by 1917, this had
increased to 650,000 tons. [132]

Even those shifts, however, were not enough to meet the steadily increasing opportunities for American shipping in distant
runs. This led to efforts to dig out all sorts of marginal shipping
which had seemed to have outlived its normal useful career.
Old steamers and old sailing vessels by the dozen were rescued
from retirement and projected scrapping, at high profit. There
was the case of a schooner built on the Maine coast to take advantage of the shipping shortage. On the day that she sailed on
her maiden voyage, each of her investors received a dividend
check for 105 per cent; the charter for her maiden voyage, with
the vessel and freight insured, more than paid for her. [133]

There were other repercussions. Immediately, the price of
cotton and wheat fell off sharply with the loss of continental markets, while finance, foreign exchange and marine insurance were
severely affected. Later, the lack of shipping meant that freight
piled up very seriously at New York. There was much more of
all this. [134]

The contacts with South Africa give a general idea of what
was going on commercially in remote regions, largely dependent upon the outside for numerous commodities. South America, Australia, and part of Asia faced much the same situation,
although it was widely conceded that the South Africans got
along more easily than some others.

The United States share of South African imports and exports
showed a threefold gain from 5 per cent in 1913 to 16 per cent in
1918, and would have been more had vessels enough been available. In that period, the British share fell from 58 per cent in
1913 to a low of 47 per cent in 1917, then went back to 51 per cent
in 1918. [135] American-flag shipping from the United States to
South Africa jumped from 1,000 out of a total of 130,000 tons in
the last year of peace to 40,000 out of 150,000 in 1918; that increase was represented entirely by sailing vessels. Particularly

prophetic of future developments was the gradual growth of two-way traffic between the two regions, with homeward traffic from South Africa to the United States jumping from four vessels in 1914 to 37 in 1918. [136]

The story in West Africa was somewhat the same, but infinitely more complicated because Liberia and the numerous colonial possessions were under so many different flags. Since it did not come into the Farrell picture until more than twenty years after South Africa, no attempt will be made to devote more than occasional references to the wartime situation there. [137]

The rapid disappearance of German ships and cargoes was the first major impact of the war in African waters. Some were lucky enough to have been in home ports; a few reached them with only a day or so to spare; others found neutral asylum, safe for a while, in Brazil, in the Canaries, or in Portuguese Africa. A few found temporary shelter at Dar-es-Salaam or other German colonial ports. The fate of the big Woermann fleet was particularly dramatic and thoroughgoing; its loss was felt most keenly in West Africa, where it had conducted a major share of the traffic in some regions, as high as 75 per cent in Liberia. [138]

Along with the ships, went the shipments to and from Germany. Many an African merchant was inconvenienced by the nonarrival of goods on those seized or interned liners. The disposition of those cargoes would still be a matter of dispute many months later. [139] The loss of further German imports would leave a significant gap in South African trade, for they amounted to about 8 per cent of the total, just below the American. They provided a respectable share of South Africa's imports of iron and steel products, machinery, cotton manufactures, and haberdashery and millinery, as well as a very high proportion of musical instruments and of drugs and chemicals. [140]

Even more, perhaps, would the South Africans feel the loss of that outlet for the export of its wool. Germany's purchases represented one-third of their total wool sales, with a modest amount of wattle bark and extract and of ostrich feathers. [141] Altogether, Germany's purchases of South African products had amounted to five times as much as those by the

United States which, unlike Germany, had no regular liner sailings back from South Africa.

As for British shipping, the Royal Navy gave a dramatic demonstration of "command of the sea," the objective of all naval effort through the years. British vessels were able to come and go at will. The British had only a handful of German cruisers and converted raiders to worry about for the time being; and relatively few vessels fell victim to them. [142]

The British themselves, however, had to remove some of their ships from the African run for other uses elsewhere. Several Union-Castle crack mail steamers were immediately taken over as armed merchant cruisers, and many other ships of this and other lines were likewise requisitioned. A heavy local demand for shipping came from the military operations against the Germans in South West Africa and also against the brief rebellion in the fall of 1914 of irreconcilable Boers in South Africa. Altogether, the usual line sailings to Britain were seriously curtailed. [143]

The modest number of sailings between the United States and South Africa, carried on, of course, mainly in conference liners, did not suffer as much, except during the first weeks of the war, while the raiding possibilities of the Germans were still a matter of conjecture. The conference liner *Tuscan Prince,* scheduled to leave New York August 10 did not dare until the 30th, while another, the *Kasenga,* was delayed from August 17 to September 20. By October, these steamships had resumed a fairly normal one-way service. [144] This continuing service by the British ships helped gain a foothold for American products at the expense of British goods in South Africa. To be sure, the conference lines raised rates from New York to South Africa twice as high as those from Britain, instead of keeping the old equal basis. [145] In 1916, up at Mombasa in East Africa, it was reported that rates from New York had gone up 675 per cent, as against only 100 per cent from Britain. [146] American goods were also taking the place of some of the lost German imports. It became increasingly obvious, however, that this was but a fraction of the commodities that might have been sold to Africa had the United States had more ships.

A corollary to the British carrying of competitive American goods was the attitude of the South Africans. It was only twelve years since the Boer War—naturally, the Boer-Afrikaner element, who outnumbered the British three to two, were not sorry to buy American instead of British offerings.

The most significant commercial event in the first year of the war was the beginning of direct shipments of wool from Port Elizabeth to Boston, instead of going by way of England. This was an initial breach in the "London entrepôt" system whereby so many American imports arrived by that roundabout route. [147]

The South Africans had feared that the loss of the usual heavy German purchases would seriously depress wool prices at Port Elizabeth and East London. Americans, however, quickly began to show a keen interest in the market, but the lack of shipping and British restrictions were a real problem. [148] There were, of course, no regular conference sailings westward to America. Finally, the Americans took matters into their own hands and chartered a neutral sailing vessel to carry their purchases to Boston. The first vessel in recent times to carry a regular South African cargo direct was the 1,522-ton Norwegian square-rigged ship *Acadia*, sailing on March 29, 1915 from East London for Boston with some 4,500 bales of wool. She arrived on May 27, which was a fast run for a sailing vessel. She was not, however, the first wool-laden vessel to arrive, for the Prince liner *Afghan Prince* reached Boston the previous day. She had sailed from New York for Cape Town in mid-February and returned from East London on April 23, taking 33 days to the square-rigger's 59. [149] That round trip by a regular conference liner, in place of the usual one-way run, was a foretaste of the future pattern of service. Altogether, three British steamships, the *Afghan Prince, Hyanthes,* and *Benin,* and five Norwegian square-riggers, the ship *Acadia* and the barks *Fido, Spica, Irene* and *Wulff,* made the homeward run to American east coast ports during the course of 1915. A few other sailing vessels from South Africa made for Gulf or west coast ports to pick up cargoes of oil or lumber. [150]

Naturally the British did not like this direct trade. The "wool and mohair interests" at the textile center of Bradford expressed themselves as "not favorably disposed." [151] More fundamental was the realization of the threat to the London entrepôt. "London still exists" so it was declared, "supreme as a market and entrepôt, and will continue to be so until the United States . . . offers greater facilities as a world center. . . . Trade, like water, always finds it own level and any South African producer or shipper, who is lured away . . . will have perforce to return to the main stream." [152] For all those brave words, the London entrepôt would never be the same again. In wool alone, the direct shipments from South Africa to the United States jumped from £7,000 in 1913 to £4,789,000 in 1918 and had fallen off only to £2,558,000 in 1920. [153]

However important those wool exports may have seemed to the South Africans, the United States regarded them primarily as simply means toward an end—and that end was selling American products to South Africa.

A new element in the South African import picture was the sudden extensive participation of Canada. Fords and other essentially United States products were being produced north of the border by Canadian branches of American concerns. Their South African popularity stemmed from the fact that coming from another British dominion, they enjoyed an imperial preference of three per cent. For years to come, many of the ships bound for South Africa would pick up cargo on the St. Lawrence.

The United States made excellent progress in penetrating the South African market, which, according to a British export journal, was being "overrun with travelers pushing business in the interests of U.S.A. manufacturers." [154] But much more could have been accomplished had more shipping been available. That plaint runs through the story month after month in a rather desperate refrain. Late in 1915, the vice-consul at Cape Town wrote that the need for increased shipping service has "impressed all who are interested in the expansion of American trade in this country. The present moment is ideal for the sale of American products in South Africa. . . . As it is, however, the sailings from New York and Boston are very irregular, and in many cases goods ordered some time ago have not yet been delivered. In other instances the exporter in America foresaw that it would be practically impossible for him to make deliveries on time and refused to accept orders from merchants in this country." [155]

That consul also told in detail about a letter from a New York exporting house regarding "the frequent congestion at New York and of the obstacles which the company was encountering in its efforts to get merchandise to South Africa—cancellations, refusals of lighterage deliveries, preference to the cargo paying the highest rate, and general uncertainty as to when any given shipment would go forward." [156]

The American special commercial agent at Johannesburg gave further evidence along those lines. He pointed out that cargo space aboard the conference liners was extremely difficult to get except for the few American export firms which had long-standing contracts. That shut off the freight of other concerns, especially in shipping windmills, plows, and similar objects paying low freight rates. One important Cape Town firm said that 300 packages of windmill parts ordered from New York had been awaiting shipment for nearly twelve weeks. [157] A similar story from London in those same last weeks of 1915 declared that "the life of a shipper or buying agent is one prolonged nightmare." [158]

A new rival with fewer distractions was taking advantage of the troubled conditions. Japan, then and later, had two powerful assets in its industrial competition—a remarkable capacity for imitation and a cheap labor supply. In its exports to South Africa, Japan came up from nothing to almost the same level that the Germans had had in 1913. The arrivals of Japanese-flag ships at Union ports jumped from 3 in 1914 and 7 in 1915 to 100 in 1916 and 84 in 1917, while the value of South African imports from Japan in those same years were £110,000, £221,000, £540,000, and £730,000 respectively. Their principal offerings seem to have been hosiery, underwear, blankets, silk goods, small bottles, crockery, chemicals, and fertilizer. They avoided returning in ballast by carrying home more wool than Britain herself. [159]

The German campaign of unrestricted submarine warfare in February 1917, which nearly accomplished its aim of starving Britain into submission, had the incidental result of stimulating American trade with South Africa, and giving the sailing vessel its last opportunity for usefulness on a large scale.

Whereas the earlier U-boat campaign had been aimed at belligerent ships and had not been pressed to the limit, Germany now went with ruthless efficiency against all shipping, neutral as well as belligerent. It hoped to bring England quickly to terms, knowing how dangerously dependent it was upon a steady supply of food, oil, and munitions from beyond the seas. The waters around the British Isles were soon strewn with the shattered hulls of torpedoed freighters and passenger liners. Bad enough in the first ten weeks, the situation became desperate in late April, when it was estimated that out of every four ships leaving British ports, one would never return. [160]

The United States, entering the war in that same grim month of April 1917, would be instrumental in urging and implementing the convoy system and other antisubmarine devices which were gradually to cut down the U-boat toll. Its generous financial support assisted Britain greatly in meeting its pressing problem of paying for its war needs. On the other hand, the transporting of 2,500,000 troops, together with huge quantities of supplies and munitions, across the Atlantic put an additional heavy burden on the available shipping already severely depleted by the unrestricted U-boat attacks. [161]

In later days of peacetime stringency, Britain would voice the slogan "Export or die," but in 1917–1918, it was an all-too-realistic case of "Import or die." Wheat and meat had to be brought in huge quantities, for England had been raising in a whole year only enough to feed her millions for a few weeks. [162] In order to have shipping enough for food and a few other commodities for survival, it was necessary to cut down drastically on nonessentials. Week after week and month after month, the responsible officials went over the situation with a keen eye upon relative values. Between 1913 and 1917, the volume of Britain's imports dropped from 54 to 38 million tons. [163] Where Britain had little need for a region's offerings, there was reluctance to allot much shipping. That was the situation of South and East Africa, which had particularly low cargo priority; they were allotted only 12,000 to 15,000 tons of cargo space (two or three ships) a month in 1917, whereas West Africa, with its palm kernels, palm oil, and ground nuts, useful for munitions or margarine, was allowed 40,000 tons. [164] The wholesale requisitioning of British shipping in 1917, moreover, took many vessels from their usual South African service. At one time only three ships of the 41-ship Union-Castle fleet were left on the usual run to and from the United Kingdom. Even those which came down from England, to meet the minimum needs of the South African market, were apt to return by way of India, which enjoyed a specially preferred position, or else they engaged in "trooping" from Australia. [165]

The British made frequent efforts, with varying success, to impose upon their overseas empire the same sort of import restrictions that were being imposed upon Britain itself. They tried in particular to curb exports from Britain and in British ships. While they saw fit to continue the usual quota of their cargo liners in the cross-trade between America and South Africa, they tried to keep that space from being utilized for "non-essential" American offerings. In July 1917, it was decreed in South Africa that in view of the acute shipping situation, no cargo space would be available on the British vessels plying to South Africa from the United States or Canada for a long list of commodities, ranging alphabetically from adding machines and advertising matter down to vacuum flasks and wood molding. [166] As one historian commented: "Owing to the opposition of the Dutch element in the population, the South African government was never able to enforce an import priority list." [167] At any rate, qualifying and mollifying comments began to appear. In August, the list was modified by the removal of baking powder, bedding, cereals, cheese, crockery, and so on but the vacuum flasks and much else remained. [168]

Before 1917 was over, Britain's shipping plight forced a far more drastic measure. It was decreed that "goods destined for allied and neutral countries cannot be transshipped in the United Kingdom in cases where means of direct transport are available." [169] Whatever might be said of the London entrepôt pattern in normal times, it was now quite out of the question to send scarce ships twice through the submarine zone at high insurance rates when they could deliver cargo easily on shorter and safer direct routes. The British re-export figures fell off almost to nothing.

To meet this situation, Americans turned to sailing vessels. Such steamships as there were had to be used on more urgent runs. As early as 1915, Scandinavian square-riggers had been chartered, and now their numbers were augmented by a fast-growing fleet of big American schooners. Some vessels already on hand were chartered; some were dug out of retirement and patched up; and still others were built for the purpose. For a while in mid-1917, some of the sailing vessels went to Europe, but they were too vulnerable targets and were formally banned from the dangerous war zones. They found rich opportunities on the distant runs to Africa, Australia, and South America, with high freight rates on all of them.

Normally, the sailing vessels on the long South Atlantic run took more than twice the normal four-week steamer time. From the very nature of their rig, the square-rigged ships or barks inclined to make better time on such an offshore route than did the fore-and-aft schooners. Few of the schooners could match the 59 days of the Norwegian ship *Acadia* which took that initial wool cargo from Port Elizabeth to Boston in 1915. The big 2,357-ton five-master *Singleton Palmer,* veteran of the Maine-built Palmer fleet of coal schooners, made the run from New York to Cape Town in 51 days, but eight months earlier she had needed 63 days. Some of the voyages, however, stretched out to double that length. [170]

Because of those varied circumstances, the United States took over from Britain a radically increased percentage of South Africa's imports. Between 1913 and 1917, for instance, the British percentage of automobile imports dropped from 40 to 1, while the American rose from 33 to 67. The shift in agricultural implements was identical. In galvanized corrugated sheets, used for roofing, the British drop was from 97 to 7 per cent, with a corresponding American rise from 2 to 90. And so it went, through item after item. [171]

South African industry received a stimulus which would last on after the war was over. "South Africa," it was remarked, "is, willy-nilly, learning to do without many products which were formerly imported, or is being compelled to manufacture goods which will take their place." [172] Altogether, between 1911 and 1917–18, the gross output of South African manufacturing climbed from £17 to £60 million. [173]

Rigid as were the British priority authorities, however, they did relax enough to allow South Africa to import generous quantities of whiskey—the South Africans had been having to drink Cape brandy. It was reported in 1918 that good Scotch had become cheaper and more plentiful in Johannesburg than it was in London. [174]

Incidentally, shortage of tonnage does not seem to have kept the Americans from doing their bit to quench African thirst. One captain with a schooner-load of gin has become legendary on the African coast. Deciding not to try to beat his way up through the Mozambique Channel, he had to wait weeks for a tug at Port Elizabeth. He appears to have spent the time sampling his cargo, for when a cable from the owner inquired its condition, he measured the distance from the rail to the waterline and sent back word that his cargo seemed to be sixty tons lighter. Other sailing vessels had already been carrying hard liquor to West Africa, judging by a Boston item from the fall of 1915 reporting the sailing of the bark *Ruth Starr* "for Guinea Coast with the fifth cargo of rum . . . in six months, about 200,000 gallons, which brings the total shipments to nearly 1,000,000 gallons. . . . Previously practically no rum was shipped from this port to the natives of Africa." [175]

An American shipment from New Orleans for Port Elizabeth and Durban, including 270 crated Ford cars, was sunk southeast of the Cape of Good Hope on November 20, 1917 by the German Surface raider *Wolf*. [176] The victim was the bark *John H. Kirby,* once the ship *Avenger,* an English 1,286-ton iron square-rigger in the annual wool races from Australia to England. Back in 1906 she had been abandoned as a hopeless wreck on the island where she went ashore off the Mississippi coast. The wartime shipping scarcity brought her a purchaser and she was rebuilt in 1916 at a cost of $80,000 by a Mobile shipyard. [177] Perhaps, as a reclaimed windjammer, she was not deemed worthy of the best in war-scarce chronometers; at any rate, hers was so faulty on that first and only voyage under her new name and flag that Captain Blom had no idea of his longitude. He was heading far out into the Indian Ocean, well past Good Hope and even Port Elizabeth, when the *Kirby* ran afoul of the *Wolf.* "She was not under full sail, but carried sufficient canvas to make a fine picture as she sailed before the great rollers coming in from southwest of the Cape." [178] She was signaled to heave to and was boarded by a prize officer in the traditional way of the pre-submarine era. The crew were imprisoned in the afterhold of the raider, already crowded with other captured crews. The American toothbrushes, soap, and other toilet goods and the ship's stores were all that the Germans salvaged before placing time bombs in the *Kirby.* She settled quickly by the stern and sank in five minutes.

Earlier in the year, the *Wolf* had laid some mines near Cape Town which sank several vessels including the steamship *City of Athens,* bound from New York for Australia. [179] Submarines caught a few outward-bound liners. [180] In view of that small number of sinkings, the Cape run escaped fairly easily.

By the spring of 1918, American shipments to Africa began to run afoul of new attitudes and regulations. With the American Expeditionary Force beginning to be shipped out of New York in full quantity, the port was congested to such a degree that an embargo had to be laid on certain exports. The railroad sidings were blocked for miles back into the country. The United States followed the British in establishing rigid priorities for shipment, and likewise did not classify South Africa as one of the more deserving destinations. South Africa had not yet developed strategic materials to its later extent; consequently the more effective use of available shipping was considered to be the transporting of such materials—nitrates, manganese, and so on—from South America, with the outward cargo being American manufactures or coal for the South Americans. [181] Liberia, with its chronic need for food, was the one African region that rated special consideration. [182]

The editor of the *British and South African Export Gazette* now found confirmation of his earlier gloomy prediction that the United States "is as little anxious to facilitate export as other belligerent countries. . . . New York advices reveal an almost incredible state of congestion at the docks and wharves and on railroads of goods destined for export. For instance, one steamer recently leaving had such an enormous quantity of freight presented that vans, horses and men had to remain in line for three nights and three days, shippers realizing that if they left they would lose their chance of making shipment. . . . Japan is virtually Great Britain's only competitor in South Africa today. The United States, having no mercantile marine of any consequence, is in a much worse position than the United Kingdom as far as export is concerned." [183] The schooner traffic to and from the Cape revived later in 1918, however, and helped to maintain American shipments at a more generous level.

The consuls on the spot in Africa remained perturbed that the United States, for lack of ships, was losing so much of the trade that it might have had. Such substantial and lasting inroads into the South African market as there were, were far from all that might have been achieved. Toward the end of the war, the consul at Cape Town wrote in that by now thoroughly familiar vein: "Despite the large volume of imports into the Union from the United States, the figures would have shown a great increase had not shipping difficulties become so acute. . . . Sailings from American ports are irregular and uncertain, and the establishment of regular American-South African service under the flag of the former country might materially assist in the extension of American foreign trade. . . . If after the war shipments revert to . . . transportation via England . . . exporters in the United States will find themselves embarrassed in competing with the products of the United Kingdom." [184]

The consul at Port Elizabeth confirmed the necessity after the war of a "regular freight service of cargo and passenger steamers" from New York or Boston because "it is absurd that American goods should be shipped to South Africa via England." [185]

Some of the vessels that would inaugurate such service to Africa and on other "essential routes" were already underway in scores of shipyards from Maine around to Puget Sound. Undertaken in part because of the shipping shortage and its accentuation by the terrific U-boat sinkings, only a few of these vessels would be completed in time for war service. Within a year thereafter, however, plenty of them would be ready to implement the new policy of service on all the important trade routes.

This immense government shipbuilding program was the most important initial achievement of the new United States Shipping Board created by the Shipping Act of September 7, 1916. [186] The Board got off to a slow start; its members were not even nominated until late in December 1916. With changes in personnel, it did not assume fairly definite form until the summer of 1917. Much more pertinent experience would be found among the members of the subordinate Emergency Fleet Corporation, set up in April 1917. [187]

The fairly general terms of the basic 1916 act had only vaguely hinted at the possibility of building ships. [188] The nation's entry into the war had inevitably changed that emphasis. The shipbuilding program might be said to date from June 15, 1917, when Congress gave President Wilson the authority to requisition, construct, and operate ships. On July 11, the President, by Executive Order, delegated those powers to the Emergency Fleet Corporation.

The actual building of the World War I emergency fleet suffers in comparison with the more ambitious and more useful emergency program of World War II. It may be said in extenuation, of course, that the later program profited by the example and errors of the earlier one. Then, too, the nation was in the second conflict long enough for most of the new ships to see war service, whereas only a fraction were at sea before the end of World War I. For all that, many things were managed better in the later program, perhaps because of its more adequate leadership. [189]

One of the most conspicuous differences lay in the types of ships constructed. The World War I program wasted a considerable part of its effort on vessels that were too small to be of general later use for the merchant marine. Of the 2,311 vessels completed, 619 were wooden, composite, or concrete of relatively small size; likewise, 575 of the steel ships were less than 6,000 dead-weight tons in size and were too small for general overseas service. That left 700 steel ships large enough to be of use on distant sea routes, and only a small portion of those had been completed before the war ended. The building of wooden ships was undertaken, partly because of the shortage of steel and partly to take advantage of the available wooden shipbuilding facilities and know-how. That program, like that for the composite and concrete ships, was pretty much a waste of time. [190]

Of the steel ships completed, 384 were requisitioned from owners who had already started or planned their construction, while 1,309 were built on contract. The requisitioned vessels, by the very nature of things, were a fairly heterogeneous lot. They were naturally among the first to be ready; by the end of the war 274 out of the final 364 had been delivered, in contrast to only 105 of the ultimate 1,309 contract steel ships.

The old-established steel yards, with their skilled technicians, were on the whole too busy with the more exacting naval construction to handle the building of freighters. This mass construction had to be undertaken in new yards, built at government expense and by executives and workers of scant experience. Government funds alone were in ample supply—more than three billions were poured into the program, to produce ships that would have been built for a third of that amount before the war. The actual cost of the emergency shipping ran to some $200 per dead-weight ton. If the cost of all the government-financed yards were reckoned in, the cost would run close to $250 a ton. [191] One particularly vicious and costly practice, which would be modified in the next war, was the frequent use of cost-plus contracts in which the builder received as profit a percentage of all his payroll and material costs. And some did not resist the temptation to pad payrolls or lay in extra material. Such abuses led to the oft-told story of one man who, upon being hired at a shipyard, was told to walk around and get acquainted with the setup. After quite a while, with his conscience beginning to trouble him at such easy money, he discovered that he was being followed. He finally turned to demand, "Why are you following me?" "I'm your helper, sir," was the answer. Directive talent was scarce, both in the higher executive posts and in the immediate supervisory roles of quartermen and leadingmen. Yards were constantly trying to pirate good talent from other yards. [192]

Unlike the World War II pattern, there was no overall uniform type of steel freighter, although there were several approaches towards one. Particularly important from the standpoint of the future merchant marine in this connection were the "Wests," built by ten west coast yards. The prefix "West" was arbitrarily added to the names of these vessels without regard to consequences. The towns of Cawthon and Isleta, for example, were turned into imaginary places by the prefix "West" on their namesake ships of the American South African Line. The "Wests" ran about 8,500 to 8,800 tons dead-weight, and 5,800 to 6,000 tons gross—a few ships were still larger, but these seemed particularly satisfactory for long-run line service.

One of the best standards for judging the relative quality of the various emergency shipbuilding programs was to see what had happened to their products by 1939, on the eve of World War II, when they had reached the 20-year normal life span of a ship. By that standard, the "8,800-ton Wests" had stood up very well. Of the 147, 102 were still in active service under the American flag, and of those, 61 were in private lines. That was a remarkably satisfactory record. [193] Three of those still active were on the American-South African run—the Ames-built *West Isleta,* and from the Southwestern yard at Los Angeles, the *West Cawthon* and *West Catnance* (renamed *Atlantic*).

The 110 somewhat smaller freighters built at the huge Hog Island yard had an even better record, with 98 still active in American-flag service. In sharp contrast, of the 40 big freighters built further up the Delaware at Harriman near Bristol, only ten survived, while only 14 of the 118 smaller steel freighters built by the Submarine Boat Company at Newark were still in service. There was similar attrition among the numerous little steel freighters built on the Great Lakes—the Ford Company secured nearly 200 of them at one time for scrapping. As for the big fleet of wooden ships, all had been scrapped by the mid-1920's. The bulk of American seagoing activity on distant runs between the wars, consequently, would be carried on by the "Wests" and the Hog Islanders. [194]

In its rush to secure ships in 1917, the Emergency Fleet Corporation also turned to Japan, where shipbuilding was flourishing. Not only was Japan expanding its own fleet, but was building also for Britain and others. It needed steel; and so a deal was arranged. American contracts were placed for 30 large steel ships, on the basis of the United States releasing one ton of steel for each two tons of ship. Inasmuch as one ton of steel would produce three dead-weight tons of ship, this gave the Japanese a good margin. The resultant ships, all named "Eastern," were highly satisfactory. The *Eastern Glade* and *Eastern Glen* served for years on the South African run. The government also acquired from the Japanese 15 vessels, already constructed. [195]

Perhaps the most crucial decision the Shipping Board was forced to make was whether or not to continue its building program after the unexpected end of hostilities in 1918. The sudden collapse of Germany was unexpected. The big emergency program after the unexpected end of hostilities in 1918. The sudden nally projected, only 1,429 keels had been laid, 746 ships launched, and a mere 470 ships delivered. There were obviously strong arguments for canceling the unfinished vessels, but the Shipping Board decided to go ahead with the building. According to Sir Arthur Salter, who represented the British shipping interests at Washington in both World Wars, he was told years later by a member of the Shipping Board of 1918, that he was responsible for that decision. It seems that at the time of the Armistice, Edward N. Hurley, then head of the Shipping Board, asked Salter, as man to man, to advise him what to do with his huge program, just getting under way. Salter said that he told him that he anticipated for a year or two shipping of all kinds would have plenty to do with the aftermath of the war; but thereafter surplus vessels would be a drug on the market, and the British were planning to curtail their building. Now Salter learned that Hurley had hurried back to his Shipping Board colleagues to urge them to go ahead and build because the British were scared to death of American competition. [196]

Whether Hurley misinterpreted Salter's advice or not, the Board went ahead with its steel ship program. Only 837 keels had already been laid but 856 more were laid down and completed after the war had ended! To be sure, a total of 4,770,000 dead-weight tons were canceled, 467 steel vessels and 491 wood, composite, and concrete. The completions were to drag on into peace—757 in 1919, 406 in 1920, 68 in 1921, and three in 1922. The emergency program came to its end formally in May 1922, five years after it had been started. At least the United States had some large steel steamships available under its flag for distant runs. The old Dark Age appeared gone for good.

Chapter V

ESSENTIAL TRADE ROUTES, 1919–1925

Two months after the fighting stopped in World War I, the Shipping Board allocated some of its freighters for line service to Africa and other regions. By spring, regular sailings were underway both to South and West Africa, beginning what would become permanent American-flag sailings on "essential trade routes" as they were called. During the ensuing decades, these services would have government financial backing of one sort or another because they were regarded as being in the national interest.

With the new services already in operation, Congress in 1920 established a major landmark in American maritime policy when it wrote the "essential trade route" concept into the law of the land. It directed the Shipping Board to determine what steamship lines should be put in operation on routes that would promote, develop, expand, and maintain "foreign and coastwise trade," as well as postal service. [197] This enunciation of principle was only a first step toward the 1936 policy which openly provided for open subsidy payments to private lines agreeing to operate such services.

This new policy was a recognition of the importance of "adequate, regular, certain, and permanent service," which the British and German cargo liners had been achieving before the war. Those four adjectives were well selected and were all significant. The Board, if possible, was to sell the necessary vessels to private citizens who would "agree to establish and maintain such lines." If no such citizen could be found, however, to take over a line deemed desirable and necessary, the Board was to "operate vessels on such lines until the business is developed so that vessels may be sold on satisfactory terms and the service maintained." [198]

This new approach was, of course, a logical outcome of the nation's maritime experience during the war. The lost opportunities because of the lack of ships had opened the public's eyes to the value of regular line service on distant runs, even though this would probably involve government funds. And now the nation had at hand hundreds of new big steel freighters produced by the emergency shipbuilding program to implement just such service. That strategy would remain fixed during the coming years, even though the tactical details for developing those services would undergo occasional changes.

The basic idea of the essential trade route was contained in that statutory phrase about "desirable for the development, expansion, and maintenance" of trade. James A. Farrell, Jr., later offered a more comprehensive definition of just what "essential trade route" involved. He called it a "linking by a direct, regular, frequent, and scheduled two-way service of an area in the United States having common economic interests and geographic unity with an area or areas abroad having reciprocal characteristics; the service on such route offering American industry, agriculture and labor attractive export markets and affording American consumers and our armed forces access to the various materials essential for the maintenance of our economy and defense." [199]

The Shipping Board, established under the emergency conditions of war, now took up its peacetime job of deciding the regular day-by-day application of policies and the control of practices under the new act. Even without the magnitude of its novel problems, the Board would have been gravely handicapped by the lack of continuity which plagued it from the first. Its membership turnover remained appallingly rapid: between 1917 and 1933, it had 35 different commissioners, with only 12 serving more than three consecutive years. Since active, experienced shipping men were barred as members, the appointees sometimes included an admiral but more often were "Deserving Republicans" or "Deserving Democrats." In its subordinate unit, the Emergency Fleet Corporation (later renamed the Merchant Fleet Corporation), there was more chance to have experienced members, but even it had five different executives in successive charge of ship sales between 1921 and 1932.[200]

At the time of the Armistice in November 1918, the Board was operating a fleet of some 1,200 vessels, half of them in the direct service of the Army or Navy. Peace brought no immediate slackening of demand for ships carrying troops or supplies, with the heavy return troop movements and the needs of hungry people abroad.

Despite those commitments, the Shipping Board lost no time in establishing line service. Early in January 1919, it allocated 33 vessels, said to have been all the tonnage available, for 13 different services, one from Philadelphia and the rest from New York. The west coast had its own allocations.[201] The Board was aware of the "unprecedented congestion at seaboard and inland of freight long delayed," by the vessel shortage, and that "American shippers . . . were quite at a loss to know how to get the physical means of moving exports."[202]

For the actual operation of these services, the Board utilized regular private shipping companies as "managing operators," a role in which they had served for running its requisitioned shipping during the war. The system had two obvious advantages; it relieved the government of the necessity of finding officials for the work, and it gave employment to the experienced shore establishments of the shipping companies which might otherwise have been broken up during the war. The managing operators were given a percentage of the gross earnings. Among the scores of shipping firms which served at the peak of the system were three types. Some were familiar old names such as Barber, Bull, Clyde, Grace, Mallory, Munson, and Ward. Others were new concerns that would be future leaders in American shipping—Dollar, Export, Lykes, Mississippi, Moore & McCormack, and Waterman. Finally, there were some of the new and less substantial companies that had sprung up like mushrooms during the immediate postwar boom which, like Green Star, would quickly disappear when the tide turned.[203]

In the postwar shipping jam, pressure for American-flag service came primarily from a group of export commission or "indent" houses, just as opposition to the conference lines had first come from that direction around 1898. At that time, they had organized the United States & Australasian Steamship Company, under which from time to time over the years they had chartered foreign-flag tonnage for the long haul to Australia and New Zealand with fairly frequent stops at South African ports. [204] In recent years, they had entrusted such operations to one Robert H. Moran. Now, five of these houses—Arkell & Douglas, Inc., H. W. Peabody & Company, Mailler & Quereau, William E. Peck, and R. W. Cameron—reactivated this company with South Africa formally included, and Moran still as the active executive.

Indent houses were naturally in a position to see the many handicaps to trade from the lack of American ships on distant routes. They rendered an important service in shopping around the United States for overseas merchants who wanted to lay in a stock of plows, cameras, men's hats, or what have you. For a modest commission, they could do a much better job on the spot than the customer himself could ever manage thousands of miles away in Johannesburg, or Sydney. These houses were aware, too, that the foreign lines often did not offer freight rates permitting effective American competition with foreign goods.

In that initial allocation of routes, "U.S. & Australasian" was made managing operator for two. [205] The one "down under" to Australia and New Zealand met relative success for several years, but the other to South Africa was slow starting and short-lived.

It was the West African allocation to A. H. Bull & Company that got off to a quick start with the assignment to it of the *Beatrice* and *Marshall,* both ready for immediate service. The sailing of the *Beatrice* for Dakar and other West African ports on February 7, 1919 was a landmark in United States-African trade, described as "the first steamer under the American flag which ever touched at the west coast of Africa." [206] The *Marshall* followed on the 24th; and the service thereafter continued with regularity.

This American West African Line, as it came to be called, was operated for nine years for the Board by the Bull concern. By the

end of 1919, that firm was also operating regular services for the
Shipping Board to Constantinople and Black Sea ports as well. [207]
A very early Bull advertisement of its West African run announced service to "Dakar, Grand Bassam, Accra, Boma, and
Matadi." [208] Some of its original ships would still be serving on
the run up to World War II: the *Cathlamet, Otho, West Hum-
haw, West Irmo,* and *West Kebar.*

Almost at once, the Shipping Board took an unusual step in
an attempt to rectify a bad competitive situation, which would
nonetheless persist for years to come. On the Guinea Coast, Elder
Dempster, the dominant British line, was keeping on with its
regular services both with the United Kingdom and the United
States. With West Africa's chronic excess of exports over imports, there was often a seasonal shortage of cargo space for logs,
palm oils, and so forth to Britain. Consequently, West African
shippers were hesitating to send their mahogany logs to New
York by the new Bull ships for fear Elder Dempster might refuse
them cargo space for Britain in the rush season. The Shipping
Board began a government-operated line from West Africa to
Britain in the hope that, by making the shippers sure of cargo
space for their products to Britain, they would use American-
flag freighters more to the United States. This was one of the few
cases where a Shipping Board line did not even touch at an
American port. [209]

On the South African run, things were not going as well. The
first two ships allocated sailed for Europe instead. After a delay,
two more ships hopefully advertised for Cape Town were di-
verted also. The ship, the *Olivant,* actually turned over by the
Board at last, was a former German freighter which had taken
refuge in Havana, only to be seized later by Cuba on its entrance
into the war; and operated for that government by the Shipping
Board. Its initial sailing to Cape Town, on April 12, 1919 cannot
be called the first American-flag voyage on that run because she
was still under the Cuban flag; that honor belongs to the *Satartia*
on August 2, apparently. The *Olivant* went as far as Durban
and returned by way of Dakar and Pensacola. [210] In 1920, this
U.S. & Australasian service had a passenger steamer on the run
for a while. The *Eten,* formerly the *Rhakotis* of the Kosmos Line

Peabody Museum of Salem

The *Eastern Glade;* built in Japan, made first
Cape voyage for Shipping Board line

Peabody Museum of Salem

The *West Isleta;* built at Seattle, made first
Cape voyage under Farrell auspices

The *Henry S. Grove*

The *Sagadahoc;* torpedoed in South Atlantic, December 3, 1941

from Hamburg to the west coast of South America, was under the flag of Peru, where she had been interned in the war. This was the peak of that service, for by the spring of 1921, the Board had cut its sailings down to one every seven weeks, because "in spite of strenuous efforts to increase the volume of business," there was insufficient cargo for more. [211] Although the line continued six ships to Australia and New Zealand for some years, the last sailing to South Africa apparently came in September 1921. [212]

Incidentally, that first year of peace found the five British conference lines in a state of transition from their one-way pattern from New York on the Cape run to an occasional round voyage. The old shipping lists show that 18 of the 30 ships made only the outward New York-South Africa run; two made only the homeward run; and ten began to follow the new shuttle pattern, with one to three round voyages. The first full-time participant in the shuttle was the Houston liner *Hypatia,* which made three round voyages between October 1918 and March 1920. The lines would not, however, emulate the consistent American round voyage service. [213]

By mid-1922, the South African trade with the United States was at a particularly low ebb, with some very uncomplimentary superlatives among all the essential routes. With only 47 ship movements in and out, it was the lowest of all, with West Africa running second at 77. In the thousands of cargo tons imported and exported, its 208,900 was almost as low as West Africa's 208,600 which was in cellar position. In the percentage of cargo carried in American-flag bottoms, its 17.5 per cent was second lowest, and was only a little more than half the overall average of 31.2 per cent. [214] In the previous year, the South and East African percentage of American-flag shipping had been even lower, at 8.7 per cent. [215] Those meager figures take on a particular significance because by the mid-1950's, South and East Africa would stand at the head of the whole list in that respect. [216]

The termination of the "U.S. & Australasian" Shipping Board service set off a clamor from both sides of the Atlantic, for that brief experience had demonstrated the usefulness of such sailings. The consul at Durban wrote "one of the greatest services that American capital could render South Africa would be the installation of a line of passenger steamers sailing at least once a month to facilitate the shipping of package freight." [217]

But private American capital could scarcely be expected to undertake such a risk while economic conditions were so unfavorable. Freight rates on general cargo, which had stood at $35 a ton in early 1919 had dropped to $23 in March 1922 and would reach $18 by the end of that year, a level where they would remain for some time. [218] Even at those reduced figures, cargoes were apt to be meager for a while. South Africa was glutted with unsold automobiles, some 1,700 of them. Imports of 7,364 cars from the United States in 1920 had dropped to 802 in 1921 and rose to only 1,944 in 1922. [219] Iron and steel shipments from the United States dropped from $17.0 million in 1920 to 1.7 in 1922, and so it went. [220] South Africa's buying power was seriously curtailed. Its diamonds and other luxury items were naturally particularly vulnerable. The DeBeers diamond mines were shut down, and in 1922, the Rand gold mines were also closed when the white miners struck. [221]

It was under such depressing circumstances that the Shipping Board once more entered the South African picture. Granting that for a while, at least, a regular line thither would lose money, it realized—and this cannot be stressed too strongly—that this was an essential service where American trade might soon lose its newly gained markets if the Government did not underwrite the venture until it should improve enough to make it a reasonable risk for private capital. The traffic department of the Emergency Fleet Corporation recommended permanent service; and on April 3, 1922, the Shipping Board voted to establish monthly service from New York to Cape Town and up to Beira, even "possibly as far as Zanzibar and Mombasa." [222]

To serve as managing operator for this service, the choice fell upon Clifford D. Mallory, one of New York's most effective shipping men. The Mallory family, originally from Mystic, Connecticut, had been engaged for years in shipping, with their major achievement the Mallory Line of good-sized steamships on the long coastal run from New York to Texas. Along with this South African route, Mallory was also operating for the Shipping

Board a fortnightly service to the Azores, Canaries, Spain, Portugal, and the western Mediterranean.

A major landmark on the South African run came on June 24, 1922, when the freighter *Eastern Glade* sailed from New York with a cargo for Cape Town and beyond. Plowing down through the South Atlantic at the leisurely 10-knot speed of that day, she reached Cape Town in just a month and then proceeded as far as Beira. After a 127-day voyage, she was back in New York on October 12. Hundreds of other voyages in the years to come would follow the same pattern, but this one had special significance for it marked the beginning in permanent American-flag service on that run.

This new service, conducted by Mallory for the Shipping Board, encountered heavy going financially at first, as had been anticipated. Every one of the first ten voyages showed a loss, ranging from $23,000 to $59,000, the average being nearly $39,000, including a proportional share of the Shipping Board overhead. The average revenue per ton was around $20 outward but only $7 homeward, for the ores which made up the bulk of the return cargoes did not command much of a rate. The whole voyage out to Beira and back ranged from 127 to 225 days. [223] That disparity between outward and homeward freights would remain a distinctive feature of the Cape run. Even that low homeward rate was something of an achievement, considering that the westbound run was in its infancy. Many more such losses explain why the line averaged almost a half million dollars a year "in the red" during its first two years, including overhead expenses but not interest or depreciation. [224] Only the deep pocket of Uncle Sam could stand deficits like that for any length of time.

Gradually, the situation grew less black. [225] Part of the improvement came from the slow process of getting organized, gaining momentum, and waiting for trade to flow into the newly developed channel. Part also came from the steady upswing in economic conditions after the bleak period of 1922 when Mallory was taking over. From the $39.9 million import and export total in 1922, the traffic rose to 56.9 millions in 1924 and then to 93.8 in 1926. [226]

Ernest M. Bull, head of A. H. Bull & Company, supplanted Mallory as managing operator of the line on October 22, 1924. The Bull family had gone into the Puerto Rican trade with sailing vessels in the early 1870's and had later shifted to steam, also engaging in the coastwise trade. The firm had been operators of the West African service since it was inaugurated in 1919. Mallory, Bull, and the Export Steamship Company, had all been operating Shipping Board lines to the Mediterranean. Now those were consolidated under Export, which became American Export. Bull received the second African service as compensation, at the expense of Mallory. [227]

Nine days before that shift, the line received the name which it would bear for almost a quarter of a century. To give some unity of appearance to the Shipping Board services, and to emphasize the national element, many of them received "trade names" beginning with the word "American." This Cape service became the "American South African Line." Bull's other service was named the American West African Line; there were also American Export, American Pioneer, American Palmetto, American Far East, and a dozen other "Americans." [228]

By 1925, the combination of momentum and improving trade conditions meant that the line was almost paying its way, even with the overhead counted in. The first ten voyages, we recall, had incurred an average loss of $38,841; the first four under Bull showed an average loss of $30,650. Then came a drastic improvement. The next eleven, the last under Shipping Board operation, saw the average deficit cut down to $980! Without counting the overhead expenses, the average voyage operations showed an actual profit of $22,000. [229] It was because of those ultimate profits that the line finally seemed attractive to private purchasers.

In its enthusiasm for trade routes, the Shipping Board had overdone the business. By mid-1920, it was operating some 1,540 ships on 209 berths. A year later, the number of ships had been cut in half to 744, but there were 410 general cargo routes and 97 managing operators. In the meantime, the boom trade of 1919 had given way to severe depression. Freight rates had fallen off drastically, a considerable part of the American, British and other merchant fleets were idle, and cargoes were dwindling. Numerous American firms that had bought freighters at $150 a ton or so and had done some lively tramping business for a while were now turning them back, losing simply the meager down payment. But the heavy overhead of Shipping Board line structure still continued at a high level and heavy financial loss.

The Shipping Board had been weak in failing to say "No" when duplicating and overlapping services had been proposed during the boom period. It was one thing to lose a modest amount in getting trade started with a single line to West Africa, South Africa, or the west coast of South America. It was a quite different matter to multiply such losses by maintaining, as the Board did, eight different services from North Atlantic ports to Hamburg, Bremen, Antwerp, and Rotterdam, with one more from the South Atlantic, and six from the Gulf ports.[230] It was small wonder that the Board's "operation of vessels" had cost $2.2 billion and had yielded only 1.4 billion in revenue up to mid-1921.[231]

Such losses naturally led to severe criticism of the whole policy. The idea of essential trade routes was in danger of being abandoned. Efforts in Congress to get the government out of ship operations and the ships transferred to private ownership were accelerated. This first took the form of a subsidy measure in 1922, but Midwest opposition killed the bill—"subsidy" was still an unacceptable idea.

The Shipping Board thereupon worked up an alternative policy. It would turn over the trade routes to private interests who would agree to maintain adequate service for a specified number of years. Under those conditions, the necessary ships would be sold at bargain rates.[232] That decision, taken in the spring of 1923, spelled out just what ultimately did take place. But first, as the Board realized, the surplus overlapping and conflicting trade routes had to be cut down to a more reasonable number, so as to give more efficient and economical service with fewer vessels.

That rather drastic consolidation of routes was carried out by Rear Admiral Leigh C. Palmer, who became president of the

Emergency Fleet Corporation on January 7, 1924.[233] Onetime
naval aide to President Taft and Secretary of the Navy Daniels,
and a wartime head of naval personnel administration as Chief
of Navigation in addition to a successful career afloat, Palmer
would stand out as one of the most effective administrators of
the merchant marine between the wars. He had retired from the
Navy in 1920 and had gone out to the Far East on business. By
the fall of 1924, the essential trade routes had been cut down
from their swollen size of 97 to only 17 managing operators. [234]
Partly because of that, the annual deficit on vessel operations
had dropped from $37.3 million in 1923–24 to $27.8 by 1924–25,
and to $16.6 in 1925–26. [235]

The transfer of the essential routes to private ownership had
gotten under way by that time. It would be a long slow process,
but by 1933 the Shipping Board had disposed of 218 cargo ships
and 27 passenger or passenger-cargo vessels to 21 different companies. All were sold with the stipulation that the buyers would
maintain scheduled line service on the route for at least five
years.

The sales price in each case was determined by bidding and
depended upon the desirability of the route. By that standard,
the two African runs rated very high. The $18.10 per dead-
weight ton, or about $156,000 a ship, paid by American South
African was the highest for three years, when American West
African established close to the maximum at $27.15 a ton or
$226,000 a ship. Some other lines, which looked less promising,
went for as low as $5.00 and even $2.55 a ton. Altogether, the
government received $49,620,000 for the various line fleets;
more important, the routes had been shifted to private hands. [236]
Palmer got that policy off to a start with the Dollar Line in
April 1925, followed by sales to Munson and American Export,
but the thoroughness he had demonstrated in consolidating the
routes annoyed the Shipping Board, which summarily dismissed
him on October 6, 1925. Palmer later recounted that his appointment had not been popular with the Shipping Board, whose
chairman had required him to submit a signed resignation for
future use at the time he assumed office. President Coolidge is

said to have been so angered by the dismissal that he contemplated abolishing the Shipping Board. [237]

It was not surprising that American South African was among the first lines to be sold, since it was to be the policy of the Shipping Board to do this as soon as a route showed reasonable prospects of breaking even. At this point in 1925, the Farrell family first come into the South African picture—James A. Farrell, then president of the United States Steel Corporation, and his two sons.

The younger Farrells, who would take over the management of American South African, represented the third generation of their family in America. Captain John Guy Farrell, their grandfather, had come over from Ireland around 1848 and settled at Fair Haven, near New Haven. Some legends that have clustered about him credit him with having been active in shipping before he migrated. At any rate, in 1864 he applied to the American Shipmasters' Association for certification as a qualified master—the closest approach to the later federal licensing of officers. [238] Around 1870, he seems to have commanded the brig *Monte Christi*, and in 1872 he did become master and part owner of the 107-ton two-masted schooner *Susan Scranton*. Built at Madison, Connecticut in 1869, she had a dozen owners from East Haven and her hailing port, New Haven. A painting of her, hanging over the desk of John J. Farrell, shows her to have been a trim craft with somewhat raking masts. During the next few years, she was frequently redocumented as she shifted from enrollment to registry and back, reflecting her changes from coasting to foreign trade. [239]

Mystery suddenly shuts down on the story at Jamaica in the spring of 1878. The preceding autumn, Captain Farrell had raised $600, mortgaging the schooner on a bottomry bond. During the next few months he made voyages between Jamaica and Mobile or New Orleans. On March 28, 1878, the *Susan Scranton* was sold to one Charles H. Schenck of New Orleans, with Richard Stark as master; early in April, the bond was paid off at Kingston. [240]

Nowhere, either at New Haven, New Orleans, or Jamaica has

a further trace of Captain Farrell come to light. According to family tradition, "When one of his ships was wrecked, Captain Farrell set out at once for the scene of the disaster. The sea absorbed him and his ship. Neither was heard from again." [241] It happened that a schooner *Monte Christi*, a name definitely in the Farrell tradition, was found abandoned in the Bahamas in September 1878, with no trace of captain or crew, but there is nothing to link that definitely to his disappearance. [242]

The failure of Captain Farrell to return to his home in Fair Haven led to one of the most remarkable "Alger" stories in American industrial history. His son, James Augustine, then only fifteen or sixteen, had to go to work to support the family. Tall, husky, and blue-eyed, he had the physique to withstand the grueling 12-hour days of hard physical labor in the intense heat of a local New Haven wire mill. The story goes that the glimpse of distant lands he had had on a voyage to Europe with his father at the age of nine led him to spend many of his rare free hours drawing maps and reading and dreaming of distant ports. In 1882, at nineteen, he moved to Pittsburgh as an expert wire drawer with the Oliver Wire Company. Four years later, he was a foreman in charge of 300 employees.

Then came a break that determined his future career. [243] When times were dull, it became customary to send the shop group out to see what they could do at sales. Farrell showed such a flair for salesmanship that at twenty-six, in 1889, he became manager of the Pittsburgh Wire Company. Ten years after, as mergers progressed in the steel business, he was foreign sales agent of the American Steel & Wire Company. Then, after the formation of the huge United States Steel Corporation in 1902, he became head of its export subsidiary.

During all that time, he was demonstrating the value of foreign markets for steel, not only in depression years like 1893, when overseas orders kept his plant from shutting down, but on a continuing basis in normal times as well. He established sales outlets for the Corporation's products in all parts of the world, and was ever on the outlook for special big contracts. Between 1902 and 1904, the Corporation's exports almost quadrupled; at the latter date, they represented ten per cent of its total sales.

It was largely the result of Farrell's extraordinary accomplishment in this job that Judge Gary, the chairman of the Board, selected Farrell to become president of the Corporation. This was at that time just about the most important position of the sort in the whole world. Farrell was the only man to rise to that post by the export path. He would remain president until 1932, and during the last four years would also be chief executive officer, a position previously held by Gary along with his chairmanship.

Farrell never lost his keen interest in shipping and in the promotion of steamship services. This had for him an extremely practical aspect, along with his love of the sea. Freight charges on the heavy material of the steel industry were a very vital matter on long hauls, where they could more or less equal the initial value of the product. The huge quantities of steel which the Corporation was exporting filled scores of ships, with part cargoes for many more. When it came to competing with foreign manufacturers, both the cost and the availability of so much ocean cargo space was a most serious matter.

The ramifications of Farrell's quest for tonnage are intertwined with much of the story of essential trade routes. His corporation had varied needs. For its 40-odd overseas warehouses—circling the world from Copenhagen, Barcelona, Johannesburg, Singapore, Sydney, Valparaiso, around to Rio—it needed regular line service to keep their stocks replenished. The huge special contracts such as rails for the Trans-Siberian or Chilean railways or structural steel for big bridges would sometimes call for full-cargo tramp loads, along with additional monthly shipments.

Farrell was ready to use ships of almost any status for the steel cargoes. Within the framework of cargo liners for regularity and tramps for flexibility, he utilized existing foreign services whenever they gave what he needed, but he also found it expedient to develop both line and tramp facilities. While considerations of "conflict of interest" kept him from personal financial participation in shipowning and operation, he exercised a not-too-remote-control over various maritime activities carried on by the company or by his family or associates. Of these, three—the Isthmian, Argonaut, and American South African Lines—combined regular line services with the owning of ships. Along with that would be patterns of lines without ships of their own and ships without line connections. The former category, including New York & South American, American & Cuban, United States & Brazil, would provide "berth services" with periodic sailings often using chartered vessels, not having a full complement or even any crew at all of their own. The latter—the early Isthmian, Seas Shipping, and Planet Lines— were essentially collections of tramps, available when needed by United States Steel for "chartering out." In addition to his utilization of regular foreign-flag shipping, Farrell generally found it expedient to use foreign registry as a "flag of convenience" in these services under his control because American-built ships were both hard to come by and expensive to operate. Until 1914, he made particular use of Britain's Red Ensign.

The foreign trade manager of the American Locomotive Company summarized Farrell's shipping policies in 1912: "The Steel Corporation has done more to keep the freight rates from the United States to foreign countries down to a reasonable figure than any other corporation or government institution. The attitude of Mr. Farrell has been right along to have the steamship companies, which are either British or German, quote American manufacturers the same rates from ports in the United States to foreign countries as they quote to manufacturers in their own countries. Whenever the steamship companies refused to do so, the Steel Corporation chartered its own steamer and carried their own shipments and also those of other manufacturers. In doing this the Steel Corporation frequently incurred a loss on shipments carried for other companies. It is not the policy of the Steel Corporation to own or control lines except when it is forced to do so by the exorbitant and discriminating rates charged to American manufacturers." [244]

Farrell began securing freighters shortly before he became president of the Corporation. It already had "fresh water" shipping in 70 ore carriers on the Great Lakes and Ohio River, of which one was named for Farrell. In 1910, the company acquired for a reported £24,000 the Bucknall freighter *Bantu*, 4,189 gross tons, built by Armstrong & Whitworth at Newcastle in 1901, and under British registry. She was the first of what was to be one of the nation's major ocean fleets. An "Isthmian Steamship Company, Limited" was formed with a capital of £100,000 and headquarters in London. Farrell held one share of stock—virtually his sole personal holding of steamship stock—and was one of the original directors of this company-owned subsidiary. By the outbreak of war in 1914, four ships had been added—the *Kentra, Buenventura, Santa Rosalia,* and *San Francisco.* And all were transferred to American registry. [245] Some 20 to 40 tramps were also normally used in 1913. [246]

Farrell himself, in discussing this situation that year in the course of an antitrust suit, emphasized that although the actual ocean freight rates were relatively the same, the "European inland rates to tidewater were lower than here. . . . The principal handicap of the American exporter . . . was the lack of adequate line service to distant places where he sought to sell his goods." Referring to the purchase of the first "Isthmian" ships, he said that they were bought to carry out contracts overseas, principally for railway materials, and for economical distribution of supplies to the distant warehouses. "There are a great many ports in the world to which steamers do not ply from this country, making it necessary for us to have our own vessels." [247]

Before long, however, these "Isthmian" ships settled down to a fairly regular service developed by Farrell. To deliver steel effectively to the west coast of South America, he had organized the New York & South American Line, operating through the Straits of Magellan with British-flag ships. Like W. R. Grace's "Merchants' Line" on that same run, it was an "industrial" service organized primarily to carry company cargo. The original impulse apparently came from a U.S. Steel contract for the development of the Chilean railroads, involving "hundreds of thousands of tons of freight which had to be moved forward periodically." [248] As only about half the cargo capacity was needed for that purpose, New York & South American, like United Fruit, Alcoa, and the later Grace and Isthmian lines, became a common carrier, transporting "considerable quantities of material for other manufacturers who have been unable to develop a business because of the lack of facilities." [249]

Later, that service was extended on up the coast to Vancouver. Farrell found that it cost $18 a ton to carry steel by rail from Pittsburgh to Vancouver, whereas it could be delivered by sea from Liverpool or Antwerp for $6 or $7, and so "it was impossible to do very much business unless we started a line of steamers." [250] The New York & South American Line, therefore, added several thousand miles to its west coast run, using four of the company's "Isthmian" ships plus a chartered freighter or two. They picked up certain business in Colombia and the west coast of Mexico, but they had to run nonstop past the whole coast of California, Oregon and Washington because "coastal" trade was barred to their foreign flags. [251]

Then, as Farrell put it in 1913, "We go into the merchandise business to get the ships back here again to load them out with steel." They would earn something carrying lumber or coal down to the Gulf of California; then they would carry unrefined copper from South American mines to Dunkirk whence they would be chartered again to come back across the Atlantic with chalk or some other cargo. Such a triangular voyage lasted from seven to nine months.

Farrell also supported, without such immediate direction or company ownership, two other steamship services designed to provide regular transportation for the Corporation's steel in markets not regularly served from the United States. In order to compete in bidding on rails and other equipment for the Trans-Siberian Railway and other roads in the Korea area, he helped to promote the American-Manchurian Line, operated by the British-flag Bucknall firm. Likewise, to furnish wire, pipe, steel sheets and other material to Bulgaria and other Black Sea regions, he backed the British-flag "American Levant Line," promising 3,000 to 5,000 tons of steel cargo every six weeks. [252]

More closely intertwined with the later Farrell maritime interests was the American & Cuban Steamship Line. In the years before World War I in recently freed Cuba, United States Steel was doing a heavy "general business of about $5 million a year, in materials for sugar grinders, railway materials, corrugated iron for buildings, pipe for water works. . . ." They built many sugar houses there, sending their "own force down there to erect them." [253] British competition was strong because the market could be furnished with British steel products more cheaply than with American. Working in the American-flag Munson Lines were two young men with ideas of making American goods more "competitive" through cheaper steamship rates. Harold J. Charlwood, an Englishman, was an acquaintance of the Farrell family, and at the request of his American friend, Arthur R. Lewis, (Harvard 1901), asked Mr. Farrell if the latter might tell their views about a steamship service for Cuban trade. This was to be a most fortunate interview for young Lewis, as it began a very generous support of him in the shipping business by Farrell.

In this immediate case, Farrell was able to secure financial backing for the proposed line from his friends Thomas and Ernest Royden. The former, later Lord Royden, of Liverpool, was one of Britain's leading shipowners, serving eventually as president of the Chamber of Shipping of the United Kingdom and as director of the Cunard Line. With a few small secondhand ships purchased by it and a few chartered ones, the American & Cuban Line prospered, aided by the sudden jump in shipping values during World War I, but more particularly did it owe its profits to the valuable and constant flow of Farrell steel cargoes, which it carried to Cuba and later also to Mexico. As time went on, incidentally, the advertisements in the *Journal of Commerce,* that had been simply under the line's name began to carry in bold type "Arthur R. Lewis, Agent." The changed emphasis was duplicated in the notices of the United States & Brazil service, which Lewis also started with chartered steamers, likewise supported by United States Steel's cargoes. Some of the later leaders of the South African service were to get their initial training in "American & Cuban": notably James A. Farrell, Jr., in his first job out of Yale, and Fred J. Unver, one of the senior traffic executives.

During World War I, United States Steel went into shipbuilding with two big new yards, Federal near Newark, in operation by July 1917, and Chickasaw near Mobile, in November.

Bethlehem Steel went in somewhat more heavily, but in ship operations, United States Steel took the lead. After the war, the company built a fleet of 27 company-owned freighters, with which Farrell soon began fairly regular "Isthmian Line" berth service to all parts of the world. [254]

At this time, American shipping interests were rushing into intercoastal service with the new Panama Canal route. Farrell was particularly enthusiastic as for heavy steel cargoes it was a "natural"—the New York-San Francisco route cut from 13,122 miles around South America to 5,263 miles by Panama and freight rates about 35 per cent lower than by rail. Return cargoes to balance the outward manufactures and steel etc., were readily available in canned goods, lumber, and so on. By the fall of 1923, 250 ships, representing 32 per cent of all American privately-owned tonnage, were in this intercoastal trade, with an equal percentage in coastal and insular possession trade, 15 per cent in nearby foreign, 10 per cent in overseas long hauls, and 11 per cent laid up. [255]

Farrell developed a diversified relationship to this intercoastal route. The prewar vessels, with their British registry, were barred from it by the coastal laws, but now hundreds of good-sized American-flag freighters were available at reasonable prices. Part of the steel cargoes were carried in the name of "Isthmian," sometimes in its regular ships, but more often in chartered vessels. Besides that formal Steel Corporation line, he also supported with cargo the Argonaut Line, which was organized late in 1922 and went into operation with the sailing of the *Sagadahoc* from New York to San Francisco on January 6, 1923. She went direct, in order to "enable San Francisco merchants to hold their own against those of Los Angeles who now have the advantage" as most of the other intercoastal ships stopped there first. The Argonaut ships continued up the coast to Portland and Puget Sound. The second sailing was made by the *Charles H. Cramp*. She and her sister ship, the *Henry S. Grove,* were the crack members of the Argonaut fleet, built by the Cramp yard at Philadelphia, where they had been started for the Grace Line and then requisitioned in the war. So successful was her voyage that she was "down to her marks with a miscellaneous cargo" and was forced to leave 500 tons for Portland on the dock for the next ship. [256]

Most of the Argonaut ships were emergency program freighters of good size, picked up in separate deals, sometimes from lines that had not made a go of it. The *Cramp* and the *Grove* were better finished than most freighters of that type and were capable of 13½ or 14 knots, and gave the Farrells almost a quarter century of good service. The *Atlantic* and the *Pacific*, slow and the least satisfactory, were the most likely to be chartered out or laid up in slack seasons. The *Lancaster*, one of the first products of the new Sun yard at Chester, and the *Sagadahoc* from Bath, Maine, came between those two extremes. [257] All these were to be taken over by a later Farrell line; Argonaut acquired a few other ships that do not come into the story in that way. [258]

This line is closely related to the Farrell story. Besides the later employment of those Argonaut ships and the dependence of that line on the backlog of steel cargoes, the elder Farrell son, John Joseph Farrell, held the controlling interest and the presidency. James Farrell, Sr., was solidly behind the enterprise with a naturally very personal interest, although with no formal connection in stock ownership or otherwise. John Farrell had had a thoroughgoing indoctrination in various aspects of shipping during the ten years since he had finished at Yale. He had become a partner in the prominent firm of ship agents, Norton, Lilly & Company, which had several close relationships with the Farrell shipping interests. The opportunity to watch "how things worked" around such a firm was naturally most valuable. He was also associated in several other varied maritime activities. [259] During World War I, he served in the Army transport service with the rank of captain.

Another unit in the Farrell sphere of maritime influence was pretty much the counterpart of a British tramp company—the Seas Shipping Company. Its principal direct holdings were the *Robin Adair, Robin Goodfellow, Robin Gray,* and *Robin Hood,* large freighters built by Skinner & Eddy at Seattle. [260] Seas also operated a sort of subsidiary known as the Planet Line; it served as ships' husband for the ships of the Planet Steamship Company. This was an organization formed by the bondholders of the

defunct Green Star Line, through the Equitable Trust Company, in 1923. In addition to the routine servicing of the seven
Planet ships, the Seas group attended to their chartering. This,
in fact, made the Planet ships, plus the *"Robins"* a sort of reserve
fleet for United States Steel, giving a flexibility to meet extra
demands. The vessels were very frequently chartered out for the
Isthmian's intercoastal service and sometimes on its other runs. [261]

James Farrell, Sr., took every occasion to stimulate an understanding of the nation's relationship to foreign trade—his original maritime concern. In 1914, he organized the National Foreign Trade Council and served as its chairman for more than a
quarter century. His keynote speeches at the annual meetings
never failed to make headlines as he emphasized what he considered the pressing needs of the moment. Along that same line, he
provided both initiative and financial support in the establishing
of Georgetown University's School of Foreign Service and particularly its foreign trade courses. Eventually some of Farrell
Line's younger executives would profit by that training. He was
the principal founder of one of New York's famous clubs, India
House, to provide a meeting place for businessmen interested in
foreign trade. He was its first president and the chief contributor
to its remarkable collection of marine art.

Farrell not only took a vicarious pleasure through his various
shipping connections, but also was able to enjoy actual ownership afloat as an enthusiastic yachtsman. He had a succession of
sailing yachts, as did his sons, as well as a large steam yacht, based
at his home on the Connecticut shore. Then there was his favorite *Tusitala*, "the last full-rigged ship under American registry to
engage in the carriage of commercial cargo." Originally built
of steel as the *Inveruglas* at Greenock in 1883, she passed through
various hands and sailed under several names and flags for forty
years. She was found among old sailing ships rotting in the James
River in 1923 by the elder Felix Riesenberg, sailor-author, who
was co-operating with Christopher Morley in a plan to restore
a square-rigger for a cruise ship. Unable to find the necessary
funds, Riesenberg went to Farrell, whose secretary said that he
could not be seen for at least a week. " 'Tell him it's about a
ship,' " Riesenberg suggested. "In a minute the reply came

back, 'Mr. Farrell will see you now.' . . . At ten o'clock the next morning the ship had been saved from the financial breakers and the wolves." She made a cruise to Brazil at a loss; then Farrell "bought out the remaining stockholders." [262]

Placed under American registry, she carried cargo for twelve years under the Argonaut house flag between New York and Honolulu or Brazil. Farrell kept in constant touch with her movements. Joseph Conrad wrote an appreciative acknowledgment of her, now posted in every Farrell ship and overseas office, in which he said, "The vital truth of sea-life is to be found in the ancient saying that it is 'the stout hearts that make the ship safe.' " [263]

Altogether, the Farrells were far from being newcomers to American maritime affairs, when the Shipping Board asked for bids for the American South African Line and its five steel freighters. A prerequisite was an agreement to maintain monthly service from New York to Beira and intermediate ports for five years. Only two bids were received. The Barber Steamship Lines offered $454,249.25, which was far below the breath-taking $780,019.50 presented by John M. Franklin, the general agent of the Argonaut Line. He was the son of P. A. S. Franklin, head of the International Mercantile Marine, and would himself one day head the United States Lines. This offer at some $156,000 a ship or $18.10 a dead-weight ton was far ahead of any other line sales price until the American West African Line came up later. [264]

Franklin represented an ad hoc syndicate formed to enter the bid, with the understanding that a corporation would be formed to take the line if the bid should be successful. Its seven members were either in the Farrell family, in the Argonaut Line, or both. Outside the family circle were Arthur R. Lewis and Franklin. The latter figured prominently in the news announcements, for he handled the Shipping Board negotiations. [265] But it was to be the Farrells' line from that time on. "We acquired the line" one of the sons was later quoted as saying, "on the strength of our father's belief in the future of the Dark Continent. The ensuing years have demonstrated how remarkable his foresight was." [266] This belief is said to have been fortified by Farrell's friend, Admiral Palmer. Another factor may have been a father's desire to have his younger son, James, Jr., in the overseas trade whereas his older son John was already well established in the intercoastal trade as head of the Argonaut Line.

The other sensation of the bidding, rivaling the high Franklin offer, was the vigorous explanation of Ernest M. Bull, the managing operator, as to why he had not submitted a bid for his company. He protested against the sale of the line, arguing that in view of the British conference pooling practices, "no American company could effectively meet such competition." He asked for deferment for further study by the Board. [267]

That such purchases were really "risk capital" was being brought home to the Board at this very moment because of the troubles of the American Palmetto Line, recently sold into private ownership. The Carolina Steamship Company, which had bought this six-ship outfit operating from South Atlantic ports to the United Kingdom and northern Europe the previous summer, were losing some $10,000 a month which they claimed was because of the action of the British and German lines in placing additional ships on the run. They asked relief from their five-year guarantee of service; the Board agreed to this. The unlucky company lost its $75,000 down payment on top of those monthly losses, and the ships were repossessed by the Board. Operations were resumed by the Board under a managing operator, to demonstrate that foreign lines could not squeeze out American competition simply by driving a private operator to the wall. [268]

With that business coming to a head, the Board took grave consideration of Bull's protest. As a leading maritime journal headlined it, "Shipping Board Hesitant over American South African." On December 22, 1925, however, it unanimously decided to sell the line to the Franklin group. A suggestion of the Farrell backing was to be found in that journal's next issue. "The decision of the Board amounts to declaration of a belief that Mr. Franklin's company, very strongly backed by American capital and backed also by the direct interest of certain important shippers, will be able to sustain itself in an independent attitude against even the most formidable British combinations." [269]

That record price of $18.10 a dead-weight ton was topped by the $27.15 paid for the West African service some thirty months later, when the Barber Steamship Company outbid the Farrells. There were two surprise aspects of this 1928 sale. Bull, who had also been operating this service for the Shipping Board, refused to bid unless assured of one of the new Jones-White mail contracts. Second, it had not been expected that the Farrells would bid so low; their American South African Line's offer of $1,228,-838 was the fourth lowest of the five bids, and barely half of Barber's winning $2,291,156 which was the highest rate yet offered in the line sales. [270] Barber, one of New York's most prominent shipping men, was of English origin and operated extensively under foreign flags on many runs, but he had also been managing operator for more Shipping Board tonnage than anyone else. [271]

The American-flag routes to Africa South of Sahara were by that time transferred to private ownership. The Farrells would still be operating the Cape service three decades later. Barber would operate the American West African Line until the end of World War II. Then, when he shifted to the Norwegian flag, the Farrells would take up the American-flag service on that run also. [272]

Chapter VI

PRIVATE OWNERSHIP, 1926–1932

THE bid of the Farrell interests for the American South African Line was accepted by the Shipping Board just before Christmas, 1925. The new company received its certificate of incorporation on the last day of that year. The first sailing under the new auspices was made by the *West Isleta* on January 30 for Cape Town and around the coast to Beira. [273]

In the meantime, most of the basic organization was taking place. The incorporators and subscribers had held their first meeting at the line's headquarters. The elder Farrell was not present but, as in so many other cases, he seems to have exercised remote control. James A. Farrell, Jr., called the meeting to order and was chosen chairman. He, with his brother-in-law, Luke D. Stapleton, John M. Franklin, and Arthur R. Lewis were named directors. John J. Farrell, president of the Argonaut Line, would become a director in mid-July. James, Jr., fresh from Yale, was elected to the presidency, which he would still be exercising thirty years later. Franklin, Stapleton, and Lewis became vice president, secretary, and treasurer respectively.

On January 6, James, Jr., Franklin, and Stapleton completed negotiations at Washington with the Shipping Board, with the purchase agreement duly executed. The company paid 25 per cent down on the purchase price of the five ships, and gave a preferred mortgage with interest at 4½ per cent for the balance, to be paid in ten annual installments. Actually it would be paid off in half that time. The day after that, the Farrell brothers and others paid in their immediate shares of the cash capital; in retrospect, considering what grew out of that investment, it could be regarded as a highly fortunate one. [274]

James, Jr., had not expected to be president; he had thought that the older and more experienced Lewis would receive that office. A second surprise followed shortly, when Lewis and he were called over to his father's Broadway office to meet Admiral Leigh C. Palmer. The distinguished former head of the Emergency Fleet Corporation, so Farrell informed them, had agreed to help run the line. Palmer was to remain as an active executive for two decades. Farrell had originally known him when he was President Taft's naval aide, and had later renewed the acquaintance. He had been out of office more than two months when approached by Farrell; he had had nothing to do with the projected sale of American South African. [275] He became a director in July, and in April of the following year, 1927, when Franklin took an outside shipping post, he was moved into the vice presidency. Along with that, he became general manager, a post which he would exercise for two decades. The directors, at his death in 1955, declared that he was "leaving a personal and business void that cannot be filled. His friendliness, his courtesy and graciousness and his special warmth under all circumstances will perpetually be remembered individually by the officers, directors and staff of the Line." [276]

To size up the African situation, Palmer immediately sailed for Cape Town by Fabre Line to Madeira, where he changed to a Union-Castle liner. His status in South Africa appears to have been something of a puzzle to the captains and agents. His encounters with the *West Isleta* on her initial voyage and the *Eastern Glade*, the Bull liner, on her last Shipping Board service, were to be of special consequence to the line. The British captain, Warren, of the former, apparently had little discipline; the whole crew were in jail for drunkenness. By contrast, the setup aboard the *Eastern Glade* was excellent; and Palmer recommended vigorously that the ship herself and her officers be taken for the new line.

The captain of the *Eastern Glade*, Allen Thompson, a Colgate graduate, had become first mate of a ship operated by Clifford D. Mallory, without previous maritime experience. He had known Mallory at Mystic, Connecticut, where he had been engaged in boatbuilding before World War I, in which he was a naval officer. Ultimately, his eyes were affected with "Uganda tick" and he retired to his native Rhode Island. He showed a real art in the selection and handling of men. During World War II, when submarines were at their worst, he returned to South Africa as mate on a Liberty ship.

The chief mate proved a most valuable find. Soon to be commanding the *West Isleta,* George Wauchope, a graduate of the New York maritime school, had had his master's ticket at twenty-one. He would be for several years virtually commodore of the new line as captain of its first passenger ship. In the mid-1930's, after taking the initiative in extending the service up into East Africa, he would be brought ashore as a sort of deputy to Palmer. He served as a reserve naval officer in World War II, and would ultimately become a rear admiral. He eventually succeeded to Palmer's executive position.

From another Bull-Shipping Board ship, the *Eastern Glen,* came another excellent commander, Captain E. I. Simmonds. Serious and very competent, he was an English-speaking native of the Dutch island of Saba in the West Indies, and had the command of the line's passenger ship until relieved by Wauchope. But not all the early captains were of such caliber. One in particular landed himself in jail on charges too serious for bail from a private fracas with gendarmerie of Lourenco Marques; he was released only on condition he never again set foot in Portuguese East Africa.

The first five ships of the new line were all products of the emergency fleet program started during World War I. They belonged to the larger class of steel freighters, averaging around 8,500 dead-weight and 5,000 to 5,600 gross tons, around 400 feet long, 54 feet in beam, and 25 feet mean draft. Their triple expansion reciprocating engines and Scotch boilers gave them a speed of around ten knots. [277] They were the *West Cawthon,* built by the Southwestern Shipbuilding Company of San Pedro; the *West Isleta* and *Western Knight,* products of the Ames Shipbuilding & Dry Dock Company, of Seattle; and the *Eastern*

Glade and *Eastern Glen,* built in the Japanese portion of the emergency program at the Uchida yard near Yokohama. [278]

The *West Isleta* and *West Cawthon* had the longest line service, each having completed 37 round voyages by the spring day in 1940 when they were sold to the British—only to be U-boat victims in short order. [279] They were built after the end of World War I and were delivered in the following summer, 1919. [280] They were not graceful ships, but tough. Fairly similar in construction, their sturdy angularity came from using straight pieces instead of curved wherever possible to make their construction quicker and simpler. The *Western Knight* had much the same design. She had originally been undertaken in a so-called "Cunard" contract for the British government; and had reveled in the prospective name of *War Helen,* before being requisitioned by the Shipping Board. [281] The *Eastern Glade* and the *Eastern Glen* had much more graceful lines than the American three; they likewise gave good service until sold around 1933. Their names were preserved in the later *African Glade* and *African Glen.*

Incidentally, except for three so-called "feeder craft," wrecked on Liberia's coast, the *Western Knight* is so far the only Farrell vessel to be lost in peacetime. She sailed from New York on the outward voyage on March 3, 1929. Leaving Cape Town for Port Elizabeth, the morning of April 8 found her groping through a heavy fog. Captain Morgan was further inshore than he realized; suddenly she piled onto the rocks near Cape Recife, just west of Algoa Bay. Some 300 tons of general cargo and 200 of rails were under water. With the heavy Indian Ocean rollers continually pounding in on that rocky coast and the ever-present chance of a real gale, salvage was a ticklish job calling for expert seamanship. The rocks kept the towboats, sent down from Port Elizabeth by the line's agents, Edward Searle & Company, from reaching the ship. Lighters had to be cast off to be carried in by the following sea; only proper handling of the lines on the ship would keep them from being dashed to pieces. With no steam aboard, hundreds of tons of cargo were hauled from the hold by hand tackle, and then lowered onto the swaying lighters. A gale struck after a full month but "all sound cargo was discharged"; so, too, was Captain Morgan. [282] As for the ship, she had long since been declared a constructive total loss with her bottom damaged beyond repair. Yet she made more money for the line by her insurance of $453,600 paid in full, than that whole year of regular shipping business.

Incidentally, an amateur salvager—a former Dutch ship officer—netted enough from cargo he managed to land by aerial railway from the abandoned ship to set himself up in the business. He had rushed to get options on all available big wire cables in various places to prevent others from using his method.

The *Western Knight* naturally had to be replaced as soon as possible. The seventeen-year-old *Chincha,* a big ship of 9,600 dead-weight and 6,346 gross tons, was built in Sunderland, England, and was obtained from the Planet Line, which had ships ever ready for charter or sale. On the eve of World War I, she had been operating under the British flag in W. R. Grace's "Merchants' Line" between New York and the west coast of South America, but early in the war was shifted to American registry. She was a bit old-fashioned in some ways, with steering chains along the decks. Her cost, however, was only $150,000, barely a third of the big insurance payment for the *Western Knight's* loss. [283]

The *West Isleta* also faced serious trouble on an outward voyage in the summer of 1936, when her only propeller dropped off in that vast stretch of South Atlantic just south of St. Helena. Cape Town's powerful tugs lacked fuel capacity for the 3,200 miles out and back. But luck was with her—the *City of New York* was near and the weather was fair. She was towed along at 12 knots—faster than she had ever traveled alone, until the Cape rollers forced a lower speed. Her passengers did not even have to be transferred to the *City of New York;* her starboard anchor chain was run out for 90 fathoms and fastened to the passenger liner. In lieu of salvage, the officers and crew of the latter received an extra month's pay.

In the monthly sailings that were established, the ships often discharged incoming cargo and picked up cargo at Baltimore and Philadelphia. The final departure point for Cape Town was normally New York. Only much later would the coastal voyage be extended to Portland, Maine and to Jacksonville, Florida. In addition to the Cape Town-Beira "main line," two voyages included Port Louis in Mauritius. [284]

The fuel problem on that lengthy run produced a unique arrangement in the three American-built ships during the first few years of service. It was a period of fairly rapid transition from coal to oil—as early as 1921, the Shipping Board had remarked that "only a very small percentage of the fleet is coal burning." [285] Fuel oil, however, was more expensive in South Africa than almost anywhere else because of the distance it had to be transported. [286] At the same time, it was one of the cheapest places to bunker with coal, thanks to the good Natal supply which reached the sea at Durban. The three would operate between New York and Cape Town on oil. Then, for the run up the coast to Beira and back, the grates would be installed, and a "black gang" of stokers and coal passers added to the crew. This was usually quite satisfactory on the northbound trip, but the black gang tended to loaf and get out of hand as Cape Town and the end of their job approached. The homebound ships, for a considerable period, put in at Trinidad for oil. The *Eastern Glade* and *Eastern Glen* did not have oil-burning facilities.

The most tangible achievement of the new American-flag service was the speedy development of homeward cargoes from Africa. The outward cargoes were a much simpler matter; except for the rapidly growing automobile shipments, they were pretty much what they had been for three decades; what was more, much of the outward cargo was secured on conference-wide contracts. [287] The British lines had shown scant interest in developing the return cargoes, but Mallory and Bull had already made a good start with their Shipping Board service. The extent of this was shown in what the *Eastern Glade* brought back on the fifth Farrell voyage, reaching New York on October 7, 1926. From Lourenco Marques she had 9,636 ingots of copper, 1,996 bags of mica waste, 40 barrels of mica skimmings, 33 bags of corundum ore, and 41 packages of beeswax. At Durban she had picked up 5,180 bags of chopped wattle bark, 2,433 more bags of corundum ore, 100 bags of chrome ore, 34 barrels of sheepskins, 76 cases of mining equipment, and 6 miscellaneous cases. The only cargo from Port Elizabeth was 31 empty cylinders. Finally, at Cape Town she had taken on 2,300 packages of grapes, 173 more barrels of sheepskins, and 1 case of jackal skins. [288] A few months later, she would probably have brought some wool, but the season had not quite started when she left South Africa.

Five months after American South African had passed into Farrell hands, and even before the Jones-White contracts became available, it had been granted a special mail contract on June 7, 1926. It was one of the first five lines to be given such treatment, which was permitted by the 1920 Shipping Act in cases where, in the opinion of the Shipping Board and the Postmaster General, the rate of 80 cents a pound stipulated in the 1891 act seemed inadequate. [289] The Oceanic Steamship Company, with its long run to Australia, had received such special terms in 1921. Now that contract was renewed and four new lines selected; Munson to South America, Export to the Mediterranean, and Dollar with its round-the-world service, in addition to American South African, which was to receive $5,000 for each of its twelve outward voyages a year. The Shipping Board gave as its reasons for this action that the "trade route involved is highly competitive, the line having as rivals several long-established British lines, as a result of which the American South African Line has been operated at a substantial annual deficit and having the disadvantage that it is the only service operated by it, whereas the competing lines are chiefly owned by wealthy British companies also operating other routes from which revenues are drawn which assist them to meet competing conditions on the route here involved." [290]

There were, of course, certain considerations that prevented British competition from affecting American South African too disastrously. It was already a member of that United States-South African Conference along with its British rivals, and had been allotted one-fourth of the sailings. Then, too, the fact that the line's president had the same name as the president of United States Steel, with only a "Jr." added, was a constant reminder to the British that it might not be expedient to antagonize the steel company which could control the allocation of so much cargo.

The line was one of the first to respond to the stimulus provided by the Merchant Marine Act of May 22, 1928, known as the Jones-White Act. [291] It ranks with those of 1916, 1920, and 1936, as one of the "Big Four" which spelled out American maritime policy between the wars.

It went much farther than the 1920 act, giving much more adequate payments on "essential routes" and making much more specific provisions for stimulating shipbuilding. Recognizing that the ships of the emergency fleet were all approaching half of a ship's normal active life span together, it established a replacement plan to offset that "block obsolescence" for the construction of "up-to-date ships . . . for an adequate merchant marine." [292] To that end, a construction loan fund of a quarter billion dollars—double the amount of the 1920 act—was set up for the construction or modernization of vessels deemed "necessary or desirable" on approved routes. This would furnish 75 per cent of the cost, the balance to be paid over a 20-year period. These vessels were to "be fitted and equipped with the most modern, the most efficient, and the most economical engines, machinery, and commercial appliances." [293]

In conjunction with that, it provided that all United States mails were to be carried to foreign ports in United States vessels wherever possible. The Postmaster General was instructed to report to the Shipping Board what routes should be set up and operated. Then, and for another eight years, subsidies were cloaked under the time-honored but thin disguise of mail service. Compensation was to be determined by the speed and size of the vessel at rates considerably more generous than anything previously granted. [294]

With the trade routes and construction loans tied in together, progress was rapid along both lines. In the course of the next three years, some fifty routes from Atlantic, Gulf, and Pacific ports to various parts of the world were established by the Postmaster General. In many cases, these simply confirmed existing services.

In its adjustment to the Jones-White terms, the American

South African Line was in the forefront. It was among the earliest of the lines to consummate a mail contract—at terms much more generous than its special previous arrangement. That had been $60,000 a year, while the subsidy would average $275,000 for the next eight years, ranging from $252,000 in 1934 to $300,-000 in 1932. [295]

The Jones-White ships made a valuable and lasting contribution to the merchant marine. With the former German liners and the swarms of freighters gradually becoming outmoded, they might be said to have killed three birds with one stone. They gave faster and more satisfactory service on several important routes; they would be invaluable as transports in World War II; and their construction enabled the major shipyards to hold their staffs together at a time when naval orders had virtually disappeared. Five years later, Senator Black and his committee would find plenty to criticize in the Jones-White setup, but the fact remains that the act did provide a most salutary stimulus on the eve of a most serious depression.

Of the nearly 30 new passenger-cargo or passenger liners built under the construction loan agreement, the first ship completed was the American South African's *City of New York*. The largest and most conspicuous were the 24,289 gross ton *Manhattan* and *Washington* for the United States Line's express service on the North Atlantic shuttle. The *City of New York* was the first new ship built by the line for its own use; all its earlier vessels had been secondhand. She was also the first passenger ship built expressly for the service between the United States and Africa, and was, moreover, "the first privately-owned American passenger and cargo vessel to be built since 1918 in American yards for exclusive use in long-voyage foreign trade." [296] She cost $1,917,-673, of which $1,350,000 was the construction loan granted on November 22, 1928.

Built by the Sun Shipbuilding Company of Chester, Pennsylvania, she was a twin-screw ship powered by diesel engines, of some 5,000 horsepower. These could drive her at 13½ to 14 knots at a time when the line's freighters averaged around ten; that meant three weeks instead of a month between New York and Cape Town. As compared with those freighters, she was 450 feet long to their 400 or 410, and her beam was 61 feet to their 54; those dimensions were reflected in her 8,272 gross tons as compared with their 5,000 to 5,600. There was less difference in their dead-weight tonnage which indicated cargo capacity, for her 9,306 tons was only slightly more than their 8,500. Unlike the line's later passenger ships, she more than held her own in that respect with the freighters. [297] She was a graceful vessel of the three-deck type, with extended forecastle, long bridges, cruiser stern, and a low, broad funnel. She had accommodations for 60 passengers, with all staterooms on the upper deck for better ventilation, and with well-appointed lounge and dining accommodations. The extra numbers in the steward's department gave her a total crew of 69. [298]

She first brought the line really into the passenger business. Like most lines, it customarily carried a small number of passengers on the freighters. The maximum number was eventually set at twelve; beyond that, it would have been necessary to carry a doctor and various other expensive features. This new direct passenger service to South Africa would fill a very special need. Not until the mid-1930's would regular air service from London to South Africa be inaugurated and even then, for some time, it was a rather uncomfortable eight-day trip, with overnight stops along the run. Passengers desiring to travel with first-class accommodations between the United States and South Africa could then, as later, make the trip by way of England. Eventually Cunard and Union-Castle would advertise such a through service, with a change at Southampton. For a brief period in 1920, there had been direct New York-Cape Town service with a former German liner operated by the Shipping Board. [299] In 1926, a British liner had made a very successful cruise from New York to South Africa, returning by way of the east coast and the Mediterranean. She started ten days before the first American South African sailing under Farrell management. [300]

Such potential cruise tourists were only one of the three categories that the line considered in inaugurating its new passenger service. There would also be some South Africans desiring to visit the United States. [301] Particularly important, in view of the hopes of developing American markets in South Africa, would be the opportunity for American businessmen to come and go with pleasure and comfort. In competition with the weekly British service by way of England, this direct run could offer the relaxation of three unbroken weeks at sea, down through the "fair weather route."

The *City of New York* was christened at her launching on October 19, 1929 by Miss Rosamond Farrell, the sister of John and James, Jr. Their father was present as one of the proudest of spectators. Fifteen weeks later, on February 1, 1930, she sailed on her maiden voyage, stopping at St. Helena and going up the coast from Cape Town as far as Lourenco Marques. She was back in New York on May 10. After discharging and unloading at Baltimore and Philadelphia in mid-May, she sailed again on May 31, four months after her original departure. [302] Like the other ships of the line, she normally made three voyages a year. The long interval, seven weeks at the outset, between the arrival at Cape Town and the ultimate departure from there would usually be utilized by tourists to see South Africa pretty thoroughly, visiting Victoria Falls and other points of interest in the interior. The South African Railways co-operated in making such trips a success. Some of the South Africans would join the ship at Cape Town and ride up the coast and back, for the line's excellent meals quickly became a byword.

During most of the 1930's, the *City of New York* was commanded by Captain Wauchope, and then, by Captain Christian W. Schmidt, one of the line's group of first-rate Scandinavian masters. Graduated from the Danish Royal Naval College, he had served in the Danish Navy and the British merchant marine before coming to America, where he quickly became associated with the Planet Line and then with other Farrell ships. Rugged and stocky, with very ample savoir-faire, he was the natural bluff sea dog for a passenger liner. Later he would become the line's first titular commodore and then resident manager at Cape Town. He was succeeded on the *City of New York* by Captain George T. Sullivan, a graduate of Massachusetts maritime school with considerable experience as a naval officer. After losing the *City of New York* and a Liberty ship by enemy action in World War II, he would ultimately become marine superintendent.

The Jones-White mail contracts would prove a godsend for this line and for other lines as well; without them, it would have been difficult to have maintained the essential trade route pattern during the depression that began late in 1929. The falling off in trade was sudden and drastic. American South African's gross revenues had climbed from $1,088,000 in 1926 to $1,971,-000 in 1929 and almost duplicated that amount in 1930, but by 1932, it had dropped to $903,000. [303] South Africa's imports of automobiles and parts, which made up the most valuable part of the trade, dropped from $19.6 million in 1929 to 7.6 in 1930, 6.2 in 1931, and 2.7 in 1932. The rest of the world would continue in its depressed state for some time to come, but South Africa would bound back well ahead of other regions, thanks to its devaluation of gold at the end of 1932. By 1934, its automobile purchases would have climbed to $17.3 million, with very interesting consequences for the American South African Line. [304]

Chapter VII

EXPANSION AND COMPETITION, 1933–1939

T HE opening of a new steamship route, by the very nature of things, has always been less of an irrevocable, costly, and time-consuming matter than the establishing of a new rail line. The latter necessitates legislative permission and very heavy capital outlay from land purchase to track laying. All this pretty well commits a company to its rail route, whether it proves a paying proposition or not. About all that a shipping company has to do, if a route proves unprofitable and it has no subsidy obligations, is to shift its vessels to another run which seems to hold out better prospects. And this is a simple and relatively inexpensive procedure. The corollary, however, is that a successful railroad is fairly secure against competition. Even when legislative permission may be forthcoming, a rival line still has the weighty matter of capital outlay to deter it. On the other hand, a steamship route that is paying well is ever liable to have a competitor move his ships in to skim part of the cream.

The Farrells were involved in both sides of that matter in the mid-1930's. In the course of a few weeks in the spring of 1935, they moved vessels from an American intercoastal run to one of their two new African services. Almost at once, a rival service moved in on their "main line" to Africa to begin more than two decades of keen competition.

A number of varied circumstances had paved the way for those rapid shifts. In the early thirties, a considerable portion of the merchant fleets of most maritime nations lay idle as exports and imports dried up in the world depression. Then, sud-

The *City of New York*. First ship built by the Farrells; engaged in passenger-cargo service, New York to South Africa, from 1930 until torpedoed in 1942

The *African Enterprise* at Cape Town

denly, the Union of South Africa devalued its pound; and shortly afterwards the United States began to buy gold at a higher price, $35 instead of $20 an ounce. With that boom in gold came such a boom in South Africa's imports that the sea lane to the Cape became a bright exception in the widespread blight of merchant shipping. Exports from the United States to South and East Africa jumped from $19 million in 1932 to 53 in 1934, 61 in 1935, 80 in 1936 and 103 in 1937. [305] Further profits in the intercoastal trade, which had been very promising in the 1920's, were threatened by severe strikes on the part of the longshoremen in American west coast ports.

This double set of circumstances placed the Farrell brothers in an advantageous position over some of the other intercoastal operators, who had no obvious alternate employment for their ships. For the Farrells, on the other hand, it would be a simple matter to shift John Farrell's intercoastal Argonaut freighters to the Cape Town route where James Farrell's American South African ships had been plying for almost a decade. It was not to prove quite that easy; merely to double the Cape Town-Beira service, where the new demands would have easily filled the shifted freighters, was not feasible. The British and German lines in the United States-South African Conference with American South African would not agree to allow the latter to have more than 25 per cent of the sailings; and they apparently did not intend to increase their own present number.

The Farrells turned to the next best solution; they inaugurated two modifications of their original Cape Town-Beira route. Almost simultaneously, American South African service was extended up the east coast beyond Beira to other ports, and a new service was opened from New Orleans and other Gulf ports to South and East Africa. This was not an entirely fresh idea; consuls and merchants at Mombasa, Zanzibar, Tanga, and Dar-es-Salaam had long regretted the lack of direct service to the United States. Imports or exports of those ports had to be transshipped at Durban or some other port to the southward or carried northward through the Suez Canal with transshipment at Aden or in ports in Britain or Germany. There were complaints that East African producers were not able with this roundabout system to sell small parcels of their goods to small consumers in the United States. [306]

Captain Wauchope, during one of the perennial long waits at Beira, decided to try some hunting in East Africa and began to read up on the region. Realizing the rich commercial possibilities, he recommended that the line send its ships farther up that coast. Eventually, he was directed to explore the feasibility of this extension of service, just as he was sent eleven years later to West Africa.

The new service was inaugurated on April 1, 1935 by the sailing of the old *Chincha* from New York, stopping at Cape Town on the 28th and following the usual pattern to Beira. Completing her loading at Beira on May 21, she turned northward up the coast on the new course instead of homeward. Six days later she made the first Farrell landfall in East Africa at Mombasa. She was at Zanzibar on the 29th, Dar-es-Salaam the next day, and back at Durban on June 6. The jaunt to East Africa had taken an extra two weeks; and this would prove to be about the average time for those additional ports. [307] After picking up further cargo at Port Elizabeth and Cape Town, she continued on her way on June 13. She made the usual stop for bunker oil at Trinidad and then discharged cargo at Boston, Philadelphia, and finally at New York, which she reached July 20, 110 days after her sailing.

The freighters on this route with their monthly schedules would follow a similar pattern until World War II. Tanga was often included and Lindi and Kilwa Kisiwane occasionally. Thereafter, with much more frequent sailings to South Africa, only one ship a month normally went on to East Africa.

The extra length of these extended voyages was compensated for by the well-paying homeward cargoes of coffee, cloves, sisal, pyrethrum, and other East African offerings, which represented also a good combination of volume and high freight rates. In the outward service from New York, however, the East African cargoes accounted for only 10 per cent of the tonnage, as compared with a quarter of the homeward. [308]

The other new service from the ports of the Gulf of Mexico to South and East Africa was inaugurated that same month of

April 1935. For the New York-East Africa extension, American South African simply used the ships already on the run, but it now had to turn to John Farrell's Argonaut Line for extra vessels.

In the combination of depressed trade and the 1934 west coast dock strikes, the Argonaut Line's *Pacific* had been tied up at Baltimore almost five years since August 1930. At New York the *Lancaster* had been idle for 25 months between July 1932 and August 1934; the *Henry S. Grove* since November 1934; and the *Sagadahoc* for ten weeks at the end of 1934, following eleven weeks from mid-May through July that same year during the strike at San Francisco. Only the *Atlantic* and the *Charles H. Cramp* had been kept steadily employed on this intercoastal run throughout 1934. [309] To use some of these ships in the new boom trade to South Africa seemed to be a good answer.

Gulf service to South and East Africa was a relative novelty. There had been occasional shipments of ore to New Orleans in the Shipping Board period, and on the West African run, some sailings from Gulf ports. Regular Gulf service on the Cape route dated from August 1932, when the Kerr Steamship Company's Silver-Java-Pacific Line began monthly sailings. With the new South African boom, these were increased to two or three a month in mid-1934. By that time, the States Marine Corporation was also beginning monthly service. One reason for this new shipping activity from the Gulf was that railroad rates on automobiles and some other commodities were lower to New Orleans than to New York or other North Atlantic ports. In the case of automobiles, for instance, the differential amounted to 17 cents per hundred pounds. [310]

This was the situation when the American South African Line decided to inaugurate its Gulf service. It was simply a one-way affair; the ships returned from Africa to New York and other northern ports. With cargoes from South Africa never too plentiful and with no apparent adequate market in the Gulf region at that time, no attempt was made to make it two-way.

The *Atlantic,* on the first sailing on this route, loaded at Mobile, and then moved over to New Orleans, whence she sailed for Cape Town by way of Trinidad on April 18. She was at Beira two whole weeks, taking on ore, and reached Mombasa just 25 days after the *Chincha's* maiden entry. She picked up more cargo at Tanga and Dar-es-Salaam, and then presumably headed nonstop for Trinidad for oil; then on to Boston and New York.

These Gulf sailings did not develop a regular pattern like those from New York. The *Sagadahoc,* leaving New Orleans May 20 on the second voyage, went out into the Indian Ocean to Mauritius instead of up the East African coast. She returned to New York after stopping at Montreal. The *Charles H. Cramp,* on the third voyage, took on cargo at Baltimore, Tampa, and Mobile on her way down to New Orleans. She turned around at Beira and came home by way of Canada, stopping at Port Alfred as well as Montreal. The fourth voyage with the *Henry S. Grove* went on to East Africa, and made the first stop at Kilwa. [311]

The Gulf service lasted only three years. It served New Orleans and Mobile in particular. In 1937, for instance, there were 12 sailings from each of those ports in addition to seven from Tampa and two from Panama City in Florida, two from Gulfport, Mississippi, and one from Port Neches, Texas. [312] At the time, there did not seem to be sufficient sources of outward cargo; the average gross revenue per voyage on the Gulf run between 1935 and 1938 averaged only $86,600 as compared with $123,700 on the regular North Atlantic run. [313] Clifford Shields, who had been sent to New Orleans to handle the traffic developments, had been instructed not to go after cargo that might well be shipped from the Atlantic ports. Ultimately, various developments extending far into the interior would mean much more extensive trade to and from the Gulf. But because of this initial unsatisfactory experience, the Farrells would not seek to establish subsidized service from the Gulf to South or West Africa after World War II. [314]

That abandoning of Gulf service in 1938 stemmed from the bitter competition with the Robin Line. For two years, 1935–37, the two lines waged a cutthroat rate war, with rates so low that they both lost money on every voyage. Robin had no service with Gulf ports, so American South African voyages on that run meant extra losses. [315] In addition, those voyages were not granted the mail subsidies of the main line to New York. In 1938, when the Maritime Commission granted a subsidy to the Robin Line on the New York run, the Farrells quickly abandoned the unprofitable Gulf service.

That rate war had started about the very moment that the new East African and Gulf services were getting under way. The story has some highly subjective aspects, and even two decades later, there is understandable sensitiveness remaining over some of the things that happened.

The rivalry grew out of the parting of the ways between the Farrell and Lewis shipping interests, originally closely intertwined under the aegis of James A. Farrell, Sr., then president of United States Steel. It will be recalled that back on the eve of World War I, he had given Arthur R. Lewis a start in the management of the American & Cuban Steamship Line and in several other shipping activities, in which he was interested though not participating personally. As time went on, Lewis and the Farrell sons, John in particular, were together in the ownership and management of some successful stevedoring concerns, as well as in the American & Cuban, Planet, Seas Shipping, Argonaut, and American South African Lines. [316]

In mid-1933, that complicated setup was suddenly unscrambled for personal reasons, with the various elements divided between the Farrell brothers and Lewis. The Farrells withdrew from two highly profitable stevedoring connections and from the American & Cuban Company. Argonaut remained under Farrell control, but Lewis retained a substantial stock interest. He withdrew completely from American South African, resigning in July as treasurer and director, positions he had held since the organization of the line in 1926. He sold all this stock to the Farrells. Conversely, the Farrells withdrew from the Seas Shipping Company, resigning their positions as officers and directors and selling all their stock to Lewis. [317]

The chief assets of Seas Shipping were those four freighters, built by Skinner & Eddy at Seattle at the close of World War I—the *Robin Adair, Robin Goodfellow, Robin Gray,* and *Robin Hood.* These had been used chiefly in the intercoastal trade, often under charter to the Isthmian Line. With the general slump in trade in the early 1930's, they had spent considerable time lying idle in port. Most of the quartet were unemployed for 18 months in 1932–33 and, even when not, found only partial employment. [318] In early 1935 only the *Robin Goodfellow* was actively employed in the intercoastal trade. The *Robin Adair* had made two round-trip voyages to Honolulu, but the rest of the record was pretty well one of idleness at New York for her and the *Robin Gray* and *Robin Hood*. [319]

These were the ships that would be used to start the rival "Robin Line" service to South and East Africa. The Farrells, father and sons, had understood that the Robin ships would not be used to compete in the African trade. This proved to have been a false assumption. Shortly after this, Lewis went to France to live, and there he soon died. The ownership and management of the Seas Shipping Company passed to his son, Arthur R. Lewis, Jr., then twenty-five years old and two years out of Yale.

By the beginning of 1935, the increased South African demand for American manufactures was resulting in an increase of shipping services. In addition to the new Gulf sailings, the Elder Dempster Line was doubling its schedule to South Africa from Montreal, which enjoyed even more favorable freight differentials than did New Orleans. Finally, at New York, in addition to the regular American South African and the British-German conference sailings, there was the nonconference British-flag service of the United States Navigation Company's "Baron Line," which had been in operation for some time. New additional competition came from another British-flag line, the Kerr "Silver" service which, as was seen, had been running from the Gulf for three years. And with this increase in sailings went some fairly sharp competitive cutting of rates.

At about that time, Sylvester J. Maddock, who had been for several years in various positions on the traffic staff of the American South African Line, left its employ, not of his own accord, it is reported. He was a persuasive promoter in developing new trade; and was about to enter the Seas Shipping-Robin picture in a prominent role. As the conference brief in the coming Shipping Board Bureau hearings expressed it: "Sylvester J. Maddock, after having been employed by the defendant American South

African Line, Inc. . . . since that line began its activity in 1926, left its employ the latter part of January, 1935. He immediately called upon the United States Navigation Company in an effort to interest them in his services. A few weeks later he called on Garcia and Diaz with a written proposal for them to enter the South African trade under his direction. About the same time he visited the Kerr Steamship Company, Inc. with like purpose, and he also approached the States Marine Corporation, although in that case he was not able to see the man he sought. In the meantime, Mr. Maddock had come into contact with young Mr. Lewis . . . who had thrust upon him the full responsibility for his father's steamship company, owing to the illness of his father. This steamship company . . . never had any connection with the South African trade and its vessels were laid up. . . . Mr. Maddock succeeded in selling to young Mr. Lewis the idea of entering the South African trade." [320]

Maddock became freight traffic manager for Seas Shipping Company's new "Robin Line." To that position he brought his detailed knowledge of American South African's customers, policies, and confidential future plans. That Lewis-cum-Maddock combination would produce aggressive and successful leadership; as to which of them contributed the most towards that end, opinions differ.

On April 18, 1935, the day of the first sailing of the Farrell's new Gulf service, the newspapers carried Lewis's announcement of his new service, to be known as the Robin Line, "under consideration some months." The Seas Shipping Company was not only entering the trade of the Cape Town-Beira range, but was going on up the coast to Mombasa, in an effort to develop trade with Kenya and Tanganyika. [321] Of course, the Farrell plans to serve East Africa had been known to Maddock.

The rival service started on June 24 with the sailing of the *Robin Adair* from New York, two days after the advertised date. She reached Cape Town July 21 and Mombasa August 7—that was the latter port's third "first time" in ten weeks with the *Chincha* and the *Atlantic* opening Farrell's new services on May 29 and June 21. The *Robin Adair* returned to New York by way of Montreal. The other three *Robins* followed at monthly intervals. In most of the ports of Southern Africa, the Robin Line secured as agents Mitchell, Cotts & Company, Ltd., a house with extensive and widely variegated business interests. [322]

Even before the first Robin ship had completed loading at New York, the U.S.A.-South African Conference had declared war. Aside from the addition of the American South African Line in 1925, it was still essentially the same combination as on the eve of World War I, for the German-flag Hansa Line had in 1931 resumed its service suspended in 1914. [323] The conference had felt the effect of the depression; the tonnage to South Africa dropped from 279,000 in 1930 to 122,000 in 1932, the number of sailings from 48 to 36, and the average cargo tonnage per sailing from 5,444 to 3,390. By 1934, the revived South African market was producing an upswing to 281,000 tons, 42 sailings, and 6,694 tons per sailing. [324]

With that revival of activity, the conference had drawn up a new set of agreements on October 15, 1934 and had filed them with the Shipping Board Bureau in accordance with the Shipping Act of 1916. [325] The arrangement for rotation of sailing, already explained, provided that with a normal 48 sailings a year, American South African was to have "one sailing each calendar month" with the other 36 divided into seven equal shares. Two of these were for Union-Castle, and one each for Ellerman & Bucknall, Clan, Houston, Prince, and Hansa. It was this arrangement that was at the crux of the coming difficulties. [326] Actually, in 1934, American South African had been making 28 per cent, not that allotted 25 per cent, of the outward sailings and carrying 32 per cent of the outward cargo, along with the major part of the homeward cargo. [327] Incidentally, it will be recalled that the line did not participate in the conference's agreement for a "pooling of revenue." [328]

In later years, James Farrell, Jr., who had been a party to those unanimous conference agreements, expressed the opinion that the line had made two miscalculations in that connection. The first was that they had underestimated Lewis's financial resources—the rate-cutting had been a device, by no means novel in shipping circles, designed to exhaust a competitor's resources. In the second place, Beaver Street had not fully appreciated the extent to which South Africa was going to buy automobiles and other American appliances during the mid-1930's. Instead of abiding by the conference limitations on American South African sailings and letting Robin carry much of the surplus, the Farrells might have done better to have increased their own sailings, whatever the foreign-flag lines might decree. As it was, American South African was entering upon one of the most stubborn and costly rate wars in American shipping history, for those "unremunerative and noncompensating" $4 rates would last for nearly two years. The Lewis pockets proved deeper than had been expected, and the Robin ships kept going.

In that financial endurance test, the Farrells were subjected to a heavier strain than the other conference members, who had their regular services on other than American-African routes, and these could help them absorb the shock of the rate war losses. [329] The Farrells, losing money with every voyage, had that drain increased by their added Gulf service.

The conference attacked the Robin Line on June 6, 1935 by the drastic step of sharply cutting its freight rates. Solicitors seeking cargo for the first Robin sailing suddenly found that the conference rates to all ports except Beira were cut to a maximum of $8 per ton, although they had ranged as high as $20. That represented just about the actual cost of transporting the goods. On September 19, the rates were all cut to $4, which was just about half that actual transportation cost and entailed a heavy loss on each voyage. [330] Those tactics were based on the incorrect assumption that Robin would thus be driven quickly off the route, particularly since the Lewis line at that time did not even have a subsidy, and the Farrells did.

Somewhat earlier that spring, Maddock had begun consultations towards seeking membership in the conference for Robin Line also, with the same terms of monthly sailings as American South African. On June 27, the conference unanimously denied the application. Upon inquiring the reason, Maddock was told by the conference secretary that in the opinion of the members it was not incumbent upon them to give their reasons. [331] They had already rejected the application of the Kerr Steamship Company.

Robin Line appealed the conference rejection to the successor of the Shipping Board, the Shipping Board Bureau of the Department of Commerce. Both sides vigorously presented their views at a hearing before a Board Examiner at New York. Robin Line claimed that the conference sailings were insufficient to move the automobiles accumulating at New York; that by reducing freight rates below a remunerative level, the conference was operating illegal "fighting ships"; and that "men who sit in London dictate where there shall be rate wars such as this." James A. Farrell, Jr., denied the charge of British control, pointing out that conference decisions had to be unanimous. [332]

The Bureau upheld the conference in its decision of August 1, 1936. "The Department is not without sympathy for the position in which the complainant finds itself, but nothing in the Shipping Act prohibits carriers from using every legitimate means to wage economic warfare in their efforts to secure or retain traffic." [333]

The rate war continued unabated, with Robin Line concentrating its efforts on the automobile exports, which were to remain its special sphere of interest for twenty years. Maddock was apparently the prime mover in this eager co-operation that was to keep Ford and Chrysler particular Robin customers. Robin willingness to go to great lengths for this industry is evident from the line's accommodation of another manufacturer, who had 1,200 cars accumulated at New York and no cargo space. It chartered extra ships for him, for double the rate war freight charges; the line made nothing on this as the chartering costs used up any surplus. The conference is said to have refused a similar double offer from another firm. [334]

In August, with the rate war more than a year in process, one newspaper commented: ". . . The disastrous rate war . . . will apparently have to continue until one of the competitors . . . is eliminated." [335]

It kept on until mid-1937, however, with neither side "eliminated" despite the heavy losses. For the Farrells it was a particularly exasperating experience. They had at hand the Argonaut fleet, which could have been thrown into the direct New York-South Africa run to take advantage of the tremendous flood of exports had not their conference membership prevented. Shipping is always apt to be a "feast or a famine," but after surviving the famine conditions of the depression years, American South African was still kept on a stringent diet with that tempting feast of exports spread before it. [336]

Midway in that rate war, Congress produced its most important and far-reaching piece of maritime policy legislation to date. This Merchant Marine Act of 1936 was built on the foundations of its 1916, 1920, and 1928 predecessors, but it provided a more straightforward and adequate means of developing private operation of American-flag vessels on a worldwide network of "essential trade routes."

Its outstanding new feature was the first provision for outright subsidies for the construction and operation of ships, instead of disguising such grants as payments for carrying mail. These subsidies, however, were not to be simple handouts; the government took elaborate precautions to ensure that the money be used for the continued development of the merchant marine. There was a definite dualism in the new provisions. As one writer aptly expressed it at the time, the government was to be pictured "as no longer a fatherly overseer, but as a cross between a rich uncle and a tough cop, holding out a blank check in one hand and wiggling a night stick behind his back with the other." [337] The final act would be a blend of two movements, one positive and the other critical and regulatory.

The critical attack on the Jones-White payments had started back in 1933 when Senator Hugo L. Black of Alabama proposed and then headed a special Senate committee to investigate the ocean mail and air mail contracts. [338] Dozens of executives of the steamship and air lines were to testify before this so-called "Black Committee" between the autumn of 1933 and the spring of 1934. [339]

Senator Black conducted much of the questioning himself and went into minute detail, confronting one shipping man after another. He sought to find out whether the ocean mail subsidies were being used to the best advantage in supporting American-flag competition with foreign lines on the essential routes. The questioning as a whole seemed to center on three main aspects: the efficiency of management of the lines; questionable expenditures, such as excessive executive salaries; and outside relationships with other foreign or domestic maritime activities. At American South African's hearing, which occupied the full morning and afternoon sessions of November 15, 1933, the first two were scarcely touched upon. [340] No question of inefficient management was raised at all, although some other lines were grilled on this point. Black's concern in regard to excessive executive salaries, which might enable a line's officials to thrive while the company finances languished, did not include American South African either. Its president's salary, $12,400, was less than half of the amount regarded as a proper maximum. [341]

On the third aspect, the committee's investigator had done a very thorough job in attempting to untangle the labyrinth of interlocking directorates and other relationships of the subsidized companies. Black apparently believed that every subsidized company should operate free from any contacts with foreign interests and from stevedoring or other domestic maritime business. Occasional questions, when this matter came up at the hearing, were directed to James Farrell, Jr., as president of the line, but during most of the day, it was John Farrell who delivered much of the testimony. This was presumably because of his partnership in Norton, Lilly. This firm was not only agent for American South African in various American ports, but was also agent for one of its principal British competitors. In addition, Black questioned John Farrell's affiliations with stevedoring and other outside activities, some of which had been terminated in the Farrell-Lewis split-up a few months earlier. Farrell answered that while he had retained financial interest in some of the stevedoring activities, he had devoted all his time since 1928 to management of the Argonaut Line. [342] In the matter of American South African having carried on its stevedoring with one of the companies in which John Farrell was interested, it was pointed out that the line's business represented less than one per cent of the gross income of the stevedoring company. [343] Not long after this hearing, John Farrell of his own accord terminated his remaining outside maritime connections, although it entailed heavy financial sacrifice. But thereafter, the Farrells concentrated on the Argonaut and South African Lines in investment as well as in management. [344]

The Black Committee reported against continuation of the existing mail subsidy system. So, too, did three cabinet members who had also been looking into the situation. Every steamship company which was then holding a mail contract had to show cause why its contract should not be suspended or canceled. American South African, after submitting such evidence, was permitted to continue along with virtually all the others. [345] Altogether, a strong prejudice against mail payments was built up in the popular mind and reflected in Congress.

Despite that, positive efforts were made to provide added financial support for American-flag shipping. Trade had fallen off badly in the depression and two big lines had gone under. Most of the freighters, moreover, were approaching the 20-year age limit and would require costly replacements. In 1935, President Roosevelt came out strongly for an "honest" form of subsidy. Bills to provide generous subsidy aid were introduced by the chairmen of the Senate Commerce Committee and the House Merchant Marine and Fisheries Committee. In both houses, those measures encountered other measures designed to police such subsidy operations. The blending of those two approaches resulted in the Merchant Marine Act of 1936 which received the President's signature on June 29. [346]

First of its provisions was the creation of a five-man independent Maritime Commission to take over the regulatory and administrative powers formerly exercised by the Shipping Board (1916–1933) and its successor, the Shipping Board Bureau of the Department of Commerce.

Subsidies were the most significant feature of the act. They were designed to enable American-flag shipowners to compete with the cheaper foreign costs of construction and operation. Those differentials would become the basis of government payments, rather than the flat rate per mile of the Jones-White mail contracts.

The so-called "operating-differential subsidy" with which the lines would be most intimately concerned was essentially a contract involving definite obligations and risks on the part of the operator. It did not guarantee him a profit, or even protect him against possible loss. Its payments would be made for services rendered.

Specifically, the operating-differential contract provided for the payment, on a specified number of voyages a year, of the difference between American-flag and foreign-flag shipping on that particular route. The operator was required to make a minimum number of voyages, "full or not full," in order to ensure regular service even in depressed periods when he might not break even. In boom periods, on the other hand, there was a limit to the number of voyages for which he would receive a subsidy, even though he might make extra sailings with chartered ships.

The principal item in such payments would be the wages of officers and crews which, at the very time the act was passed, were beginning to soar far ahead of the foreign rates under aggressive union pressure. [347] Ultimately, wages would account for about 87 per cent of the operational subsidy payments which, in turn, would virtually be paying three-quarters of the inflated pay rates. The other items for which operating-differential payments would be made were subsistence, supplies, maintenance and repairs, and insurance. That subsidy did not, however, include fuel oil, stevedoring, and other charges which fell equally upon foreign-flag and American-flag shipping.

To avoid excess profiteering in boom times, the act provided that half of the profits over ten per cent of the necessary capital would be paid back to the government, up to the amount of the accrued subsidy. There would be times when a line's whole subsidy would thus be repaid. From 1938 through 1955, with four years out during the war, the total of $549.0 millions was accrued in operating-differential subsidies, of which 129.1 was recaptured, leaving a net total of 419.0 actually due to the lines. The estimated totals for the various companies, showing the amounts repaid in parentheses, were, in order of size: United States Lines, 103.4 (25.3); American Export Lines, 67.8 (5.3); Moore-McCormack Lines, 76.3 (18.8); American

President Lines, 70.2 (15.5); Lykes Brothers, 65.7 (33.7); Grace Lines, 43.9 (13.3); Farrell Lines, 27.2 (1.4); Mississippi (Delta), 26.1 (6.0); Seas (Robin), 18.1 (2.5); American Mail Line, 18.5 (4.2); Oceanic, 8.3 (.7); New York and Cuba (Ward), 7.4 (.8); Pacific-Argentine-Brazil Lines, 5.7 (o); Pacific Transport Lines, 3.0 (.7); Gulf and South American, 1.5 (o); Bloomfield, 1.1 (o). The last four lines were in operation for only a part of that period. [348]

It was also stipulated that, in order to have funds on hand to keep going in the bad years and to purchase new ships, each line must set up a general and a special reserve fund into which depreciation and other items must be deposited. If a line sought to save a part of its profits instead of distributing them as dividends, it might, with the permission of the Commission, deposit the full amount in its special reserve fund and thus avoid the heavy corporation income tax. Finally, each subsidized operator was required to keep elaborate specified accounts, and its books were to be open to inspection by the Maritime Commission, or the Maritime Board-Maritime Administration which would succeed it in 1950.

Those reserve funds were important because part of every operating-differential contract would be the operator's agreement to build new tonnage. If the operator were free to build his ships in British, Dutch or other foreign yards, they would cost only about half as much as in an American yard. Congress realized, however, that the American yards had had hard sledding in the depression years and were having difficulty in holding onto their skilled technicians and workers. From the standpoint of national defense it was vital that the shipyard facilities and key personnel be maintained at least at a safe minimum level. The act therefore specified that all ships built in connection with operating-differential subsidies must be built in American yards.

To compensate the subsidized operator for the extra cost of that required domestic construction, the act also made provision for "construction-differential" subsidies. These would meet, up to 50 per cent (later 55 per cent), that difference in price. The Maritime Commission would contract with the selected shipbuilding yard for the full cost of the new ship. Then it would contract with the subsidized line to purchase the ship at about half that amount, the difference representing the "construction-differential" subsidy, which was never actually paid to the steamship operator.

It could be said that the shipyards were the real beneficiaries of the construction-differential subsidies, just as the very expensive seamen were the ones who profited most by the operating-differential subsidies. The latter payments, however, were essential to the shipowners if they were to maintain regular service during the lean years. Time and again, that subsidy would make the difference between profit and loss. In 1949, for instance, the Farrell Lines directors were told that for the first half of the year the operations would probably show a loss of $3.25 a share before subsidy, and a profit of 85 cents a share after subsidy. [349] If things went very well, on the other hand, the government might recapture the whole subsidy; during the first decade, the entire accrued subsidies of American Export, Lykes Brothers, and Delta would be thus recaptured. [350] The new system did not guarantee the shipowners against loss, but it did make them more willing to risk the necessary heavy investments.

During the next 20 years, the number of the subsidized "chosen instruments" of maritime policy would fluctuate between 11 and 16 lines. Some of the recipients, notably Lykes Brothers, would spread out over several routes. [351]

American South African on June 17, 1937 received one of the first temporary operating-differential subsidy agreements, pending the working out of permanent details. On July 1, these supplanted the old Jones-White mail contracts. During the next 15 months, the line would receive $140,000 in operating-differential subsidies; this was barely half of the old Jones-White rate. Then, for the next 19 months, from October 1, 1938 to April 23, 1940, it would receive no subsidy at all, thanks to a new aspect of the Robin competition.

The bitter two-year rate war with the Robin Line came to an end on the very day that American South African began its first operating-differential contract. That day—July 1, 1937—the Conference restored almost all of its rates to the level of June 1,

1935; Robin Line had already raised some of its charges. [352] Their heavy losses had not caused either rival to succumb. The real beneficiaries, as so often in price wars, were those who profited from the reduced prices, the South Africans in this case. Also, as it was pointed out early in 1936, the rate war was giving "American manufacturers, especially in the automobile trade, a great advantage over British manufacturers in the South African market." [353]

But the difficulties with the Robin competition grew worse, in spite of the return to normalcy on rates. Seas Shipping made formal application on November 30, 1937 to the Maritime Commission for an operating-differential subsidy for its Robin ships on that same run. It based this request on the provision of the 1936 act which stipulated that no contract should be made "which would be in addition to the existing service, or services," unless the Maritime Commission should deem the existing service inadequate. [354] In the phrase quoted above, the words "or services" had been added by Congress after persistent efforts by the attorney for the Robin Line. Back in 1935, even before Robin had started its operations, he began his appearances before Congressional committees to secure such a modification of wording that would give the line a chance for a subsidy along with American South African. [355]

American South African, in view of its twelve years of service on the run, its Ocean Mail subsidies, and its existing temporary operating-differential subsidy, countered the Robin petition with one for an exclusive subsidy for both its regular Atlantic service and its Gulf route as well.

There seemed plenty of reasonable doubt as to the outcome when the Maritime Commission began its hearings at Washington in mid-April 1938, for each side had strong basic arguments. The Robin case, as later summarized, ran: "The Merchant Marine Act of 1936 must be construed as a definite prohibition against the granting of an exclusive subsidy to a single operator. . . . Every effort should be made to build up the business of each of the applicants in order that they as American companies may carry more and more of the American commerce in vessels flying the American flag. To give a subsidy to one and refuse it to the other would be of undue advantage or prejudice to one citizen as against another." [356]

To such arguments, the American South African line countered: "For the government at this juncture to subsidize the Robin Line, competitor of the American South African line, would, we think, definitely be regarded by the shipping community as a breach of faith. The effect of such action in discouraging the investment of further private capital in subsidized shipping services cannot be overestimated. . . . [357] We make the statement categorically: there is no service under the American flag in the long voyage or transatlantic trade where the American participation approaches that which we have built up, or where the number of sailings has been increased as has our own. If our service is inadequate, then the service of every American operator is inadequate, and none is safe from the danger of having, upon a moment's notice, to fight government money in the hands of any other citizen who can find American vessels not otherwise employed." [358]

However even the logic behind those two positions might be, the Commissioner who presided at the hearing later declared that the decision was based essentially upon what was presented at the hearing, and there Robin scored a marked advantage. It had been the general expectation that the regular legal counsel of each line would represent it; but Robin included in its legal force an additional admiralty lawyer, reputedly one of New York's most skillful. Robin also rounded up 18 American shippers, carefully handpicked, who all declared that "they used both lines, as well as most of the foreign lines, and that in the interest of service they desired to see both lines continue in operation." [359] In addition, it was apparently a serious tactical error, of which opposing counsel took full advantage, when the American South African Line bluntly questioned whether Robin would be able to raise the $750,000 necessary for the required building program. [360]

On August 5, 1938, the Maritime Commission voted to deny American South African's application for an exclusive subsidy. Instead it granted subsidies to both companies on the route from New York and other Atlantic ports to South and East Africa and also, to American South African, on the Gulf run as well. The Commission concluded that the present service was inadequate and that "neither of the applicants here is able alone to provide adequate service." [361] Before receiving long-range subsidy contracts, the lines would have to meet certain requirements, some of which would be unacceptable to the Farrells. [362]

Naturally, American South African questioned the wisdom and justice of that decision. As the Farrells stated their position on September 19, 1938:

> Dear Admiral Land:
>
> In reply to your letter of September 14, 1938, we are obliged to state that in our considered opinion the Commission's Report of August 5, 1938, and Order dated August 8, 1938, are:
>
> (1) contrary to the facts adduced at the hearings,
> (2) contrary to the letter and the spirit of the Merchant Marine Act, 1936,
> (3) a violation of our legal and moral rights,
> (4) inimical to successful operation under private ownership.
>
> Accordingly, we are compelled to advise your Commission that we cannot concur in said Report and Order. [363]

Blunt and direct as the letter might seem, the Congressional Information Bureau on September 30 informed its subscribers that: "Commission officials declared that as far as they could determine it amounts to neither an acceptance nor a rejection of the subsidy. They . . . are in disagreement as to its meaning and further termed it 'vague.' " [364] Not until the spring of 1940 would American South African finally agree to accept the "double tracked" agreement.

During the intervening year and a half, the line's finances were in an extremely straitened condition. Already weakened by the two years of operating at the suicidal $4 a ton rate, the line was now, for the first time since mid-1926, cut off from governmental aid. The first victim of the new situation was the Gulf run, which would have received a subsidy had Farrell accepted the "double track" subsidy. Instead, the line had to terminate it with the sailing of the *Charles H. Cramp* from New Orleans on September 1, 1938. The total number of Farrell sailings to

South Africa fell from 26 in 1937 to 20 in 1938 and 13 in 1939. Some of the surplus ships were chartered out for the intercoastal trade.

In the meantime, the Robin Line had entered upon a long-term contract with the Maritime Commission on October 4, 1938. This yielded up to mid-1940 $343,798 in operating-differential subsidies. [365] In addition, the line received for four new ships, for which it had negotiated, $4,833,455 in construction-differential subsidies. [366]

The Maritime Commission kept urging the American South African Line to participate in an operating-differential contract without success. Early in 1940, the company finally decided that a construction-differential subsidy was needed in order to compete with the new ships contracted for by the Robin Line. So American South African applied to the Maritime Commission for the subsidies, which were granted on April 23, 1940. Under these contracts, the line agreed to undertake a minimum of 12 and a maximum of 24 sailings a year on the Cape run. It was also agreed that new ships would be added to the fleet: three passenger-cargo liners and three C-2 freighters.

The final ship in the Farrell "first fleet," the *Challenger*, was purchased early in 1937 from the Sun Shipbuilding Company at Chester, Pennsylvania. She was the most capacious of all the liners in that group, having a dead-weight tonnage of 11,620. Built in 1918 as an emergency program freighter at the Bethlehem yard at Alameda, California, she was one of 23 such freighters converted in the 1920's to diesel propulsion. In her case, this took place at the Sun yard, which also produced the *City of New York,* the only other Farrell "motor vessel." [367]

This American South African and Seas Shipping situation was the first, and for many years the only, case of what came to be called "double tracking" of operating-differential subsidies on essential trade routes. Two other instances occurred in 1949 and 1954, while a case of "triple tracking" on a transpacific run occurred in 1953. The whole policy would come up for scrutiny by the House Committee on Merchant Marine and Fisheries in 1956. [368]

The Robin Line continued a vigorous and efficient competition on the run to South and East Africa for another 17 years. [369] During the big profits of the period of neutrality in 1940–41, its earnings were ahead of Farrell and also during the war years of government control, but finally, in the immediate postwar period, Farrell went into the lead with an average profit of $1,334,000 to Robin's $984,000. [370] Despite frequent invitations on the part of American South African to join the conference, Robin declined and remained a free agent.

Chapter VIII

THE SECOND FLEET

THE Farrell fleet, like all the others on essential trade routes, was completely transformed during the 1940's. The old slow ships of the World War I emergency program, after reaching or passing the 20-year life span, had been sold, sunk, or scrapped. In their places came faster, more capacious, more efficiently equipped, and more expensive vessels. These were part of that "long-range program" called for in the 1936 Act. The Maritime Commission was instructed to work out an effective plan for replacement of the aging Hog Islanders, "Wests," and other emergency ships. It decided that fifty new ships should be built in each of the following ten years. In this way, "block obsolescence" from building too many at once would be prevented. It would also avoid too heavy a strain upon the shipyards by thus spreading out the construction load.

The immediate emphasis was upon cargo carriers. Three types were planned under the designation of C (for cargo); each represented a different degree of size and speed, with the C-3 the largest and fastest. Much of the American-flag cargo carrying on the essential trade routes was to be performed by these ships for the next 20 years. The even larger C-4's were a later development, and never numerous. Certain marked economies were possible from this concentration on those few types. Ships of each class had so much in common that many of their component parts could be produced in quantity, even at some distance from the shipyards. Instead of scattering single ships among various yards, several ships of a type were ordered from a specific yard at one time.

The C-2 was the first of the new classes to be put in production, because of the urgent need for freighters of moderate size and speed. With steam turbines or diesel engines of some 6,000 horsepower, which was double that of the old "Wests," the C-2 was designed for 15½-knot speed, half again the old rate. Her cubic content was one-third greater than that of the "Wests," yet, when one of the first C-2's made her maiden run in 1939, it was found that her cost of operation was little more than the older, slower ships. [371] Most of the C-2's were originally named for celebrated clippers of the age of sail.

The need for a type with greater cargo capacity and greater speed next led to the C-3. This had 16½- or 17-knot speed and measured 12,500 dead-weight tons. The C-3 also allowed flexibility in respect to modifications of design. In particular, it made possible the PC-3, a combination passenger and cargo liner. Incidentally, the lines, upper works, and funnel of the C-3 made a better-looking ship than the C-2.

Later, for runs which did not call for such speed, and where large cargoes might not always be available, the C-1 was evolved with a speed of 14 knots.

By the end of 1947, the Farrell fleet would consist of six C-3's, all on the South and East African run, and eight C-2's, several of which were on the West African. By 1949, two passenger-cargo liners, similar to PC-3's, were added. Its three original PC-3's never served in the line, as the Navy took them immediately for war service. With the construction-differential subsidy to offset the extra cost of building in American yards, these ships cost a great deal more than those bargains of the 1920's. [372] The Farrells, as was seen, had paid $18.10 per dead-weight ton for their original five ships in 1926, but their first C-2's in 1942 would cost nearly $160 per dead-weight ton.

The Farrells, like the other companies with operating-differential contracts, were aided in meeting those heavy costs by the provisions of the 1936 Act in respect to reserve funds. Some of the deposits in those, we recall, were compulsory. There were also inducements to deposit further amounts instead of distributing them as dividends.

The readiness of foreigners to pay high prices for their old ships further helped the operators. Within eight months of the outbreak of World War II, the price for old ships had risen sharply to $400,000 or more. An offer of only $67,000 for the *Chincha,* however, came from a Yugoslav and was approved by the directors on August 17, 1939, just two weeks before the war. That was the difficult year when the line was operating without a subsidy, and it is said that one reason for the premature sale was to meet a payroll. [373]

The Farrell ships have fallen into three distinct fleets, in addition to the little "Feeder Fleet" in Liberian waters. The "First Fleet," except for the passenger-cargo liner *City of New York,* consisted of thirteen rather heterogeneous secondhand vessels. Some of these were part of the American South African fleet proper; the rest were in the Argonaut Line. The "Second Fleet" would be composed of the various groups of "C's" and passenger-cargo liners acquired during the 1940's. The "Third Fleet" will consist of faster, more modern, and infinitely more costly replacements for those sixteen "C's."

With the granting of the new subsidy by the Maritime Commission in April 1940, the line agreed to build new ships. On that very day, the directors decided to sell the last two ships of the original quintet, the *West Isleta* and the *West Cawthon.* The British bought them for $440,000 and $430,000 respectively. The *West Isleta* (renamed *Empire Merlin*) was sunk by submarine gunfire within five months, and the *West Cawthon (Empire Bison)* was torpedoed two months later. The *Eastern Glade* and *Eastern Glen,* sold out of the line in 1933, had been resold to the British and shared the same fate. [374]

During the summer of 1940, two of the former Argonaut ships were also sold for foreign registry—the Neutrality Act was keeping American-flag shipping out of the war zone. The *Pacific,* sold on British account for $414,000 early in September, was torpedoed in March 1941. The *Atlantic* was more fortunate, possibly because she went under Panamanian colors instead after being sold in August for $400,000. She was still under that "flag of convenience" in 1953, when resold for scrapping. [375]

At the close of the war, the only survivors of the whole "First Fleet" were the *Charles H. Cramp* and *Henry S. Grove;* both served throughout the war and then were traded in for scrapping in partial payment for new ships in 1946. Four others—the *Sagadohoc, City of New York, Challenger,* and *Lancaster*—would be lost during wartime service with the line. [376]

In the interim, the "Second Fleet" was coming along. The names of all the line's vessels would thereafter start with "African." That was a convenient device, allowing more flexibility than some of the other line name devices which would produce such gems as *Mormacdove* and *Exochorda.* It was about this time that a black band was added to the previous plain buff funnels while enameled plates of the house flag with its alternate fields of blue and red, were attached to each side.

The first Farrell venture into the "long-range program" was an ambitious one. By their subsidy contract, they agreed to build three PC-3 passenger-cargo liners, each with accommodations for 110 first-class passengers. They were designed to be capable of 16½ knots or better, since their turbines could develop 9,350 horsepower. The contract was awarded to the Ingalls shipyard at Pascagoula, Mississippi, which laid the first keel, the *African Comet's,* on July 1, 1940, and launched her on June 28, 1941, one year less than three days afterwards. Miss Mary Farrell was her sponsor. The *African Meteor* and the *African Planet* followed shortly.

The *African Comet* was not only the first of the "Africans" but she also represented an interesting first time in American ship construction. Welding, which would generally replace the traditional riveting in the great World War II shipbuilding program, was just coming into use. Admiral Emory S. Land, head of the Maritime Commission, declared at the launching that "No country has ever before built an all-welded passenger liner." [377]

These three ships never really served in the Farrell fleet. Three weeks after Pearl Harbor, on December 30, the line was notified by the Maritime Commission that all three were needed for national defense and would not be delivered. [378] They were immediately taken over as Navy Transports U.S.S. *Arthur Middleton (African Comet)*, U.S.S. *Samuel Chase (African Meteor)*, and U.S.S. *George Clymer (African Planet)*. Captain Christian W. Schmidt took the *African Comet,* which he had brought north before the requisition, out to the Pacific for the Navy. The *Planet's* name was later used for one of the line's C-3 freighters. That these, and other new liners, were on hand for such essential service was a result, in part, of the 1936 maritime policy.

The line was never given back the ships, and appears to have had no regrets on that point. They seem to have had a serious lack of stability, and the Navy had to pour more than a thousand tons of permanent concrete ballast into the hold of each ship to keep it upright. That would have meant the loss of valuable freight capacity on the Cape run.

A second, and more modest, trio of "C's" built for American South African would serve under its flag. These were C-2 freighters, with some special features which would make them more generally useful than the conventional C-2's acquired later. In particular, they each had 27,400 cubic feet of refrigerated space, as compared with only 3,000 cubic feet for the other C-2's. This space would be particularly useful for the newly developing rock-lobster and fruit cargoes on the Cape run.

The contract for these three ships, which would continue the new "meteorological" nomenclature as the *African Star, African Sun* and *African Dawn,* was to some extent "in the family." It went to the Federal Shipbuilding & Dry Dock Company at Kearny, New Jersey, near Newark. This yard, it will be recalled, had been established by the elder Farrell during World War I as a subsidiary of the United States Steel Corporation, and was rated as one of the "Big Five" of American shipbuilding. [379] Its president, at the time, Lynn H. Korndorff, had been appointed by Farrell; was a close friend of the family; and was one of the nonfamily stockholders in the closely held American South African Line. Altogether, Federal would build nine ships for the Farrell "Second Fleet," and they would rank among the most satisfactory of all its ships. A thoughtful touch was the use of South African champagne, of which the Cape was very proud, when the wife of the South African minister at Washington christened the *African Sun*. [380] One of this C-2 trio from Kearny did not survive for the postwar fleet, for the *African Star* was torpedoed off Rio in mid-1943; the name would be passed on to the first of the 1946 C-3's.

With the nation at war, its shipyards were busier than ever before in its history. As in 1917, submarine sinkings called for a tremendous building program for emergency ships to offset the terrific losses. Once again, mushroom shipyards sprang up around the coasts, all the way from South Portland, Maine to Portland, Oregon and beyond. For rapid mass construction, the basic features of an old British tramp design were applied to the new Liberty ship. With old-fashioned reciprocating engines used to avoid the serious congestion in turbine and diesel production, the Liberty could make only ten or eleven knots. Her ample holds had good cargo capacity, and she became the "work horse of the seas." As the more efficient turbines became available, the Liberty gave way to the Victory ship, similar in size and capacity, but capable of making some 16½ knots, the speed of a C-3. Luckily, this was rather too fast for most of the submarines of that day to catch.

Many of the worst features of World War I shipbuilding were avoided, even though performance was spotty. That nation-wide uniform design greatly simplified the fabrication of parts at a distance; the use of welding instead of riveting enabled women to participate in the work and speeded up the process; and this speeding enabled far more use of each building slip. In particular, the Libertys were completed in time to be of very real service while the war was still on.

The Liberty ship thus had the same slow speed of the World War I emergency ships, but it had the size of the new C-2's—in fact, it was officially called the EC-2 and the Victory ship the VC-2. In length, the comparative figures for the seven main government-built dry cargo types were: Hog Islanders, 390 feet; "Wests," 409; Libertys, 441; Victorys, 455; C-1's, 417; C-2's, 439; and C-3's, 492. Their respective dead-weight tonnage was around 7,800, 8,500, 10,400, 10,700, 9,100, 10,100, and 12,100. [381]

The Maritime Commission made some sound policy decisions. One of the best was to continue with the "long-range program" of "C's" along with the huge emergency program. It was realized that the emergency ships would not be particularly useful after the war, except as tramps, and that the nation should have an adequate supply of good custom-built ships as well. The original 1937 "long-range program" goal of 500 "C's" in ten years was speeded up, so that the total was attained even before the war was over. As far as merchant marine development went, those ships, while amounting to not quite one-tenth of the total, proved more useful than all the others when peace came.

Altogether, the Maritime Commission during the war built 5,777 vessels, totaling 56 million dead-weight, or 39 million gross tons. Just about half that tonnage represented the 2,708 Liberty ships. In addition, there were 414 Victory ships, 705 T-2 and other tankers, 727 minor types, and 682 military types, as well as the 541 C's of the "long-range program." [382] The nation's ship-yards at the same time, of course, were turning out tremendous additional tonnage for the Navy.

In that whole World War II construction between 1939 and 1945, the Maritime Commission produced about three times as many ships as the Shipping Board had turned out in 1917–22, and they had more than four times the total tonnage. The over-all cost of its shipbuilding came to some $13 billion, while the Navy's shipbuilding cost an additional $18 billion, in addition to ordnance equipment. [383]

The Farrells would have a temporary connection with some of those emergency ships. During the war, as will be seen, when all vessels had been requisitioned by the government, they would act as general agents or "ships' husbands" for scores of the Liberty ships. Later, in the period of readjustment at the close of the war, they would charter a number of Victory ships for the run to South and East Africa. [384] During all that time, however, they would be looking forward to the time when their own full fleet of "C's" would be ready.

The largest group of ships added to their fleet, and in many ways the most satisfactory, consisted of six C-3's built by Federal at the close of the war. In the middle of the war, the Maritime

Commission canceled some of its building contracts, including one with Federal at Kearny for eleven C-3's. Korndorff suggested to the Farrells that he undertake them for American South African. The idea appealed to them, but they felt that they could not at the time afford more than six of the eleven. At their suggestion, Lykes Brothers agreed to take the other five, which were completed in 1945.

On October 23, 1943 the Maritime Commission contracted with Federal for building the six; and at the same time contracted with American South African for their purchase. Two bore the names of earlier Farrell vessels. The *African Planet* was named for one of the PC-3's taken over by the Navy, and the *African Star* for the C-2 sunk in 1943. The other four, continuing the "meteorological" pattern, would become the *African Crescent, African Lightning, African Moon,* and *African Rainbow.*

Instead of taking job-lot C-3's, the company spent months determining exactly the particular features it wanted for the South African run. Its chief consultant was Herbert Lee Seward, professor of marine engineering at Yale, who had served as consultant to the Shipping Board, the Maritime Commission, the Navy Department, and various companies. He was assisted by the firm of Gibbs & Cox. The line followed standard C-3 equipment in the construction of the hull, in topsides and in motive power. These particular vessels had two steam turbines generating 8,500 horsepower, with double reduction gear to the single-screw shaft. Their machinery was produced by the General Electric Company at its Lynn, Massachusetts plant.

The deviations from the conventional C-3 design were estimated to have amounted to about 20 per cent of the total cost, as "owner's features." By providing four deep tanks, the usual 12,250-barrel fuel capacity was increased to 17,500 barrels. Oil was expensive in Africa; and this important change enabled a ship to make the round voyage way to East Africa without refueling. Three more tanks were installed for those important outward cargoes of lubricating oil. Another feature was very ample refrigerating space—35,000 cubic feet gross, or 25,000 net —for the lobster and fruit from Cape Town. The holds, too, were arranged for the particular nature of the traffic on the route. One of the later inducements for shipping by Farrell Lines would be the ventilating and dehumidifying equipment installed in all dry cargo holds to ensure maximum protection to the cargo even in the extremes of weather likely to be encountered in a January run between New York and Mombasa. Low fireproof deckhouses at the base of the masts for special cargo, such as explosive and inflammable materials, helped safeguard the general cargo, if anything happened. [385] The heavy deadweight and cubic capacity of the ships was to make it possible to lift larger cargoes and carry them faster than any of the line's previous ships. What was more, they proved to be amazingly economical. The cost accountants were to find that these C-3's were cheaper to operate than the later C-2's, despite their superior speed and size. [386] The line had additional cause for satisfaction by the fall of 1946 for having been "first in the trade" with many of its innovations: "commercial radar, cargo oil tanks, fruit cooling, refrigerating cargo space, bullion strong rooms, and scientific temperature control for the better protection of cargo entrusted to us." [387]

A construction-differential subsidy agreement was signed by the company and the Maritime Commission on March 8, 1945. [388] In view of the cheaper cost in foreign yards, the subsidy amounted to half the building cost which, because of rising labor costs, increased sharply before the ships were finished. As it turned out, the Federal yard received something over $4 million apiece for the six ships and the line paid around two millions apiece, or about $165 per dead-weight ton. It was agreed that the *Charles H. Cramp* and the *Henry S. Grove,* the only survivors of the "First Fleet," would be traded in for scrapping, with an allowance of $451,776 for the *Grove* and $450,690 for the *Cramp* toward the purchase of the new ships.

These six C-3's were among the last vessels built by Federal, for the United States Steel Corporation decided to discontinue shipbuilding. The yard saw to it that particularly thorough workmanship went into their last building. The five Lykes ships were completed in 1945, but it was not until February 2, 1946 that the first of the sextet, the second *African Star,* was christened by Mrs. John J. Farrell, wife of the chairman of the board, and six weeks later, the second *African Planet,* by Mrs. James A. Farrell, Jr., wife of the president. [389] The ships, delivered in April and June, soon sailed for South Africa. The *African Rainbow* was completed on July 19; the *African Crescent* on September 13; the *African Moon,* the largest of all Farrell ships by a few tons, on December 27; and finally, the *African Lightning* on February 11, 1947. [390]

The other eight ships of the "Second Fleet" were purchased secondhand from the government's huge surplus. More intelligent and vigorous leadership was to handle that surplus infinitely better than in the bungling experimentation of the Shipping Board after World War I. The Navy Department and the Maritime Commission in June 1944 asked the Harvard Graduate School of Business Administration to undertake "a comprehensive review of the shipbuilding and shipping industries . . . and probable postwar shipping requirements . . . to develop the facts necessary to the formulation of a program for the disposition of surplus ships and shipbuilding facilities." The government also wanted "recommendation of a program to be adopted for the disposition of surplus ships and shipbuilding facilities." [391] The study was undertaken by James W. Culliton, Harvey P. Bishop, James M. Knox, and Paul F. Lawler. Their 325-page report on *The Use and Disposition of Ships and Shipyards at the End of World War II,* commonly known as the "Harvard Report," appeared in June 1945, midway between the surrender of Germany and of Japan. It is one of the significant documents of American maritime policy, for it influenced strongly the Merchant Ship Sales Act of 1946, nine months later. [392]

In brief, the Report recommended as follows: "(a) sell ships; (b) avoid delay in selling ships; (c) fulfill contractual obligations; (d) refrain as a rule from operating commercial services; (e) adopt a 'one-price' policy; (f) make the adopted price policy 'firm'; (g) put some ships in reserve and effectively sterilize them." [393]

Some of their points had a definite bearing on the terms under which the Farrells would acquire their ships. The report advised the scrapping of all obviously unfit ships, while those to be sold should be put in safe operating condition in private yards at government expense. The basic price for all ships less than 15 years old, except Libertys, should be "the estimated prewar reproduction cost in a representative foreign yard" with allowance for depreciation at five per cent a year from the time of construction. For the better freighters and passenger ships, private American operators should have first choice. Finally, as a provisional measure, the government should charter vessels to operators "who need ships temporarily until ships suited to their requirements can be built." [394]

The Merchant Ship Sales Act, which became law on March 8, 1946, implemented those suggestions. It stipulated that the "statutory sales price" of a dry cargo vessel (tankers were to sell at a higher rate) would amount to 50 per cent of the prewar cost, with depreciation at the rate of five per cent a year since construction, and with adjustments made for special improvements or deterioration. A war-built vessel might be sold by the Maritime Commission to any American citizen with the proper qualifications "necessary to enable him to operate and maintain the vessel under normal competitive conditions." Charter rates were to be not less than 15 per cent annually of the statutory sales price and not "less than the prevailing world market charter rate for similar vessels for similar use." [395]

The Farrell decision in 1946 to enter the West African service raised questions as to the type of ship best adapted for that run, where port facilities were not yet well developed. [396] The Maritime Commission's trade-route study had recommended the C-1, because of its light draft, and the Delta Line would later use that type on its Gulf-West African run. A Farrell study in 1946, however, estimated that on the New York-West African run, the superior capacity of a C-2 would earn $30,000 more freight than a C-1 and cost $12,800 more to operate. The net gain, with all items evaluated, would be nearly $4,900 more per voyage for a C-2. [397]

The line settled upon war-built C-2's, some of which were available at reasonable rates. [398] By the Ship Sales Act, one would cost around $960,000, as compared with the C-2's *African Dawn*

Pier fire and explosion, December 3, 1956. Flames from the Luckenbach 35th Street pier extending toward the Farrell 33rd Street pier; the *African Lightning* in stream; the *African Grove* just emerging from pier

The first *African Star* in war gray. This ship, the first of the "Second Fleet" C-2's,

Painting by Worden Wood

and *African Sun* built to order, new, in 1942 at a cost of some $1,500,000 to the line after deduction of the construction-differential. In mid-1946, the line was operating a number of C-3's, C-2's, and Victorys on charter on the South African run. That gave it an opportunity to judge the relative merits of the ships which it had been using. The Maritime Commission sold the line three of those—the *Ann McKim, Gauntlet,* and *Golden Racer*—but the demand for C-2's was so heavy that its other two were sold elsewhere. All had been built in 1944 by the Moore Dry Dock Company at Oakland in San Francisco Bay, with turbine engines by the General Electric plant at Lynn, Massachusetts.

In changing these old clipper names, the line kept the prefix "African" but began a new device of having the names of each group start with the same letter. There would be these "G's" and then the "P's" and the "E's." The *Ann McKim* as the *African Glade,* and the *Golden Racer* as the *African Glen* perpetuated the names of the pioneer *Eastern Glade* and *Eastern Glen.* The *Gauntlet* was renamed the *African Grove,* honoring the long-lived and highly successful Argonaut freighter *Henry S. Grove,* but it would scarcely have been appropriate to bestow a similar honor on her equally satisfactory sister ship, as the *African Cramp.*

The line took possession of the *Golden Racer-African Glen* on February 7, 1947, with the other two following on March 4. Each was sent to Baltimore, where the line for years has carried on its major repair and refitting work. Tanks were installed for the latex (liquid rubber) shipments from the Firestone plantations in Liberia. Refrigerator boxes, that would be found useful by the housewives of Monrovia, were also installed, but on a very modest scale compared with the "reefer" capacity on the ships for Cape Town.

In April 1947, a week before the first of these sailed for West Africa, the line began negotiations to get three more Moore-built wartime C-2's. It was learned that the Bloomfield Steamship Company of Houston, Texas had three to sell. The Farrells had taken a 20 per cent interest in this projected Gulf service to South Africa. Lykes opposition crowded it out of a hoped-for

operating-differential subsidy, and its Texas backers lost enthusiasm. [399] It had already bought these C-2's from the Maritime
Commission, which now approved the Farrell's purchase of the
remaining 80 per cent of Bloomfield Line stock for $1,365,000
and their assumption of the Commission mortgages on the three
ships. These were to be immediately bareboat chartered until
the negotiations were completed. [400] That was how the line acquired its three "P's," for the *Argonaut* became the *African Patriot,* the *Archer* the *African Pilgrim,* and the *Mandarin* the *African Pilot.*

The final pair of vessels brought in to round out the new fleet
enjoyed a clear primacy in prestige from the very outset. They
were acquired to provide more elaborate passenger service than
the 12-passenger limit on the freighters would permit. The recollections of the *City of New York's* 12 years of service were still
rosy. The line went after two passenger-liner ships, similar but
not exactly like PC-3's, that had been used for the Delta service
to the east coast of South America from the Gulf, and then requisitioned as transports in the war. They had been built in 1940
at the Bethlehem Steel Company's Sparrow Point Yard at Baltimore, with engines from the company's Fore River Yard in
Quincy, Massachusetts. These were now lying in the reserve fleet
in such deplorable condition that it was hard to imagine that
they had once been crack passenger liners and would soon be
again. The government had agreed to restore liners used as
transports to their prewar condition, but Congressional appro-
priations had not been forthcoming.

Under the circumstances, the Maritime Commission agreed
to sell the hulls for $100,000 apiece on condition that Farrell
Lines would pay for the reconditioning, with such "betterments"
as it wanted. A construction-differential subsidy would be
granted to cover the extra domestic cost of this work. The line
turned to Gibbs & Cox for specifications. Several yards bid on
the reconstruction with the Gulf Shipbuilding Company at Mobile the lowest. Altogether, these ships, already eight years old,
cost the line around $2,250,000 apiece, a little more than the
new cargo C-3's. Taking possession in late December 1948, the

line had them towed by two Moran tugs to Mobile—a stormy 17-day trip from New York.

In the construction, every effort was made to give the ships the best in passenger accommodations in the 30 staterooms and in the public rooms. Their broad, straight funnels were a special indication that William Francis Gibbs had had a hand in the reconversion—the funnels on many other liners were beginning to narrow at the top. The passenger accommodations of the "E's" aroused nothing but enthusiasm, but there were those at Beaver Street who regretted the loss of cargo space. With hulls of virtually the same size as the C-3 freighters, but with four feet narrower beam, they averaged only some 8,500 dead-weight tons as compared with the freighters' 12,000. The extra demands of the steward's department, moreover, meant that the "E's" carried double the 50-man crews of the freighters, almost one extra man for each passenger. For all that, the E's were to be a constant source of pride, if not of profit. They each received a new and third name, as the first "E's"—*African Enterprise* (Delta's *Delargentino* and Army transport *J. W. McAndrew*) and *African Endeavor* (Delta's *Delbrasil* and Navy transport *George F. Elliott*).

One of the celebrated Farrell dinners was given aboard the *Enterprise* before her maiden voyage on July 30, 1949. John Farrell, who had followed the conversion process with constant guidance, paid individual tribute to those who had brought about so happy an achievement. Out in South Africa, she received a warm reception, with parties at every port. A month later, on August 31, the *Endeavor* likewise made her maiden sailing. Both ships sailed with capacity passenger lists. [401]

The "Second Fleet" would remain at that 16-ship strength for the next decade. Totaling 169,000 dead-weight tons (137,000 gross tons), it stood just midway among the subsidized lines in 1955. Six of the fleets were larger: United States Lines, 48 ships at 562,000 dead-weight tons; Lykes Brothers, 54 at 539,000; Moore-McCormack Lines, 36 at 400,000; American Export Lines, 30 at 313,000; American President Lines, 19 at 224,000; and Grace Lines, 25 at 223,000. Smaller than the Farrell fleet were those of the Seas Shipping Company (Robin Line), 12 at

142,000; Mississippi Shipping Company (Delta Lines), 14 at 130,000; American Mail Line, 9 at 106,000; Pacific Transport Lines, 6 at 63,000; Pacific-Argentine-Brazil Lines, 4 at 50,000; Gulf and South American Steamship Company, 4 at 42,800; and Oceanic Steamship Company, 4 at 42,700. Altogether, the 281 ships totaled more than 3,000,000 dead-weight tons. [402]

Aside from a few big passenger liners of 20,000 tons or more, a large part of all those fleets was made up of C-3's, C-2's, and C-1's from the "long-range program." The wisdom shown in conceiving that program, and then in keeping it going along with the Liberty and Victory emergency ships during the war was evidenced by their performance in the postwar decade, when they were able to compete successfully with the cargo ships of other nations.

Chapter IX

WORLD WAR II

THE First World War brought the new American merchant
marine into existence; the Second World War demonstrated its great value. Even in the 27 months before the United
States entered that second war, the increased shipping needs on
distant sea lanes were being met far more adequately than had
been possible in the earlier similar interval in the years of 1914–
1917. The new network of government-sponsored line services
were even from the beginning able to provide many of the essential requisites for this expanded role. There were at hand a respectable fleet of American-flag cargo and passenger ships; a
substantial body of American officers and seamen; widespread
commercial contacts with distant regions; and, in the shipping
offices of New York and other American seaports, a wealth of
managerial "know-how" developed during the past two decades.

After Pearl Harbor, the government took the whole shipping
industry into its own hands for the next four years. It determined
where all ships should go and what they should carry; but it left
the actual management of those wartime voyages to the experienced shipping lines. The merchant fleet, under the government's huge building program, mushroomed from 1,100 to
5,500 vessels. And along with this, the purely commercial role
of the prewar merchant marine was overshadowed by its military functions. It had an indispensable part in the transporting
of millions of men and billions of tons of material to implement
the nation's operations across the Atlantic and in the far Pacific.
That tremendous logistical performance would bring an in-

creased appreciation of the merchant marine in postwar years.

Wherever possible, the established steamship lines continued to serve the same regions as they had before the war, in order that full advantage might be taken of their experience and contacts. In some cases, of course, this was not possible. At the outset, the Neutrality Act banned American-flag vessels from the war zones in Western Europe and the Mediterranean. After Pearl Harbor, the usual runs to the Far East and Southeast Asia were obviously impossible. In Africa, South of the Sahara, and South America, on the other hand, relatively normal contacts continued in this war as in the earlier one. Not only were these regions not immediately involved in military operations, but they could provide materials essential to the war effort, and, in return, could afford to purchase pretty much all the goods that they could get from the United States.

At the same time, the outbreak of war in 1939, as in 1914, suddenly cut the normal commercial contacts of the remote continents with Europe. German shipping and shipments once more immediately disappeared, while trade with Britain and other European nations was drastically curtailed. Once again, as one spokesman had so aptly phrased it in 1914, the United States was faced with a great responsibility and a great opportunity by that commercial vacuum. [403] Its larger merchant marine of the late 1930's enabled the United States to move into this situation in a manner far more satisfactory to American exporters and to the merchants of the faraway lands than had been possible before.

In the case of the Union of South Africa, the United States in World War I had handled only a quarter as much of the trade as had the war-distracted British; now they handled almost as much. The trade with the Belgian Congo in World War I averaged less than $3 million a year; in World War II that rose to more than 92 millions. [404] There were substantial, if less drastic, increases in the case of other African regions. If one compares average annual United States trade with the ports South of the Sahara for the six years 1934–39 with that for 1940–45, the suddenness of the sharp increases becomes evident. In millions of dollars, American exports jumped from 93 to 163 and imports from 43 to 150 millions. [405]

In two major fields of manufactures where South Africa normally drew upon Britain and the Continent, the United States made rapid wartime gains. Iron and steel products jumped from a prewar average of only 8.0 millions to a wartime 28.7, while cotton manufactures rose sixfold from 1.5 to 9.0 millions. Automobiles, however, showed a reverse trend after an initial boom; by 1942, with their automobile plants shifted to war industry, the Americans did not even have new cars themselves. [406]

In imports from Africa, the radically increased demand for strategic metals and minerals was the outstanding feature. These had been on an extremely modest scale in World War I, partly because the major mines were still undeveloped and partly because there was no regular westbound steamship service. Africa in World War I had thus lagged far behind South America as a source of critical materials. [407] During the intervening years, as already noted, chrome from Southern Africa, copper from Rhodesia and the Belgian Congo, and manganese from the Gold Coast had become major return cargoes. [408]

As World War II approached, with the possibility of jeopardized sea lanes, the United States gradually came to the realization that the stockpiling of critical materials was important. The Farrells were among the first to give instructions that homeward-bound ships were to give priority to ore and other minerals. In fact, in the autumn of 1938, around the time of the Munich crisis, their last two ships to make the Gulf run to South Africa returned with full cargoes of nothing but manganese from Durban, and carried it to the big Bethlehem steel works at Sparrows Point near Baltimore. [409] Some of the line's overseas agents were dismayed at a policy which would inevitably result in leaving some better-paying commodities for its rivals' cargoes.

Altogether, imports of nonprecious metals from the ports South of Sahara rose almost tenfold from an average of 7.4 millions for 1934–39 to 72.7 for 1940–45. Part of that increase came from the accustomed sources of chrome, manganese, and asbestos, but even more arose from shipments of the products of the rich Katanga region in the Belgian Congo. As war came on, the British, in their far-reaching efforts to keep strategic materials out of the hands of the Germans, refused to let the great Union

Minière du Haut Katanga ship its copper to its usual Belgian refineries near the German border, where the finished product might easily be seized. Thus denied British "navicerts" or shipping permits, the Union finally secured the agreement of the American South African Line to carry part of the copper from Beira, along with its regular cargo of Rhodesian copper from that port, while American West African would pick up the rest at Matadi. As a result, copper shipments to the United States rose from an average of $1.6 million in 1934–39 to 20.5 in 1940–45. Tin likewise jumped, from 0.2 to 13.2 millions in that same period, and "other nonprecious minerals" from 1.0 to 25.2 millions. That last category included, besides cobalt and other traditional offerings, uranium for the initial atomic project. [410] After the war, the Belgians continued to trade with the United States, but they carried almost everything in their own ships, shunning the American shipping lines that had co-operated in carrying their minerals to a safe destination.

Those same considerations also rerouted South African diamonds in the same direction. A large part of them had ultimately reached the United States, after going to Holland or Belgium for cutting by the way of Britain, but now they began to be sent direct. There was virtually no income for the shipping companies in diamonds, impressive as they appeared in the trade statistics. They usually went by air mail or were carried by passengers aboard ship. In the war years, their value as imports to the United States rose three and a half times higher than on the eve of the war, to $42.6 million. [411]

Another commodity that began to move directly to New York was gold, usually in consignments worth some $2,700,000. [412] This was a good source of profit to the steamships, as it paid a high rate and took up relatively little space. A great deal of gold in the Union was earmarked during the war years for various foreign owners and was shipped to various destinations as the opportunity arose, but the actual details were kept secret even in later years. [413] The story goes that a heavy cut in the steamship lines' gold freight came when one huge shipment was transferred in West Africa to a heavy cruiser for safe shipment to America.

The only other important deviation from the prewar commodity pattern was wool. As in World War I, this began to
move from Port Elizabeth and East London to Boston, instead of Britain. From a prewar average of $0.9 million, the value
of the wool shipments rose to 15.4 millions for the war years,
with 1942 the peak year at 40.3 millions.

The ships on the Cape run naturally felt the impact of these
new wartime influences. There was an immediate scramble for
passenger accommodations, when the usual European services
were suspended or curtailed. When the *City of New York* sailed
from Cape Town on December 11, 1939 she carried the first
shipment of gold bullion for New York. During the next ten
weeks, three other ships carried similar treasure loads.

The fifth wartime American South African voyage, made by
the *Challenger,* set several records. Outbound from New York
on December 3, 1939, she carried 13,132 payable tons of American exports, exceeded only by the *African Moon's* 13,600-ton
cargo in 1948 for an all-time Farrell record. Her homeward
9,158 tons of minerals included 3,519 tons of copper, and 5,047
tons of chrome. She also carried better-paying cargo of wool,
karakul, hides, and wattle, in addition to $2,707,911 worth of
gold. [414]

At this time, the line made a significant new extension of its
Cape service. In the desperate shipping shortage of World War
I, the British had had to maintain regular service from New
York to South Africa to meet the region's basic needs because
adequate American shipping had been lacking; now it was different. [415] At the beginning of 1940, American South African
agreed with the British conference lines to take over as many
sailings as possible on their account on a percentage basis. [416] The
German Hansa Line had already suspended its sailings, of course.
For this service as a whole the Farrells used their Argonaut ships.
The first to sail was the *Charles H. Cramp* on Union-Castle account on January 21, 1940 from New York. By June 1, the sixth
sailing was underway. [417] The British conference lines would
never again return in full force to the run.

During the spring and summer of 1940, the Argonaut ships,
as already noted, were formally taken over by the American

South African Line, which soon took advantage of the current high prices to sell four vessels for foreign registry. [418] New ships were ordered in accordance with the line's recently acquired subsidy contract. Until those new vessels were ready, the line used two old vessels, the *Polybius* and *West Cheswald* on bareboat charter from the Maritime Commission. [419] This arrangement simply provided the use of the ship, or "bareboat," itself, with the charterer "finding" everything else, in contrast to time charter, where the owner provided crew, supplies, and so on. A few other freighters were time chartered from other American lines, along with five foreign-flag freighters. These last voyages not only proved useful to South Africa in meeting its import and export needs, but most of them were also highly profitable to the company. One of those vessels carried the biggest wool cargo ever recorded on the Port Elizabeth-Boston run.

American South African had some violent ups and downs in the five years before Pearl Harbor. In 1937, with its sailings on both the Atlantic and Gulf runs, it made 26 voyages, including five by Argonaut ships and one by a chartered vessel. By 1939, that had been cut in half, with its regular ships making only ten voyages and Argonaut, three. Then, with war starting in Europe, that jumped back to 33 voyages in 1940 and 35 in 1941; in the latter year, 19 of the voyages were made by chartered ships. [420]

Lykes Brothers, who had the largest of American cargo fleets, began what would be permanent American-flag service on the run from the Gulf to South and East Africa early in 1941. With their lines to Britain, the Continent, and the Mediterranean barred by the spread of the war zone, they sought other employment for their displaced ships. One answer was to move into the Gulf-Cape run which the Farrells had given up in 1938. The new service was inaugurated by the *Effingham,* which sailed from New Orleans on January 31, 1941. It would be just nine years before Lykes received an operating-differential contract for that route.

For a year and a half after Europe went to war, the American-flag vessels came and went safely. German surface raiders and submarines picked off occasional British vessels in the South Atlantic, but until the spring of 1941, the only American-flag victim was the American Pioneer Line's *City of Rayville* in late 1940; she was presumably sunk by a mine laid in Australian waters by a German surface raider, and not by deliberate attack.

In 1941, with American neutrality wearing thin, the African runs became the principal enemy target. [421] Of the next six American-flag vessels sunk by the Germans, four were on voyages involving Africa. On May 21, 1941, the Robin Line's *Robin Moor,* formerly American Export's *Exmoor,* en route from New York to Cape Town, was sunk by a German submarine off the bulge of Brazil, the only American-flag victim of a submarine in the first two years. The passengers and crew put off in lifeboats and were picked up safely. President Roosevelt denounced the act as "piracy by an international highwayman." [422] American indignation and protests had less justification when a German plane sank the Isthmian Line's freighter *Steel Seafarer* in the Gulf of Suez on September 7, 1941, for she was carrying 5,700 tons of munitions. Her crew got clear just in time, as she rolled over and sank quickly. She was one of the numerous American-flag freighters that had been carrying, under very lucrative charter terms, munitions for the British operations in North Africa. On the return voyage, some of these were stopping in East or South Africa to pick up ore, sisal, or other cargo. The next victim was the freighter *Lehigh,* torpedoed without warning on October 19, en route from Spain for a cargo of ore in West Africa.

American South African's turn came just four days before Pearl Harbor, some 250 miles southeast of St. Helena. The freighter *Sagadahoc,* a Maine-built veteran of the Argonaut intercoastal service, had sailed from New York on November 7 with a heavy 12,074-ton cargo, destined for all the South and East African ports except Cape Town. On December 3, 1941, she was torpedoed without warning by a surfaced submarine. The big United States flag painted on her side did not save her; the first torpedo, in fact, hit just below it. The second one was a direct hit on the engine room. The only fatality was an oiler, who had managed to climb out of the demolished engine room, to be trapped by shifting deck cargo. All the others got away safely in two lifeboats before she sank, within twenty minutes of the first attack. One boatload, with Captain Frederick I. Evans and 15 men, was picked up six days later by the American-Hawaiian freighter *Kentuckian* and taken to Durban. The other boat, with Chief Officer Norris J. Chadbourne and 19 men, was picked up after seven days by the Alaska Packer's freighter *Bering*. These survivors were carried to Trinidad. Chadbourne established what would be a precedent for torpedoed officers of the line; reaching New York on December 29, he put to sea again in fifteen days as chief officer in the *Charles H. Cramp*. Captain Evans shortly afterwards went into naval service.

Years later, a survivor of this sinking was chatting with a German sailor at a bar in Hamburg. The name *Sagadahoc* happened to come up, whereupon the German produced a snapshot of a surfaced U-boat entering Kiel Canal proudly displaying two life rings with the sunken freighter's name. [423]

After Pearl Harbor, the government quickly completed the process of gaining control of the seagoing merchant marine. Some of the vessels, especially passenger liners, were taken over as transports by the Army or Navy. The rest came under the jurisdiction of a new operating unit created as a semidetached part of the Maritime Commission on February 7, 1942. While the Commission proper concentrated on the building and manning of ships, this new War Shipping Administration (WSA) was charged with the direction of where the ships should be used and what cargoes should be carried by them. The titular head of the WSA was the same as of the Maritime Commission proper, Admiral Emory S. Land, but much of the actual burden of guidance fell upon the Deputy Director, Lewis A. Douglas, later ambassador to Britain. Some of the personnel of War Shipping came from the staff of the Maritime Commission, but far more were shipping men, economists, and other outsiders brought in to man the complicated setup. Besides its Washington headquarters, WSA had branches or representatives in the major ports of the United States and also abroad.

For the actual operations, the War Shipping Administration depended upon the various private shipping houses. This arrangement was of mutual value; the government had the services of the men with the best pertinent experience and the shipping companies were able to afford to keep their shoreside organizations intact, even though the government had taken all their ships. Those firms with operating-differential subsidies under the 1936 Act had these suspended for the duration early in 1942. Incidentally, at this same time, American South African's last sailing on private account until early 1946 was on February 5, 1942, two days after the War Shipping Administration had been set up. [424]

The government requisitioning of merchant tonnage was complete by April 1942. In some cases, particularly with passenger ships needed for transports, the requisition was "for title"; that is, the vessel was taken over "for keeps." That was what happened to American South African's three new passenger-cargo liners as soon as they were completed and also to many passenger ships built as a result of the Jones-White Act of 1929. [425] The *City of New York* escaped that process, however, as she was the only passenger ship linking the United States and South Africa; she would be sunk even before she went under the Time Charter Agreement with the rest of the Farrell fleet.

The second category in contracts was the "General Agency Agreement" or "GAA," which was developed to look out for the ships actually owned by the War Shipping Administration. Some of these were old veterans of the World War I emergency fleet, such as the *Polybius* and *West Cheswald,* which American South African had had on bareboat charter since 1941. The bulk of the vessels were the new Liberty ships, produced by the tremendous building program of this war. The first two Libertys were ready for sea in December 1941, and thereafter they came along rapidly. Each was assigned to a particular shipping firm under this General Agency Agreement for "husbanding." The firm as general agent or "ship's husband" would select the officers and attend to the crews, maintenance, and supplying of the vessels, as it would do for its own ships in peacetime. Overseas, the company's agents would perform similar services in foreign ports. Altogether, American South African served as general agent for some 70 ships, most of them Libertys. By the time the GAA program was terminated in 1946, it had completed 946 voyages on government account. [426]

The third category concerned cargoes, rather than ships. A company's traffic division handled this Berth Sub-agent Agreement (BSA), whereas the General Agency Agreement was under a company's marine division. The Berth Agreement was linked up with a particular overseas region, the same one wherever feasible, with which the company in question had already developed commercial contacts. It was thus appropriate that Robin and American South African, along with Lykes Brothers to a lesser degree for the Gulf traffic, should be the lines to handle the berth traffic for South and East Africa.

By the middle of the year, these arrangements were pretty well straightened out, but in the early months of 1942 no one seems to have been entirely sure about what was happening. When one of the Farrell officials tried to get definite answers at Washington in March, he found that the WSA official with whom he talked "was very vague on the whole subject." Then he was invited to come down to Washington to organize one of WSA's new divisions, but declined. [427]

With the complications of these new wartime contracts with the government, the Farrell headquarters at Beaver Street became short-handed as several of its top executives left for war service. James A. Farrell, Jr., the president, served in naval intelligence at the Third Naval District Headquarters, rising to the rank of commander. George Wauchope, also a naval reserve officer, established and commanded the great maritime training school at Sheepshead Bay; then, in the Pacific, he participated in eleven amphibious landings, commanding attack transports or serving as chief of staff of an amphibious command. Clifford Shields went to Cape Town as representative of the War Shipping Administration. Various others of the headquarters staff or from the ships also served in the Navy or in the Army, or in civilian capacity.

That left the burden of carrying on the line operations principally in the hands of John J. Farrell, chairman of the board. Admiral Leigh C. Palmer was general manager; Fred J. Unver, in charge of traffic; E. C. Arthur, marine superintendent; George H. Hoeft, superintending engineer; and after his return from the sea, Captain George T. Sullivan became port captain. John

J. Monahan maintained liaison with Washington until his sudden death in 1943.

Once the United States entered the war, five of the regular Farrell ships and nine of their "general agency" charges would be sunk, with the loss of 130 officers, crewmen, and passengers. Most of the remaining prewar Farrell fleet quickly followed the *Sagadahoc* to the bottom. The most shocking sinking was that of the *City of New York* with the loss of 20 lives. She had left New York on December 28, 1941. After discharging her outward general cargo at various ports from Cape Town to Lourenco Marques, she took on a capacity homeward cargo, including 4,500 tons of manganese from Durban. But it was the safety of his 42 passengers of various nationalities, including children, that concerned Captain Sullivan, leaving Cape Town on March 2, heading toward the danger zone. All the way north, he sounded the alarm for lifeboat drills, again and again, at any hour day or night.

For four weeks, it was the "fair weather route" at its best until Palm Sunday, March 29, near the Hatteras area, when it turned cloudy and cold. From time to time, the radio picked up alarms from ships being chased by U-boats. They were taking a heavy toll along the east coast, for anti-submarine measures were very slow in developing.

Around noon, and some thirty miles east of Hatteras, as the passengers gathered for luncheon, a torpedo crashed into the port side just below the bridge. Thanks to the constant drilling, everything moved along in quick, orderly fashion in abandoning ship, until, with most of the passengers and crew in the lifeboats, a second torpedo struck. One lifeboat was capsized by it, and spilled its occupants into the water; most were picked up by boats or life rafts, but the wife of a New York businessman was drowned. The radio operator, one of the last to leave the ship, had managed to get off an S.O.S. by pressing two wires together; his regular equipment had been smashed. The ship went down stern first; for a moment, she was poised almost perpendicular, and then disappeared, within 20 minutes of the first attack.

Most of the survivors were rescued 36 hours later, when the

destroyer *Jesse Roper* located their lifeboats and rafts and took them into Norfolk. During the first night, with waves running 15 feet high, the wife of a Yugoslav consular official gave birth to a boy, who was named after the rescuing destroyer. Captain Sullivan had had the foresight to put the doctor, who had had two ribs broken in the crash, in that boat. [428]

Fifteen men, four women, and a girl of three in the remaining boat were not located for 13 days and by then were off the Delaware Capes. Seven of the men and one woman died. That anyone survived the ordeal was attributable in no small measure to the firm leadership of the First Assistant Engineer, Norman Lee, and the Third Mate, Duncan MacNichol.

One passenger, Anna Zurcher of Berne, en route to the Swiss Consulate at New York, kept a diary of those grueling days and nights. [429] She told of the rationing of the meager canned supplies and of the Yugoslav general who went out of his head as he lay dying and struggled for Engineer Lee's automatic. [430] On the eleventh day, she wrote: "Sleep and rest were impossible. During the night it got too rough to sail any more, so the sail was ordered down and the sea anchor put out again. It was so wet and cold that there were no high spirits left. . . . The General died after breakfast and left lots of useful warm clothes. I know it sounds dreadful, but anything warm is useless to the dead and makes such a difference to those who are left. It started to rain hard, so we all got busy with tins and canvas and sail, trying to catch some water. . . . We opened the last tin of tomatoes, and had half of it for lunch. Mr. Lee said, rather grimly, that we must keep the other half until the day after tomorrow. . . . We've even forgotten to look for ships or planes." [431] Three days later, things were even worse: "During the night I took the baby from Mrs. Etter because she seemed so weak. . . . When dawn broke we found Mrs. Etter dead. It's hard to believe because she was so strong. There was not enough combined strength among the men left to bury her! Also Mickey was crying, 'Don't throw my Mummy in the sea!' The wind was cold, and the sea so rough Mr. MacNichol called to start sailing, but Mr. Lee just looked at him and shook his head. Poor man, he was done in.

Only two nights in all these thirteen that he has been down out of this awful wind." [432]

Relief, however, came later that day, Saturday, April 11. It was a joint achievement, amazingly long-delayed, of the Army, the Navy, and the Coast Guard. An Army bomber spotted them first; it called up a Navy blimp, and finally a Coast Guard cutter took the survivors aboard and carried them to the hospital at Lewes, Delaware.

By the late spring of 1942, the U-boats, having at last found the east coast too well protected, were gradually moving southward to the Caribbean. There the big diesel-powered *Challenger,* en route to Trinidad, was sunk. Captain John G. Waller and all but one of the crew were saved.

In the meantime, the old *Lancaster* had barely escaped from a serious dock fire in New York; had safely negotiated the perilous "Murmansk run" though some in her convoy were lost; and was on her way to North Africa with supplies for the American forces. She reached Casablanca safely but too late to enter, for the submarine gates were closed for the night; with morning came a gale that drove her ashore and she was wrecked with the loss of twelve lives. Her loss was eventually declared to be a war risk after long insurance litigation over war risk or ordinary marine risk.

By then only the *Charles H. Cramp* and the *Henry S. Grove* of the prewar fleet were still afloat, and engaged steadily in dangerous missions of one sort or another. Two of the new "C's," the *African Dawn* and *African Sun,* likewise kept going safely throughout the war. The first *African Star* never completed her first South African voyage for she was torpedoed off Brazil, Captain Waller's second such experience in fourteen months. The War Shipping Administration had canceled some of her prospective cargo at Durban, where the agent in evident annoyance wrote in the voyage record, "1,000 tons of lifting wasted"; but underneath was another entry, "Lost at sea, July 1943." [433] This was no hit-and-run sinking. The submarine surfaced near the captain's lifeboat and asked for him. He instructed the second mate, James Neary, to say he had been killed. Thereupon, Neary was taken abroad the U-boat and questioned; this was wound up by the inquiry if medical assistance were needed and the gift of a package of cigarettes and he was returned to the lifeboat. Years later, the German lieutenant who had given Neary the cigarettes came to the United States on a Fulbright fellowship and looked up Neary. Waller's lifeboat was picked up by a British destroyer. [434]

The two sister ships of the *African Star* happened to spend part of their time on the regular Cape Town run. They were routed for a while, however, some 3,400 miles out of the way to avoid the heavy convoy activity to North Africa. This 10,200 mile detour as against the usual 6,800 mile trip took them through the Panama Canal, down the west coast of South America, back through the straits of Magellan, and then across to Good Hope. The *African Sun* made the round trip that way to Beira on her maiden voyage early in 1943. On her second voyage, she went out the same way, but returned through the dangerous waters off Rio. Her third voyage took her to India and back: Charleston-Bermuda-Suez-Aden-Abadan-Bombay-Colombo-Aden-Suez-Gibraltar-New York. [435]

The line's contacts were naturally somewhat closer with the four surviving ships of its own than with the others that it "husbanded." The relations with the masters, although they were all picked by the line, were usually less continuing or intimate; and only occasionally did it arrange the berthing. More often these ships were given routes more closely associated with the fighting than the South African, such as North Russia, North Africa, Italy, Normandy, and the far Pacific.

One of the first Farrell "GAA" experiences—in mid-1942— was involved in what has been called "the grimmest convoy battle of the entire war." [436] Two of the line's "GAA" Liberty ships, fresh from the builders, the *William Hooper* and the *Daniel Morgan,* were under Captains E. L. Graves and G. T. Sullivan. Barely ashore from the sinking of the *City of New York,* the latter had insisted on getting back to sea at once, and so took the *Daniel Morgan,* which was loading munitions for the North Russian run. With him went another undaunted survivor of that sinking, the radio operator, Albert Vida.

This convoy was engaged in the hazardous and thankless

task of carrying war materials to the Russians, by what came to be called the "Murmansk run," although these ships were headed for the port of Archangel. Arctic ice forced vessels fairly close to Norway, where the Germans lay in wait, well fortified with planes, U-boats, and surface vessels, even including the giant battleship, *Tirpitz*. This luckless "Convoy PQ-17" sailed from Iceland on June 27. Two weeks later, only seven of its 22 American freighters were still afloat. [437]

It set out from Iceland with very ample naval protection. The Germans were eager to smash this convoy. They struck on the Fourth of July, 240 miles above the North Cape, in full force. Just as the situation was growing extremely serious, the British Admiralty called off all the protecting Allied naval vessels; the unlucky merchant skippers were told to scatter and look out for themselves.

As it was, the unhappy freighters caught incessant punishment from dive bombers, torpedo bombers, and occasionally from U-boats. The *William Hooper* went down the first day, but the *Daniel Morgan* kept going through another day in "a magnificent effort to carry her cargo through." [438] But a swarm of five attacking dive bombers were too much for her late on July 5, and she had to be abandoned. After her boats got off, a U-boat finished her off. Its commander asked Sullivan what her cargo was and advised him on the best course to take for rescue. They were soon picked up by a big Russian tanker and landed at Archangel. On his way home, the American authorities in Britain consulted Sullivan on his suggestions for convoy protection. [439] Thereafter, he stayed ashore, first as American South African's port captain at New York and later as marine superindent. One other Farrell-operated ship was lost on that grim passage. The *Richard Bland* was torpedoed while in convoy on March 3, 1943; Captain Dodd and 17 others were killed.

In addition to the *Lancaster's* loss, the North African and Mediterranean operations took a toll of three Farrell-operated Liberty ships. On January 27, 1943, a submarine wolf pack, some 300 miles south of the Azores, sank three stragglers from a convoy bound from New York to Casablanca, one of which was the

Charles Cotesworth Pinckney. The heaviest loss of life in any Farrell-connected sinking occurred in this one, with 47 killed, including young Captain Woolverton, who had been married just a week before sailing. [440] In September 1943, the *William W. Gerard* was either mined or torpedoed in the Mediterranean near Malta and the *Bushrod Washington* was bombed at Salerno; both were supporting the invasion of Italy. The latter's captain, Jonathan M. Wainwright V, the son of the general left in command in the Philippines, rushed to another ship and set up active antiaircraft fire.

Two more of the Farrell "General Agency" vessels were lost in the Normandy landings in June 1944. One of these was the Liberty ship named for James A. Farrell, Sr.; she was sunk off the beachhead on June 29. The other, the old freighter *West Cheswald,* was one of the ships selected to be sunk to form a breakwater for the artificial port at "Utah Beach."

Thanks to the fact that the Japanese failed to use their submarines much against cargo ships, the only victim from the Farrell group in the Pacific was the *Jeremiah M. Daily,* sunk on November 12, 1944 off the Philippines by a Japanese kamikaze suicide plane. Captain Manwaring and three others were killed.

In the meantime, the regular fleet of Barber's American West African Line had lost five of its seven ships between April and November 1942, two in African waters, two in the Caribbean and one in the North Atlantic.

Along with the courage and perseverance of the officers and crews, the managerial "know-how" of the shipping houses was an essential contribution in keeping ships and cargoes moving on such an unprecedented scale. That skilled experience must be rated as one of the valuable by-products of the national shipping policy between the wars.

There was, on the other hand, an impression during and after the war that the shipping interests had "cleaned up" financially during those years. It is true that freight and charter rates were high during the early neutral period and old ships could be sold off at high profits. Even the Farrell firm, which was relatively conservative in performance, had profits of 1.7 millions under the conditions of neutral trading in 1940, after not quite breaking even in its net earnings of the two preceding years. In 1941, the year of maximum profits, Farrell profits more than doubled to 3.5 millions. At the same time, the Robin Line, which had its subsidy in 1938–39, and made $119,000 for those two years, rose to 2.8 millions in 1940 and to 5.2 millions in 1941. Both lines were subsidized in 1940 and 1941, and according to the agreement with the Maritime Commission, had to return to the government half of all profits over 10 per cent up to the amount of the subsidy in those peak years. [441]

Once the nation was in the war and the government took control of the shipping industry, those earlier profits diminished. It was later stated that the net operating earnings of the subsidized lines "were substantially below those of any other American industry making a real contribution to the war effort." In 1943, for instance, the profits of the subsidized steamship lines were only 6.6 per cent as compared with 25.6 per cent for the aircraft and equipment industry, 22.4 per cent for shipbuilding, and so on for seven other industries all yielding higher returns. [442] Farrell profits dropped to an average of $814,000 a year in 1942–45. [443]

The official charter rates that came in with the War Shipping Administration were only a fraction of what they had been in the neutral period. The head of the Maritime Commission admitted officially that if the subsidized lines had sued for more, it might have cost the government a half billion dollars more. [444] Of this, American South African received $6.4 million. For the time charters of the vessels of the subsidized lines, "leased" by the government, the total was 194.2 millions, and for the vessels purchased outright by the government, or lost, $159.1 million. American South African's share was 5.7 millions for the first and 4.1 for the second. [445]

Such war profits as the subsidized lines did achieve, were in large part plowed back into their fleets through the purchase of new ships. In the immediate postwar years, the Farrells did this. They bought six new C-3's; and regretted, it will be recalled, that they did not have enough to buy all eleven of the Federal yard's final lot of them. [446] They also purchased six secondhand C-2's. Such investments, of course, contributed heavily to the net worth of the lines, but the need for plowing back profits demonstrated again that shipping was not the quickest road to rapid riches.

Chapter X

LINE ORGANIZATION

THE Farrell Lines in the 1950's had some 1,150 persons regularly employed; of these, 900 or so were aboard ship and 250 ashore. That last group did not include the hundreds of longshoremen, shipyard repair workers, and employees in the offices of the line's agents in ports at home and abroad, all of whom spent part of their working hours and earned part of their living in connection with the comings and goings of Farrell ships. The regular shoreside employees were mainly at the company's headquarters on Beaver Street in New York's shipping district, with some at the line's pier in Brooklyn and a few others scattered in various American and African cities.

The American South African-Farrell Lines setup has been from the beginning an owner-management company, in the hands of the Farrell family. Such close family control is a fairly rare phenomenon in American shipping circles. Whatever the influence of the elder Farrell may have been, the actual ownership and direction have been for the most part in the hands of his two sons, with John as chairman of the board, and James, Jr., as president. The two brothers were said to own 60-odd per cent of the stock in 1956 and to be in a position to exercise control over more than 90 per cent.

A practice of many of the old British family-controlled steamship lines to plow back into the company a large part of their earnings has become a consistent Farrell policy. [447] It seemed the sensible thing to do, as one member of the family pointed out, especially under the terms of the 1936 Act. [448] With the pattern

171

of family ownership, savings could be set aside advantageously without the constant pressure for a bolstered dividend rate, encountered by firms with swarms of stockholders.

A New York newspaper article in 1950 called the Farrell brothers "one of the most successful family teams ever to enter the maritime industry. . . . John Farrell, as chairman of the board and the elder of the two, is a quiet, reticent man who seeks to avoid the limelight. Yet his knowledge of shipping and keen insight into its problems command the respect of all who know him. James Farrell, as president . . . is one of the most active executives along 'Shipping Row.' He is an accomplished public speaker with a sense of humor and a gift of repartee. Despite the apparent differences in their characters, there is complete harmony between the brothers. Connecticut Yankees, they are shrewd businessmen, but they readily admit that they owe their success in no small measure to the foresight and encouragement of their father." [449]

John Farrell's prime interest is in the ships and seamen; to be captain of a ship appeals to him more than being behind a desk. Officers and seamen who know him, and they are numerous, speak warmly of his habit of rambling around the dock and the ships to talk with them and pick up suggestions for making their life aboard more comfortable and more efficient. This knowledge that they have such a friend at court contributes to the generally high morale of the men in the fleet.

James Farrell's concern, on the other hand, has been more with the cargoes to fill the holds of those ships, and with the problems of the shipping industry as a whole. Like his brother, he lives in Connecticut, some forty miles out on the shore of Long Island Sound, and commutes regularly to keep his nine to five hours in his office. Virtually all important papers go over the desks of both brothers. James has become one of the leading spokesmen for the subsidized steamship operators, heading one organization or committee after another. He has his father's flair for persuasive expression of pertinent arguments, and has shown himself particularly good in negotiations with organized labor.

The board of directors, normally around eight in number, is

an "inside" board, very closely intertwined both with operation and with ownership. Aside from the initial temporary organization set up in January 1926, only eleven men in addition to the Farrell brothers have sat on the board during the whole 32 years. Of those eleven men, nine have been top officials of the line as well as directors. Two of those director-officials (Luke D. Stapleton, Jr., and Thomas J. Sartor) were also members of the Farrell family. Two other Farrell relations (Ralph G. Farrell, Sr., and Joseph B. Murray) have been in the group, but did not serve as officials. [450]

This trend was further emphasized by the creation of the executive committee of the directors in January 1945. [451] They really run the line, except in matters of high policy. At first, the committee consisted of the Farrell brothers and Admiral Palmer. Before long, two much younger officials of the company succeeded the latter—George Wauchope and C. Carlton Lewis.

In January 1946, after his return from naval service, Wauchope was appointed executive vice-president. Along with oversight of the line's widespread activities, he has traveled repeatedly, representing the company beyond the seas, all the way from Monrovia, where he has headed the port authority, over to Mombasa and Cape Town. He has engaged as well in negotiations in Europe where many of the principal cargo allotments are made. [452]

Lewis has been with the company since 1944, serving as vice-president, finance, since 1945, secretary since 1946, and treasurer since 1948. After the sudden death in 1943 of John J. Monahan, who had been a director three years and was being groomed to take full charge of finance, the Farrells turned to the accounting firm of Price, Waterhouse & Company for a successor. They recommended Lewis, a graduate of Virginia Polytechnic Institute with graduate work in business at Columbia, and with substantial experience in the accounting field. He is said to have been the first man to hold such a high position in the shipping field without previous maritime experience. In addition to overall fiscal responsibility, Lewis became the channel of liaison between the company and Washington.

As in most shipping firms, the shoreside business of the com-

pany falls into three major divisions—Operations, Traffic, and
Finance. Operations includes the "husbanding" of the ships,
with responsibility for the selection, supervision, and subsistence
of the crews and the maintenance, repair, and supplying of the
ships; the loading and unloading of cargo, with the provision
of terminal facilities; and control of the movements of the ships
on their appointed schedules. Traffic falls into two distinct
parts—solicitation or "sales" in quest of cargo, and "freight"
which involves detailed routine keeping track of bills of lading,
manifests, and the other steps in the movement of inward and
outward cargo. Finance today includes more than the traditional
"accounting" details, for it has special duties in meeting the
government's call for multitudinous data from subsidized lines,
and the maintenance of contact with those government maritime authorities.

Operations might be called essentially a negative field. Its
performance is regarded as perfect when there are no delays in
schedule, no breakdowns of machinery, no running afoul of
rocks, mudbanks, or other vessels, and no excessive extortion
on the part of the unions. Normally, Farrell Lines measured up
very well in those negative respects; its relative freedom from
accidents gave it very low "hull and machinery" insurance rates.
Things could happen, however, even in the best-regulated lines.
Between mid-November and mid-December 1956 the line sus-
tained three heavy blows, for none of which it was responsible.
A ten-day longshoremen's strike began to disrupt schedules. A
fire, breaking out on an adjacent pier, reached some chemicals;
the explosion not only ripped that pier apart but damaged and
set afire the Farrell pier, where two men were killed, and the
African Lightning and *African Grove* were threatened. Cool,
quick work saved both, the *Grove* escaping with great difficulty.
Four men, including the injured marine superintendent, received Farrell Medals for their heroic work. [453] Two weeks later,
the *African Star* was rammed in the harbor by another freighter,
the *Alcoa Pilgrim,* which cut a 20-foot hole in her side. Captain
Chadbourne beached the sinking vessel close to the Statue of
Liberty; he was cleared by the Coast Guard of all blame, the
other ship being held responsible. [454] She was finally repaired

at a cost of $800,000, which was just about a record. Fortunately, such months have been very rare in Farrell annals.

In Traffic, on the other hand, cold statistics hang heavily over the heads of the sales staff, since the volume of freight earnings determines profit or loss. Theirs is a constant, aggressive quest for business, partly to keep other lines from getting existing freight and partly to develop new fields. [455] Most of the line's organizational growing pains have centered around the traffic setup. When the Farrells called in a firm of management engineers, their principal recommendation was that the head of the solicitation activity should be freed entirely from all routine "freight" responsibility, and should be able to devote his full time to planning and the maintaining of major contacts. [456]

In a major company reorganization in 1956, one member of the executive committee was placed in charge of each of the three major divisions, while the chairman of the board was regarded as representative of the stockholder interests. James Farrell, in addition to his overall administrative responsibilities as president, was in immediate charge of Traffic, while Wauchope headed Operations, and Lewis, Finance. To maintain constant administrative oversight, the executive committee meets every Tuesday with the top traffic officials; on Thursdays with operations; and on Wednesdays by themselves, to discuss high policy. Another case of integrated control occurs in Wauchope's supervision of the not always clear-cut frontier between Operations and Traffic, involving schedules, commodities, and much else.

Besides these top executives, six others rate the title of "officials." Two are senior experts in finance; Frank H. Matthews, the controller, and Charles F. Witt, assistant treasurer and assistant secretary. As neither Farrell brother has a son, they were naturally concerned for the future of the line. For several years, they had been looking over the best possible men to take over the top positions in Traffic and Operations. In 1956, John C. Gorman became vice-president, traffic. William H. Farrell, son of the late director Ralph G. Farrell, was made assistant vice-president, traffic. Thomas J. Smith, already terminal manager, received additional duty as Wauchope's right-hand man. The post of marine superintendent went to Lawrence A. Renehan, who was only thirty, having become a master at twenty-four; he later became an assistant to the president and was succeeded by Norman Lee who had commanded that *City of New York* lifeboat in its harrowing experience.

Below that "management" group came some two dozen at New York and others outside who were rated as staff. Scores of assistants, clerks, secretaries, typists and so on, about equally divided between men and women, rounded out the shoreside organization. The groups at New York in the spring of 1958 totaled 231, with an annual payroll of nearly $1,500,000. Functionally, 16 of these were rated as Executive. The Traffic Division included 23 in sales, 36 in freight, and seven in passenger. Operations Division was made up of 33 in the marine section and seven in terminal. Finance included 25 in financial statements and estimates, ten in inventory and receiving, 35 in auditing, bookkeeping and cashier, four in claims, 13 in ships' payroll, eight in purchasing, and 14 in central service. [457]

The line has been a pioneer in providing various benefits to its shoreside staff. In particular, it set up a "profit-sharing trust" in 1934, setting aside six per cent of the company's stock to pay eligible employees $7\frac{1}{2}$ per cent of their base salaries additional in each year when the company's profits reach a certain level. Payments were made into the trust every year except 1949. There are also the more conventional provisions for medical protection, group life insurance, and retirement benefits, all fully paid by the company. Earliest of all the benefits, dating from 1926, was the reimbursing of employees for tuition paid for courses related to their jobs. [458]

Part of the New York shoreside activity is carried on at the pier in Brooklyn, important because a larger part of the freight dollar goes for loading and unloading cargo than for any other purpose. The line has been in the Gowanus Bay section of Brooklyn most of the time since the start. In 1946, needing more ample accommodations for its expanded fleet and frequent sailings, it turned to the pier at the foot of 33rd Street. With a length of 1,616 feet, it is said to be the longest in New York Harbor except for the adjacent 1,739-foot 35th Street pier which would also ultimately be acquired by the Farrells. Each pier can comfortably berth six ships at a time, which is equivalent to the total dockage facilities of many an African port.

Another significant "Farrell first" occurred in connection with the acquisition of the 33rd Street pier. Like many of the other city-owned piers in Brooklyn and Manhattan, its rundown condition called for extensive rehabilitation. In 1947, James Farrell, Jr., in his capacity as president of the Maritime Association, urged the City Planning Commission to approve a $300 million project to build new piers and modernize the existing ones, to prevent the diversion of shipping to other ports. Since funds were not forthcoming the Farrells suggested an arrangement whereby they would furnish the necessary capital to modernize the 33rd Street pier and deduct a tenth of that amount from each annual rental payment. This proved of mutual advantage; the total advance finally came to $796,000 and the annual rental to $232,000. The arrangement proved so successful that it became known in shipping circles as the "Farrell contract," as numerous other lines followed suit. When the original 1948 contract came up for renewal in 1958, the Farrells not only continued it for another ten years but also arranged to take over the still larger 35th Street pier as well. [459]

A hundred longshoremen, more or less, work at the loading and discharging of every Farrell ship at an American port, but they are not regular employees of the line. The stevedore acts as the intermediary between them and the steamship company. At New York, the Farrells have had long and satisfactory relations with the Universal Terminal & Stevedoring Company. The role of the stevedore is to contract for putting cargo aboard ship or unloading it at the going rate per ton, and to furnish certain capital equipment. Then he arranges with the longshoremen's union to have the proper number of men on hand for each particular job, normally a "gang" of 20-odd men for each of the five holds of the ship.

Of the total amount spent by the Farrell Lines for loading and discharging cargo in America and Africa—$3,326,000 for stevedoring and $1,042,000 for other cargo handling in 1955—five-sixths went for the American handling and only one-sixth for the African, although naturally the same material was handled in both places. [460] The principal explanation is that the average American longshoreman receives more pay for an hour's work than his native African counterpart for a whole week. It is true that American stevedoring equipment is efficient, but the stevedores in Africa can afford to put such swarms of low-priced labor on the job that it can be accomplished almost as quickly.

Outside New York, both in America and Africa, part of the line's business has been handled by its own employees, but a considerably greater portion is entrusted to agents, who receive a commission for their services. There were definite reasons for this dual system. For the normal grist of business, the Farrells preferred to use local agents. In particular reference to Africa, this was "because this prevents the company over-expanding the staff, expense being proportionate to revenue, and local people are the best judges of local conditions and best accepted by local populations of similar nationality." [461] On the other hand, the direct Farrell branch offices were needed also, as they "supplement but do not direct or replace local agents, having proved to be of utmost importance in improving the company's public relations, in conferring with government officials on important problems, and in stimulating canvassing. Perhaps the greatest benefit . . . is the training opportunity provided for future executives." [462]

The overseas agent performs many services. Not only does he handle all the details of assembling and distributing cargo, with all the attendant paper work, but also anything else that may come up. That may range from being on hand to greet arriving captains, to planning parties with shippers, and the occasional bailing out of misbehaving crew members. An essential responsibility is the all-important stevedoring; not infrequently the agents, directly or through subsidiary firms, went into that lucrative business themselves. The Farrell agents were paid a guaranteed fee, similar to a lawyer's retainer, and a commission amounting usually to one or two per cent on incoming cargo, which simply involves routine detail, but five per cent on outgoing cargo, as an inducement to drum up as much business as possible. In 1955, the total fees and commissions paid them in America and Africa amounted to $580,795. [463]

The Farrells preferred not to utilize companies heavily engaged in importing and exporting because that might lead to a conflict of interest with rival shippers. This differed from the policy of the Robin Line, whose agents in many South African ports, the house of Mitchell, Cotts & Company, described themselves as "world-wide traders; shipowners, coal exporters and bunkering depot proprietors; stevedores and warehousemen; shipping, airways, forwarding, clearing, and insurance agents; importers and exporters; engineers; chemists; and manufacturers." [464]

The primacy among the Farrells' South African agents rests with the house of John T. Rennie & Sons, based at Durban. This old Scottish firm dates from 1849, when John T. Rennie, a stockbroker at Aberdeen, first acquired an interest in a trading vessel. By 1854, the family was operating clippers to Durban, continuing until 1879 when they shifted to steam, with liners so graceful that they were known as "Rennies' yachts." In 1911, they sold the ships to the Harrison Line—and as good Scots regretted ever after not waiting until ship values soared in World War I. The Rennies continued in insurance brokerage in London and in the general ship agency business, with bunkerage and stevedoring on the side, at Durban, with branches in several other cities of Southern Africa. [465]

When Clifford Mallory was organizing American South African in 1922, he asked a Glasgow shipping friend about an agent for Durban. The Scot unhesitantly named the Rennies, and the contact with the line has remained unbroken ever since. Like Farrell Lines, Rennie is a family concern with similar ideas about how business should be conducted. The Rennies have held the local Farrell agencies at Durban, Lourenco Marques, Johannesburg, and eventually at East London and Cape Town. They are also general agents for the whole Cape Town-Beira range, with overall direction of Farrell loadings and ship movements, and for Europe through their London headquarters.

Edward Searle & Company at Port Elizabeth even antedated the Rennie connection with American-flag shipping, dating back to 1919, when the United States & Australasian Steamship Company appointed the Schlesinger interests with their widespread South African connections as general agents. They in turn appointed the Searle firm as sub-agent at Port Elizabeth. That arrangement was continued under the Mallory, Bull, and Farrell operations. That concern was active in the automobile business, naturally an important asset there. The present Edward Searle has been one of the line's most helpful agents in many ways.

The East London agency was long held by Deary & Company, which was eventually taken over by the Rennies, though the old name was retained to some extent. At Cape Town, the firm of Sturrocks, a name well known in South African transportation, held the agency for many years. When the Sturrocks became agents for the South African Marine in 1946, the Rennies were persuaded to set up a Cape Town agency. At Beira, the original agent, Mann, George & Company, was supplanted later by Allan, Wack & Shepherd, whose business centered in Rhodesia. Mann, George & Company later became Farrell agents at Walvis Bay.

In East Africa, the big commercial house of A. Baumann, active in many fields, particularly coffee, was selected. To accommodate the Farrell preference for shipping specialists, this firm set up a subsidiary, the Steamship & General Agency, which served Mombasa and Dar-es-Salaam, and also acted as general agents for the whole East African area. The local agency at Tanga was Bird & Company, traders in sisal; and at Zanzibar, the general trading firm of Smith, Mackenzie & Company.

When the Farrells moved into West Africa, they encountered so difficult an agency problem that the inauguration of their service was delayed. Resentment against the projected service blocked one effort after another to secure agents for British and French colonial ports. A British steamship line passed the word that it would regard acceptance of the new agencies as unfriendly acts. That was a potent threat, for space was at a premium at certain seasons, and a denial of cargo accommodation could be serious. The Delta Line was in the same fix; and American South African acted for both concerns in all the frustrating negotiations. [466]

A Dutch firm in the first refusal stressed its gratitude to "Mr.

Three generations of Farrells: left to right, James A. Farrell, Jr., James A. Farrell, Sr.,
John J. Farrell, under the portrait of Captain John Guy Farrell.
In the case is a model of the Farrell square-rigger *Tusitala*

OTHER EXECUTIVE COMMITTEE MEMBERS

Fabian Bachrach

C. Carlton Lewis

Flying Camera, Inc.

George Wauchope

Leigh C. Palmer

Farrell, Jr., that he had been willing to trust this important agency to our organization and we would have liked it very much indeed. . . . In view of our relationship with other lines in the West African trade, that is, however, not possible." [467] This was particularly disconcerting because American South African, with negotiations already going forward, had so informed the Maritime Commission in applying for the route. Rumors had reached that Commission hearing of the probability of this foreign-flag hostility.

The company sent Captain George Wauchope to London late in January 1947, to see what could be arranged on the spot. He was blocked at every step by the constant pressure on prospective agents by that hostile British firm. His only encouraging discovery was that the great Lever subsidiary, the United Africa Company, Barber agent in several ports, "would not interpose any objections" to Farrell entry into the trade. The senior partner of another British house, well established in West Africa, the next contact, told Wauchope: "he would like to have the business but he could not take it" after the warning given him directly by that other British firm. Wauchope then went to the source of the trouble, that latter firm, where he was told bluntly that inasmuch as the United States-West African trade was already overtonnaged "there was no room . . . and we could expect to meet (his firm's) opposition at all points." Neither the "good offices" of the United Africa Company nor the unofficial interest of the British government shipping authorities was able to modify that tough stand.

With the projected date of the first sailing to West Africa close at hand, in the middle of February Wauchope turned to two French houses, again with negative results. The original Farrell choice, meanwhile, had reopened the matter in New York; but all that was accomplished was two more weeks of delay.

Then, as American South African was about to set up its own branch offices, another French firm that had been sounded out cabled a surprise acceptance of agencies in all French and British ports for Farrell and Delta. The Société Commerciale de l'Ouest Africain (SCOA) was a general trading company, which was, of course, never the Farrell preference. The main difficulty, however, was that SCOA's staff had virtually no experience in the details of shipping, nor did it have the lighters, surfboats, and other equipment essential to port operations. Eventually, that situation would be improved, when in 1953 at Farrell suggestion SCOA got together with Société Ouest Africain d'Enterprises Maritime (SOAEM), a prominent French shipping and stevedoring firm with ample boats and other equipment along the coast. They formed a joint subsidiary called the Union Maritime et Coloniale (UMARCO). [468] But whatever SCOA may have lacked in the beginning, it had been a godsend to American South African to find at last a company that dared to risk joining with a newcomer in that well-entrenched and hostile trade.

South of that Anglo-French sphere at Matadi and Leopoldville in the Belgian Congo, the agency was at first with the Nieuwe Afrikaansche Handels Vennootschap, sometimes called the "Dutch House" or NAHV. In 1957, that agency was transferred to the house of Van Ommeren Congo, Ltd., who had already served as Farrell agents in various European cities. At Luanda, Lobito, and the other Angola ports, the agents were the Sociedade Luso-Americana. Later, the agencies at Teneriffe and Las Palmas went to the three Pavillard brothers, whose father had for years been the Elder Dempster agent in the Canaries. [469]

Although Farrell ships seldom visit European ports, the company has agents in a dozen cities, with the Rennie firm's London headquarters as general agents. Some of the most important tonnage allocations are made there—from chrome to cocoa.

In the United States, the company lists agents in 30 cities, but most of the work falls upon those in the main east coast ports of call: Norton, Lilly & Company at Boston, Baltimore, Norfolk, Newport News, and part of Philadelphia, where the Lavino Shipping Company handles the rest; the Fred E. Gignoux firm at Portland, Maine; Goff & Page at Fall River; the Wilmington Shipping Company at Wilmington, North Carolina; the Charleston Shipping Company at Charleston; and the Strachan Shipping Company at Savannah and Jacksonville. Direct Farrell branch offices, mainly devoted to traffic solicitation, are at Chicago, Baltimore, Detroit, and Windsor, Ontario. The line has a "port engineer for the fleet" at Baltimore, where much of the repair and maintenance work is done.

The representation in Africa began in the late 1920's when Clifford Shields was sent to Johannesburg. Since then three other top traffic men, John C. Gorman, William A. Farrell, and John B. O'Reilly, Jr., have held that key post. Cape Town has had mariners: Captain C. W. Schmidt, 1950–59, and then Captain C. W. Swenson. Monrovia, Farrell's only agency of its own except New York, also had a succession of captains. [470] The other two African outposts are Nairobi and Takoradi; some of the overseas representatives have served at two, three, or even four different posts, particularly Captain Paul Duffy, William F. Toohey, and John T. Byrne, Jr. At all five centers, the Farrells have provided not only adequate offices but also attractive homes and ample entertainment allowances.

For centuries, under many flags and on many sea lanes, mariners have hammered out a way of running a ship, many features of which still survive. But along with those time-honored practices, the American-flag merchant marine has developed some new and costly features. Reflecting modern labor developments, the crews have won for themselves standards of pay and working conditions far beyond those in any other nation's shipping.

The men aboard a steamship fall into the two basic categories of "licensed" officers, corresponding to the commissioned officers of the armed services, and the "unlicensed" hands, the equivalent of the enlisted men. At the same time, they are all divided functionally into the three departments of deck, engine, and steward's.

On a Farrell freighter in the late 1950's, for instance, there would normally be 50 men altogether; including 12 licensed officers. By departments, they would fall into 20 deck, 16 engine, and 14 stewards.

The master stands no regular four-hour watches, nor does the chief mate. Below them come the three watch-standing deck officers—the second, third, and the junior third or fourth mates; often known as "chief officer," "second officer" and so on. The radio officer rounds out the licensed deck personnel. The chief engineer wears four stripes—as does the captain—but is not in the line of command. The first assistant engineer is roughly the counterpart of the first mate; so, too, are the officers below him of the corresponding deck officers—the second, third, and junior third or fourth assistant engineers. There is also a "licensed junior engineer."

Not licensed and corresponding somewhat to military warrant officers are the chief steward, chief electrician, second electrician, boatswain, and carpenter. The Farrells gave up pursers some time ago, except on the passenger liners. That middle group used to be known as "idlers" because they did not stand watches.

Then come the costly members of the crew, taking their relative capacity and responsibilities into account. Each watch usually has two able-bodied (A.B.) seamen, with a stipulated period of experience, and one ordinary seaman, with less time afloat. One of them steers, one serves as lookout, and the third stands by for odd jobs. Down below in the engine room, there is a fireman-water tender and an oiler on each watch; in the old days of coal, a larger "black gang" of stokers, trimmers, and coal-passers was needed. Others who do not stand watches include deck maintenance men, wipers, a chief cook and two assistant cooks, a storekeeper, a pantryman, a utility man, and seven messmen. By and large freighters in other merchant marines have crews of similar size and functions, except that some British ships with lascar or Chinese crewmen may have as many as 85.

Shipboard controls, by the very nature of things, are vested by time-honored tradition of the sea in one man. Consequently, much has depended upon the experience, character, and competence of the captain. Engineers often claim, in their after-dinner bull sessions, that their functions are much more exacting and complicated, but nevertheless, the captain is responsible even for what may happen to their engines. A newly appointed captain is warned by the marine superintendent to this effect: ". . . you are assuming complete charge of the vessel and all the responsibilities attendant thereto. You will be responsible to the Government of the United States, to the Farrell Lines, Incorporated as owners, and to the underwriters. . . . Your responsibility endures through all the time that you hold this position, whether the ship is at sea, in inland waters, at anchor, or secured alongside a dock." [471]

Before cable and radio, the master was unquestionably on his own always; but instantaneous communication makes this a less clear-cut matter. A new captain radioed from mid-Atlantic: "Gale increasing. Shall I head south?" The marine superintendent flashed back, "You are master of the *African*—." The reverse of that story comes from Port Elizabeth, where in times of serious congestion agents often radio incoming ships, calling the master's attention to the desirability, if consistent with safety, of putting on some extra speed to get in ahead of other vessels. The Farrell files are full of such messages, and its captains have always gladly complied—but not one Britisher. His ship not only put on no extra speed, but the agent heard from England to the effect that "One does not even make suggestions to masters of our line."

Before becoming a master, four Coast Guard examinations must be passed progressively for licenses for third, second, and first mate, and then for master. The stipulated minimum time must be spent in each of the lower grades. Those licenses represent the indispensable stamp of governmental approval upon a mariner's competence, but the actual jobs depend upon the steamship operators who select their captains.

In this, the Farrells have normally preferred the policy of "promotion from within" from among their mates. [472] One of the first of these to be promoted was Wauchope. Very few, after the start, achieved command without line service as mate.

The company's marine division calls for periodic evaluations by the captains in "fitness reports" of the capacity and performance of their officers. In a vacancy, the choice is made by the marine superintendent, usually in conference with Wauchope and John Farrell. New captains are customarily broken in on the West African run on a provisional voyage-by-voyage basis. Eventually, they would, if successful, be shifted to a C-3 on the Cape run, unless they preferred the Guinea Coast.

The Farrell officers have been fairly typical of those in the American merchant marine as a whole. Some have approached command "through the hawsepipe," having served as unlicensed hands. Some, such as Alden D. Graham with his law degree, have special backgrounds. Between the wars many Scandinavians, Britons, and other Europeans were to be found on the bridges and in the engine rooms of American ships. The suddenly expanded merchant marine had had to turn to them in the scarcity of trained officers. Bargain terms were given in the matter of licenses and naturalization. The Farrell ships were no exception. Christian W. Schmidt, Anders R. Mortenson, and Ole P. Stender were among those who started in with the tramps of the Planet Line and then graduated to Argonaut and American South African ships.

Maritime academy graduates became suddenly prominent in the Farrell picture after World War II. This was partly because, in addition to the traditional state schools, the new federal academy at King's Point near New York had trained large numbers of merchant marine officers during the war. Already several of the earlier state "schoolship" graduates were prominent in the line, including Wauchope, George T. Sullivan, Paul S. Maguire, and George R. Hickey. [473] With rapid postwar expansion of the Farrell fleet, many "boy captains" have risen to command at the average age of thirty. They are an amazing phenomenon to the South Africans, accustomed to the seasoned Britishers often waiting twenty years for their commands. Eight of this group of fourteen are King's Point graduates and a ninth comes from New York's Fort Schuyler. Of the twelve captains and engineers on shore duty, all but one are maritime academy men, with eight from King's Point.

In mid-1958, the line had 19 masters afloat, rotating with the 16 ships. They fell into the two groups of the 14 "boy captains" and five senior masters from the prewar fleet. The latter's first commands had come to them at the average age of forty. Of these, Stender had trained on a Danish schoolship and Hickey at the Massachusetts maritime academy. Among all the masters of this time, there were none between the ages of forty-one and fifty. [474]

The engineers as a whole present a special situation. [475] Only 16 per cent in the Farrell Lines in 1957 were merchant marine school graduates as compared with 54 per cent of the deck officers. This was mainly because of the more numerous and far more lucrative posts ashore awaiting engineers at this period.

The union situation would seem to make it questionable how long the Farrell Lines will be able to continue that high proportion of "schoolship" masters. The two principal officer unions— the Masters, Mates and Pilots (MMP) and Marine Engineers Beneficial Association (MEBA) began during World War II to assign officers for all except the two top deck and engineer positions as they became vacant. As time went on, they have been insisting more and more upon that right. James Farrell on one occasion called this trend "inimical not only to owners and officers, but also, I firmly believe, to the ultimate interests of responsible maritime unions." [476] Of the fifty men aboard a Farrell freighter today, the master is the only one entirely free from union contacts. In fact, this is one of the very few lines where they may not even belong to the union, on the ground that they are part of "management." The company has a free choice in selecting a chief mate and the two top engineers, but they retain their active union membership. The unions are more and more insisting upon naming the officers whom the company shall take.

It is, however, in connection with the unlicensed personnel and with the longshoremen that the American-flag merchant marine faces a continual and dangerous economic threat to its very existence. As it is, the unsubsidized American-flag lines are gradually disappearing, and the subsidized are naturally troubled by the situation. When the Farrells went into the African trade in the mid-1920's, the average seaman and longshoreman were making not more than 75 cents an hour in base pay. By the late 1950's, each was getting about four times that amount, exclusive of overtime and the increasing fringe benefits. Of course, against the estimates that have been made of annual incomes of $4,600 or more, must be weighed the matter of recurrent unemployment in this industry. Most of this increase has been accomplished by the unions' exploiting the vulnerability of every transportation service to the costly consequences of delayed departures.

The rise to power of the National Maritime Union (NMU) and the International Longshoremen's Association (ILA)—the two unions with which the Farrell Lines have been concerned—

dates from the mid-1930's. Each has bargained collectively with
the steamship industry, the NMU through the American Merchant Marine Institute and the ILA, at New York, through the
New York Shipping Association. They have successfully used
the strike threat, sometimes working together and sometimes
separately, especially at the periods when their contracts come
up for renewal. Each has developed vigorously many provisions
for overtime and other extra charges, in addition to base pay.
And, as a result of that success, their members have made tremendous strides in increased earnings, but this has meant millions annually added to the cost of operating American shipping.
Also the margin between the earnings of the licensed personnel
with their required years of training and experience has been
sharply narrowed so that the green, untrained workers appear
to be receiving more than the actual value of the services rendered.

There have been certain differences as far as the subsidized
lines have been affected by the two groups. In the case of the seamen's gains, these have been absorbed to a considerable extent by
the operating-differential subsidies. The longshoremen's gains,
which fall upon foreign-flag as well as American-flag shipping,
have not been so compensated. Also the National Maritime
Union has been relatively responsible in its leadership compared
with the International Longshoremen's Association. [477]

By the time the new unionism went into action in 1934, there
had been years of effort to achieve some much-needed improvements in the seamen's lot, on the part of a persistent, devoted,
Norwegian-born mariner, Andrew Furuseth. [478] Some of the
younger element on the west coast grew impatient at his moderate methods, and in the summer of 1934 the seamen joined the
longshoremen in a crippling strike at San Francisco and other
ports. The man primarily responsible for shifting the movement
to the east coast was Joseph Curran, who might be called an
alumnus of the American South African Line, for he had served
in rather turbulent fashion under Wauchope on the old *City of
New York*. He was primarily responsible for some strikes at New
York in 1936. The following year, he organized the National
Maritime Union, affiliated with the overall new CIO: the seamen

of Farrell Lines elected to associate themselves with it, rather than with its rival union, affiliated with the AFL. It includes all unlicensed personnel—deck, engine, and stewards.

The so-called "hiring hall" was an achievement of these maritime unions. It replaced the informal methods of selecting crews. Seamen, now as almost always, are "signed on" on a voyage basis. At the end of the voyage, if mutually satisfactory, the seaman may continue. Otherwise, he reports in at the union headquarters under the new system and receives a dated certificate. When Farrell needs an able-bodied seaman, for example, it now notifies the NMU headquarters, with its separate "hiring halls" for deck, engine, and stewards. When this job is announced in the deck hall, the man selected is the one who has been waiting longest. His name is sent over to the line; if he passes his physical examination and satisfies the company's records and recollections, he gets the job. It is generally understood that if he has a criminal record for assault or narcotics smuggling, the company will be justified in rejecting him, but the mere fact that he has been found stupid or lazy is not usually regarded as adequate grounds for turning him down. That is how unlicensed crews are picked today.

In contrast, the ILA deliberately continued the unfair "shape-up" system of selecting gangs, finding it a profitable means of exploiting its members. Its "hiring bosses" could determine which longshoremen, of the crowd at the pier, would get the jobs. This was a vicious system because it exposed the worker to favoritism and extortion. [479] Some of the worst aspects of the longshoremen's unions would be modified when, after amazing exposés, New York and New Jersey in 1953 set up a Waterfront Commission, and the American Federation of Labor expelled the ILA.

The Farrells had naturally felt the impact of such movements from the outset. In the initial 1934 strike, the *Sagadahoc* had lain idle at San Francisco 76 days at a loss of more than $50,-000. [480] The *West Cawthon* and *Pacific* were detained at New York in one of Curran's 1936 strikes. [481] In the severe 1946 and 1948 strikes, involving both the seamen and longshoremen, several Farrell ships were delayed at a time when South African trade was enjoying its tremendous postwar boom. At the close of 1948, the line's annual report read: "The Company's relations with organized labor (seagoing and shoreside) can be considered better than average for the industry. Severe work stoppages, totally unwarranted and unnecessary, have occurred in 1948, costing the company in excess of $250,000. That such stoppages occurred can be attributed to unwise labor leadership. . . . Through economic pressure, organized maritime labor has forced wages to a breaking point." [482]

The unions succeeded, however, in gaining more and more, year after year. Some of this was in base pay, which rose until all three watches on a British, Norwegian, or other foreign-flag ship cost less than a single watch under the American-flag, while a mess attendant, the low man of the shipboard hierarchy, received more pay than the first mate or possibly the captain under a foreign flag. [483] By securing a nominal 40-hour week along with actual 56-hour work at sea, a large automatic overtime addition was made to base pay. The costly "penalty" overtime, insisted upon by the unions, moreover, required constant oversight by the responsible officers. On a freighter, for example, passengers as well as crew are supposed to finish their evening meal by six o'clock; if a waiter could engage an unwary passenger in conversation for five extra minutes, it would run up an hour's overtime for six men. An example of the "pistol at the head" union tactics came in 1956 after two seamen had been drowned returning to their ship in a native boat at a West African surf port. The line thereupon instructed their captains to forbid shore leave when the seas were running too high. One captain did that; the NMU demanded penalty payments for the lost shore leaves, and when Beaver Street demurred, the union held up the departure of the passenger liner *African Enterprise* until the line agreed.

For all that, James Farrell, in criticizing certain union trends, declared, "I believe in, and try to encourage and foster within my own company, good labor-management relations. I believe in responsible trade unionism, just as I believe in responsible management. I support the right of any man to join a union, just as I support his right to choose his own employer and the right of the employer to select his supervisors." [484]

The extent to which union pressure had run up the cost of seamen's wages and stevedoring is evident in contrasting the average voyage expenses on the Cape Town-Beira run at the end of 1925 with the costs on that same route 30 years later. Fuel, the most expensive item in 1925 at $23,630, had risen only about one-third to $31,816. Stevedoring costs for the voyage had more than doubled, from $20,630 to $44,500. Wages of officers and crew had soared even higher, increasing more than threefold, from $22,000 to $74,640, but since the earlier 162-day voyage was almost double the later 85 days while the number of men rose from 38 to 50, the average daily pay per man (including officers) rose from $3.50 to $17.50. [485]

Those ever-rising costs have naturally caused concern in many quarters. Fear has been expressed in Congress that the American merchant marine is being priced out of the market. [486] The operating-differential subsidies have actually been paying the equivalent of three-quarters of the mariners' basic pay, overtime, and fringe benefits. Most of the unsubsidized lines have either given up American-flag operation and are shifting their vessels to the "flags of convenience" of Panama or Liberia, or else are lining up for subsidies which they formerly did not want to bother with.

Stevedoring, in the meantime, has risen to such a cost that on many runs it costs more to move a box or bale into the hold of a ship and unload it in another port, than it does to carry it hundreds or even thousands of miles. [487] That situation, combined with trucking competition, helped to kill the protected coastwise trade and has become a real problem in foreign trade as well. To avoid the crushing costs, shipowners and shippers have been experimenting with loaded railroad cars, trucks, containers or other devices that will eliminate or greatly reduce normal handling.

The latest development has been the organizing of steamship office staffs under the aegis of the longshoremen's union. For the moment, at least, Farrell Lines can still pick its own shoreside staff, just as it picks its top officers afloat.

An article on American shipping men in the spring of 1949 remarked that "once a year they foregather at the annual dinner of the Propeller Club and drink a toast to the future of the American merchant marine. But they don't tell each other any secrets or act in concert much beyond that." [488] Shortly thereafter, Farrell Lines began to play an important part in getting one major segment of that industry to "act in concert." During the next few years, the heads of the subsidized lines holding operating-differential contracts gradually worked out an organization designed to meet their specific needs. Abbreviated CASL and pronounced like "castle," this Committee of American Steamship Lines has demonstrated its effectiveness both in public relations and in its contacts with the Government.

There were, to be sure, various steamship organizations already in existence when the movement toward CASL got under way. But they represented widely varying ownership interests —Atlantic versus Pacific ports; long offshore trades versus protected domestic runs; liners versus tramps; dry cargo ships versus tankers; and finally subsidized versus unsubsidized lines. Some companies belonged to more than one group. Towering above all the others in size was the American Merchant Marine Institute, whose bargaining role with the maritime unions has already been noted; it included most of the Atlantic and Gulf operators, but not those of the west coast. One of the chief difficulties of that situation was the inability of the shipping industry to present a united front at Washington; senators and representatives got so many varying arguments that they could not find out just what the merchant marine really wanted. To rectify that situation, the National Federation of American Shipping had been created in 1944, but its weakness was implicit in that word "federation." It was not a merger, but a sort of loose holding corporation of five organizations which retained their full identity. Differing in size and interests, they had difficulty in determining positive policy without weakening compromise.

The subsidized lines, 13 at the time, had additional cause for concern. Since the Black hearings of 1933–34, the lines had been somewhat suspect as "kept lines," and subsidies in general are anathema to some economists. There was particular need for action because most of the original operating-differential subsidy contracts would be coming up for renewal during the next few years, involving costly replacement of the existing fleets. It was also realized that the lines might profit by co-operating in presenting their common problems to the Maritime Administration. With all that in mind, the top officials of the subsidized lines began to meet frequently for luncheon in 1950 to discuss ways and means.

James Farrell was especially active in this movement and headed the first special public relations committee of that informal group. Always a believer in turning to experts outside of shipping circles for objective advice on special subjects, he now called on one of the outstanding public relations firms to make a thorough study of the shipping situation and advise the subsidized lines what to do. In their 48-page report in mid-1952, they recognized the general air of frustration in shipping circles and advised a course that would be "aggressive, self-respecting, forthright . . . prepared to fight if necessary." [489]

It was recognized that the ideal setup would be along the lines of the British Council of Shipping, with a unified overall organization for the whole merchant marine having direct membership of all lines instead of the "federated" arrangement. Along with that there would be subordinate autonomous units to look out for the particular interests of the subsidized, tanker, tramp, or other special groups. During the summer of 1952, Farrell was host at a series of small dinners at the University Club in New York, each including leaders from the major segments of the merchant marine. At the end, it was conceded that while every individual present wholly agreed that a national organization was highly desirable, "everyone was pessimistic that such an organization could be brought together." [490]

It was decided by the subsidized lines to go ahead with their own group anyway, whether or not there might eventually be a larger group into which it might fit. Avoiding the unpopular word "subsidy," it was originally named the "Committee of the American Shipping Lines serving Essential Foreign Trade Routes," but after one newspaper referred to "the committee with the long name," that was cut to the "Committee of American Steamship Lines." James Farrell was its first annual chairman and also headed its public relations committee. The Beaver Street participation was furthered by Carlton Lewis, whose office was the committee's virtual headquarters. As the regular Farrell liaison with Washington, he had useful contacts at the capital. At times, he said later, he was spending more time on the committee's business than on the company's.

In 1953, with the end of the National Federation of American Shipping, the Committee took over its secretary-treasurer, Alexander Purdon, who became executive director of CASL. He was unique in refusing to become an "empire builder." He kept the headquarters staff to an absolute minimum; five years later, it numbered only three men and three women. It became the Committee's policy to utilize the part-time services of first-rate experts for particular tasks. For high-level public relations advice, for instance, members of the firm of Ivy Lee and T. J. Ross, which made the 1952 survey, are constantly on hand in New York; when a special research job is needed, an experienced scholar is "chartered" for the task.

The corollary of that modest headquarters overhead has been the "do-it-yourself" participation by the line executives themselves. It is essentially a committee of steamship presidents, and the chairmanship rotates annually; Farrell was followed in that post by Rudolph S. Hecht of Delta; C. C. Mallory of Grace Lines; Albert R. Lintner of American Mail; William T. Moore of Moore-McCormack; Solon B. Turman of Lykes Brothers; and Lewis A. Lapham of Grace Lines, in succession. Each has devoted much time and effort to the position. Much has also been done by the executive committee, consisting of the chairman, his two predecessors, and his successor-designate. Finally, most of the specialized work has been carried out by the sub-committees for public relations, operating-differential subsidies, vessel replacement, finance, budget, and technical matters. Staffed in large part by the executive vice-presidents or financial vice-presidents of the lines, these groups have run up an impressive total of man hours spent on committee work, but if each line had had to handle all those things for itself, the total would have been still higher. The overhead of the Washington headquarters uses up only a third of the annual CASL budget, which is met by assessment among the lines on a tonnage basis.

Another third of that budget goes for public relations activity which, as Farrell anticipated, is doing its part in creating a better general understanding of subsidized shipping. Research unearths some of the pertinent facts, and these are presented through various means. Sometimes, *Maritime Affairs,* one of the Committee's periodic bulletins, points out just how the residents of Kansas, Oklahoma, or Texas profit by foreign commerce. The other bulletin, *Shipping Outlook,* presents, for editorial or Congressional consumption, pertinent data replete with cold facts on "An Appraisal of the Economic Role of American-Flag Shipping," or on "U.S. Government Insured Merchant Marine Bonds: A New Source of Prime Investment Securities." Extracts from talks by the various steamship presidents, sometimes based on CASL research, are disseminated in printed or mimeographed form. The Committee has made arrangements with the Transportation Center of Northwestern University for a thorough study of the role of the merchant marine in the national economy. Finally, Purdon, sometimes accompanied by a steamship president and by traffic representatives of various lines, has made successful "saturation" visitations in various inland industrial centers to acquaint them with how their factories can be geared to foreign trade.

Along with that, CASL has been in constant contact with the Maritime Administration over matters of mutual concern in connection with the contractual relationship between the lines and the government. It stimulated the production of a manual of subsidy procedure. It helped to arrange that the new operating-differential contracts be made on a uniform 20-year basis, equivalent to the normal life of the ships, and it suggested a means of prompter subsidy payments, which were badly in arrears. In the difficult matter of arriving at foreign shipbuilding costs as a basis for construction-differential payments, it has retained foreign naval architects to analyze the costs in Japan, Germany and elsewhere; then the Committee can compare those findings with those reached independently by the Maritime Administration. In the interest of increased efficiency, CASL has arranged, despite much initial hesitation on the part of the lines, for an interchange of technical experience. Last but by no means least, CASL, like almost every organization with headquarters in Washington, has maintained continual contact with the appropriate committees on Capitol Hill. Altogether, the subsidized operators have had good cause for satisfaction in its achievements.

Those same lines, of course, have maintained their connections with various other steamship organizations. The American Merchant Marine Institute, in addition to handling maritime labor relations, carries on public relations and numerous other activities of concern to the industry as a whole. The Propeller Club, similar in its general purpose to the Navy League, annually brings together several hundred leaders of the industry for a three-day conference on dozens of aspects of shipping problems; Admiral Wauchope, incidentally, is president of its New York branch. James Farrell and Clifford Shields are directors of the venerable National Foreign Trade Council founded by Farrell's father; it not only holds annual plenary sessions where problems are aired with due publicity, but in mid-1958 it gave a special luncheon for Prime Minister Nkrumah of Ghana, with James Farrell as one of the speakers. Nor does the list end there —Farrell Lines plays its part in the New York Shipping Association, the Maritime Association of New York, the Africa Society and much else.

Chapter XI

DAKAR TO LOBITO

THE cliché that Africa is a continent of contrasts and contradictions is never more evident than between the west coast
and the south, and, to a lesser extent, between the west and the
east coasts. The Farrell ships, when their service was first extended to the west coast in 1947, found conditions vastly different
from their earlier experience with the ports of South and East Africa. Climate, terrain, size of population and kind, products, communications, governmental status, living conditions, and much
else made this seem in whole or part another world. And it was
a much more primitive one that was beginning to emerge in
twentieth-century guise, decades later than had been the case on
the other two ocean coasts.

The region was humid and tropical with all the discomforts
and risks of equatorial living for the white man. That high central plateau, that covers much of central Africa and makes life
tolerable for the white man even closer to the equator, as in Nairobi, did not extend to the west. Many legends still cling to West
Africa as the "White Man's Grave" though medical research and
modern sanitation have done much to rob it of this gloomy title.
There is, for instance, the old story that every colony on the
Guinea Coast had three governors: one on his way home in a
box, while his successor was dying in the colony, and a new ap-
pointee just setting out from home. It was said, too, that if the
seas should dry up, a trail of bones would be found all the way
from the coast to the Canaries—remains of the poor devils who
tried to reach that refuge from the west coast's pest holes and

failed. In contrast, by the 1950's, two at least of the Farrell representatives had their wives and children living with them there under apparently normal health conditions.

Even with the fevers pretty well conquered, the European population remained a very small one, except in Dakar at the northern and Angola at the southern ends. Even in the latter places, their numbers were trifling compared with temperate South Africa. Unlike the South and East, these ports had no highly developed hinterland such as the Rand, which could and did buy large quantities of expensive commodities from Europe and America. Railroads, to be sure, penetrated from several of the ports into the back country, but there was nothing comparable to the strenuous competition that tapped the Johannesburg market.

From the maritime side the principal ports developed with dramatic speed and thoroughness, practically from scratch. In 1920, according to the United States consul at Lagos in Nigeria, "Lagos is the only port south of Dakar in West Africa provided with ocean wharfage and warehouse accommodations at which a limited number of ships can be dispatched reasonably." [491] A few of the others were sheltered lighterage ports, where cargo could be carried fairly easily to and from the anchored ocean freighters by small craft, called lighters. Many, however, still required the use of surfboats, because of the great Atlantic rollers constantly pounding on the open shore, and there was no shelter at all for an anchorage. Some of the busiest were among the ports still dependent upon lighters or surfboats that had to be loaded and unloaded while the freighters were well outside the surf line in the open sea. And then, even the most dexterous handling was not always able to get the cargo safely through the high surf to and from the beaches.

The busy cocoa port of Accra in Gold Coast was the last of the major west coast ports to cling to that primitive method. Into the 1950's, until the new port at Tema should be completed, this was the way cargo had to be handled, with very small surfboats, not even towed by a tug, but "paddled out by 10 to 20 natives with a helmsman at the long oar. They sing a chant to keep the rhythm and the helmsman clicks some instrument that sounds exactly like an upper and lower plate. Discharge is intermittent. The boys paddle in and out all day; the round trip is two miles." Passengers had to come and go between ship and shore the same hard way; landing in a so-called "mammy chair." "Once over the side your destiny rests with the native paddlers since you have to ride over the bar. . . . The cargo and you are landed in the same manner, only we were carried to the beach in a chair instead of on their heads. One surfboat overturned crossing the bar and lost its cargo of auto parts, refrigerators, etc." [492]

By that time most of the other major ports had achieved new, well-equipped quays, along which vessels could load and unload. At some of the lesser ports where ships still put in occasionally, the primitive methods still prevailed. That was one of the reasons why the West African run was considered excellent experience for a new, young captain. Here anything might happen and very often did—and he would have to handle the job himself. It was very unlike ports such as Cape Town, Durban, or Mombasa, where he could depend on the usual pilots, agents, and stevedores to attend to most matters.

A dozen of these West African ports might be considered major ports of call. Taking them from north to south, these would be Dakar at Cape Verde in Senegal (French); Freetown in Sierra Leone (British); Monrovia in Liberia (independent); Abidjan in Ivory Coast (French); Takoradi and Accra in Gold Coast (British until it became independent Ghana in 1957); Lagos in Nigeria (British); Douala in Cameroons (French); Pointe Noire in French Equatorial Africa; Matadi in the Belgian Congo; and Luanda and Lobito in Angola (Portuguese). Three others might be considered in a fairly similar category: Teneriffe and Las Palmas in the Canaries (Spanish), and Conakry, capital of French Guinea which voted itself independent of France in the autumn of 1958. Some of these major ports were relative newcomers as ports of call but were overshadowing once-prominent neighbors which had not been modernized. Abidjan, the most recent and conspicuous case of this, had replaced Grand Bassam and Port Bouet. Likewise, Lobito had lured shipping away from Benguela and Takoradi from Sekondi, while Monrovia had absorbed the former traffic of Marshall. [493]

American-flag shipping on this coast was brought face to face with the lasting effects of the imperialistic "scramble for Africa." All but the Liberian ports were in the hands of European colonial powers, when the Farrell ships began to come here. Despite a growing tendency to disclaim any excessive colonialism in West Africa, economic if not political pressures were constantly encountered by other nations seeking to penetrate that field. This was rather the reverse of South Africa, where the self-governing Union was inclined to go its own way despite membership in the British family of nations. Most of the West African regions were ready enough to sell their products to build up dollar exchange, but shipping them in American-flag ships and buying American goods in return were a different matter. The obstacles were not always as rigid as Britain's insistence that Gold Coast, for instance, do virtually all its importing from the sterling area. In most of these places, trade had followed the flag and had become well-entrenched. This was particularly true of the Belgian Congo. In the Portuguese and Spanish colonies, trade conditions were somewhat more flexible. By 1959, of course, the British and French were relaxing their hold. Between plebiscites, riots, and new shades of autonomous status, in fact, most colonialism was changing on the Guinea Coast as well as in other parts of Africa.

West Africa's sea route is much shorter than South Africa's from New York; it is some 3,300 miles to Dakar, which is just about the distance to London. A C-2 freighter can do this in only seven or eight days. Even with the occasional stops in the Canaries at Las Palmas and Teneriffe, which add much to the pleasure of the trip for the passengers aboard, the mileage is only 3,825 miles. The direct run from New York to Monrovia with no stops en route, a course that is used on alternate Farrell sailings, comes to 3,965, about equal to a trip from New York to Marseille, and takes twelve days. [494]

At the westernmost tip of the "bulge," Dakar lies athwart several important sea lanes. This has made it one of the world's greatest bunkering ports. Further strategic advantage comes from its being at the eastern end of the shortest route across the

Atlantic. Only 1,620 miles separate it from Natal at the tip of the bulge of South America in Brazil. Thus, unlike the usual seaport, Dakar's significance comes from its harbor and its geographical setting rather than its hinterland, which is the Sahara.

A small island, Goree, two miles off Dakar, was the original center of activity in the Cape Verde area. During its long history, reaching back to the time of Columbus, Goree has been in the hands of many nations: the Portuguese, first; the Dutch, who named it; the English, who seized it more than once; and the French, who have held it longest. Its newest buildings date from 1829, which makes them older than the oldest buildings in the glistening-white, modern city of Dakar, which the French built on the mainland. As late as the 1880's in a manual of world port facilities, the name of Dakar appeared only at the end of the Goree account in the notation that its harbor "has only ten feet of water." [495] It was about this time that the status of Dakar and Goree shifted, when France took over the great mass of West Africa and selected Dakar as its military and naval base. The city which gradually grew up included a large number, ultimately some 30,000, of French residents who made it their permanent home—a rather unusual phenomenon in view of the average Frenchman's aversion to settling outside his native land.

The shallow harbor was dredged and fitted with breakwaters and well-equipped docks. It would be for many years the one place on the west coast where major ship repairs could be made. Its extensive bunkering, ship repairing, and service as a base, have made it a commercial center to a certain extent, but it lacks the hinterland to become a flourishing port of call. Aside from peanuts, materials for export are not heavy. There are two railroads, an 800-mile one to the upper Niger River region and a shorter one along the coast northward to the old Senegal capital, St. Louis. The American freighters that bring grain for the local flour mills, machinery, and a few other things, however, do not stop in on their homeward voyage. They are more apt to find return cargo at Conakry, down the coast in French Guinea. It also has a railroad to the Upper Niger, and there are bauxite deposits in its hinterland that may one day mean expanded exports, in addition to its present palm oil.

Although French colonialism predominated in the "bulge," from the Atlantic far across the Sahara, the British developed four colonies on the Guinea Coast. Jutting back into that French area are Gambia, Sierra Leone, Gold Coast (now Ghana), and Nigeria. The oldest and the smallest, Gambia, has no good port and negligible commerce. In Sierra Leone, Freetown, the capital and chief seaport, has the finest harbor in all West Africa. It is deep and spacious, and beautifully situated at the foot of one of the rare hills along that monotonously flat coast. After the American Revolution Freetown was established by Britain for Negroes who had served in its army or navy or who had come over to England with their masters. With them to Africa were sent sixty shanghaied white prostitutes. It was further populated by other former slaves, freed by the Royal Navy, which was then engaged in suppressing the slave trade on that coast after Britain abolished slavery in 1807. The descendants of those early settlers are still known as "creoles" in Sierra Leone. But, as at Dakar, this is another case where more than a harbor is needed to make a successful port. Its hinterland, while less meager than Dakar's, was not rich enough for plentiful trade. A very inadequate railroad, completed in 1897 with a gauge narrow even for Africa—2' 6"—has handicapped further the development of commerce. Many ships calling there still unload by lighters out in the harbor, although Freetown has eventually acquired docking facilities for a couple of ships. Like Dakar, however, it has served very well as a naval base. Britain used it in both World Wars for the assembling of convoys. [496] Leaving Gold Coast and Nigeria for later, Liberia comes next along the Guinea Coast.

Monrovia, its present chief port, was founded, like Freetown, for the benefit of former slaves. Some groups in the United States sought to solve its Negro problem by sending the Negroes back to their ancestral land. Under the auspices of the American Colonization Society, a little settlement named for President Monroe was planted at Cape Mesurado, a small hill at the mouth of a river on that part of the Guinea Coast known as the "Pepper" or "Grain" Coast.

Other coastal settlements followed; and in 1847, the region

established itself as Liberia, an independent republic. The United States government maintained a friendly interest, but not any official relationship with it. The so-called Americo-Liberians, descended from those freed slaves with their Anglo-Saxon names—King, Barclay, Harmon, Tubman, Dennis—still monopolize most of the political and economic activity of the republic, though they number only a few thousands in a population of more than a million.

Monrovia gradually developed as a port, but remained one of the lesser ones of the west coast until after World War II. One German trading house was established there as early as 1852; and a few others followed. The region did not have much to offer in return cargoes. In 1908, the port had seven wharves, belonging to the various trading firms, near the custom house on the river. One of these belonged to the Woermanns, which had been one of the earliest firms to establish itself and which controlled two-thirds of the steamers calling there. The United States consul that year mentioned as one of the "most pressing drawbacks to shipping" there the time-consuming distance between the "anchorage and the landing on account of the shifting of the bar . . . fully four hours or more are consumed in making the trip." [497] Conditions had improved little four decades later: "The anchorage . . . offers little or no protection and ships frequently roll so heavily as to make loading or discharging impossible. . . . At times the sea is so heavy on the bar as to prevent surfboats from crossing it; this also stops work." [498]

By that time, however, events were in progress, thanks to official as well as to private American initiative and capital, that would change the situation at Monrovia. It had not been directly affected by the Firestone decision in 1926 to establish rubber plantations some fifty miles away at Harbel. [499] Nor did the port feel any immediate reaction from the United States-Liberian defense agreement of March 31, 1942, which led to the building of an American air base, Roberts Field, alongside those rubber plantations at Harbel. But at the end of that year, a third project was suddenly concerned with Monrovia itself. After the Casablanca Conference in North Africa, President Roosevelt visited Liberia. At a luncheon at Roberts Field, he is said to have asked President Barclay what Liberia wanted most, and to have been immediately told that it was a real port for Monrovia.

On December 31, 1943, United States funds were made available for a survey of the best sites. The Firestones are said to have preferred that it be located at Marshall, the closest outlet to their Harbel rubber facilities, but the estuary of the St. Paul River at Monrovia was selected. It was a larger, less sluggish, river and so was less inclined to keep silting back than the one at the Marshall bar. Early in 1944, an agreement was made whereby Lend Lease funds would be available for the construction of an artificial harbor there. It was to be built by the Raymond Concrete Pile Company, an American concern, under the supervision of the United States Navy's Seabees.

Despite the wartime scarcity of materials, work was started that same year on plans which resulted in two breakwaters of rock from nearby Mamba Point. One was 7,702 feet long and the other 7,250 feet. These provided protection for some 750 acres of water inside them, of which 150 acres would be dredged to accommodate ocean-going vessels. A marginal wharf, capable of accommodating four large ships at once, was to be built, with three large storage sheds, ample petroleum storage, and a generous fenced-in area to accommodate the "free port" status of the project. [500] A stipulation of the Lend Lease agreement was that the port was to be under American management until those funds, some $20 million, were repaid. This is being done slowly in installments. Monrovia would become the principal West African center of Farrell Lines. [501]

The new port, which was not officially opened until mid-1948, was to give the coup de grace to the rival port of Marshall, some 35 miles down the coast and named for the American Chief Justice. Marshall enjoyed several years of lively business with the coming of the Firestone rubber project and the adjacent Roberts Field air base at Harbel only nine miles away up the Farmington River. But it had an almost insurmountable natural handicap in a big sand bar that blocked ocean freighters from reaching its harbor. The depth of the water over the bar changed constantly, so only very shallow draft vessels could be used. Dredging was not considered practicable because of the silting.

Freighters with the incoming general cargo and outgoing rubber had to anchor outside the bar in a rough, exposed roadstead, for loading and unloading by lighters. Delays of days were common because often the surf was too heavy for the lighters to cross the bar or the swell outside made loading too hazardous. The baled sheet rubber was difficult enough to handle this way, but the latex presented worse problems. At first, it was shipped in drums, but in 1940 the Barber freighter *West Lashaway* was fitted with a deep tank to carry it. This meant pumping it into the freighter from small Firestone lighters, which brought it down the river from Harbel—and this was far from easy outside the bar in those rough waters. The gasoline for Roberts Field was able to bypass the bar because tankers would discharge it into a buoy which had pipe connections with tanks on shore.

With the eventual operation of a feeder system between Harbel and Monrovia, which coincided with the opening of the latter's new port, Marshall lost the rubber traffic. But as late as February 1950, a few weeks before this shift, vessels were still having to cope with the bar, as is shown in this report of the loading of the *African Grove* by "four lighters equipped with latex tanks" and carrying 23 tons each, which means a loading of 180 tons a day if they each make two trips to Harbel. "They make it out to the ship in 35–40 minutes" when the surf is light. "It takes approximately 20 minutes to discharge one lighter. . . . It takes 29 lighters to fill No. 4 tank. . . . It is often impossible to load the tanks on the lighters 100 per cent because of the heavy rolling. Lighters without tanks carried out the 90 tons of baled rubber. . . ." [502]

Two years earlier that same ship did not have as easy a time, for she grounded on the bar while anchoring one January night. Efforts to back her off were unsuccessful, and the ship soon broached to, broadside to the shoal. One of the lighters tried in vain to pull her off and a call was sent to one of the line's other freighters for help, but she managed to work herself free by the third day. [503] Eight years before, the *West Lashaway* had brought out a young couple to join the Firestone staff; they came out to see their shipboard acquaintances when the freighter stopped on her homeward run. A heavy sea rose, and on the way back across the bar, their lighter capsized and they were drowned along with the Dutch harbormaster and several natives of the crew. Altogether, 26 lives were lost in 23 years on Marshall bar.

At Cape Palmas, which is the border between Liberia and Ivory Coast, the coastline of West Africa rounds the "bulge" and runs in a fairly straight easterly slant for about a thousand miles. Here, in succession, come the Ivory Coast, the Gold Coast, and Dahomey and Nigeria, once called the Slave Coast. This Guinea Coast proper, like most of the coastline to the northward, is low and monotonous with practically no good natural harbors. From the navigation standpoint, it is not as rugged and inhospitable as the coast of Natal over in South Africa, but at times, it, too, can be difficult. This is especially true in the rainy season and also when the "harmattan" winds from the Sahara sands cut visibility to a minimum. In a typical experience, a Farrell captain reported in 1950 missing Accra and a week later Marshall also. "The harmattan along the Nigerian and Gold Coast was very thick." [504]

From the maritime standpoint, until the amazing recent rise of Abidjan, the Ivory Coast was a case of a hinterland with no good outlets. It was, thus, the exact opposite of Sierra Leone with its magnificent harbor at Freetown and few exports to be shipped. The Ivory Coast's hinterland was potentially rich in coffee, mahogany, and other commodities, but its whole 500 miles of shore had little in the way of a natural port. The virtually continuous lagoons along the eastern half of the Ivory Coast have been a valuable asset in the sheltered movement of heavy materials; but the outer bar cut those lagoons off from easy access to ocean shipping. Steamships sometimes stopped at Grand Bassam, Port Bouet, or Vridi, small places in the same customs district; but they were open roadsteads with very difficult access to the back country.

The tantalizing aspect was that the spacious Ebrie Lagoon along the shore here would give good access to the interior; but an outer sandy barrier, a mile and a half wide, prevented ships from reaching it. Between 1904 and 1933, attempts to pierce the barrier had quickly silted up. During World War II, however, with all normal outside contacts by sea cut off by British power, since French West Africa was on the Vichy side, there was a chance to make permanent progress with no sea traffic in the way. [505] This lagoon system was potentially a great asset to the commerce of Ivory Coast. The Farrell survey in 1946 called it fortunate to have this "series of fresh-water lagoons, extending in an easterly direction from Grand Lahou to Assinie, approximately 180 miles. Where separated these lagoons have now been connected by the canals completed during the war. . . . A depth of six feet of water is maintained through the entire length . . . a number of rivers empty into the lagoons. The rivers and the lagoons are used for rafting down mahogany logs to the shipping ports. . . . At Abidjan the lagoon is very wide and of considerable depth. It will provide plenty of anchorage area." [506]

Eventually, once the channel was opened, all Ivory Coast felt the quickening effect. Abidjan, which a few decades earlier had been simply a barren lagoon, was suddenly transformed into a beautifully laid-out city of 140,000 population. As a port, it acquired a 3,700-foot deepwater quay, capable of accommodating seven ships at a time. The loading of mahogany logs, which had been a very difficult process under the old Grand Bassam setup, was greatly simplified. Both coffee and cocoa exports also flourished; "Ivory Coast" became a major trade name in world coffee circles. There have been widespread doubts as to whether France broke even on its African possessions as a whole, but no one has questioned that Ivory Coast, with the Abidjan stimulus, has become a most profitable unit.

While such prosperity was a novelty on the Ivory Coast, its next neighbor to the eastward, Britain's Gold Coast, had long enjoyed well-being. A map of the Guinea Coast in the eighteenth century shows virtually all the European contacts concentrated in the Gold Coast area, where various nations had built strongholds—Cape Coast Castle, Christiansborg, Dixcove, and others. They were seeking slaves as well as the gold that gave the region its name. The gold had been a lure as early as 1482, when the Portuguese set up a prefabricated castle at Elmina (the mine), which Columbus is said to have visited. Even in the twentieth century, gold was often the colony's most valuable export. In 1940, for example, gold headed its exports to all countries at £6.8

million, followed by the celebrated cocoa output at £4.0 million, and manganese at £1.0. But, of course, as with the Rand output, bullion calls for almost no shipping space nor the port facilities essential for cocoa and manganese.

Gold Coast has had two major ports, its capital, Accra, in the east, and Takoradi in the west. Each has direct rail connection with Kumasi in the interior; and this region has been ahead of the rest of the west coast in roads possible for motor transport. Takoradi has become a well-equipped seaport since World War I; before that, the adjacent surf port of Sekondi was used by shipping. It was between 1921 and 1928 that Takoradi was developed at the cost of $16.5 million; later extensions after World War II would run the total cost up to $25 million. The investment has proved a good one, for the valuable manganese and bauxite, as well as the mahogany logs, for which it was an outlet, needed something better than surfboats for their proper handling. Takoradi has two breakwaters. A slender main one heads out toward the open sea, and then turns parallel to the shore, thus giving excellent protection. A second one, serving as a pier, has seven deepwater slips for unloading general cargoes and loading ore. There are also eight stout mooring posts, where vessels can lie for loading logs.

In contrast, Accra, a hundred miles to the east, has the dubious distinction of being the last and only major port to rely upon primitive surfboats to unload and load the steamships that have to anchor a mile or so off the surf-swept shore. Despite this, Accra handled so impressive a share of the cocoa exports that "Accra" was the trade name in world markets for Gold Coast cocoa. Takoradi, for all its facilities, could not handle all this rich offering; and Accra has rail connections with the cocoa country. Also Accra had been much more of a general business center than Takoradi, with well-stocked department stores managed by the big trading companies. This meant that some of the imports were marketed there. One of the annual Farrell calendars shows a C-2 freighter unloading a crated automobile into two surfboats at the Accra Roads. Whether or not that particular one got ashore, the bottom of the sea out at that anchorage is said to be well stocked with motors, refrigerators, and much else that missed

the boats at one time or another. The Accra waterfront, especially at low tide, has an aroma that is definitely distinctive—
with the accent on the second syllable. Accra's days as a busy
surf port are numbered, however, for the new independent state
of Ghana has inherited from Gold Coast the plans for a new
$20 million harbor twenty miles to the eastward at Tema.

Another major port that competes with Accra in aroma is
Lagos, capital and principal seaport of the huge British colony
of Nigeria, slated for independence in 1960. Some 220 miles east
of Accra, it lies on the Gulf of Benin, well under the "bulge,"
where the coast begins to bend to the southward again. As late
as 1946, it consisted for the most part of "nothing but tin shacks
and mud huts," its "squalor and filth" were indescribable, and
its situation on a low swampy island was not good for health or
sanitation. Ten years later, it was much the same; the stench
from the open sewers followed ships well down toward the open
sea. By then, however, there were at least remedial plans on
paper.

The British had taken Lagos around 1860 to break up one of
the last big strongholds of the slave trade. Its palm oil and the
desire to forestall German and French imperialist ambitions
were to make Nigeria one of the largest of Britain's "dependent"
colonies, with a tremendous native population. It has very few
resident Europeans. Lagos became the capital and the principal
port of entry, handling ultimately some 70 per cent of the import
and 45 per cent of the export tonnage.

As a seaport, Lagos has two parts. The steamship schedules
refer to "Lagos-Apapa" which is equivalent to referring to "New
York-Brooklyn." The incoming cargo for the city of Lagos itself
is still unloaded at the old custom-house wharf in Lagos proper,
on an island which is across the harbor from the mainland.
Apapa, the newer part of the port on the mainland, was opened
in 1926 with four berths for steamships; five more were added
in 1956. The rail connections are here, so Apapa handles the
trade with the interior.

Like Beira on the southeast coast of Africa, the name of Lagos
has become synonymous with port congestion and delays. Although back in 1920 it was praised as the only port south of

Dakar with ocean wharfage and warehouse accommodations, its facilities had not kept pace with the increase in Nigerian commerce. The West African Lines Conference of ships connecting the coast with Britain and the Continent kept track of the "number of days' delay awaiting working berth" during the first half of 1956 at the various ports. The score was 54 days for Takoradi; 67 for Accra; 139 for Port Harcourt, the second Nigerian port; and 481 for Lagos-Apapa, of which 356 were accounted for by the primitive conditions at the customs wharf on the Lagos side. [507] Some blame at Lagos was placed upon the failure of the railroad to remove landed cargo promptly. This railroad runs 705 miles inland to Kano, the principal center in northern Nigeria. There was also the extreme inefficiency of the local longshoremen, in getting cargo out of the ships, to add to the delays. In 1950, a freighter was delayed because "the agent couldn't keep the natives working. To do so would require one European to supervise each gang. It looked like a slow-motion picture instead of a ship discharging." [508]

Nigeria has numerous lesser ports. Chief among them is Port Harcourt near the Niger River delta, terminus of the eastern railroad line connecting with Kano in the interior. Some of the port names bring back memories of tales of the slaving days, such as Old Calabar and Bonny. Smaller vessels than ocean freighters serve these ports, with some even ascending the Niger. The whole region is dotted with trading posts for incoming "merchandise" and outgoing "produce." [509]

Just beyond Nigeria, where the west coast turns sharply southward, the once big German colony of Cameroons, divided as British and French mandates after World War I, will also be free in 1960. The narrow northern British slice, with its sea outlet at Victoria, has been administered with Nigeria. Douala is the chief port of the much larger French Cameroons. Other French possessions bound it on the south and east.

Douala, 300 miles north of the Equator and apt to be the hottest and stickiest of West African ports, lies 27 miles up a river from the Cameroons Estuary. Palm oil and kernels, coffee, cocoa, and mahogany are available as cargo. The docking facilities are moderately satisfactory; and there is railroad connection with Yaoundé, the Cameroons capital, 150 miles in the interior.

Four hundred miles south of the Equator is Pointe Noire, and it too, flies the French tricolor. By this time, a ship is well out of the Guinea Coast area and is becoming involved in the Congo complex. One tends to associate the Congo with Belgium alone, unmindful of the fact that the vast region called by France Equatorial Africa, which lies just to the north of Belgium's holdings, also belongs to the Congo River area. This includes several hundred miles of the north bank of the great river itself. The capital of French Equatorial Africa, Brazzaville, is just across the Congo from Leopoldville, capital of the Belgian Congo.

From those two cities may be heard the roar of the rapids, which block navigation on the Congo for some 200 miles below them toward the sea. The river above them stretches broad and navigable for nearly a thousand miles into the heart of the continent. But for that turbulent stretch of rapids, the maritime story here would have been a simpler and far different one. As it is, Belgium and France have both had to find ways to transport imports and exports from tidewater to their capitals and the immense hinterland.

Belgium was the more fortunate in this dilemma; it controlled the lower Congo to the head of navigation. France had to find an overland route all the way to the sea from Brazzaville and the interior beyond. For years, French engineers and hydrographers studied the various possibilities. In 1922, they settled upon Pointe Noire, which is about 100 miles north of the mouth of the Congo. There was a small natural bay there, partly sheltered by a sandspit; the French constructed an outer breakwater that extended the sandspit. On the inner side of the breakwater, warehouses, cranes, and berths were built for five or six ships. A second breakwater in the harbor, built in the shape of a right angle, gave further protection. Work was begun on the project in 1934 and the port was opened for traffic five years later, but the equipment was not fully installed until after the war. In the meantime, the "Congo Ocean Railroad" was being built to link Pointe Noire with Brazzaville, where material could be shifted to and from Congo steamers for trade with the interior. A new

city sprang up at Pointe Noire, white and glistening, like the
other French colonial towns of Dakar and Abidjan.

This was another case, however, where it takes more than a
good harbor to make a flourishing port. Unlike the rich hinterland behind Abidjan to the northward and down in the Belgian
Congo to the southward, Pointe Noire tapped an extremely
unproductive region in French Equatorial Africa, enormous
though it was in area. Exports have been fairly meager as a result,
and since this was also a very sparsely populated hinterland, the
imports have been low, mainly some building materials and
petroleum products. Pointe Noire has hopes, though, for future
exports because of new mineral wealth from the interior.

Belgium, too, has Congo problems. Although possessing the
head of navigation on the lower river, its share of the seacoast
is a meager 25 miles or so; and to get even that took sharp dip-
lomatic pressure in the days of the great scramble. As it is,
Portuguese Angola possesses the southern or left side of the river
almost up to the Belgian port of Matadi, the head of navigation
before the rapids block the way. Belgium has two other ports
below Matadi, on the Belgian north side of the river, but Banana
at the mouth of the Congo is simply a control port with virtually
no commerce. The other downriver port, Boma, onetime capital
of the Congo, is about halfway between Matadi and the sea. It
still carries on a moderate amount of trade for the immediate
region, with banana exports as its particular specialty. Most of
the Matadi-bound ships do not stop there.

The 85-mile trip up the Congo to Matadi is a decided contrast
to the hundreds of miles of flat, monotonous coastline between
Dakar and the mouth of the Congo. Hills along the river are
reminiscent of the Hudson River beyond Poughkeepsie, and
there is little to suggest this is the same river as the usually pictured upper Congo. The current is strong; in some places, old
slow tramps can scarcely hold their own against it. Just below
Matadi, the Devil's Cauldron runs at eight to ten knots, so that
vessels with insufficient speed sometimes have to turn around
and put in at the oil docks below the city. A pilot is needed for
the whole 85 miles, although the river is well marked with scores

THE OPENING OF THE NEW PORT OF MONROVIA,
July 26, 1948

Monrovia Port Development

The *African Patriot*, first ship to be docked at the new port

Monrovia Port Development

President Tubman at the dedication ceremonies

J. Walker Grimm

The *Saint Paul,* one of the little LCT's; carried the first
latex from Harbel to Monrovia in May 1950

Morris Rosenfeld

The *Kpo*

of successively numbered buoys, with the usual Belgian thoroughness.

Matadi is crowded on a hot hill on the south bank of the river, at the foot of those 200 miles of rapids. It has been credited with "the best loading record of all West African ports." [510] Its waterfront has a well-equipped quay, some 3,500 feet long, that is capable of handling seven large ships at once. In the pursuit of speed, the Belgians have developed the device of loading and unloading ships not only from the pier side but also, simultaneously, from the outer side. Oil cargoes from tankers are handled at Ango Ango, which is just before the rapid current of the Devil's Cauldron below the city.

At Matadi is encountered the great problem of Congo commerce—transshipment. Had there been no rapids, seagoing freighters could have sailed straight up the river past Matadi to Leopoldville; once there, they had ahead almost a thousand miles of deep and easily navigable waters, before having to unload or load cargo for the interior. Instead, virtually all incoming and outgoing cargo had to be transferred at Matadi to the 200-odd mile rail line to Leopoldville, where some imports would be bound and where most would have to be placed aboard the big river steamers. Deep in that vast interior or away from the Congo, material had to continue to be shifted at numerous points, anyway, between river or train or lake and perhaps back to railroad again.

Around 1950, serious congestion began to cause shipping delays at Matadi. The cause was not the usual one of poor facilities or inadequate labor force in that very efficient port. The delays resulted from the overloading of its one ocean outlet by Belgium in an attempt to prevent transit profits from going to other African seaports and railroads. A major bottleneck resulted, when the Belgians tried to ship bulky mineral cargoes through Matadi, in addition to the palm oil, palm kernels, and other vegetable shipments already being handled by that port. Copper and other minerals to reach Matadi from the Katanga mining area had to be sent by the rail line, completed in 1928, to Port Francqui on the Kasai River; there they were put aboard a steamer for Leopoldville; and again back to rail travel from

Leopoldville to Matadi. In contrast, freight cars loaded in Katanga could go straight to ocean piers, where freighters waited, either at Beira in Portuguese Mozambique on the Indian Ocean, the original outlet, or to Lobito in Portuguese Angola on the Atlantic where the port was completed in 1931. As time went on, the pressure became so heavy on Matadi that the Belgians reluctantly had to divert more traffic to the Lobito route. There were other rival ports. On one occasion, a heavy order of copper for France was permitted by the Belgians to go out through Pointe Noire. Coffee and other products from the eastern Congo, and the trustee regions of Ruanda-Urundi, as previously mentioned, were apt to find their way, by lake steamer and rail, through British East Africa, either to Dar-es-Salaam, where Belgium had its "Belbase," or Mombasa. A trickle of Congo traffic even passed through the distant harbors of Durban and Port Elizabeth in South Africa.

In 1955, Matadi led all those outlets with 1,827,000 metric tons, followed by Lobito at 572,000, Boma at 163,000, Beira at 88,000, Dar-es-Salaam at 71,000, Mombasa at 11,000, and Durban at 89. Belgium's efforts to concentrate as much traffic as possible through its own ports moved 78 per cent of the Congo imports through Matadi and Boma, but only 60 per cent of the mineral exports, for Lobito handled 60 per cent of the bulky Katanga minerals and Beira 13 per cent more, with Dar-es-Salaam handling all the coffee. Matadi's big export specialty was palm oil and allied products from up the Congo. Distant Durban's tiny share consisted chiefly of automobile exports. [511] In the commercial statistics in this appendix, the Belgian Congo is included in West Africa, as less than seven per cent of its tonnage moved through Indian Ocean ports; earlier, that percentage had been somewhat higher. [512]

As far as possible, Belgium has seen to it that both the exports and the imports of the Congo went in its own Belgian Line ships. Farrell and other American freighters called regularly at all these outlets, but at Matadi, Boma, and Lobito, the lion's share of the cargo was generally already booked for the holds of the Belgian-flag ships. Along the waterfront at Matadi, it is a common sight to see perhaps five Belgian vessels, completely outnumbering the occasional American, British, Dutch, French, or German ships. At Lobito, almost 40 per cent of the tonnage goes in Belgian ships; this is as much as the American, British, and Portuguese cargoes combined. This Belgian monopoly has been a matter of constant frustration in other shipping circles. That Belgians might carry the imports that they had purchased was one thing; but to have them also transport the Congo exports, bought by Americans or British, was quite another matter in the latter's eyes, with their ships losing that business also.

The Belgian Line not only had a formal monopoly of all cargo on the colonial government account but also on the traffic, in both directions, of the Katanga mines and other affiliates of the parent Société Générale de Belgique. One American shipper, who used Farrell Lines, was warned that he would be penalized if he did that again. Only about 15 per cent of the Congo trade was open to free steamship competition and even there the Belgian Line received its share. Farrell Lines more than once made formal protests against this situation. It was pointed out that for their ambitious projected development support may be needed from American investors and American industries, if not from the American Government, and that the clannishness of the Belgian group and the treatment of the Congo as a closed Belgian preserve might well discourage such co-operation.

Toward the southern end of the west coast, the remaining pair of its dozen major seaports—Luanda and Lobito—lie in Portuguese Angola. Angola has had a longer continuous history than its opposite number, Mozambique, on the other side of Africa. In sharp contrast to the situation at Matadi and some other ports up the coast, the possessive practices of European colonialism have been less of an obstacle here to American penetration than at any of the other major ports, except of course, Monrovia. Both ports had a good start in the matter of natural harbors, for each was protected by a sandspit created by the northern flow of the cold Benguela current. Their modern growth was long delayed because of the slow development of the hinterland.

Luanda, formerly São Paulo de Loanda, was founded in 1575, and became a center of the flourishing slave trade to Brazil. Un-

til the 1940's, it had only a few primitive jetties, and ships had
to load and unload from lighters; this was true of all the Angola
coast. Luanda stands more on its own feet than do Lourenco
Marques, Beira, and Lobito, which are primarily transit ports,
owing their prosperity to the handling of other people's commodities. Luanda's rise as a modern port ties in with the rapid
growth of coffee production in its hinterland. About two-thirds of
the coffee comes to the United States, which furnishes in return
trade a generous amount of automobiles, agricultural equipment, and other materials. Incidentally, it seems the consensus
of west coast captains that Luanda, with its mellow, centuries-old
atmosphere, is the pleasantest of the major west coast ports of
call.

Lobito, already discussed in its role as the rail outlet for the
Katanga and the Copperbelt, lies some 240 miles south of Luanda, and has an even better harbor. [513] Instead of a centuries-
old city, however, there was nothing here but lonesome sands
until very recent times. Benguela, twelve miles away, had long
been the center of commerce in the area, and had given its name
to the current which comes up the coast from the Cape and also
to the railroad from the Katanga and Copperbelt in its early
days. That railroad was completed to the border of Belgian
Congo in 1928 but its final link to the Katanga was delayed for
three more years. Even then, Belgium's interest in the new Port
Francqui route and Rhodesia's desire to keep as much traffic as
possible for its own route to Beira delayed the full potential use of
this Lobito route until postwar congestion at Matadi and Beira
made the shift imperative. The first quay suitable for seagoing
vessels was not built until 1937; and it was another twenty years,
before a second, with accommodations for eight or nine vessels,
was completed. By that time, Lobito was handling all the Belgian Congo cobalt and manganese, half of its zinc and a quarter
of its copper; on the other side of the ledger, it was the port of
entry for large amounts of coal for the Katanga and Copperbelt.
Only Abidjan could be considered a competitor with it in the
matter of its sudden rise to first-rate importance.

Chapter XII

SERVICE TO WEST AFRICA

THE commencement of regular service to West Africa in 1947 now made it possible for the American South African Line to state with pride that it had become "the only steamship company linking the United States with all three ocean coasts of Africa." The following spring it became the Farrell Lines since its old name was no longer applicable to that newly extended service.

The Farrells were not the American-flag pioneers here as they had been in South and East Africa. West Africa had had American-flag service since early in 1919 when the Shipping Board claimed the *Beatrice* to be the first American steamship ever to serve West Africa. [514]

There had been American ventures under sail, of course, ever since the Newport colonists had started their highly profitable triangular trade in rum, slaves, and molasses. Even after the slave trade was outlawed, American slavers kept going out to the Guinea Coast from time to time. The fast schooner *Wanderer*, which had borne the flag of the New York Yacht Club, was captured in that trade; and a mariner from Maine was hanged in 1860 at New York for taking part in that traffic. Other American vessels had found their way out to the Guinea Coast on somewhat less irregular missions, swapping rum, flour, and gunpowder for palm oil and occasional ivory. That West African commerce was never conducted on such a regular basis as the Salem trade with Zanzibar had been, officially backed as it was with a treaty and a succession of consuls. [515]

In mid-Victorian days, long before the European nations began their great scramble for African colonies, steamship contacts
between Europe and West Africa had gradually been developed.
Outstanding in this field, then and now, was Britain's Elder
Dempster fleet, a name as dominant in West African shipping
as Union-Castle was in South African. One of its component
parts dating back to 1852 had operated three small steamers between London and the Guinea Coast. A rival line between Glasgow and Liverpool and West Africa started in 1869. The two
gradually merged under Alexander Elder and John Dempster. [516] They were succeeded upon retirement in 1884 by Alfred
Lewis Jones, later Sir Alfred, who for the next quarter century—
the great years of the imperial scramble—was head of the line,
generally known by the good maritime nickname of "Davy Jones."
The rapidly growing Elder Dempster fleet offered passenger and
freight service to all the major and minor ports of the West African coast. The nature of this trade called for numerous relatively
small ships rather than a few large ones. As late as 1950, the 38
Elder Dempster ships averaged only 5,160 gross tons, with only
two of them at more than 7,500 tons. In contrast, Union-Castle,
with its big mail steamers on the Cape route, averaged 14,000
tons for its 27 ships. The largest of these was 28,700 tons and ten
of them were larger than the biggest Elder Dempster liner. [517]

Next to Elder Dempster, the most familiar name in West African shipping has been Woermann. The family's century of activity has been interrupted by two World Wars. It began under
Adolf Woermann of Hamburg, whose operations were on such
an extensive scale that Bismarck called him the "royal merchant." His steamers were simply an adjunct to his general commercial activities and were used to link up the West African
warehouses and stores, established by him in Liberia in 1852
and elsewhere later. When other nations began to entrench
themselves in West Africa and impose duties and restrictions
that hurt his trade, Woermann became one of the most persuasive advocates of Germany's setting up its own African empire.
Down through the years, the Woermann ships, named for members of the family, shared much of the West African trade with
the Elder Dempster vessels. Later on, the Belgians began their

own steamship line to enjoy particular privileges in the Congo trade. Likewise, the French, the Dutch, the Portuguese, and the Spaniards set up their own flag lines.

The possibility of American steamship service to West Africa was discussed even before Elder Dempster or Woermann got under way. In 1850, the House Committee on Naval Affairs reported favorably on the proposal of an Alabama judge to establish a subsidized line of mail steamships "to the Western Coast of Africa, and thence via the Mediterranean to London; designed to promote the emigration of free persons of color from the United States to Liberia; also to increase the steam navy, and to extend the commerce of the United States." [518] The project, of course, did not materialize.

A half century later, however, the need of direct steamship contact with West Africa began to be voiced from time to time. In 1907, an American consul on the Guinea Coast, for instance, passed on word from an American businessman who had been at Grand Bassa that a "merchant of that place" who was importing American lumber, had asked him to "try and interest our Government" in having a vessel put on for direct trade. This was followed up by letters, citing "the danger of theft on the vessels for West Africa via Europe." [519] Such little direct service as existed was carried on in tramps or sailing vessels.

Shortly after that, the Woermann Line, in conjunction with the Hamburg-American service to Africa and the Hamburg-Bremen-Africa Line, inaugurated direct service between New York and West Africa, jointly with the Elder Dempster Line. In an agreement of March 2, 1911, freight and passenger services were pooled, with alternate German and British sailings every two months. [520]

With the Woermann liners swept from the sea by World War I, direct contact with the United States became more urgent. They had carried not only most of the trade in Liberia as well as in the German colonies, but also some 17 per cent of the Gold Coast's. The British and French saw to it that their own colonies were taken care of after a fashion by their ships, particularly as they needed palm oil and other West African offerings. Liberia

and the Canaries, however, sounded loud complaints at being
cut off from the outside world.

As in the case of South Africa, steamers could not be spared
for these new American opportunities, and large numbers of
sailing vessels had moved into the trade. The bulky Gold Coast
logs were a case in point. According to the consul at Accra, practically all of these now went directly to the United States whereas
before the war the bulk of them had been transshipped by way of
Europe. In 1918 none went to Europe. The same thing was happening in cocoa and other West African products. This short-
circuiting of the London entrepôt was the equivalent of what
happened with South African wool. The same consul, showing
the shift in national shares of Gold Coast exports between 1913
and 1919, pointed out that the United Kingdom's 68 per cent
had dropped to 46 per cent; Germany's 17 per cent had vanished;
France's 9 per cent had risen to 15 per cent; and the United
States' had jumped from 2 per cent to 32 per cent. [521]

That extraordinary increase in the American share of West
African trade was largely the result of that new Shipping Board
service operated by A. H. Bull & Company, that had, it will be
recalled, begun regular line service in 1919, well ahead of the
similar service to South Africa. The latter did not get on a lasting basis until 1922. In that year, there were 77 vessels arriving
or clearing in the West African trade to 47 for South and East
Africa; of these 25 and 13 ships respectively were under the
American flag. The Shipping Board was operating ten ships on
the West African route to only half that number to the Cape.
That was one reason why the West African route, as already
noted, commanded one of the highest prices per ship of the
Shipping Board sales, when sold to Edward J. Barber in 1928. [522]

From that time on the name Barber, like that of Elder Dempster, would remain very closely linked to the New York-West
African run. This was a seasoned maritime professional coming
to the west coast, as well as a family firm of long standing that had
built up an interlocking group of companies, that included shipping and stevedoring. As a shipping journal commented in 1919:
"The Barber Steamship Company must be reckoned with as one
of the shipping companies best equipped financially and in point

of experience to meet any conditions." [523] In 1933, including his own runs and those for which he was agent, Barber claimed his company was operating 59,000 tons of shipping under the American flag and 12,750 under foreign flags. [524]

One of his shrewdest steps taken in developing the West African trade was the selection of the United Africa Company as agents in several ports of Gold Coast and Nigeria. This was a subsidiary of the huge British soap manufacturers, Lever Brothers; it was the biggest of big business on that coast. It had, to be sure, its own ships for the run to Britain, but it could throw plenty of import and export trade of its own to American West African, and receive its agent's percentage for its services. That important "UAC" connection was to remain in Barber's hands. [525]

He was granted a Jones-White Act mail subsidy averaging $270,000 a year. [526] Even with that, he lost $113,000 in 1928. He did make a substantial profit of $422,000 the following year but with the effects of the depression making themselves felt, he dropped to $47,000 the year after and then to $11,000. In 1932, he lost $123,000. Altogether with the mail subsidy there was a net profit of $264,000 over five years; without it the loss would have been $1,088,000. [527] With conditions that bad in the early 1930's, Barber persuaded the Shipping Board to take back three of the ships that he had bought in 1928. [528]

On the eve of World War II, the role of American-flag shipping on the two major African routes presented a strange contrast. In the West African trade, 21 per cent of the dry cargo imports and 61 per cent of the exports were being carried in United States vessels; with South and East Africa it was just the reverse. In the same year, 1938, of the latter's trade, 92 per cent of the dry cargo imports, but only 36 per cent of the exports were shipped under the American flag. [529] Incidentally, compared with other American trade routes, exports to West Africa ran second highest, just behind those to the west coast of South America, and imports from South and East Africa were the highest.

The American West African Line's ships made 24 voyages, averaging 121 days, in 1937, and visiting 52 ports in West Africa and the United States, altogether, on those voyages. The way the service was arranged, virtually all voyages touched at certain important African ports, especially in Gold Coast and Nigeria, but beyond these, there was a branching out with less frequent visits to many less active sources of trade. Those time-wasting minor ports of call, which would be bypassed by the later Farrell service, included such dots on the map as Salt Pond, Grand Popo, Opobo, and Koko, most of which were little more than beaches where surfboats or lighters were needed. Surprisingly, the pivotal point of the later Farrell Lines, Monrovia, was not on any of the regular Barber schedules. [530]

By the eve of World War II, Barber was still just about breaking even. Altogether, for 1937, the line showed a profit of $109,-000, after depreciation allowance of $178,000. The previous year had been somewhat better, with profits of $168,000 after similar depreciations. [531] At this point, the Jones-White mail subsidy was approaching the end of its term, and Barber was not putting in for an operating-differential subsidy under the new 1936 act. [532] Had he decided to do so, he would have had to buy expensive new ships to replace his old ones, fast reaching their maximum age.

This situation was being watched with interest by the Farrells. As James Farrell explained to the Maritime Commission in September 1946: "As long ago as 1928, we tried to enter this trade. . . . Barber topped our bid but our interest never declined. We continued to collect data, to inform ourselves and to watch the situation. . . . Our application is not a casual, last minute preparation. . . ." [533]

Farrell headquarters had underway an elaborate study of the African route, but its first report in February 1946 was virtually useless as it had been based on the mistaken assumption that Barber was going to sell his interest, including his two surviving old steamers, while continuing as agent on the route. [534] Discussions to that effect had been going on between James Farrell and Edward Barber. The latter's staff understood that he planned to turn it over and, to their later chagrin, talked freely of the details and mysteries of the trade. Suddenly, by the middle of the year, came the surprise announcement by Barber that he was staying on the route, but with ships of Norwegian, not American, registry. Shifting flags was becoming a custom with him. [535] Now, under the name of Barber-West African Line, he would act as managing agent for regular berth service to West Africa from American Atlantic ports.

On July 19, 1946, on the day that the Maritime Commission announced its agreement to his abandonment of American-flag service on that essential route, the American South African Line wired the Commission its willingness to operate without subsidy pending the decision "rather than see this important area without any American-flag service for some months to come." [536]

A high point in the history of the Farrell shipping enterprises was the line's highly effective presentation of its case before the Maritime Commission examiners at Washington on September 6, when it applied along with Robin and Delta for an operating-differential subsidy. One examiner was to compliment the line on its "wonderful presentation," which would serve as a model when other lines later appeared before the Commission. [537] Much thoughtful work had gone into a well-developed plan for operation, a wealth of firsthand information, pertinent statistics, and numerous striking exhibits. Unlike the earlier session when Robin had secured its "double-track" subsidy for South and East Africa, that line was completely outclassed and apparently inadequately prepared. [538] Part of the credit for American South African's performance belongs to its general counsel, Donald D. Geary, and part to James Farrell, who said that the Commission and the earlier Shipping Board had each twice determined the essentiality of the route, which "stems from reciprocal commerce and community of interest between the North American continent and West Africa, including the paramount defense area usually described as the 'bulge.' West Africa produces seven of the essential strategic materials denied to us in the early stages of World War II. The United States produces in exportable surplus every essential need of the peoples of Africa." [539]

What probably clinched the case was the lengthy presentation by Captain George Wauchope of the plans of operation, based on his recent five months "on the spot" survey all along the West African coast. It had been a rugged experience; in places he had found no transportation, no living facilities, and no food. James Farrell, in explaining Wauchope's role, said: "We selected Wauchope for this assignment as the best-qualified man we could find for the job, either within or outside our organization. He possesses a rare combination of knowledge and experience. . . . Wauchope visited every principal port and area which we expect to serve. He developed an immense amount of factual data on trade and commerce (past, present, and projected) . . . and presents a plan for immediate and long range operation. . . . We are ready to begin operations." [540]

This report represented a pattern of service that was quite different from the way Bull and Barber had operated and would be a fairly close preview of the service Farrell would render. Wauchope's major emphasis was upon speeding up the service with the ships ready to sail on a new voyage in 81 days instead of the old 120-day arrangement. In his analysis of the Barber methods, he declared that "even the roughest calculation" shows that the only way to make the run economically sound under postwar high costs is by "reduction in the length of the voyage." This "can be accomplished in three ways; by increasing the speed of the ships in the service, by reducing the number of ports of call, or by improving the dispatch at the various ports." [541]

His most radical innovations to save the time of the ocean-going freighters were three feeder services by small craft to the lesser outports. One of these, for a Landing Ship Tank (LST) to operate from Lagos east and west along the coast, did not materialize. The other two services to be based at Monrovia developed very successfully, as will be seen.

He further advocated cutting the length of the sea voyage by using C-2 freighters with their 14½-knot speed instead of the 10 knots of the World War I veterans. He also suggested that instead of 25 regular ports of call, that number be cut in half. He anticipated further saving from the new port improvements under way not only at Monrovia but also at Abidjan, Luanda, and several other places because there would be faster port turnaround with the ships able to lie alongside quays with cranes to handle the cargo.

Instead of Barber's three separate prewar routes, he suggested two, a so-called Northern and a Southern, with alternate sailings every three weeks. Five ports—Monrovia, Abidjan, Takoradi,

Accra, and Lagos—would be on both, and so would get a ship every three weeks. Ten other ports would have a call at six-weeks' intervals. Wauchope figured that the Northern Route would have a total round voyage of 12,337 miles, and the Southern 13,353 miles. If close 80-day schedules could be maintained, each ship would make four and a half voyages a year, with five days out for overhaul. That estimate would prove to be over-optimistic and five ships would prove necessary. Port delays would stretch the voyage to 90 days rather than around 80 for a while.

In contrast to that well-worked-out program, the Robin presentation was decidedly sketchy. Carroll C. Pendleton, its executive vice-president, cited its South African performance, declared that it was "the best qualified of all applicants to give an efficient American-flag service," and proposed 18 annual sailings from North Atlantic ports and six from the Gulf. Sylvester J. Maddock, vice-president in charge of traffic, made the bold prediction that "Firestone are determined that they are going to ship their rubber from Marshall, and as long as Elder Dempster and the Barber Lines continue to serve Marshall, then there is no point in getting off on a feeder service to Monrovia that is not going to bring any cargo." [542]

The Maritime Commission had regarded this route (14) as a unit, combining services from the North Atlantic and the Gulf ports. That proposition was dropped when the attitude of Farrell and of Delta, based on New Orleans, became clear. Theodore Brent, the Delta president, declared, "If the route is divided, we are not an applicant for a North Atlantic service, but we are an applicant for a Gulf service." [543] James Farrell had already said that in case the Commission decided to "split the route . . . we would only tender for the Atlantic range and interpose no objection to Mississippi Shipping Company or any other responsible Gulf operator being awarded the Gulf range provided the Atlantic berth is not involved." [544] He later amplified that final remark to explain that the line would not approve of their competing with homeward cargoes to North Atlantic instead of Gulf ports. [545]

The Maritime Commission made its awards on January 9,

1947. Route 14 was divided into "Service 1" from and to North Atlantic ports, with its award to the Farrell line, and into "Service 2" from and to Gulf ports, with its award to Delta. Robin Line received nothing on the West African run. This divided arrangement was similar to what the Commission would later do with the South and East African run. [546]

The West African service went into operation two months later than originally scheduled because of the delay in obtaining agents for the British and French ports. That frustrating experience, it will be recalled, was not easily solved. It had seemed well in hand at the time of the Maritime Commission hearings, to recapitulate briefly, but the opposition of a British steamship line on the run had been persistent. This reached the point where the Farrells informed the Commission they would establish their own branch offices, but then came the acceptance of the French company, known as SCOA, a trading house primarily, without the usual experience and equipment for berthing services. This was remedied with its later merger with another company. [547]

In the meantime, the Maritime Commission had delivered the first of the promised C-2's, the *Golden Racer*, renamed the *African Glen*, early in February in good season for her scheduled sailing on the 28th. Instead, she sailed for South Africa on March 29. It was April 26, 1947 when the line at last went into operation with the sailing of another C-2, the *African Glade* from New York. Title to her had been taken on March 26; she was the former *Ann McKim*, earlier chartered by the Farrells on the South African run. [548] She had to be refitted at Baltimore for West Africa, and deep tanks for latex were installed. She loaded part of her cargo there before leaving for New York to take on the main portion of her modest lading.

The Delta Line had had the same agency difficulties, with American South African representing both lines, and was also accepted by the SCOA firm. It did not get its first ship off, the *Del Oro*, from New Orleans until May 10.

That sailing of the *African Glade* was another major landmark in the line's history, comparable to that of the *West Isleta* in 1926 and the *Chincha* in 1935 to open new services. The *African Glade* had two captains aboard—her master, Captain George R. Hickey, and, as a passenger, Captain Paul S. Maguire, who would take over at Monrovia for the next eighteen months as the Farrell's West African representative.

The African landfall came ten days out at Dakar on May 6. The new agent was not on hand to meet the ship as is customary, but everything went well thanks to the head of the stevedoring firm, which would take over the Farrell business as part of UMARCO five years later. [549] Another American there told Maguire that "our competitors feel very sorry for us—they feel we are going to have a lot of trouble—no lighters, etc. I told (him) to tell them not to waste any sympathy on us—we thrive on punishment." [550]

At Monrovia on May 12, after unloading at Freetown two days before, the arrival of the first Farrell ship was celebrated with a luncheon aboard. Among the guests were the Liberian Secretary of State and the Secretary of the Treasury, the Firestone manager, the third secretary of the legation, and the head of the Bank of Monrovia, who was serving temporarily as the line's agent. "I think the party was a great success, thanks to Captain Hickey," wrote Maguire. Hickey saw to it that the line got off to a good start in its public relations in every detail, including gifts of hams to each guest along with nylons for the wives and pens for the men.

Additional crew was taken on, according to the general custom of the coast. These so-called Krooboys were from one of the maritime tribes of the area and handled the unloading and loading of cargo aboard the ship, while local native longshoremen attended to the shore end. The Krooboys stayed with the ship down the coast and back; they lived on the after deck, doing their own cooking, in which rice figured heavily. In later days, some of the coast ports insisted on doing all their own stevedoring; but the Krooboys still went along to clean the latex tanks.

At Takoradi, the next stop, the Swiss agent had the native labor assembled at dockside, having persuaded them to work overtime at night. It was a novel experience for the agent: as this was the "first venture of this SCOA branch in the steamship agency business and Paris did not give them much time to make preparations." Again, there were somber comments on the attitude of the competing lines. The agent said that "the only time he realized how unfriendly they were was just prior to the arrival of the *Glade* when he tried to borrow or rent hand trucks . . . and people he knew disappeared at his approach."

At Accra, a heavy black squall kept the surfboats from coming out. That cost the ship a whole extra day there, although she had only thirty tons of cargo to discharge.

So it went down the coast—Lagos, Douala, Pointe Noire, Matadi, Luanda, and Lobito—dropping off cargo and picking up information of all sorts, and always beset by delays. Not until June 3, four weeks after the landfall at Dakar and 38 days from New York, did they at last come to Lobito.

Up the coast, homeward, it was the same slow progress. Port delays occurred in one stop after another, just as at Beira and Mombasa on the other side of Africa. At Takoradi, for example, eight days, instead of the three scheduled at New York, were spent loading. Monrovia and Freetown were the only other stops, but it was July 3, 68 days after she sailed, that the *Glade* reached New York.

The *African Grove,* which made the second voyage, was gone 80 days. Her itinerary was somewhat longer with extra calls at Marshall, Cape Palmas, and Abidjan outward and again at Marshall on returning. She was delayed 17 days at Takoradi, while Marshall added a further five days. [551]

Those slow coastwise passages on the west coast were in the traditional pattern there, but they gave food for thought. Five months after the original late arrival at Lobito by the *African Glade,* the line took action. Direct service was announced from New York to Lobito, with Luanda and Matadi the next stops, because of "increased American interest in the Belgian Congo and Portuguese Angola market opportunities." [552] Beginning November 26, 1947, this new course cut the running time to those ports virtually in half. Thereafter, Farrell west coast sailings were to alternate between the original "Northern Route" by way of Dakar, Freetown, and sometimes, the Canaries, and this "Southern Route" straight to Angola. Later on, Monrovia was included regularly on both. Similar direct service by the Belgian Line was to give strong competition.

The Farrell Lines, as they had just come to be called, appeared well satisfied with the first West African year in the executive committee's report to the directors. It speaks of the welcome extended by "all American exporters and importers" and in particular by the "numerous and growing independent traders." Much faster progress was made "than was anticipated in attracting support from the relatively few . . . large trading combines long entrenched on the west coast. Only one firm . . . continues to avoid our ships. . . . With only one exception, our line has participated in the transport of every commodity moving in either direction" with "shipments from over 2,900 firms. . . . We have had to compete against experienced, competent and determined opposition of two long-established lines and two others of more recent advent. In most instances this competition has been fair and above board and a needed spur to our endeavors. . . . The West African trade is highly specialized . . . there is much to learn. . . . In perhaps no other trade does the seagoing personnel play so large a part in success or failure of cargoliner operations." Despite fewer sailings than its competitors, Farrell Lines ranked second among the five lines doing business between West Africa and the American Atlantic ports, and in the matter of cargo tonnage per vessel, the Farrell ships stood first. [553]

Monrovia, with its freedom from colonial influences and as the base of the feeder services, was the natural choice for the Farrell supervision and base facilities. It was also the one exception to the usual Farrell pattern of utilizing local residents as agents. By the end of 1947, the company remodeled a substantial and attractive building, formerly occupied by the Bank of West Africa, for its small American staff. Two houses for executives—the resident manager and the office superintendent—were built in the outskirts at Sinkor, overlooking the constant surf of the Atlantic rollers. In addition to the resident Americans, there was a considerable staff of native clerks, mainly from Gold Coast and Nigeria, many of whom proved very proficient. The office has received efficient and continued direction from Thomas W. Griffith, one-time Barber purser, who came out at the end of 1948 and was still there a decade later.

Although Farrell representatives at inland cities such as Johannesburg and Nairobi were apt to be businessmen without nautical experience, the post at Monrovia has been held by a succession of mariners. The presence of the feeder fleet was doubtless the controlling factor in this. Maguire, taking over in April 1947, was followed in turn by Captain Thomas A. Donnelly in December 1948; Captain Paul Duffy in July 1955; Captain George R. Hickey in May 1956; and Captain Howard J. Kayser in December 1957. During Captain Donnelly's long tenure, there were two periods of "time out," with Captain Arthur Jensen serving in an acting capacity for six months, and a former junior officer, William F. Toohey, for nine months in 1953-54.

Those who saw Monrovia for the first time in the mid-1950's could scarcely picture that thriving city in its almost primitive conditions of only ten years before. Maguire wrote back at that time that money meant "very little in Monrovia in so far as food and transportation are concerned—there is no place to buy or rent a car—I have been sponging everywhere for transportation and meals. Some of the distances . . . are not too far, but the roads are filthy, with dust and filth making a car a requisite." Later he emphasized his complete isolation. "There are no telephones, and communications to West African ports are slow, not dependable, and the charges excessive. It may seem paradoxical, but you are closer to Lagos than I am." Without ice or artificial refrigeration, fresh meat and other perishable provisions were a problem, temporarily alleviated with each arrival of a Farrell ship with "reefer" accommodations. [554] The wise leadership of President Tubman, combined with the influx of American capital and business personnel, would soon change many of these conditions considerably.

The completion of the new port project gave a marked stimulus to the Farrell setup at Monrovia. It was not formally opened for business until July 26, 1948, although it was to have been completed the previous year. [555] The first ship to dock was the Farrell liner *African Patriot*. The reception given aboard her that day for President Tubman was an event to be remembered. Thousands went wild with excitement. The guards tried to keep the number aboard at any one time down to around fifty persons; finally the accommodation ladder had to be raised out of reach. The scene aboard sounded like the accounts of the White House at Andrew Jackson's inaugural in 1829. [556]

Just before the party, the opening of the port had been signalized at the Liberian State Department, when the Monrovia Port Management Company, Ltd. came into being. This was in accordance with the terms of the original agreement between the governments of Liberia and the United States, by which such a group would operate the port until the Lend Lease advance from the United States was paid off in full. [557] The company would exercise the usual governmental activities involved in managing a free port, and would receive ten per cent of the gross fees for the port's operating expenses. It was composed of the Liberian Government and the seven American corporations most closely concerned with the Liberian economy.

The seven corporations involved would have much to do with the transformation of Monrovia and Liberia as a whole. Senior in point of local contact was the Firestone Plantations Company, there since 1926. Farrell Lines and the Mississippi Shipping Company represented the American subsidized steamship firms. The Socony Mobil Company and the Texas Company had oil installations in the new port area. The Liberia Mining Company, under Lansdell K. Christie, had the concession of valuable iron ore forty miles inland in the Bomi Hills, from which a rail line would soon connect with the port. The Liberia Company, known as "Stettinius Associates" had a very comprehensive development, its most conspicuous feature being the wholesale use of Liberia's colors as a "flag of convenience" for world merchant shipping. Christie was elected the first president of the port group for a four-year term and would be succeeded by Wauchope of Farrell Lines. Donald Inskip, an American port engineer, was selected to manage the port.

In contrast to that profitable but questionable use of the Liberian flag on ships that never came near Monrovia, Farrell Lines was making a beginning with what might be called the "legitimate" Liberian-flag merchant marine. These were in the coastal—as contrasted with the Harbel—feeder fleet, both being Wauchope's projects that were now being implemented. Maguire suggested to President Tubman that he would think Liberia would welcome registering these small vessels under its flag since the crews would be mainly Liberian. The law forbidding foreign-owned ships in Liberian registry was subsequently repealed; and on June 10, 1947 a formal agreement was drawn up with the company. The *African Guide* became the first such vessel in Liberian registry; she was followed by others in the feeder group.

These small vessels were soon being assembled in the United States. Of the nine that were to serve in the next decade, the *African Guide,* a former Army feeder ship, was the largest. [558] Like all the other feeder craft, she had diesel engines; she could make 12 knots. Her draft of more than nine feet prevented her use on the Harbel rubber shuttle. The *African Guide,* in consequence, would spend most of her time on the 222-mile coastal run to Cape Palmas. The other two original feeder craft, former naval Landing Craft Tank (LCT) vessels, were the *Cavalla* and *Mesurado.* Like all the later feeder craft, these were named for Liberian rivers. The *African Guide* towed the two LCT's across the Atlantic, a month's voyage to Monrovia. A few weeks later, President Tubman visited the *African Guide,* receiving a snappy salute from the native crew as he boarded this first vessel of his new merchant marine.

The coastal feeder system developed regular service down the coast to Cape Palmas on the edge of Ivory Coast; the run up the coast to Freetown was less permanent. The service opened during the last week of December 1947 with the *African Guide.* She distributed and picked up cargo at the little ports en route—Marshall, Grand Bassa, River Cess, Sinoe, and Grand Cess. The small Firestone rubber plantation at Cape Palmas occasionally had some rubber to be loaded. Passengers, too, both in cabins and on deck, took full advantage of this round-trip service.

In fact, to the Liberians, the new coastal contact meant much more than the C-2 ocean service from New York or the rubber shuttle from Harbel. In later days, one could fly from Monrovia to Cape Palmas, but at this time, coastal travel was primitive and uncertain. Even a decade later, big surfboats were to be seen making their leisurely way along the coast with dozens of native passengers patiently enduring exposure to the weather for several days to get to Monrovia or other ports. As the Farrell's Liberian lawyer told Maguire, President Tubman and others felt this coastal service on regular schedule was "the most valuable contribution Farrell Lines can give to Liberia. . . . While they appreciate the ocean service, the Liberian clamor is for a . . . coastwise passenger service." [559]

Back in New York, however, this coastal service generated far less enthusiasm among company officials. The *African Guide* came to be regarded as a white elephant; and the early history of the Cape Palmas route was written in red ink.

The shuttle feeder service between Monrovia and the Firestone rubber plantations at Harbel would, as time went on, have infinitely more to offer from the company's point of view. Wauchope had visualized that with the protected port in prospect at Monrovia, the dry and liquid rubber could be carried there for loading by way of the Farmington River from Harbel, across the shifting Marshall bar, and along the coast. On the return run, the feeder craft would carry the American cargo consigned to Harbel. The Firestone lighters used at the bar were too small to go along the coast to Monrovia, but he learned that while Roberts Field was being built, considerably larger vessels had been able to negotiate the bar and the river. From his war experience he knew that Landing Craft Tank (LCT) vessels could lift tons of cargo with a draft of around $4\frac{1}{2}$ feet which would be about right for the bar and the river; and their speed of seven knots could make the round trip in three days. With tanks for latex installed on them and tanks for storage on the pier at Monrovia, the ocean-going freighters could load in only a fraction of the time it was taking at Marshall. The delays and uncertainties will be recalled of that loading and discharging by lighters in the rough waters off the bar there. [560]

The first two LCT's of the feeder fleet, the *Cavalla* and *Mesurado,* had been rushed over, towed by the *African Guide,* to be ready for the opening of the port, but that was delayed for months. The third LCT, the *Saint Paul,* arrived later already equipped with her tanks for latex, but still the full service was delayed as the Monrovia storage tanks were not ready until two years after the port began to function. In the interim, a service of sorts was developed with the feeder craft in dry cargo on the Harbel run. They were also often used to pinch hit for the *African Guide* on her coastal route, a job for which they were not intended. The *Mesurado* was soon wrecked in that coastal service, and her namesake, the *Mesurado II,* and the *St. Paul* were lost within five years. The *Cavalla,* however, served for more than eight years. For the most part, non-Americans commanded the feeder craft; and with a single officer "on his own" on some of the smaller ones, it is not surprising that there were accidents. [561]

Altogether, the beginning of the feeder service was financially discouraging. The company had invested $515,000 in vessels and facilities at Monrovia; the losses were $316,000 in 1948, the first year. [562] And in the second year, the investment had been increased to $672,000, with the balance still in the red, though cut down to $42,000. [563] Only a strong optimist would foresee that those dollars invested in this fleet would before long be paying off at a higher rate than in the line's ocean freighters.

The full Harbel latex service at last went into operation in May 1950. In eight days, the *Saint Paul* carried some 200,000 gallons from Harbel to Monrovia, just in time for the sailing of the Elder Dempster liner *Cargill,* the first ship to load latex there instead of at Marshall. With ships now able to load in one day at Monrovia what used to take five to eight days at the Marshall bar, the new service, so wrote a Farrell official, has been "a great money-saver for the ocean carrier, including Farrell Lines." [564]

Eventually new vessels were especially built for the trade, with greater cargo capacity but still with the all-important draft of 4½ feet. The *Mesurado II,* lost in her first month, the *Cestos,* and the *Farmington* were identical and carried around 140 tons or 40,000 gallons on each trip at eight knots. The other two, the *Kpo* and the *Lofa,* were fairly similar but somewhat larger. These vessels, as well as much of the repair and maintenance equipment, including a disassembled marine railway, came from the United States, along with most of the necessary supplies.

Three other lines, Delta, Barber, and Elder Dempster, also carried these rubber cargoes to the United States. By agreements between them and Farrell Lines in January 1950, it was arranged that 20 per cent (later raised in the mid-1950's to 27 per cent) of the full freight from Harbel to the United States would go to the 50-mile run of the feeder service, and the remainder to the ocean carriers for the 3,900-mile ocean voyage. An agreement was also made by Farrell with Firestone by which the latter would ship all its rubber output by the Farrell feeders; and in turn, Farrell would take all this as it came along.

In 1954, Farrell Lines carried 21,887 of the 47,563 tons of Harbel rubber exports, with Elder Dempster second. It carried 3,835 of the 14,767 tons of Firestone imports, more than half of which total was rice brought by Delta from the Gulf. [565] Of that outgoing rubber, about three-quarters was latex to one-quarter dried rubber. With the average ocean freight rate around $30 a ton, or $8.10 for the feeder portion, this would mean total feeder earnings of some $385,000 a year for the rubber plus some $156,000 for the Firestone imports. Altogether that came to more than a half million dollars earnings on relatively low capital investment and operating cost. Farrell Lines also saved an estimated $132,000 a year on their ocean voyage expenses by loading at Monrovia. [566]

The ocean-going end of the West African service after 1950 became definitely profitable, reflecting the growing amount of United States traffic with the region. While there were the competing lines, the Farrell ships were acquiring the lion's share. The total United States exports and imports in the West African trade rose from $38 million in 1938 to 163 in 1946 and 517 by 1954. [567]

Once again, the Farrells had come into a trade just in time to rise with the tide—and, as in South Africa, their entrance had doubtless contributed to that rise. Several factors were involved in this West African boom. By no means the least of these was the opening of the port of Abidjan in 1949 as the well-equipped outlet of the French Ivory Coast. [568]

Other reasons for the expanding traffic came from a sudden boom in coffee exports, particularly from Portuguese Angola, and in cocoa exports. Total coffee exports from West Africa had been $6.6 million in 1946; they had jumped to 10.1 millions in 1949 and had become 63.3 millions in 1955. And coffee, of course, paid an excellent freight rate. So, too, did cocoa exports which rose from $26.4 million in 1946 to 80.3 in 1949, and to 113.7 in 1954.

The Farrells had to wait patiently to gain a share of the latter lucrative traffic; cocoa was the one export that they did not carry in their first year. Hershey, Baker, and other American firms bought a good share of Gold Coast and Nigerian cocoa, but it took time to secure an allotment of one-quarter of the American-bound cocoa tonnage to the only American-flag line. Barber had another quarter, because of its earlier presence there, while one-half went to Elder Dempster with both seniority and the advantage of being a British line in trade with British colonies. At Abidjan and other ports of the French areas, on the other hand, the Farrell share reached well over 50 per cent of the rapidly expanding cocoa exports.

Finally, there was the great increase in rubber exports, particularly from Firestone, in the first postwar decade. Back in 1939 these had been only $2.9 million, but by 1946 they had jumped to 13.8 millions, and continued rising to 36.8 in 1955. Farrell, of course, had a double cut on the rubber profits as they not only carried almost half of the Firestone rubber to the United States, but also were getting that 27 per cent as feeder freight on the rest.

The outward cargoes to West Africa continued to lag behind the homeward, except in 1949, when for once they drew ahead— $161 million to 142 millions homeward. The close of the war saw a sudden boom in American cotton manufactures, but by 1948, with the combined impact of revived British manufactures and the heavy inroads of Japanese textiles, they fell off from $51.3 million to $8.0. To offset that loss, automobile shipments were increasing steadily. This reflected in part the growing prosperity of the Gold Coast and of the Belgian Congo, as well as the improvement of roads in both those regions. In 1939, the total value of these shipments of automobiles and parts had come to $2.7 million; by 1946, this had jumped to 6.3 millions. Six years later, in 1955, it had reached 39.9 millions. In the early 1950's, the Farrells brought out a considerable part of the equipment for the 37-mile railway from Monrovia to the iron mines at Bomi Hills —the only normal 4' 8¼" gauge South of the Sahara. Incidentally, another steamship company had the agency for those ore exports.

Despite these good aspects of the West African trade, the company was concerned in 1952 because "congestion and concomitant heavy delays have made a joke of any attempt at regular service to the West African ports." [569] More fundamentally unfavorable were the holdovers of colonialism. For a long time during the postwar years in British West Africa, rigid trade controls from London allowed nothing to be imported from outside the sterling area if anything of the sort, irrespective of quality, was available in Britain or elsewhere within it. Discriminating currency controls made difficulties in French West African areas. In the Belgian Congo most of the cargoes continued to be "routed by Belgian flag steamers." With trade thus dutifully following the flag in those regions, the relative absence of such restrictions and of mother-country competition was particularly appreciated in the Portuguese and Spanish colonies. Above all, there was cause for gratitude that Liberia had never appeared on any map in the color of a great colonial power.

For all that, Farrell Lines after a decade of operation had plenty of reason to be glad that it had extended its shipping routes to West Africa in 1947. The traffic, to be sure, was only about half of that from South Africa, but it was fairly steady and still growing. The West Africans kept on buying their flour and tobacco from the United States even in bad times when South Africa stopped buying as many new automobiles.

Chapter XIII

THE POSTWAR "MAIN LINE"

A t the close of World War II, cargo-carrying immediately boomed as never before, because overseas markets were starved just as they had been in 1919. American merchant shipping began to be returned to private operation after its four years of wartime governmental control of ships and cargoes. It would take many months, however, before the status of the ships themselves would be back on a normal peacetime basis. In the meantime, the shipping firms would have to charter part of the vessels that they needed from the government on provisional interim arrangements.

The American South African Line was in a particularly favorable situation, for South Africa once again was able to pay generously for its immediate needs and desires. The line's emancipation from the War Shipping Administration control was signalized by the sailing of the *African Sun* on April 2, 1946 for Cape Town; she had only been returned by the government a few days before. This ship and the line's other C-2 on the Cape run were shortly to be joined by the new C-3's, already beginning to come off the ways of the Federal yard at Kearny. [570]

The executive committee had vigorously expressed the line's optimism at the beginning of that year, predicting that for "at least three years, there should be a satisfactory volume of outward and inward traffic. That the Company will enjoy more than the prewar share of this business is certain." [571] At the end of that year, optimism was still evident in a review of the line's first 20 years. "During this entire period our Company has pros-

pered; it has doubled, and completely renewed its fleet, provided
employment for as many as 2,500 persons, expanded the commerce of the United States, and trained numerous officers for
our Navy, and paid our shareholders moderate dividends. True,
we are now earning, and have at other times earned, substantial
profits, but certainly not because of unduly high freight rates.
The reason has been increased efficiency, in ship utilization and
a constantly increasing volume of business." [572]

This estimate of three good years ahead would show prophetic
skill of a high order; business did continue up and up until the
end of 1948. Then, just at the end of three years, conditions
suddenly deteriorated with the imposition of drastic import controls by the Union of South Africa.

In the matter of the status of the ships, the year 1946 was a
fairly bewildering one of transition. The Beaver Street headquarters had to operate ships under three different sorts of
status. The company would still be acting as "ship's husband"
on General Agency Account (GAA) for a slowly diminishing
fleet of Liberty ships and other government-owned vessels. [573]

The second category consisted of vessels "leased" from the
government on bareboat charter. [574] The Harvard Report, upon
which a great deal of the postwar shipping policy would be
based, had recognized that this bareboat device would be necessary for a while, but it recommended that the rates for this not
be so temptingly low that shipping men might prefer chartering
to the risks of ownership, nor that the terms of the charters be
so short that vessels could be used for a quick profit and then
turned in. [575] The charter rate was fixed at about $13,000 a
month for C-2's or Victory ships. This was later raised to absorb
abnormal profits. [576]

The third group of vessels consisted of the ships owned outright by the Farrells. These various new *Africans* kept coming off
the ways all through 1946 until there were eight of them. [577]
Eventually these would make chartering unnecessary. This tripartite division into General Agency Agreement, bareboat chartered, and "owned" ships was still further complicated because
a vessel would often slide from one category into another.

A mixed succession of chartered and owned ships followed

the *African Sun* down through the South Atlantic after she left New York on that first private voyage since February 1942. The second *African Star,* the first of the new Federal-built C-3's, was on her maiden voyage. After her came six chartered C-2's. By June, the second new C-3 started her maiden voyage. And so it went, a constant procession, but far from enough to meet the insatiable South African demand for cargo. During the next two years, various other chartered ships, principally *Victorys,* would supplement the fleet of *Africans.* [578]

During the course of 1947 and 1948, Farrell ships would carry more than a million long tons of cargo between the United States and South and East Africa. That million broke neatly into fairly even parts by three separate counts. The totals for each year were close: 1947, 527,000 tons and 1948, 539,000 tons. Likewise, the outward tonnage to Africa for the two years was almost equal to the total homeward—498,000 to 569,000 tons. And as a third close balance, the total 556,000 tons carried on subsidized voyages was only slightly more than the 510,000 tons on extra nonsubsidized voyages beyond the operating-differential quota. [579] On the other hand, the value of the cargoes showed a far from even balance, with the outward general cargo as usual worth far more and paying much higher freight than the chrome and manganese that loomed large in the holds on the return passage.

As in the past, there was ample competition from other vessels on that long haul to Cape Town and beyond. Some of these were under foreign flags, but still more were American. The rivalry assumed a rather different pattern, however, in 1947–48 from what it had been earlier.

The most conspicuous difference lay in the diminishing role of the British "conference" lines. The old U.S.A.-South African Outward Conference was entering upon a new stage. [580] With the postwar boom, the British lines, but not the German Hansa, were back, but with a relatively smaller share of the trade than before. Their 66 outward voyages from New York to South Africa in 1947–48 were at just about the prewar rate, whereas the American-flag sailings had jumped tremendously. In those two years, the British conference ships carried a total of only 228,000 tons of cargo to South Africa as compared with Farrell's

1,067,000 tons and the probably equal amount for the other subsidized American ships. [581]

What was more, their voyage pattern still showed traces of the old pre-World War I neglect of the return Africa-New York run. In contrast to the 66 outward passages from New York in those two years, 1947–48, there were only ten in return from Africa. Those ten westbound voyages were all made by the so-called "American and African" joint services of Ellerman-Bucknall and Union-Castle, which gave monthly outward service, sometimes returning by the way of Canada. The other major joint service, shared by Clan and Union-Castle, had outward sailings to the Cape about every three weeks, a total of 30 for the two years. As in earlier years, some of the vessels came back by way of India and Suez to the United States, while others proceeded from South and East Africa to the United Kingdom, whence part went on to the United States and others went back to Africa. The Prince and Houston Lines made only eight and seven outward passages respectively in the two years, but all returned by way of the United Kingdom. [582]

Even for that meager service, the days were numbered. To the British, the New York-South Africa run was a "cross-trade" in contrast to the more desirable "direct trade" from the mother country. After South African import controls drastically curtailed the trade with the United States in 1949, the British lines began now and then to skip occasional sailings and eventually to withdraw from the run altogether. In 1955, the departure of a Prince Line ship from New York for Cape Town marked the end of British-flag conference service, which had previously only had brief interruptions by war since 1893. On one of the lower floors of 26 Beaver Street at New York below the Farrell headquarters the U.S.A.-South Africa Outward Conference and its companion Homeward Conference still continue to function. Farrell Lines, however, constitute the sole active membership and bear most of the overhead expense, believing, as its management does, in the importance of maintaining a rate-regulating organition for that trade. In 1958, most of the lines active on the Cape run joined in a formal rate agreement which was expected to develop before long into a regular conference. The American

West African Freight Conference, in the meantime, had continued with an active membership representing services under several flags.

An even more significant result of the withdrawal of British service from the Cape run is that three decades after the Farrells entered the trade, the proportion of American-flag participation in the trade with South and East Africa is higher than any of the other 30-odd "essential trade routes."

Foreign-flag competition, however, was emerging from a new source. In April 1947 came the announcement that the flag of the Union of South Africa would be seen for the first time in "deep-water" trade. The new line was the South African Marine Corporation, or "Safmarine" as it was often called. Its flag would give it a very definite tactical advantage in attracting cargo, and also it would have certain international aspects. The credit for establishing it goes in part to Dr. H. J. van de Bijl, who was also a prime mover in creating the government-owned South African Iron and Steel Corporation (ISCOR) and also the Electricity Commission. [583] The rest of the initiative came from an American, Henry D. Mercer, the aggressively successful head of the unsubsidized States Marine fleet. As a later account put it, "States Marine helped set up a company headed by Henry Mercer's old friend, former Air Marshal ('Bomber') Harris, famous for his blanket bombing of Germany . . . The two firms whack up fifty-fifty such cargo as they can corral that is headed either east or west between the U.S. and South Africa." [584] States Marine served as agents in America and furnished part of the ships. It also helped the South Africans secure three American-built Victory ships as soon as surplus tonnage was thrown open to foreign purchase. The *New Bern Victory, Westbrook Victory,* and *Westerly Victory* became overnight the *Constantia, Vergelegen,* and *Morgenster* hailing from Cape Town. [585]

A spokesman for the new line pointed out that with most of South Africa's consumer goods imported, it would be an advantage not to have to pay the freight charges, as well as the cost of the goods, in dollars. He added that the line did not have a government subsidy, nor did it seek one. [586]

It did, nevertheless, have something else that was to prove very useful along that line. For some time, the Union government was to decree that all its purchases from the United States—and these included all material for railroads, harbors, and certain industries—must come in South African ships. On top of that, South Africans were urged to do their own individual importing and exporting under their own flag, as a patriotic duty. [587]

"Safmarine," which in its second year carried almost as much cargo as all the British conference liners, meant severe competition for the Farrells. [588] In spite of that, there was an occasion when the latter line backed up the South African ships in litigation. In earlier days, the United States and other countries had levied "tonnage and light duties" on shipping entering their ports as a means of lighthouse maintenance. Since April 19, 1949, by a presidential proclamation, the United States had put this on a reciprocity basis, with duties waived on vessels of nations that did not tax American ships. That policy exempted British vessels, but not the independent members of the Commonwealth. Some $3,700 light duties, consequently, greeted the *Constantia* under the South African flag at New York. Back in Africa, the government threatened to impose similar levies on American shipping. The case went to Federal court at New York, and the Farrell Lines instructed their attorneys to support the rival's case. A token amount was paid under protest but no further fees were levied. [589]

In 1949, as part of its drastic import control regulations, the government would go still further in giving exceptional advantages to Safmarine. The Minister of Economic Affairs declared: "Too long has South Africa been wholly dependent on foreign shipping lines. These shipping firms are undoubtedly of great benefit to South Africa—and at the same time to their shareholders. But the government welcomes the flotation of our own South African shipping companies and will assist them wherever possible. Furthermore, the government is not prepared to stand indifferently should any attempt be made to stifle South African ventures in this direction. The Union government will, as far as possible, see that our shipping companies are not placed in a disadvantageous position." [590] That was, of course, the same sort of seagoing nationalism which has helped revive the American merchant marine, and which would send many other flags, from Israel's to Ghana's, out upon the sea.

Safmarine's special privileges were modified somewhat during the boom years of the mid-1950's but were revived again when trade fell off in the late 1950's. There were rumors of a possible new South African flag service, with financial backing from outside the Union.

This British and South African shipping competition combined was mild compared with that with other subsidized American lines. Farrell, which had had the only American-flag line on the Cape route until 1935, now not only had the continuing strenuous competition of the Robin Line but also that of a third line, Lykes Brothers, who had been operating from Gulf ports since 1941.

At the end of the war, the Maritime Commission was carefully studying the whole question of the essential trade routes before it resumed the operating-differential subsidies, which had been in abeyance since mid-1942. The matter had been considered by the authors of the Harvard Business School report of 1945, already mentioned. They felt that there was no question about the desirability of continuing private operation of shipping with the help of subsidies when needed, because "government operation is less flexible and more costly." Private ownership was necessary in their opinion because ". . . one real requirement of the most effective operation is to have private capital at risk." [591] They especially stressed the importance of selecting routes with "sufficient potential traffic to warrant the United States-flag service. In the past, the United States-flag ships have secured their highest proportion of foreign trade in the routes where the foreign nation served has possessed no merchant marine." [592]

The Maritime Commission's Trade Routes Committee was instructed to disregard all previous actions and attempt to set up an ideal system of essential routes. The 23 routes under 12 companies of the 1936 Act had had only a brief period of operation before the war came. This left only the figures for 1938 as really tangible data on which to base predictions; beyond that, it was to be too often necessary to guess about postwar conditions in various parts of the world. By November 1945, the committee asked the

SENIOR SHIPMASTERS

George T. Sullivan

Christian W. Schmidt

John G. Waller

Flying Camera, Inc.

Anders R. Mortenson

Flying Camera, Inc.

Ole P. Stender

Flying Camera, Inc.

Alden G. Graham

Gibbs & Cox, Inc.

Projected "Third Fleet" replacement ship

shipping industry for its comments on a proposed program of 33 essential routes. The list had a fairly high common denominator with the earlier official schedules, which went back to the mail pay act of 1891. [593] Hostile or skeptical critics have pointed out from time to time that every overhauling of the essential route system has ended up with much the same routes, and pretty much the same shipping operators thereon. [594] By and large, the number of essential routes, in one program after another, has boiled down to some 20 or 30 basic ones, and the operating companies to around a dozen. That had been, of course, a rather inevitable result, considering the relative importance and possibilities of the various routes, and the limited number of companies that were "ready, willing, and able" to undertake the responsibility of regular service.

However searching the Maritime Commission's postwar evaluation of the various possible routes may have been, they were apparently satisfied with the arrangements made on the eve of the war. They notified American South African and the other subsidized operators that "At its meeting on July 16, 1946, the Commission authorized the resumption of subsidized operations by the twelve holders of operating-differential subsidy agreements," on condition that they file proper applications. [595]

That blanket renewal of the subsidies suspended early in 1942 was naturally gratifying to those operators. They more than once expressed appreciation of the extent to which the Commission had consulted the industry in the formulation of its postwar plans. Along with the basic "status quo ante" policy numerous new route arrangements were made. There would be, in fact, three new "essential routes" to Africa South of Sahara resulting from the postwar readjustments. By the time that the Maritime Commission's allocations were eventually arranged by 1949, there would be four subsidized companies, all members of the original dozen, on four routes to South, East or West Africa. To South and East Africa, Farrell and Robin would still be double-tracked on Route 15A from the Atlantic ports, while Lykes would cover 15B from the Gulf. On the West African run, Farrell would have 14-1 from the Atlantic ports, and Mississippi (Delta), 14-2 from the Gulf. [596]

On the route to Cape Town and beyond, the principal novelty was the Lykes award for service from the Gulf. After their 1935–1938 experience with the Gulf service, the Farrells did not care about securing direct participation again, but they did attempt to develop an indirect interest in that trade, acquiring 20 per cent of the stock of the Bloomfield Steamship Company, being organized by B. M. Bloomfield, a former Lykes executive, at Houston, Texas. The project, which had generous Texas financial backing, was to develop Gulf trade with South and East Africa. The Maritime Commission sold Bloomfield three C-2's for the run but the expected operating-differential subsidy ran afoul of powerful Lykes opposition. A subsidy for the same route was being sought by that big Tampa-New Orleans concern with its ubiquitous fleet of 50-odd ships, which was already being subsidized on services from the Gulf to the United Kingdom, Continental Europe, the Mediterranean, the Orient, and the Caribbean. They had moved into the South and East African run in 1941 after their European services were interrupted. The Maritime Commission rejected the applications of both lines for this "Route 15B" from the Gulf ports to South and East Africa. Thereupon Bloomfield sold his three ships to the Farrells, who also purchased the remaining 80 per cent of the stock. These C-2's became, it will be recalled, the *African Patriot, African Pilgrim,* and *African Pilot.* [597]

Eventually, on December 29, 1949, Lykes received an exclusive operating-differential contract for the 15B route. The first subsidized sailing was made by the *Mason Lykes* on January 11, 1950, just nine years after the company had first begun service on that run. Bloomfield later received a contract on Route 21 from the Gulf to Europe.

The Farrells offered no objection to the Lykes service on Route 15B so long as the vessels returned from South Africa to the Gulf. They would not approve, however, of those ships returning to New York or other Atlantic ports as the Farrell ships themselves had done in 1935–38. They also made a similar proviso concerning the Mississippi (Delta) participation in Route 14-2 between the Gulf and West Africa. At the time, the competition from the Gulf route did not seem serious, but later it became clear that it was growing increasingly competitive through many parts of the American hinterland. Ores and other heavy cargo, for example, could be hauled by cheap inland river transportation from the Gulf not only up the Mississippi but also even further inland by the Ohio River to Pittsburgh. In reverse, the Farrell ships could sometimes draw cargo away from the Gulf ports to Charleston or Savannah from the Mississippi and beyond.

In the postwar decade, competition with the Robin Line remained just as strong and continuous as it had been in the later 1930's. It was felt all along the Atlantic coast from Portland to Jacksonville, and out in Africa from Cape Town to Mombasa. When the pressing postwar demands for outward cargo space were greater than even the weekly schedules of the two lines could accommodate, Robin managed to steal a march. The automobile manufacturers in particular were cramped by this shortage. The United States exports of automobiles and parts jumped from $5.3 million in 1945 to 29.0 in 1946 and 69.7 in 1947; and a car naturally took up more room than the shipments of several lesser consignees. The question arose in both lines of chartering extra ships to carry the automobiles to Port Elizabeth. Beaver Street headquarters decided against doing so because the freight would be insufficient to compensate the charter costs; but Robin went ahead and chartered extra ships. As Farrell had foreseen, money was lost on the deal; but there was a valuable by-product. In the long run, that temporary loss was made up many times over by Robin because of the lasting gratitude of the automobile manufacturers.

Those skyrocketing car shipments were only part of the tremendous postwar purchasing of American goods by South Africa. Through the war, unspent reserves had been piling up from the payments for gold, minerals, and other exports because nonessential commodities were not available. Now all tastes could be gratified from Cadillacs to bubble gum; and South Africa was turning more and more to the United States for what it wanted.

For the first time, in 1947 and 1948, it actually bought more from the United States than from the United Kingdom. In that latter peak year, combined American imports and exports to

South, East, and West Africa for the first time reached a billion dollars, more than half of which consisted of exports to South and East Africa. This was repeated, at a slightly higher level, in 1956. [598] In normal times, Britain had had a very strong lead in its traditional industrial offerings. Now, America's cotton goods had a brisk temporary boom in 1947, while its iron and steel manufactures rose substantially to six times their pre-war value in all three years, 1947–49. The growing demand for tractors brought agricultural machinery and implements up to almost that same high level in 1948 and 1949. [599] Outside those major categories, appliances and other expensive consumer goods were in high demand.

The month of April 1948, in which the American South African Line became Farrell Lines, was the busiest in the history of the family's service to South and East Africa. Seven ships sailed to Cape Town and beyond; four of them belonged to the line and the three others were chartered to carry the surplus, chiefly automobiles, piling up on the piers of Brooklyn and other ports along the coast, at this peak of the South African spending spree. Altogether in 1948, 54 Farrell sailings were made for the Cape, of which 21 were by chartered vessels. The freight revenue from that outward service totaled $11,500,000 for the year, with $1,545,000 of it for April alone. [600]

The exact nature of the cargoes in those boom years may be seen in the appendix analysis of what the *African Planet* carried out and back on her ninth voyage, between August 14 and November 5, 1948. It shows what was carried to and from each port and the freight rate on each principal commodity. The ship earned $324,574 on that voyage, principally on the outward passage. While giving a generally good idea of the pattern, it differed from the usual routine in that little American cargo was picked up outside New York, and that the *Planet* did not continue beyond Lourenco Marques. [601]

This voyage was among the ten most lucrative of that lush year of 1948, but it did not hold first place. The *African Moon* set a tonnage record at 13,600, even greater than the *Challenger's* in 1939. [602] The *African Crescent*, sailing on October 9, had the largest outward freight earnings at $308,100. The *African*

Planet herself on her next sailing in early December, before the import controls got in their deadening effect, had the highest total voyage freight earnings of any of the Farrell ships—a total of $444,000, with $294,000 outward and $150,000 homeward. That was, however, a 124-day voyage, as she went on up the coast to East Africa with its richer opportunities.

At the end of 1948, the South African trade suddenly went sour. By the following summer, freight earnings had dropped to only a little more than a quarter of what they had been in the floodtide of the previous year. The Union of South Africa had decided to act in its increasingly unfavorable situation in international trade. Its exports to the United States were paying for only a fraction of what the imports cost. Even its current gold production could not make up the difference; and as a result the gold reserves, accumulated during the war, were being raided. No longer, the government felt, could the Union afford those cargoes of automobiles, refrigerators, and gum that had been jamming the holds of every liner from the United States. [603]

South Africa's position in international finance was midway between the "hard" American currency and the "soft" currencies of Britain and much of the Continent. It was a sort of associate member of Britain's "sterling bloc" and its pound was geared in value to the British pound. At the same time, its gold ingots from the Rand were "hard" enough to command dollars in large quantities. South Africa had refused to follow the dutiful example of New Zealand, Malaya, and others in the Commonwealth in depositing its dollar exchange in the common sterling fund. Between June 1946 and March 1953, the South African Reserve Bank shipped almost a billion dollars worth of gold to the United States by sea. Of that total $998 million worth, Farrell Lines carried 428; Robin Lines 384; Safmarine 123; Ellerman & Bucknall 57; and Union-Castle $4 million worth. By ports of shipment, 688 millions went from Durban, 241 from Cape Town, and 68 from Port Elizabeth. [604]

To make matters worse, from the standpoint of the financial authorities, the United States was not only outstripping Britain in shipments to South Africa, but it was taking less of African

products than ever in return. The situation was further aggra-
vated by the fact that the Union was losing the dollar exchange
on some of its indirect exports to America. This was happening
because some sharp operators in Britain and on the Continent
were buying karakul and other valuable commodities from
South Africa for "soft" currency and then reshipping them for
sale to Americans. In this way, they, rather than the original
sellers in South Africa, obtained the resultant dollar exchange.

Action was somewhat delayed because of a pending election.
One of the top officials in the Department of Commerce and Industry advised earlier, in 1947, of the danger of this drain; but
the answer was "You are an economist, but as politicians, we
can't do anything with the election ahead." Early in 1948, that
general election swept the veteran Marshal Smuts from office
and put the Afrikaners of the Nationalist party in the saddle.
They soon felt free to act.

The blow fell on November 3, 1948 in the form of a decree
that imposed drastic import restrictions to stop the drain on the
gold reserves. The importation of many luxury items ceased
completely. Most of the remaining commodities were put on a
quota basis, with an importer cut down to just half of the amount
he had spent in 1947. Only in the case of construction machinery
and certain other items, deemed essential, was a relatively free
inflow of imports still allowed. The road scrapers would still
be going to the Union, but the passenger automobiles, appliances, and much else, would either be cut down in numbers or
forbidden altogether.

The Farrell headquarters were not taken by surprise. Their
usual competent intelligence service had been warning for some
time that such a move was in the air. [605] A further ruling by the
South African government, however, disturbed them gravely.
This was that freight charges by ships from without the sterling
area would be deducted from the already drastically reduced
allowance of an importer. Even when it was agreed to accept
payment in South African pounds, Pretoria ruled the freight
charges would still be deducted from the importer's quota for
buying exports, unless the shipment had been by the South African Marine. This situation was gradually rectified to some degree

by the good offices of the State Department and some of the less arbitrary South African officials.

The next action to hit that trade was somewhat milder in effect; the South African pound was devalued in September 1949. It was reduced 44 per cent in value from $4.03 to $2.80, to keep pace with the pound sterling. This obviously gave the British a marked advantage in competition with the United States in the matter of price.

Such a threefold handicap naturally affected sharply all three American-flag lines—Farrell, Robin, and Lykes from the Gulf. Apparently Robin Line's "intelligence service" was less in the know than Farrell's. On the very day that the import restrictions were imposed, the Robin officials were down at Washington trying to persuade the Maritime Commission to increase the number of sailings per year for which they could receive the operating-differential subsidy. During these years of the postwar boom, both this line and Farrell had been making many extra voyages on which they received no subsidy. Now they were soon to be faced with the exactly opposite side of the picture; subsidy contracts stipulated, as a corollary to the maximum sailings that could be made, a minimum number that must be made "full or not full." Shortly, both lines would be making voyage after voyage at a loss because of this contractual obligation. Thus the subsidy system was giving the shippers of the United States and South Africa continued regular service, albeit reduced, under circumstances that unobligated shipping lines might well have abandoned as unprofitable. And that was just what the British conference lines were doing.

By 1950, the full impact of those restrictive measures was at its worst—and then the picture was a gloomy one. The Farrell sailings had first fallen off from four a month to three; then, as cargoes and freight earnings kept dropping, to two. In the 54 sailings of 1948, the outward cargo revenue had totaled nearly $12 million; the next year, with only 25 sailings, that would drop to not quite $5 million. At the same time, the earnings on each of the voyages were still respectable. But by the bad year, 1950, the revenue from 27 sailings totaled only about $2 million, and the average voyage earnings now had fallen to about $80,000, as compared with an average of around $220,000 in 1948. [606]

This sudden change in trade pattern demonstrated the value of the chartering process as an element of flexibility. Obviously, a line kept in its regular fleet just enough ships to meet the demands of normal trade. In busy seasons, when extra sailings could be used, the custom was to "charter in" extra tonnage from the government or from other lines; conversely, in slack times, a line could "charter out" to other shipping interests its surplus vessels. During 1948's rush of cargoes, Farrell Lines "chartered in" ten ships, which made 21 South African voyages. Seven were Victory ships, provided by the Maritime Commission on "bareboat" charter. Three others were time chartered: the *Mormacdove,* from Moore, McCormack, the *Hawaiian* from American-Hawaiian; and the *Suzanne* from Bull Lines. Before the last of the "chartered in" vessels, the *Great Falls Victory,* from the government, had returned from her eighth voyage, January 20 to April 6, 1940, the reverse process of "chartering out" had had to be started.

Despite the import restrictions, there were still ores and other materials to bring back from South Africa, and also the rich unrestricted trade of East Africa. In consequence, the Farrells time-chartered out three of their ships to American-Hawaiian for outward voyages to the Far East. Then, on returning from Singapore to Beira or Lourenco Marques, they were redelivered to the Farrells and carried the latter's homeward cargoes from there. The *African Planet* made the first of these "chartered out" voyages in the spring of 1949, followed on the same course by the *African Sun* and the *African Dawn* in the summer and autumn. The pattern shifted slightly in the next three ships, which were chartered out to the Prudential Steamship Company. Both the *African Lightning* and the *African Dawn* during the first four months of 1950 went out through Suez and touched at various colorful spots around the Persian Gulf before they were redelivered to Farrell service at the oil port of Abadan. These two returned home by way of East and South Africa, where they picked up Farrell cargo. The *African Glade,* the third Prudential charter, stopped at Trieste, Istanbul, and other eastern Mediterranean ports; then, at Aden, it was turned back to Farrell for its homeward journey around the Cape. [607] The Maritime Commission finally decided not to pay subsidy on those single homeward passages. Consequently, Farrell abandoned the charter pattern as no longer profitable.

The directors were considering the sale of two of the ex-Bloomfield C-2's (*Patriot, Pilgrim,* or *Pilot*) when the Korean situation suddenly gave them a chance to be of national service, with the heavy demand for shipping on the long transpacific haul. Instead of being sold, the "P's" were time chartered to the Military Sea Transport Service. Along with them went the C-3 *African Rainbow* for eight months. The line also husbanded a number of government-owned vessels on General Agency Agreement during the Korean operations.

On the regular Cape run, Farrell vessels, like their rivals, were finding very slim pickings. On several occasions, even, the homeward cargoes made more money than the outward—and that was contrary, of course, to the normal pattern. Perhaps the smallest outward cargo to be carried by a Farrell ship from New York to Cape Town was the $21,400 freight list of the *African Endeavor,* which, on January 21, 1950, sailed with less than 900 tons on her third voyage.

The Farrell Executive Committee minced no words in its vigorous comments on the fact that 1950 was an unusually bad year. It was reported first that the line was operating at a loss before the subsidy was taken into account, but as the year progressed, this loss increased until even with the subsidy payments included, the story was written in red ink. It was remarked that had it not been for the West Africa service and the chartering-out, things would have been still worse. [608] That new route has been credited by some West African enthusiasts with having saved the company in those dark days. Fitting in with that, the possibility was discussed of opening an additional service from the west coast of the United States to Africa, as a possible outlet for the surplus vessels. The idea would crop up again later. [609]

With West Africa as an anchor to windward at this time, Farrell was not as thoroughly dependent upon the vagaries of South African trade conditions as was Robin. This 1950 experience demonstrated the danger of having all one's eggs in one basket. Best situated of all was the third subsidized line to South Africa; Lykes Brothers had several other services that could absorb losses from this one.

Gradually, there was partial relaxation of the ultra-rigid import restrictions; and trade conditions improved. After the heights of 1947–48 and the depths of 1950, United States exports to South and East Africa leveled off at a fairly stable amount, part way between those two extremes until a slump in 1958.

The Farrells had had some hard luck, quite beyond their control, in the timing of their acquisition of passenger ships. The depression of 1929 had broken only a few days after the *City of New York* had been launched, while the South African import restrictions were imposed within two weeks after the *African Enterprise* and *African Endeavor* were taken over from the government. They at least were to sail with full passenger lists to offset a little the cargo lack. It was, too, gratifying to all concerned to have such first-class passenger service resumed at last, more than six years after the sinking of the *City of New York* during the war.

One new element that had been coming into the ocean travel situation since the days of that pioneer liner was the competition of the airplane. The war had given a tremendous boost to trans-oceanic air travel, and as early as 1944 some of the American steamship companies were contemplating such service as soon as the war should end. Among the applicants was American South African Line which in December 1944 requested the Civil Aeronautics Board for permission to develop regular service between New York and Johannesburg via the Caribbean and West Africa. Martin Mars flying boats were to be used with accommodations for 58 persons and nine tons of mail and cargo. [610] The Civil Aeronautics Board finally decided against permitting steamship lines to operate air service and many of the best routes were awarded to Pan-American Airways. [611] This "chosen instrument" eventually began operations from New York to Johannesburg by way of the Azores, Lisbon, Dakar, Roberts Field in Liberia, and Leopoldville.

In 1950, Farrell Lines concluded an agreement with Pan-

American, whereby travelers might secure, at ten per cent discount from the regular rates, round-trip service between New York and South Africa, when going out by ship and returning by plane, or vice versa. In 1951, a similar arrangement was made with British Overseas Airways Corporation (BOAC) and with the Royal Dutch Airlines (KLM). Even with such arrangements, ships and planes continued to compete on all the major routes. The air service naturally had the tremendous asset of speed on its side, but to those travelers not pressed by the time element, ships had much to offer, well expressed by one line's slogan, "Getting there is half the fun." And in Farrell's case, plenty of people still would prefer the leisurely 17 days down through the South Atlantic, either in the comfortable luxury of the "E's" or the less expensive but also pleasant accommodations of the freighters. In 1953, for instance, about 70 per cent of the direct travel between the United States and South Africa was by sea. As compared with 404 passengers who went from the United States to South Africa by air, 1,094 traveled by sea, including 407 on the *Enterprise* or *Endeavor* and 209 on the freighters. The return pattern was similar, with 421 by air and 901 by sea, including 571 on Farrell ships. [612] By 1956, figures on a somewhat different basis show that 2,162 tourists from the United States reached South Africa by air and only 1,242 by sea. [613]

Aside from that direct travel, there was also keen competition by sea via British or Continental ports. This had the advantage of more frequent sailings and, as a particular appeal to South African travelers, it gave an opportunity for a stopover in Britain. In the travel sections of New York newspapers, for instance, one could find the rival superlatives almost alongside each other. Farrell Lines, catching the eye with the symbol of the two springboks which decorates their shipboard china, announced "No other trip in all the World Offers so Much" and then, continuing in the vein of those earlier *City of New York* brochures, "A glorious ocean passage: 17 relaxing days of sun between New York and Cape Town. . . . And then, the wonder of South Africa . . . a trip to another world." But nearby, a joint advertisement of Cunard and Union-Castle would counter with "Holiday at Sea en route to South Africa! Your holiday begins the moment you step aboard a famous Cunarder in New York, and continues for nineteen glorious days till you leave your Union-Castle liner at Cape Town. . . . What's more, you can break your journey at Southampton for a visit to Britain or the Continent if you wish. There's no finer service to the fabulous 'Land of Contrast.' " There might be frequent questioning of the accuracy of that final remark on the Blue Train from Cape Town to Johannesburg when passengers from the *African Enterprise* or *African Endeavor* compared notes on the cuisine and the spirit of the service with those who had arrived by the rival route.

By the mid-1950's, Farrell Lines became concerned at the falling-off in passenger traffic, and, as of March 1, 1956, lowered all fares $100 each way. Passage on the *Enterprise* or *Endeavor* dropped from $650 to $550, on the C-3 freighters from $500 to $400, and on the C-2 freighters (*African Dawn* and *African Sun*) from $475 to $375. At that time, first class accommodations on the Cunard-Union-Castle combination were "$574 up," and cabin class, "$423 up." The first-class air rate to New York was around $800 and the tourist rate around $625. [614]

In addition to that reduction of basic fares, the Farrell Lines at the same time announced a further 20 per cent cut for "off season" travel—March, April, and May outward to South Africa, and October, November, and December homeward. Those were the months when travel was normally light because of the reverse season pattern of winter in one region while summer in the other, and vice versa. At times, a sailing for Cape Town around the turn of the year might be booked solid a year ahead; yet, that same vessel might be returning with only two dozen or so passengers, sometimes only half the number of extra stewards carried to look out for them.

The *African Enterprise* and the *African Endeavor,* as the crack commands of the 16 Farrell ships, normally went to the two senior captains, one of whom had the title of commodore, formally created in 1950. Captain Schmidt, already noted as master of the *City of New York* and first to hold the title, began the new passenger service with the first voyage of the *Enterprise* in July 1949. [615] He soon went ashore as resident manager at Cape Town, and the title passed to Captain John G. Waller, who had commanded the second passenger voyage, with the sailing of the *Endeavor* in the late summer of 1949. Waller, an Englishman, had already served four years as a mate on British ships when he began his World War I service as a lieutenant in the Royal Naval Reserve. Coming to America, he was with the Argonaut Line and then American South African. Two ships were torpedoed under his command in World War II, it will be recalled. [616] He continued on the *Endeavor* until illness forced his retirement in 1952. The third commodore, Anders R. Mortenson, tall, red-haired, taciturn, and highly competent, was born in Sweden and started at eighteen on a Swedish square-rigger. Migrating to the United States, he served on a Maine schooner, and then shifted to steam. In 1936, he was given command of the *Sagadahoc* just in time for the second Gulf run to South Africa. That was the first of several Farrell commands; in 1950 he succeeded Schmidt on the *Enterprise* and in 1952 Waller on the *Endeavor*.

Three other prewar officers would continue into the postwar period in the line's senior group. Ole Peter Stender, born on the Danish island of Bornholm, was trained as a cadet on the government square-rigger which ultimately became the *Joseph Conrad*. As in the case of Schmidt and Mortenson, his Farrell connection started with the old Planet Line; then he became master of the *Pacific* of the Argonaut Line. [617] In 1942, bound from Cape Town for New York in the chartered *Polybius*, he was torpedoed and sailed his lifeboat to Trinidad. Round-faced and merry, he looked, as one Farrell put it, "like Santa Claus with a shave." From 1950 onward, he has been perennial master of the *African Planet*, by preference. George R. Hickey, a graduate of the Massachusetts maritime school, served as a naval officer in World War II, and then won superlatives as a cargo expert. He would serve for a while as resident manager at Monrovia. Alden G. Graham, a native of Portland, Oregon, was a sea lawyer in the best sense of the word, having his law degree from Stanford. He first came to command in World War II; and in 1952 took over the *Enterprise* from Mortenson. Along with his sea duties he wrote numerous articles.

The "E's" followed on the whole the pattern established by the *City of New York*, but with their superior speed they could make a faster turnaround. The schedule called for a sailing from New York about every forty days, and the line advertised all-expense 62-day cruises, including nearly two weeks of "overland side trip" to special points of interest. As before, the passenger liners stopped briefly at St. Helena on the outward passage. For a while, the "E's" went close enough to Ascension Island to put overboard a "Farrell barrel" filled with magazines and other reading matter for the inhabitants of that still more lonesome rock. At first, the "E's" went only as far as Lourenco Marques, but finally continued on to Beira with the clear understanding that if they encountered any serious delays, the practice would terminate. Many South Africans took advantage of the opportunity for a trip up and down the coast and were always enthusiastic over the excellent meals.

Occasional other modifications were made in the freighter schedules, largely to avoid congestion and to extend service. For a while, as the bad delays at Beira lessened, Mombasa became a similar trouble spot. In order to get the valuable coffee and sisal cargoes back to America more quickly, the East African schedule was changed. The homebound ships, instead of stopping for ore and other cargo all the way down the coast, picked up their return chrome cargo at Lourenco Marques on their way up to East Africa and then ran nonstop from the last East African stop back to Cape Town. Outside of its traditional range of ports, Madagascar was seldom visited, but over on the other side, in South West Africa, stops at Walvis Bay became more frequent, with occasional visits to Luderitz Bay as well. [618]

The 1950's saw plenty of competition on the South and East African route. The Robin Line, with its continuing hold on certain automobile exports and its vigorous traffic policies, ran at times neck and neck with Farrell. Eventually in 1956, the heirs to the line did not see fit to undertake the heavy responsibilities of a renewed subsidy contract and the line was absorbed by Moore-McCormack, which had long-standing interests in trade with South America and the Baltic. [619] The South African Marine still attracted a fair amount of trade, though it did not retain the extreme advantages it had enjoyed early in 1949 as South Africa's highly favored "chosen instrument." For a while the

French ships of Louis Dreyfus skimmed some of the cream of the East African trade, but then abandoned that for what seemed richer opportunities in tramping. A Dutch line also offered competition in East Africa, with service back to the United States by way of Suez. Gradually, the subsidized Lykes service on Route 15B from the Gulf to South Africa increased its trade considerably more than had seemed likely in 1946. With all those varied competitors, the Farrell performance fully held its own.

The year 1957 saw American commerce with Africa South of Sahara at an all-time peak, with exports and imports totally more than a billion dollars once again as in 1948. Then came one of those periodic recessions and American exports and shipping fell off around the world. The impact was especially serious for all the lines on the South African run. In particular, the four decades of American automobile primacy in South Africa since World War I ran afoul of heavy imports of the cheaper little British and German cars, a situation further complicated by the remaining import controls. Farrell and the other lines for a while curtailed their sailings on the Cape run.

Chapter XIV

TRADE PROMOTION

A FTER 30-odd years of American-flag efforts, the trade of the United States with the three ocean coasts of Africa has risen faster than with almost any other part of the world. In regions fenced off at the outset into rigid imperialistic spheres of influence, American products have been penetrating in greater and greater volume. At the same time, that much more difficult achievement, the return trade, has gradually been helping Africa to pay for those products. Some of that trade would doubtless have developed without American-flag service, as the United States and Africa became more aware of what the other had to offer, but such worthwhile results in so comparatively short a time would have been another matter. Despite what some of its critics have to say about the maritime subsidy policy, the African experience at least would seem to justify the Government's initiative in setting up "essential trade routes" and then in keeping up modest financial support of them. That support has cost less than one per cent of the billions of dollars worth of American products exported to Africa.

Tribute to the mutual benefits of that American shipping experience has come recently from two distinguished South Africans, who have had an excellent opportunity to observe its workings. Eric H. Louw, who had been South Africa's first Trade Commissioner at New York at the time the Farrells were taking over the Cape route and who eventually became Minister of External Affairs and Minister of Economic Affairs, declared "that the Farrell family have, by their initiative and enterprise, made a valuable contribution not only to the promotion of trade relations between our two countries, but also to friendly relations between our respective peoples." [620]

A more comprehensive estimate came from Michiel H. de Kock, governor of the South African Reserve Bank, in referring to the direct and indirect contribution of American-flag shipping "to the economic development of our two countries. In the first place, there were obvious economic advantages to both countries in having a direct shipping service between them. This not only saved time, but also expense and, I am sure, has led to a greater variety of each country's products being available in the other. In addition, these services do not serve the Union alone, but also other African territories, so that the Union's trade with these areas has been facilitated. . . . Directly, too, the presence of these ships in Union harbours has, of course, increased harbour income. . . ." As indirect advantages, he refers to "the attractions which the pleasant sea voyage offers" in increasing tourist traffic, which "may bring in its train" greater understanding as well as "the increase in business"; and also, to the far reaching value of the "advertising campaigns which a number of these lines, especially the Farrell Lines have undertaken." [621]

By no means the least of Farrell achievements has been that effort to make Americans conscious of Africa in general, and of its trade and investment possibilities in particular. By the mid-1950's, Africa was beginning to lose some of its mystery for the average American; and perhaps, to fascinate him even more. In that widened interest in all things African, the American-flag operators deserve much credit. It was not always so; Louw himself told of a call at his New York office in 1926 of an American businessman who sat and stared at him. "Just before leaving," said Louw, "he told me somewhat sheepishly that he had not expected me to be a white man." [622]

No small amount of Farrell advertising had been highlighted by descriptions of Africa itself and its opportunities for Americans. This emphasis gained rapid momentum in the late 1940's. The line brought out two strikingly illustrated brochures— "African Markets" and "African Resources"—with descriptions of the chief commodities of export and import. This educational advertising was carried further in a series of full pages in color each month in a Sunday magazine section of a major newspaper. Boldly designed to catch the eye, these dynamic layouts played up the exotic and amazing contradictions of today's Africa with its witch doctors and skyscrapers, along with hammering away for trade and investment. A distinctive product might be the focus point, or a glamorous port of call, and once there were lions, sitting calmly in a row watching the automobiles drive by. But above all, one sensed the vast potential strength of this awakening continent. It was good advertising and it disseminated much factual information to a wide audience.

One week, for instance, the public would be told: "In the shadow of Mount Kilimanjaro, through the fertile highlands of Kenya and Tanganyika stretch huge coffee plantations, the glossy green leaves and glistening berries shining in the hot sun. . . . Quite likely many more of Africa's fine food products have appeared on your dining table: Cape rock-lobster tails, grapes and wines from South Africa, cocoa from the Gold Coast and Ivory Coast, tea from Rhodesia and Mozambique, pungent Zanzibar cloves, cashew nuts, and exotic spices. . . . On Farrell Lines ships, dehumidifying equipment protects coffee, tea, and spices from excess moisture; fish and fruit are carried in refrigerator compartments." [623] Another time businessmen would be reminded that "South Africa is a rich market and a fine field for investment . . . profitable to investigate right on the spot," and a good trip "in our fine transatlantic liners." [624]

But it has been a slow process to divert long-standing commercial connections into new channels. Fundamentally, of course, the scheduling of regular American-flag sailings per se was the biggest impetus to promoting African trade with the United States. All four subsidized lines share the credit. The Farrell Lines, however, alone served all three ocean coasts, and made some innovations. Its record of continuous service has been the longest. The slowness in penetrating new regions was one reason why the Shipping Board had absorbed the losses during the early years of Mallory and Bull, and continued to help with subsidies, after the lines were sold into private ownership.

Even more than colonial domination and entrenched economic interests, probably the greatest single handicap under which American exports labored was the regular, frequent, and dependable steamship service of various foreign-flag lines, linking the ports of Africa and Europe. The average purchasers South of the Sahara normally followed the line of least resistance and traded with Europe. Inertia and habit would explain much of that. More than one study of American shipping, to be sure, has minimized such discrimination. [625] Yet, the evidence would tend to back the report of the United States consul at Durban in 1907 that "American cargo cannot be carried in the vessels of our strongest commercial competitors, and the United States still hope to secure the trade it should have." [626]

A by-product of the coming of the American-flag lines has been the apparent tendency toward the improvement of all steamship service on such runs. The competition stimulated the foreign-flag lines to offer better direct services than they had given previously, both to South Africa and on the west coast. There the manager of a leading American interest substantiated the changed attitude by the remark that ever since the new Farrell service had been announced, the two foreign-flag lines had been tumbling over themselves to be co-operative in place of their former indifference. [627] It had long been a byword in shipping circles that one old pioneer foreign-flag line—the name is apt to shift in the telling—always acted as though the people of Africa should constantly get down on their knees and give thanks for the comings and goings of its ships. The important aspect for American trade, of course, was that such newly expanded traffic made it all the easier to sell American goods to African markets.

From the standpoint of justifying government support of shipping, the traffic story has varied aspects. By and large, the swelling traffic on the African runs has been credited to the fact that frequent sailing and good service have made it as easy, if not easier, to import from New York as from Europe. Many of the hundreds of American-made items in the usual general export cargoes now carried from New York would in earlier days have been European. [628]

Granting that service is the first essential in attracting cargo, there are two other ways. Most obvious and constant is the scramble for freight that would probably be moving anyway by some shipping line or other carrier. That is naturally of keen importance to management, for therein lies the profit. Of more significance here and highly elusive is the indirect quest for freight through the development of new business projects or markets that might not have existed had it not been for the subsidy lines. The national economy would be just as well off whether a consignment of appliances from Dayton or St. Louis is carried to Durban by Farrell, Robin, or Lykes. But it would be a different matter if those appliances only found their African market through the imagination and persuasive efforts of the tariff experts of some particular line.

Much of the effort of the Farrell traffic force all the way from New York to Nairobi has been directed toward the search for additional outlets for new as well as current commodities. The offices of the representatives in Africa have been flooded with catalogues from American firms with requests about African markets for their goods, which the traffic staff try to find. On their own initiative, too, they scout out the possibilities of developing special projects. They keep in frequent contact with the line's shippers and consignees, as do the representatives at the regional offices in the United States. [629]

In this connection, the traffic personnel of all 14 of the subsidized lines made 1,069,000 personal visits or telephone contacts in the interests of trade promotion in 1957. These lines, moreover, spent more than $14 million in promoting foreign trade between the United States and the 423 foreign ports they serve in 102 countries. [630]

A recent case of Farrell initiative concerned the railroads in South Africa, where for years the well-entrenched British had enjoyed the lion's share of sales, as in mining and other fields, and the American part had been relatively slight. By the mid-1950's, the government-owned South African Railways still used mostly coal-burning locomotives, some 2,800 of them on its 13,000 miles of roadbed, of which a scant 800 were electrified. For years, Clifford Shields and other Farrell officials had been pointing out to the South Africans the advantages of diesel locomotives, especially for barren regions devoid of coal and water. When South Africa sent out its railway mission in 1956 to study the situation in various foreign countries, Farrell Lines went out of their way to facilitate their contacts in the United States.

The Mission was "impressed, if not overawed" by what they saw in the American plants. At any rate, they recommended the purchase of 50 diesel-electric locomotives. In this, the Farrells had an extra interest, of course, because speeding-up of the railway service was such a vital answer to African port congestion. They next took the initiative in arranging reduced freight rates to enable the manufacturers to compete in price with the British and Germans.

General Electric received a contract for 45 of the diesel-electric locomotives, at about $8 million including spare parts. Thirty of the railroad's experts came over to supervise the building and get some preliminary training in operation. "If we . . . can be of any help to your group, please do not fail to let me know" wrote one Farrell vice-president. The first two were carried out by the *African Dawn* at the special rate of about $12,500, and others followed. As usual in such orders, Robin Line got a share of the business, as did Safmarine. In fact, the whole shipment, being government-controlled, might have been required to go under the South African flag. Later in the year, a further order for 115 diesel locomotives for use in South West Africa also went to General Electric after competition with 28 other bidders. [631]

The Farrell Lines wanted to introduce American locomotives in Rhodesia's overtaxed railways, too. There, colonial controls had remained much stronger; so it was not surprising that most of the diesels came from Britain. Farrell had a hand, however, in arranging that General Motors send out two on approval, with reduced freight rates.

Along with this diesel engine promotion went certain movements of American capital investment. The Wall Street firm of Dillon, Read was floating a $15 million bond issue earmarked for transportation development in the Union of South Africa. [632] Considerable American capital from one source or another had already gone into the improvement of the Rhodesian railways. [633]

That rapidly increasing investment of American capital in Africa was part, but only part, of the story of the even faster growth of commerce and shipping between the United States and Africa. The value of the American exports alone to South Africa in the one year 1957 was equal, for example, to the total permanent American capital investment of $300 million in South Africa. The two were sufficiently interdependent to explain the interest of the shipping lines in stimulating such investment, but their trade was by no means dependent upon it.

Large-scale American investment in Africa went back to the mid-1920's when the Farrells were entering the trade. Some of the ventures were associated with American exports, through the assembling, processing or distribution of American products, whether automobiles, tires, harvesting machines, petroleum, or soft drinks. The rest represented projects for developing products for importation, such as rubber, coffee, and minerals. The rate of American investment accelerated rapidly after World War II. Up to 1939, Britain and the United States each had about equal net investments in outside countries; after the war, the British owed the outside world more than it owed them, whereas United States foreign investments were steadily increasing. In 1954, the Department of Commerce brought out an elaborate brochure on investment opportunities in South Africa. [634] Between 1950 and 1955, such investments jumped from $140 to 257 millions, and two years later had gone on to about 300 millions. [635]

Liberia, the only other African region differentiated in the official figures, showed an even sharper rate of increase, with the investments there jumping between 1950 and 1955 from $82 to 261 millions. [636] It was incidentally the only region where Farrell Lines made any outside investments, and those were relatively small. They held $25,000 worth of the stock of the Monrovia Port Management Company, and participated actively in its direction. They invested a similar amount in the American-owned Liberia Mining Company. The major Farrell investment, however, was the million dollars, more or less, in their shore establishment at Monrovia and their feeder service from there to the Firestone plantations at Harbel. This venture was of mutual advantage to the Farrells and to the Firestone establishment, which was the largest concentration of American investment in that area. [637]

In Ghana, the principal manganese mine, "the largest producer in the world," and the ore-loading pier at Takoradi are owned by an American firm. The Congo, as already mentioned, is controlled by a few great Belgian corporations, with only one wholly American-owned company and a total of about $20 million American investments.

In South Africa, American capital has gone primarily into utilizing the Union's industry to complete the processing of American export products. In 1954, for example, there were 56 such plants of varying size with seniority going to seven automobile assembly plants, and the rest in seven major categories, ranging from a $20 million oil refinery near Durban down to plants which produced tooth paste, shaving cream, and soft drinks under American names. There was a relationship of mutual advantage between these firms and the steamship lines. The constant shipments of knocked-down automobiles, empty Pepsi-Cola bottles, and so on meant steady business for the lines. At the same time, the efficient operation of those African plants was dependent upon the regular arrival of those cargo liners.

The mining industry of South Africa, which had long been its economic mainstay under strong British control, finally began to feel the impact of American capital. By the mid-1950's, Americans had purchased numerous mining activities, ranging from copper, chrome, and manganese to gold, diamonds and platinum. [638] In 1958, Charles W. Engelhard of New Jersey, owner of various plants in America engaged in refining precious metals and making precision machinery, organized the "American-South African Investment Trust," formed to give Americans an opportunity to invest in South African gold mining companies and, to a lesser extent, in industrial shares and gold bullion. In connection with Dillon, Read, an initial investment of $30 million was oversubscribed. Similar extension of American holdings was going on in Rhodesia. [639] One could assume that much of the equipment for those mines would be brought by sea from

America, and that a good share of the minerals extracted would return thither.

To the average rural South Africans, there was something very remote about those big corporations and their minerals. They were more receptive, it was found, to the purchase of American products when the United States was buying their wool. [640] Now, the Farrells made some special arrangements to open an American market for the products of Cape Province, in hopes of boosting the sales of American manufacturers.

Although nearly nine-tenths of South Africa is not arable and three-quarters of the region has a rainfall of less than 25 inches a year, Cape Province is the exception. From early Boer days, grapes and other fruits have been raised there, with wine, brandy, and other liquors as by-products. Dried fruit was gradually exported in modest amounts, along with some of the wine. Farrell ships sometimes carried these products to Trinidad or Canada, but very seldom to the United States.

The fact that it is summer in South Africa when it is winter in Europe and North America suggested the possibility of getting larger profits from shipping fresh fruit to those regions out of their seasons. Sir Donald Currie, founder of the Castle Line, had experimented with refrigeration on his ships. The first grapes attempted in 1889 spoiled, but by 1892 Cape peaches were being sold in London. Thereafter, both Union and Castle steamers carried modest amounts "practically for nothing" in order to stimulate the trade, which ultimately developed to very substantial proportions. [641]

Once the westbound sailings on the Cape Town-New York run became general after World War I, the South Africans saw similar possibilities in the United States, but nothing happened for another ten years. [642] Then in 1936 American South African provided its first refrigerated space with 4,000 cubic feet (100 tons) on the *City of New York*. Thereupon, the Co-operative Winegrowers' Association (KWV) of Cape Province decided to try out the American market with wine and fruit. The first shipment came to grief. The chairman of "KWV" had neglected to check on the United States regulations for such imports. The wine was not properly labeled, and the Agriculture Department's protectionist precautions against the fruit fly called for such a long period of cold storage that the fruit was apt to be damaged. Instead of admitting that he had failed to find out those regulations in advance, the chairman called for a boycott of American manufactures, which developed an alarming following among the farmers of the Western Cape Province. [643] There was even an agitation for a punitive 25 per cent import duty on American products. As one South African official said later with gusto in describing this episode, "We may be a small nation, but no one is going to push us around."

The situation obviously had bad implications beyond the mere shipment of wine and grapes, for this was the flood tide of South Africa's prewar purchasing of American goods. [644] The unfortunate angle was that the United States imports from South Africa were at a very low level, far below Britain's purchasing. The British journal devoted to the South African market took full advantage of this, declaring that it was inevitable that the South African farmer who bought much of his equipment from the United States should be "painfully alive to the anomaly" that the products raised with the help of that equipment were refused a market in the United States. As a result of this "most glaring example of one-way trade," the journal predicted hopefully that South Africa was likely to turn from America to Britain for its agricultural implements and automobiles. [645]

The Farrells immediately became leaders in organizing a South African Reciprocal Trade Committee. In its name, they went to Washington, where the Department of Agriculture eventually agreed to modify its ban on South African fruit, provided it would be marketed only in the off-season. On May 5, 1937, James Farrell, Jr., presided at a luncheon of this committee at India House in New York to celebrate the arrival of the first shipment of 5,000 cases of grapes. A spokesman from Cape Town declared that the hostile attitude toward American goods had been completely reversed. [646] Had shipping contacts with Africa been dependent upon foreign-flag lines, it is highly doubtful if they would have gone to such lengths to save the market for American exports. Here, as in 1949 when South Africa imposed

its drastic import controls, "enlightened self-interest" led the
subsidy lines, with their well-established contacts to combat the
threat both to their own freight earnings and the sale of American manufactures. [647]

The importation was interrupted by the war, but early in
1946 the *African Dawn* brought over 5,300 cases of fresh grapes.
That July, the line signed a five-year agreement with the South
African Perishable Products Export Control to place 1,100
measurement tons (44,000 cubic feet) of refrigerated space at
its disposal monthly. [648] This was a welcome new device which
left to the South Africans, rather than to the line, the delicate
question of deciding how much of the line's precious "reefer"
space would be given to fruit and how much to the rapidly increasing rock-lobster shipments. The fresh fruit imports continued thereafter on a modest scale during the appropriate season. The refrigeration aboard ship for this delicate cargo had
to be kept between 30 and 40 degrees, and extreme care had to
be taken in loading and unloading. Because California and Florida fruit is available much of the year in America, South African
fruit has enjoyed much less seasonal advantage than in Britain.
American production was even more of an obstacle to South
African wines. One further modest agricultural product traveled
in refrigerated space just before the Christmas season—a cut
flower with tiny white blossoms, the chincherinchee or Star of
Bethlehem, which stays fresh for weeks.

Those relatively small shipments with their difficult requirements would probably not have seemed worth the bother as a
purely business proposition, but they were not an end in themselves. They helped make an important section of the Union
more receptive to American products,

Far more lucrative was the other cargo from that same Cape
Town region which was developing about the same time. Frozen
rock lobster, or crayfish, have been perhaps the most spectacular
instance of Farrell trade promotion. By providing refrigerated
space of deep-freeze temperature from Cape Town to New York,
the line made possible a trade which jumped in value in a quarter century from $200 a year to some eight millions, almost ex-

actly equal to the cost of those 45 diesel locomotives, which were moving in the opposite direction in 1958.

These crustaceans came from the cold waters of the Antarctic currents around the Cape of Good Hope, and this gave them a sweeter flavor and more tang than similar crayfish from other parts of the world. They differed from the "down east" American lobsters in having merely a few feelers instead of big claws. As early as 1874, an enterprising South African captain set up a cannery. By 1890, there were three such plants in Cape Town, which provided a modest output for export. The product went principally to France, with a small amount to the United States. [649]

By the mid-1930's, John M. Stubbs, son of an English fish dealer who had migrated to the Cape, decided that frozen lobster tails would be much more of a delicacy than the tinned products, and would yield a greater profit. Utilizing the newly installed refrigerated space on the *City of New York,* he began shipping them to New York. Stubbs himself more than once came over to the United States to organize the sales promotion, which he placed in the hands of Richard Kulze, a New York lawyer specializing in international trade. Those two men would still be handling their respective ends of the business more than twenty years later.

The success was immediate. In 1934, South Africa sent the United States only $200 worth of frozen lobster, transshipped at Southampton, as against $4,100 worth of the canned. In 1936, the frozen exports rose to $101,000; in 1937, to $349,000; and by 1941, $428,000, while the canned shipments trailed far behind at $14,000, $33,000, and $13,000 respectively. The business gradually outstripped the capacity of the *City of New York.* To provide more frequent service, the Farrells equipped three of their freighters with "reefer" space as well.

Stubbs managed to keep the exports to the United States going throughout World War II, though the shipments fell as low as $75,000 in the worst year. He had cause to appreciate the convenience of the prewar line service when refrigerated space became short in those war years. His most trying experience came one hot day when he went down to the dock to supervise the loading aboard a Dutch ship for New York, on which he had been promised "reefer" space. To his dismay, he found his cases of frozen lobster lying in the sun, while the refrigerated compartment was being filled with cases of gold by a force of soldiers. The lieutenant in charge was stubborn; Stubbs rushed up to the Castle and only in the nick of time could he persuade the Commandant to let him have his "reefer" space.

The Farrells, as already noted, had those lobster shipments in mind when they designed their new freighters during and after the war—eight of them each had more than 20,000 cubic feet of "reefer" space—about five times as much as the prewar freighters. Special techniques were developed both at Cape Town and at Brooklyn for efficient handling of the frozen tails, packed in 24-pound cases. They paid about four cents a pound, or $50 a measurement ton freight. [650] Although this was a much higher rate than most of the homeward cargo, it was not all clear gain; in addition to the expensive equipment and extra care, there was little use for the refrigerated space on the outward voyage. Profitable or not, the Farrells did well by the lobsters; Kulze could report in 1958 that in more than two decades, there had not been a single case of damage in transit. Even when the *African Star* lay partly submerged after a collision in New York Harbor, with its power dead for more than forty hours, the lobsters were found to be in perfect condition.

The rock-lobster business flourished more than ever in the postwar years, reaching the million dollar level in 1946 and then climbing steadily to several times that amount. Thanks to the aggressive sales organization under Kulze in New York, which launched a very ambitious advertising program, "South African Rock Lobster Tails" found their way into menus and kitchens all over the country except northeast New England. The State of Maine strenuously resisted this foreign competition to its "real" two-clawed lobsters. In 1941, its legislature declared that "No person, firm, or corporation shall sell or transport for sale within the state African crawfish, so called, in any form." Later, the word African was omitted because crayfish were coming in from other countries also. Massachusetts passed a similar law. [651] In 1951, the Maine delegation in Congress introduced bills in the Senate and House aimed to limit the use of the word "lobster" to the *Homarus americanus,* found in North Atlantic waters from Labrador to Hatteras. [652] The measure did not pass, nor did a similar effort in 1958. [653] On the latter occasion, Clifford Shields explained the continuing interest of Farrell Lines in the broader aspects of the lobster imports: "If we destroy the source of dollars provided by shipments of South African rock lobster to the United States, the South African public may rise up—as it did once before, when we prohibited the import of South African grapes—and campaign publicly against the importation of American goods. . . . We cannot reduce South Africa's dollar earnings without, almost automatically, reducing South Africa's dollar purchases." [654] Rock lobster continued to arrive in Farrell and Robin ships, and to be advertised and sold as such, except "down east" where an occasional grocer would be hauled into court for trying to sell "crawfish." [655]

The Farrell brothers have regarded their passenger liners as potential instruments of trade promotion, as their advertisements indicate, with the suggestion constantly running through them that business and pleasure be combined in a trip to South and East Africa. One of the outstanding exponents of that practice has been E. Winthrop Hall, president of F. J. and J. C. Codman Company of Rockland, Massachusetts, manufacturers of buffing and polishing wheels. Around 1950, he began to use Farrell ships in what expanded into a triple role of exporter, importer, and passenger. South Africa was selected for his company's introduction to the exporting field because it appeared to be the "fastest-growing nation in the world at that time." He used the Farrell Lines first because of "the ad in the *New York Times.*" [656] Visiting Johannesburg and other industrial centers, he found ample use for the buffing and polishing equipment by the manufacturers of steel, tinplate, knives and forks, kerosene heaters and cast-iron stoves for the native trade, and also in the automobile assembly plants. In particular, the buffing tools were useful in shining up the large amount of chrome which the natives insisted upon in their bicycles. Orginally the company had used sisal from Yucatan, but later Hall began to extend his trips up to British East Africa and turned to its sisal as well. These business trips were usually fitted in between the arrival of the *African Enterprise* or *African Endeavor* at Cape Town and its departure thence after going up the coast and back. Describing his habit of regular trips there for six years, in Farrell ships, he wrote in 1957 how those ships "have the comforts and fine appointments of big liners with the pleasant intimacy of a yacht." Consequently, he finds that the "leisurely 17-day crossing goes by almost too fast." The people whom he has met aboard have meant "some lasting friendships and in some cases extremely helpful business contacts with African companies." [657]

Testimonials to Farrell cargo service as well as to the amenities of life aboard their ships could be produced by the dozen. There has been a general appreciation of what the comings and goings of their ships have meant, in African as well as in American industrial and business circles. In 1948, as will be recalled, the review by the Executive Committee of the first year of West African service pointed out the enthusiastic support and welcome from all American exporters and importers. [658]

The relative success of the nation's maritime policy may be judged in part by the extent to which the merchant marine has stimulated new sales of American products abroad. From the days of the mercantilists centuries ago, nations have sought a "favorable balance of trade," selling more than they bought in overseas commerce.

The trade with South and East Africa has been particularly valuable in that respect. In the first three Farrell decades, 1925–1955, American exports thither rose from $55 to $295 million a year. That 530 per cent rate of increase was far ahead of the 320 per cent rise for the nation's exports as a whole. What was more, the South and East Africans have been "cash customers," able to pay for virtually all that was shipped to them, whereas a very large part of the nation's overseas shipments during the latter half of the 30-year period have been given away to other nations under Lend Lease, Marshall Plan, Economic Co-operation, or other generous free programs. At the outset, the large proportion of British-flag ships on the run coincided with Britain's large share of South Africa's commerce. Eventually the American share of that commerce began to approach, and in the years 1947 and 1948 even exceeded the traditional British share. There is an apparent link between that achievement and the fact that a larger proportion of United States exports on that run move in American-flag vessels than to any of the other 17 major trade areas. On the South and East African run, in 1957, 71 per cent of the exports were carried in American bottoms whereas for all the sea routes the average was only 17 per cent.

There was also a respectable record on the West African run. In that same 1925–55 period, American exports to West Africa rose from 18 to 141 millions a year, a gain of 783 per cent. Imports, the more distinctive feature of that trade, jumped 1515 per cent, from $21 to 323 million. In the matter of the American-flag share of the export tonnage in 1957, the West African run, at 33 per cent, was in third place among all the routes.

A further encouraging aspect of the export trade with Africa was its marked acceleration in the postwar years. Between 1950 and 1955 its 64 per cent increase was well ahead of any other region, with the rate to Europe next at 41 per cent and with the old favorite, Latin America, at only 18 per cent. It is small wonder that the Farrell Lines remarked in 1950: that an "unbiased view confirms that at present, in the 25 years past, and in the foreseeable future, no trade routes based on the United States were or are any more secure, more essential, or offer anything like the growth possibilities of our established routes." [659]

The government has aided the African services most of the time since World War I, paying some $70 million. That was about one per cent of the almost $7 billion worth of American exports shipped out on those African essential routes during that period. In the case of the Farrell services, they received in all $28,793,000 for the whole period 1926–55: $125,000 for mail contracts under the 1920 act, $2,358,000 under the 1928 Jones-White Act, and a net $26,309,000 in operating-differential subsidies under the 1936 act. The total accrued amount was reduced by the "recapture" of $1,400,000 because of profits over ten per cent in certain years. The original $17-odd million in construction-differential subsidies were canceled by other items. Those payments had at times made the difference between profit and loss.

During its shorter period of operation, the Robin Line had received a net $15.6 million in operating-differential and a net 4.9 millions in construction-differential contracts. For their post-war periods of service from the Gulf, Lykes and Mississippi (Delta) received smaller amounts, merged in the totals with payments for their other services, while Barber had received some Jones-White mail contract payments during a decade of early West African service.

Those maritime payments fade into insignificance alongside what the government has been pouring out in agricultural subsidies in a similar period. In the year 1956 alone, the Soil Bank payments for *not* raising crops came to $242 millions, with the single state of Iowa receiving twice as much as the 30 years of subsidies to Farrell Lines. [660]

The tangible results of the operating- and construction-differential subsidies, on the other hand, were decidedly impressive. On the subsidized lines, nearly 300 cargo or passenger liners were making, in the mid-1950's, about 1,500 voyages a year, visiting most of the worthwhile ports of the world with service that was regular, frequent, and dependable.

American shipping policy was strongly attacked in 1956 in a study sponsored by the Council of Foreign Relations. The author presented a strongly international point of view, based on the fact that foreign shipping can operate more cheaply and contributes to the foreign economies, so its use would relieve the United States of some of its foreign aid obligations. His particular propositions were that "cargo-preference legislation should be repealed"; that "attempts should be made to open the coasting trades to foreign-flag vessels"; that the "United States merchant fleet should be internationalized to the fullest extent consonant with mutual military necessity"; and that "shipbuilding activity should be maintained at the lowest level consonant with adequate national defense." [661]

In rebuttal, the shipping industry and the Maritime Administration came up with some significant figures. The American merchant marine was contributing about $5.3 billion to the

United States economy a year. It was creating jobs for 225,000 persons, including 70,000 aboard its ships, 90,000 in shoreside work including stevedoring, and 65,000 in shipyards. [662]

The most surprising feature of this research was the argument that the maritime subsidies were really little, if any, burden to the taxpayer, because the subsidized shipping generated taxes that more than offset the actual subsidy outlay. It was estimated that during the 20-year period of the 1936 subsidy program, federal income taxes from the contract lines came to $172 million, with 140 millions from the seagoing personnel and 110 millions from shoreside personnel and labor, making a total of 422 millions. If the taxes paid by allied industries such as ship repair yards and ship suppliers were included, they "would probably show that the government is earning more in taxes from the shipping industry than it is paying out in contracts to shipping companies." [663]

The whole question was an important one at the time because most of the operating-differential contracts would be coming up for renewal in the near future. This presented every company with a major decision. However desirable their business might seem at the moment, they had to commit themselves to maintain the service "for better or for worse" for two whole decades. What was more, they would have to agree to replace their entire fleets, for their C-2's, C-3's and passenger liners were gradually approaching maximum active age. Nevertheless, nearly all the lines made new contracts with the Federal Maritime Board.

The Robin Line was one of the few exceptions. It gave up its 22-year independent career early in 1957, as already mentioned, to become part of one of the largest subsidized lines, Moore-McCormack. Robin having been a closely held family concern, similar to Farrell and Lykes, the death of the younger Arthur Lewis left no relatives interested in continuing the service.

The Federal Maritime Board on April 25, 1957 approved the transfer of its subsidy on the South and East African run to the new owner. Moore-McCormack agreed to build eight new ships for its "Robin Line Division." The selling price was $17 million, about half in stock and the rest in cash and mortgages. Moore-McCormack had just acquired some surplus freighters in absorbing the Pacific-Argentine-Brazil Line with which it had been double tracked; consequently it sold off some of the twelve Robin ships. These two "Moore-Mac" acquisitions reduced the number of subsidized operators to fourteen. [664]

Farrell Lines were now the sole survivor of the old steamship competition of twenty years earlier on the New York-South African run. The British lines, as already noted, had gradually suspended regular service after the 1949 slump. The German Hansa Line went with the war. Their names still remained as nonvoting members but Farrell Lines alone was an active member of the old United States-South African conference.

That spring of 1957 brought rumors along Shipping Row that Farrell Lines were also about to sell out to another major company. Beaver Street decided that it would be well to scotch such speculations with a brief advertisement on the shipping pages of the New York newspapers. It called attention to the fact that it was "a privately owned American-flag steamship company devoting all effort to the development of African trade and travel," and concluded with a list of the seven directors with the three family members in the top row.

For months thereafter, Beaver Street was to weigh the relative advantages, however, of renewing the contract or selling the line. The circumstances were unique in the 32 years of the company's history. At the expiration of the contract, the Farrells would be free agents under no obligation to the government. They had built up a valuable fleet, and for the second time in the line's history, it was completely out of debt. In the boom influence following the Suez crisis, moreover, they could sell the fleet at a figure several times the amount paid recently for the Robin Line. There was, of course, a calculated risk in going on. There might be more bad years like 1932 and 1950, yet the contract would require a minimum number of voyages, "full or not full." It would also require the replacement of the fleet at a heavy cost. If the Farrell brothers, the principal shareholders, were interested in cash alone, the opportunity was a rich one, of a sort that did not come often in the shipping business. Money, however, was not the only consideration. Their services to South,

East, and West Africa, now so closely associated with the family name, were an achievement of which they were proud, and would like to see continued. All through the summer and autumn months, they explored every angle of the situation. There were continued negotiations with the Maritime Administration over the terms of new operating and construction-differential contracts and details of new ships involved, should the firm decide to sign up again.

The momentus question of going on or selling out was finally threshed out in an all-day session in a private room at the University Club on November 25, 1957. The seven men participating represented "the principal stockholders and the management of the line in their various capacities." In addition to the Farrell brothers and their brother-in-law Joseph B. Murray, it included Wauchope and Lewis from the Executive Committee; Donald D. Geary, the general counsel; and his law partner, H. Maurice Fridlund, a tax expert. James Farrell opened the session with a statement setting forth the purpose and scope of the meeting, calling particular attention to "the financial exposure of the venture" and "the advisability of investing the Company's funds in a twenty-year program versus liquidation or sale." Geary outlined the new contract, which was discussed point by point. Then, after lunch, Lewis reviewed the financial implications of the proposed commitments, and Wauchope discussed the proposed new ships. Then came "considerable additional discussion," in the course of which it was estimated that the trade with Africa would probably increase 15 per cent in the first decade of the contract and around ten in the second ten years. Finally came the unanimous agreement that the line should go ahead. [665]

The new operating-differential contract was signed with the Federal Maritime Board on December 16, 1957 to continue service on Trade Route 15A to South and East Africa until December 31, 1979. This involved an agreement to replace their whole 16-ship fleet during the course of the contract. The total cost of such a program would cost the line some $96 million. The line's conservative policy of plowing most of its profits into reserves, year after year, put them in a position to undertake such an ambitious program. That, of course, was one of the purposes of the 1936 legislation.

The company agreed to contract by September 30, 1959 for five new ships, to be somewhat larger, considerably faster, and very much more expensive than the present excellent C-3's. The rest of the freighters would come along with successive contracts—three each by 1963, 1964 and 1966, with the remaining two by 1968. These new ships would be placed on the "main line" to South Africa, relieving C-3's for the West African run, where the C-2's could be gradually retired.

The cost of ships had been going up steadily, much faster than freight income, since 1926 when the nucleus of the "first fleet" had cost only $18.10 a dead-weight ton, secondhand. The new C-3's of the "second fleet" twenty years later had cost the line and the government each around $165 a ton, thanks to construction-differential subsidies. This "third fleet" was expected to cost a great deal more than that.

In a statement at the time, the Farrell brothers declared that their signing of the contract was "an expression of faith on the part of our company that through the co-operative efforts of private American shipping and the Government of the United States, within the framework of the shipping laws, a strong American merchant marine can be maintained. The cargoes that our ships are bringing into the United States are of growing importance and the cargoes that we are carrying to the continent of Africa are helping to build that area and to increase its wealth and ability to continue to trade profitably with us. We have not yet even scratched the surface of the potential that the trade and commerce between Africa and the United States could achieve to the mutual benefit of both areas. Africa is an awakening giant that needs more of the things that America can supply in abundance." Neither the sharp decline on the Cape run in 1958 nor the spreading political ferment throughout Africa shook that faith.

And they still believed, as each had expressed it on more than one occasion, "We have our ambitions, but we do not seek to be the biggest American-flag steamship company. We want a balanced business and to be considered among the best." [666]

APPENDIX A

U. S. COMMERCE WITH AFRICA SOUTH OF SAHARA, 1913-1957
GRAND TOTALS

| | Millions of Dollars | | | Exports from U. S.; Imports into U. S. | | | | | |
| | South of Sahara | | | South & East Africa | | | West Africa | | |
	Tot.	Exp.	Imp.	Tot.	Exp.	Imp.	Tot.	Exp.	Imp.
1913	28	23	5	21	17	4	7	6	.7
1914	27	23	3	20	17	2	7	6	.9
1915	36	24	12	28	17	10	7	6	1
1916	63	34	28	46	26	19	17	8	9
1917	80	37	42	56	29	27	23	8	15
1918	100	46	53	73	36	37	26	10	15
1919	174	106	68	90	50	40	83	55	27
1920	150	102	47	99	70	29	50	32	18
1921	60	43	16	39	29	9	20	14	6
1922	64	36	27	40	25	14	24	11	12
1923	91	46	45	51	33	18	40	13	27
1924	96	56	40	57	42	14	39	14	25
1925	120	73	47	81	55	26	39	18	20
1926	139	82	57	94	60	33	45	21	23
1927	140	85	54	74	62	11	65	23	42
1928	137	93	64	84	69	15	74	23	49
1929	162	100	61	93	75	17	69	24	44
1930	118	70	48	60	49	10	58	20	37
1931	73	47	26	43	35	8	30	12	17
1932	45	28	17	25	19	5	20	8	11
1933	53	33	19	33	25	7	20	7	12
1934	84	63	21	61	53	8	22	10	12
1935	102	74	28	69	61	8	32	13	19
1936	132	95	36	93	80	13	38	15	23
1937	196	127	68	128	103	24	68	24	44
1938	147	103	43	108	81	26	38	21	17
1939	159	95	64	121	80	40	38	14	24
1940	256	135	121	188	122	66	67	13	54
1941	381	235	146	288	204	84	92	30	61
1942	341	163	178	241	120	121	100	43	57
1943	487	302	184	313	201	111	174	100	73
1944	428	223	205	282	168	113	146	54	91
1945	463	213	249	298	153	144	165	59	105
1946	607	336	270	442	264	177	163	72	90
1947	917	637	280	622	487	135	294	149	145
1948	1012	657	355	706	539	166	306	117	188
1949	767	467	300	463	306	157	303	161	142
1950	664	258	405	345	143	201	319	115	204
1951	921	418	502	497	279	217	423	138	285
1952	900	403	496	456	249	207	443	154	288
1953	861	367	493	441	242	199	419	125	293
1954	954	444	509	436	261	174	517	183	334
1955	968	435	531	503	295	208	464	141	383
1956	987	463	524	584	295	198	493	167	326
1957	1064	531	533	556	326	229	508	204	303

Compiled from annual reports of *Foreign Commerce and Navigation of the United States* through 1946; thereafter from *U. S. Exports of Domestic and Foreign Merchandise: Commodity by Country of Destination* (FT 410,420) and *U. S. Imports of Merchandise for Consumption: Commodity by Country of Origin* (FT 110, 120). Same sources for next two Appendix tables.

Total Belgian Congo commerce included under West Africa though a minor part of it moved through ports of South and East Africa.

APPENDIX B

U. S. COMMERCE WITH SOUTH AND EAST AFRICA, 1913-1957
BY PRINCIPAL AND DISTINCTIVE COMMODITIES
In Millions of Dollars; Amounts under $100,000 not recorded here

	Exports from U. S.						Imports into U. S.								
	Automobiles & Parts	Lubricating Oil	Iron & Steel Manufactures	Agricultural Machinery & Implements	Mining & Construction Machinery	Cotton Manufactures	Wool	Hides, Skins & Furs	Wattle & Mangrove Bark & Extract	Copper	Chrome	Other Non-Precious Minerals	Sisal	Coffee	Lobster
1913	1.2	.6	4.1	1.2	.9	1.1			.1	.4	.3				
1914	1.6	.7	4.8	1.4	.9	.6	.1		.1		.3				
1915	.9	.6	2.9	2.9	.9	.5	3.6		1.8		.2				
1916	2.6	.9	4.3	.9	.7	1.5	14.3	.5	1.0	1.3	.1				
1917	2.9	1.3	5.2	1.1	.7	1.9	10.7	.2	.7	1.7	.9	.1			
1918	1.6	1.8	8.8	1.1	1.7	2.8	29.5		.1	4.9		.4			
1919	4.5	1.2	15.1	1.5	1.0	2.8	28.2	5.8	.8	1.4					
1920	10.7	2.8	16.0	1.9	.7	3.8	11.1	5.2	1.2	1.3	.3	.2	.1	.1	
1921	1.4	2.0	8.4	1.3	.8	1.2	4.1	.8	.3	1.4		.2	.3		
1922	2.4	1.4	1.7	.4	.5	2.2	3.9	.9	.2	6.6	.3		.1		
1923	5.1	1.8	2.5	.8	1.2	2.5	6.7	1.5	.5	2.5	.5	.3	.6		
1924	3.7	2.6	2.9	7.0	1.4	3.1	3.0	.8	.2	4.3	.5	.5	.9		
1925	9.3	2.2	2.5	8.2	1.4	4.0	4.2	2.7	.3	12.7	.7	.7	.8		
1926	15.6	2.3	2.9	3.3	2.0	4.3	6.9	2.7	.6	16.9	.8	.9	.5		
1927	19.0	2.3	3.0	4.7	2.2	4.0	2.5	2.8	.6	2.7	.8	.9	.1		
1928	21.6	2.4	2.5	6.6	2.2	3.8	2.3	3.2	.8	2.5	.8	2.1	1.0	.1	
1929	20.7	2.4	3.0	6.6	2.0	3.6	1.7	4.6	.3	1.4	1.2	2.5	1.4	.5	
1930	8.8	1.7	2.1	2.8	2.3	2.4	1.3	2.4	.2		1.3	.8	.9	.1	
1931	6.5	1.0	1.3	1.1	1.9	1.7	.4	2.0		1.3	1.1	.1	.2	.3	
1932	3.0	.6	.6	.7	.7	1.0	.2	.4		1.4	.3	.1	.4	.7	
1933	6.2	1.5	1.1	.8	1.1	.6	.4	1.5		1.8	.1	.2	.6	.5	
1934	18.7	1.8	2.4	3.3	2.3	.7	.2	1.3	.1	2.2	.7	.6	.4	.3	
1935	23.3	2.0	3.5	2.8	2.4	.7	.1	1.4	.4	.2	1.5	.8	.8	1.0	
1936	27.4	2.0	5.1	3.8	2.9	.8	1.1	2.2	.5		2.0	.7	2.1	1.7	.1
1937	31.6	3.4	10.5	5.0	5.1	1.5	1.6	3.0	.5	.6	4.1	1.3	1.8	1.6	.3
1938	12.8	2.3	6.0	3.7	5.4	1.5	.2	3.0	.2	1.2	2.6	1.1	2.4	1.5	.2
1939	19.9	3.6	6.8	2.5	3.8	1.7	2.3	4.9	.4	5.6	.7	1.4	1.1	1.4	.3
1940	18.8	6.1	23.5	3.9	4.6	5.4	7.6	10.9	.4	6.1	3.6	10.1	1.7	.2	.4
1941	28.5	5.0	31.8	5.1	4.7	9.0	11.4	18.3	1.0	19.9	6.5	7.1	1.0	1.8	.2
1942	6.5	3.6	18.5	1.6	1.6	3.8	40.3	12.4	1.5	2.6	6.4	10.6	7.1	1.7	.1
1943	7.5	3.6	15.0	3.8	3.0	6.0	12.0	11.2	.9	1.5	4.9	8.8	8.5		.1
1944	9.4	6.3	25.6	6.1	2.3	11.5	7.6	5.6	1.1	.1	3.0	5.0	8.4		
1945	5.3	4.5	23.8	7.9	3.3	17.7	13.6	11.9	2.5	21.2	4.0	5.2	10.1		.1
1946	29.0	5.5	18.2	7.5	4.8	32.7	36.4	26.0	2.4	4.1	3.9	15.0	3.9		1.1
1947	69.7	11.8	35.6	18.7	14.6	95.2	18.3	20.8	2.8	5.7	3.3	8.9	6.0	.1	2.2
1948	21.4	10.5	36.5	33.5	16.6	21.0	19.3	10.9	3.9	8.9	4.1	10.1	5.1	.9	2.4
1949	21.3	6.2	36.0	33.2	22.1	21.1	18.9	19.1	6.6	13.5	7.8	26.5	15.3	.9	2.2
1950	17.2	3.9	12.4	13.3	8.7	6.4	16.9	16.2	2.4	21.1	6.9	26.2	5.0	11.6	3.8
1951	32.1	6.6	19.0	23.4	12.4	34.9	60.0	18.3	3.5	35.0	6.6	38.2	18.1	11.7	4.8
1952	25.0	7.4	18.7	19.5	17.4	.1	33.2	13.6	8.5	25.4	5.5	31.2	33.5	13.4	5.2
1953	22.4	2.1	18.8	21.0	15.8	9.1	17.5	10.2	4.3	55.9	16.7	24.8	20.6	9.2	6.6
1954	26.6	5.6	21.5	18.1	11.1	14.7	20.4	8.5	1.8	46.1	6.9	39.3	11.2	19.1	4.1
1955	51.9	5.9	20.8	23.8	15.7	20.0	20.8	7.2	1.4	59.5	15.0	24.0	6.0	31.1	6.1
1956	50.7	5.2	19.2	17.3	19.7	13.5	14.2	7.3	3.2	38.0	16.6	39.7	3.9	32.5	7.2
1957	55.0	11.4	20.4	23.9	22.8	18.7	11.7	4.7	2.5	42.8	28.2	38.5	3.2	47.6	7.4

Same sources as for Appendix A. Since World War II, tractors were the principal item in agricultural machinery, and "earth-moving" apparatus in mining and construction machinery. Furs, chiefly karakul, exceeded hides and skins in value after 1939.

APPENDIX C

U. S. COMMERCE WITH WEST AFRICA, 1913-1957
BY PRINCIPAL AND DISTINCTIVE COMMODITIES
In Millions of Dollars; Amounts under $100,000 not recorded here

	Exports from U. S.						Imports into U. S.								
	Automobiles & Parts	Lubricating Oil	Other Petroleum	Tobacco	Flour	Cotton Manufactures	Cocoa	Palm Oil & Kernels	Mahogany & Other Logs	Hides & Skins	Manganese	Copper	Other Non-Precious Minerals	Coffee	Rubber
1913			3.8	2.0	.4	.2		.5							
1914			1.6	1.5	.5	.1		.6							
1915			1.2	1.0	.4	.1		.4							
1916	.1		1.6	1.7	.5	.1	4.2	.9	.4	.1					
1917	.2		1.9	2.0	.5	.1	4.6	1.1	1.0	.8					
1918	.4	.1	1.8	3.1	.2	.1	9.6	1.6	.7	.2					
1919	.7	.5	3.7	7.7	1.4	.2	19.3	3.7	1.2	3.3					
1920	3.0	.4	7.2	7.1	4.3	.4	12.0	2.0	1.5	1.8	.1			.1	.1
1921	.4	.6	6.0	2.4	.8	.2	3.7	1.2	1.7	.4				.1	
1922	.8	.2	2.9	3.0	1.5	.2	8.4	1.6	1.7	.4	.1				
1923	1.0	.1	3.3	4.3	1.3	.2	11.0	4.8	1.3	.1	.3	7.7			
1924	1.2	.3	3.6	4.0	1.4	.1	8.1	3.6	1.4	.3	.2	11.0			
1925	2.5	.4	5.1	4.2	1.7	.2	11.0	6.4	1.4	.3	.3			.1	
1926	2.6	.3	11.8	3.2	2.0	.1	12.9	6.4	1.3	.1	1.0				.2
1927	4.3	.5	6.8	3.3	3.3	.3	17.2	7.8	1.1	.4	13.9			.1	.2
1928	3.4	.6	8.8	3.0	2.3	.3	15.6	7.3	.9	.4	.1	13.7			
1929	3.4	.7	9.3	3.6	2.2	.3	19.4	12.2	.7	.6	.3	9.0			
1930	2.0	1.6	6.4	3.4	2.0	.2	10.0	10.7	.6	1.5	1.2	10.8	.9	.5	
1931	1.3	.2	6.3	2.0	.9	.1	6.1	7.2	.4	1.0	1.1			.8	
1932	.6	.1	3.6	2.0	.5	.1	6.9	2.5	.1	.3	.3			.7	
1933	.9	.3	3.1	1.5	.4		7.1	2.7	.9	.4				.2	
1934	.9	.5	3.9	1.6	.7		6.9	4.6		1.2			1.6	.3	
1935	3.2	.6	2.8	2.2	.8		11.4	3.7	.2	1.0	1.2		1.1	.1	.1
1936	3.5	.5	3.6	2.3	1.0		14.0	3.1	.4	.7	3.1		1.2	.1	.2
1937	5.8	.7	7.5	2.0	1.2		28.8	6.2	.7	2.1	2.9		.8	.7	1.0
1938	2.4	1.2	4.1	1.8	1.9		6.6	1.3	.6	1.2	3.0		.2	.8	.4
1939	2.7	.9	3.0	1.8	.6		13.6	1.0	.6	2.0	3.0		.2	.2	2.4
1940	2.6	.7	1.2	1.3	.5	.1	17.5	.9	.7	2.0	4.4	4.9	18.6	.6	2.8
1941	3.8	1.2	.8	1.0	.6	.6	16.7	1.1	.4	2.6	3.2	11.2	30.5	1.4	4.2
1942	11.0	2.6	1.7	1.1	.9	2.3	1.8	1.8	.5	2.7	2.0	7.0	35.7	1.5	6.0
1943	3.9	1.4	1.6	1.6	.9	8.9	11.1	3.0	11.1	2.2	6.4	13.8	39.4	1.7	7.4
1944	2.0	1.4	1.5	1.6	2.5	7.4	22.3	5.6	1.2	2.5	2.3	9.5	43.9	.2	10.0
1945	2.1	.7	.7	3.9	2.8	17.3	25.4	3.3	1.3	2.7	2.0	25.5	39.3	.6	21.6
1946	6.3	1.4	.6	5.2	1.4	21.5	26.4	2.2	2.7	1.6	3.1	2.6	29.9	6.6	13.8
1947	15.4	3.1	.8	4.5	6.1	51.3	75.4	10.1	5.6	4.6	3.0		35.4	9.8	11.2
1948	11.4	3.3	4.6	6.5		8.0	101.6	12.2	6.4	6.4	1.7		46.0	7.9	13.6
1949	10.6	3.3	4.6	6.4		8.0	67.8	7.6	2.1	8.8	5.0		27.8	10.1	17.0
1950	15.4	1.4	2.3	5.6	5.8	4.1	80.2	7.5	5.2	8.0	7.1		22.1	22.8	22.8
1951	27.5	2.5	4.7	7.9	5.5	8.2	116.9	12.5	5.9	7.2	10.1		29.1	29.0	51.5
1952	27.6	1.6	5.9	6.6	9.3	5.5	105.8	6.6	2.4	2.8	13.7		34.5	32.4	38.4
1953	22.4	1.1	5.1	6.7	7.3	3.1	87.7	3.8	4.9	3.3	22.8		46.4	53.3	36.4
1954	26.6	1.8	3.4	9.0	3.7	3.2	113.7	4.5	3.1	2.8	10.1	9.0	51.2	69.3	22.0
1955	39.9	1.2	1.7	10.2	9.9	2.2	86.8	4.5	3.5	4.4	8.6	10.3	66.6	63.3	36.8
1956	28.9	1.6	4.8	8.0	9.9	2.5	74.2	7.6	4.3	4.6	19.7	11.2	68.5	76.7	40.0
1957	27.4	5.3	8.1	7.1	13.5	4.4	62.9	7.2	1.7	2.4	19.0	6.2	40.8	81.7	37.1

Same sources as Appendix A. Most of the recent sharp gains in automobile exports and in imports of "other nonprecious minerals" represent trade of the Belgian Congo, some of which may have moved by ports of South Africa.

APPENDIX D

SHIPS OF THE FARRELL FLEET

Name	Type	Completed	Line Service	Built at—Yard	Dwt.	Gross	Net	Length & Beam Feet	Engines & Horse Power	"Baled" Cubic Feet	Refrig. Space Cu.Ft.
WEST ISLETA		My 1919	1926-40	Seattle, Ames	8,472	5,680	3,508	409—54	R-3000	431,600	
WEST CAWTHON		Ap 1919	1926-40	Los Angeles, SW.	8,576	5,611	3,483	410—"	R-2800	413,000	
WESTERN KNIGHT		D 1918	1926-29	Seattle, Ames	8,500	5,579	3,578	409—"	R-3500		
EASTERN GLADE		Mr 1920	1926-33	Yokohama, Uchida	8,500	5,057	3,171	400—"	R-3000		
EASTERN GLEN		Je 1920	1926-33	"	8,500	5,169	3,545	399—"	R-3000		
CHINCHA		O 1912	1929-39	Sunderland, Thompson	9,600	6,348	3,983	403—52	R-2600	435,000	
CITY OF NEW YORK		Ja 1930	1930-42	Chester, Sun	9,306	8,272	5,025	450—61	D-5000	449,000	4,000
CHALLENGER		O 1918	1937-42	Alameda, Bethlehem	11,620	7,667	5,842	410—56	D-3060	547,000	4,000
CHARLES H. CRAMP		O 1920	c1935-45	Phila., Cramp	9,395	6,220	3,812	404—53	R-3300	383,000	4,500
HENRY S. GROVE		Ja 1921	—	"	9,412	6,220	3,812	"	R-3300	384,000	4,500
ATLANTIC		Mr 1919	" 40	Los Angeles, SW.	8,500	5,524	3,455	410—54	R-2800	435,000	
PACIFIC		N 1915	" 40	San Francisco, Union	8,850	6,034	4,300	400—56	T-2600	353,000	
LANCASTER		Je 1918	" 42	Chester, Sun	11,572	7,615	5,409	434—57	R-2900	510,000	
SAGADAHOC		Jy 1918	" 41	Bath, Texas Co.	9,832	6,275	3,969	420—54	R-3000	516,000	
(AFRICAN COMET)	PC-3	D 1941	—	Pascagoula, Ingalls	6,790	11,812	8,148	465—69	T-9350	473,000	
(AFRICAN METEOR)	"	F 1942	1942	"	"	"	"	"	"	"	
(AFRICAN PLANET, I)	"	Je 1942	"	"	"	"	"	"	"	"	
AFRICAN STAR, I	C-2	Ag 1942	1942-43	Kearny-Federal	9,777	8,329	5,018	439—63	T-6000	471,000	27,400
AFRICAN DAWN	"	N 1942	1942-	"	"	"	"	"	"	"	"
AFRICAN SUN	"	D 1942	"	"	"	"	"	"	"	"	"
AFRICAN STAR, II	C-3	Ap 1946	1946-	"	12,031	7,971	4,624	468—69	T-8500	613,000	21,400
AFRICAN PLANET, II	"	Je 1946	"	"	12,069	"	"	"	"	"	"
AFRICAN RAINBOW	"	Jy 1946	"	"	12,095	7,972	4,618	"	"	"	"
AFRICAN CRESCENT	"	O 1946	"	"	12,031	7,974	4,619	"	"	"	"
AFRICAN MOON	"	F 1947	1947-	"	12,100	"	"	"	"	"	"
AFRICAN LIGHTNING	C-3	F 1947	"	Oakland, Moore	12,068	6,117	3,518	438—63	T-6000	534,000	3,200
AFRICAN GLEN	C-2	F 1945	"	"	10,032	6,116	3,513	"	"	"	"
AFRICAN GLADE	"	Ja 1944	"	"	10,006	6,111	3,514	"	"	"	"
AFRICAN GROVE	"	Ja 1944	"	"	10,038	6,223	4,917	"	"	"	"
AFRICAN PILGRIM	"	Mr 1944	"	"	10,187	"	"	"	"	"	"
AFRICAN PATRIOT	"	My 1944	1944	Baltimore, Bethlehem	10,062	6,132	3,544	468—65	T-7800	427,000	6,500
AFRICAN PILOT	"	My 1944	"	"	10,112	6,130	3,544	"	"	"	"
AFRICAN ENTERPRISE		N 1940	1949-	"	8,602	7,922	4,327	"	"	"	"
AFRICAN ENDEAVOR		My 1940	"	"	8,542	7,922	4,327	"	"	"	"
LIBERIA FEEDER FLEET											
AFRICAN GUIDE	FP	My 1944	1947-54	New Orleans, Higgins		575	278	168—32	D- 800	24,000	
CAVALLA	LCT	Ap 1943	1947-56	Buffalo		169	102	119—32	D- 495	10,000	
MESURADO, I	"	Je 1943	1947-48	No. Tonawanda, Bison		169	102	"	"	"	
ST. PAUL	"	Je 1943	1948-53	"		170	104	"	"	"	
MESURADO, II		My 1949	1949-50	Balt., Wills-Spedden		238	148	121—28	D- 330	13,000	
CESTOS		My 1950	1950-	Camden, N. J., Mathis		238	148	123—28	"	"	
FARMINGTON		Je 1951	1951-	"		258	148	"	"	"	
KPO		N 1954	1954-	Oyster Bay, Jakobsen		366	227	142—31	"	23,000	
LOFA		My 1956	1956-	"		344	240	153—31	"	22,000	

D—Diesel; R—Reciprocating:

APPENDIX E

REMARKS ON INDIVIDUAL FARRELL SHIPS

West Isleta. Made first Am. So. African-Farrell sailing, Jan., '26. Sold British (Ropner) April, '40; renamed *Empire Merlin;* sunk by submarine gunfire Aug. 25, 1940.

West Cawthon. Also sold Ropner April, '40, renamed *Empire Bison;* torpedoed Nov. 1, '40.

Western Knight. Stranded in fog near Port Elizabeth, April 8, '29; constructive total loss; only Farrell peacetime loss except in little feeder fleet.

Eastern Glade. Made first Shipping-Board-Am. So. African sailing, July 1922; sold '33 to Postal SS. Co., N. Y. Sold British (Smith) 1940; renamed *Empire Jaguar;* torpedoed Dec. 8, '40.

Eastern Glen. Also sold '33; renamed *American Oriole.* Sold British (Barberrys) '40; renamed *Barberrys;* torpedoed Nov. 26, 1942.

Chincha. Formerly in W. R. Grace British-flag service to Chile, etc.; later in Planet Line; purchased as replacement for *Western Knight,* made first Farrell sailing to East Africa April '35; sold Aug., '39 to Ant. Barbarovic of Sisak, Yugoslavia; renamed *Milena;* survived war.

City of New York. First Farrell passenger-cargo ship; for other "firsts" see text. Torpedoed March 29, 1942, 30 miles east of Hatteras, with loss of 20 lives.

Challenger. Entirely reconditioned, with diesel engines at Sun yard, Chester, '24. Most capacious of early Farrell ships; torpedoed May 17, '42 in N. Y.-Trinidad convoy; 1 killed.

Charles H. Cramp and *Henry S. Grove.* Named for top officials of Cramp yard; fastest and best appointed of "first fleet" freighters, and only ones still in service by '43; traded in toward new C-3's in '46. These, and next four ships originally in Argonaut intercoastal service from 1921-22.

Atlantic. Originally *West Catnance;* opened Gulf service April, '35; sold Aug., '40 for Panamanian registry; resold for scrapping '53.

Pacific. Only "first fleet" ship with turbines; sold British (Jacobs) Sept., '40; torpedoed March 1, '41.

Lancaster. Stranded at entrance to Casablanca harbor Dec. 30, '42; 12 lives lost.

Sagadahoc. Originally *Bath;* made first Argonaut intercoastal sailing, Jan., '22. Torpedoed Dec. 3, '41 in South Atlantic; one life lost.

African Comet, African Meteor & *African Planet, I.* Requisitioned as Navy transports before serving in line; became U.S.S. *Arthur Middleton, Samuel Chase* and *George Clymer;* first all-welded U.S. passenger ships and first to have "African" names.

African Star, I. Torpedoed July 12, '43 off Rio, returning from first voyage to South Africa.

African Moon. Largest of all Farrell ships by a few tons.

African Glen, ex-*Golden Racer; African Glade,* ex-*Ann McKim; African Grove,* ex-*Gauntlet; African Pilgrim,* ex-*Archer; African Patriot,* ex-*Argonaut; African Pilot,* ex-*Mandarin.*

African Glade. Made first Farrell sailing to West Africa, May, '47.

African Enterprise. Ex-*Delargentina* (Delta Line), ex-Army transport *J. W. McAndrew;* revived regular passenger service, July, '49.

African Endeavor. Ex-*Delbrasil* (Delta); ex-Navy transport *George F. Elliott;* both ships reconditioned by Gulf Shipbuilding Co., Mobile.

LIBERIA FEEDER FLEET

African Guide. Ex-FP-188 (Army feeder ship); first foreign-owned vessel in Liberian registry; towed the LCT's to Monrovia; used for coastal service; sold to Babun Line for Cuba-Gulf freight service.

Cavalla. Ex-LCT 516; made 422 voyages in 8½ years; sold to Monrovia Port Management for barge.

Mesurado, I. Ex-LCT; wrecked near Sinoe July 15, '48.

St. Paul. Ex-LCT 623. First feeder craft with latex tanks; made first Harbel-Monrovia latex runs, May 1950; stranded 5 miles SE of Monrovia, Aug. 24, '53.

Mesurado, II. First vessel built specifically for Harbel run; stranded Jan. 22, '50, after less than month of service, close to where *St. Paul* was wrecked; hull salvaged and used at Lagos.

Cestos and *Farmington.* Fitted with latex tanks for Harbel run.

Kpo. Fitted with mast and booms for handling coastal cargo; pronounced "Po."

Lofa. Similar but without mast. Can carry 219 tons of cargo with 4½ ft. draft for Harbel run; more with 8½ ft. draft for coastal service.

APPENDIX F

CARGO AND EXPENSE DETAILS, *AFRICAN PLANET* VOYAGE 9, AUG.-NOV., 1948

Showing Cargo Revenue in Dollars

OUTWARD CARGO

	Rate Per Ton	Total	Cape Town	Port Eliz.	East London	Dur-ban	Lour. Marq.
AUTOMOBILES & PARTS							
Unboxed cars (156)	$18.00	$40,818	$8,649	$ 8,360	$8,375	$15,435	$
Knocked down etc.	15.00	49,626	7,053	32,294	1,177	9,102	
Parts & accessories	19.00	10,195	1,901	3,613	1,627	2,947	106
Tractors & parts	15.00	1,050	792		258		
APPLIANCES & PARTS							
Refrigerators	28.00	7,446	1,034	2,612	910	2,803	5
Washing Machines	26.00	2,879	944	121	1,100	713	
Sewing Machines	32.00	.284	167			117	
Phonographs & Radios	26.00	1,102	5	413		652	30
Office Equipment	34.00	2,127	718	240	181	987	
VARIOUS "LUXURY" ITEMS							
Toys	28.00	3,075	932	774	755	559	54
Cigarettes	34.00	608		44	60	502	
Candy & Gum	34.00	634	319	144	40	226	
TEXTILES & CLOTHING							
Cotton & Piece Goods	32.00	26,759	1,778	1,065	600	23,300	1,627
Yarn	32.00	1,550		1,036		410	
Women's Dresses, etc.	32.00	690	195	495			
Hosiery	34.00	656	271	138	42	205	
Corsets & Brassieres	34.00	625	19	539		66	
Men's Clothing	32.00	325	19	52	71	181	
Men's Straw Hats	34.00	1,261		1,261			
Oil Cloth	26.00	268	35	166	66		
Floor Coverings	26.00	901		587		313	
MACHINERY							
"Earth Moving"	26.00	5,021		5,021			
Pumps	26.00	1,637	208	1,223	92	113	
Various	var.	14,331	6,985	1,086	688	5,978	282
METALS & MFRS.							
Iron Fence Posts, used	14.00	3,190		119	1,175	993	901
Aluminum Sheets	26.00	2,083	1,580	64			439
Galvanized Wire	14.00	687	687				
Hardware & Tools	var.	545	43	187	92	222	
Copper Pipe & Tubing	32.00	479	479				
FOOD							
Crackers & Toast	32.00	4,680	1,378	768	906	1,059	
Canned Goods	28.00	1,173	308	169	45	399	246
Various	var.	1,833	57			1,776	
VARIOUS							
Glassware	32.00	16,997	4,955	1,281	1,332	7,329	2,098
Chemicals	28.00	8,183	2,363	562	851	4,407	
Drugs, Med. Supplies	34.00	3,614	2,351	20	824	254	165
Cooperage	28.00	1,925	1,925				
Enamelled Ware	32.00	1,217	34	365	164	653	

	Rate					
MINERALS						
Manganese, 2250 tons	8.50	19,125			19,125	
Chrome, 1002 tons	8.25	8,267				8,267
Vermiculite, 512 tons	9.50	4,871				4,871
Asbestos, 2950 bags	16.00	2,149	1,785			364
Corundum, 1605 bags	16.50	1,698				1,698
Scrap Tinplate	11.00	1,080	949		131	
Scrap Copper, Brass	19.50	1,381	247		205	929
OTHER CARGO						
Wool, 1694 bales	50.40	11,783	2,391	9,392		
Lobster, 7020 cases	50.00	6,586	6,586			
Wattle Bark, 3850 bbl.	13.00	4,550			4,550	
Wattle Extract, 3520 bags	20.00	2,978			2,978	
Wines, etc.	25.00	1,500	1,500			
Rags, 30 bales	35.00	393			393	
Ostrich Feathers	1½%	248		248		
Dried Fruit	19.50	197	197			
Misc.	var.	3,938	309	217	112	3,300

Compiled from outward and homeward manifests. Rates for "payable tons" based, at line's choice, either on weight (2240 lbs.) or "measurement" (40 cu. ft.). Rates cited here are for Cape Town; extra for other ports: Port Elizabeth, 50 cents; East London, $1.00; Durban, $1.50; Lourenco Marques, $2.00 on outward cargo. This voyage did not include Beira, where rate was still higher.

OTHER VOYAGE STATISTICS

Nautical miles traveled, 17,419; Days at sea, 43; Days in port, 49.
"Freight payable tons of cargo carried": Outward, 12,243; Homeward, 5,097.
"Vessel Operating Revenue": Total $338,822; Outward freight, $254,727; Homeward freight, $66,251; Passengers, $9,936; Mail, $3,300; Misc., $4,592.
"Vessel Operating Expense": Total, $234,470; Wages, $55,203; Fuel, $46,200; Subsistence, $9,725; Stores, etc., $8,913; Other maintenance, $2,924; Repairs, $1,265; Insurance, $22,585; Agency & Brokerage Fees & Commissions, $8,746; Wharfage & Dockage, $5,175; Other Port Expenses, $7,067; Stevedoring, $48,332; Other Cargo Expenses, $12,646; Misc., $6,412.
Direct Profit from Vessel Operations: $104,357.
Tabulated from "Vessel Operating Statement" to Maritime Commission.
This was one of the last and most profitable of the voyages during South Africa's "buying spree" just before import controls drastically curtailed such cargoes (see text, Chapter XIII).

APPENDIX G

FARRELL LINES SHIPMASTERS, 1958

ACTIVE SEA COMMANDS	Born		First Farrell Service	First Farrell Command — Age		Advanced Education
Anders R. Mortenson	1896	Brantevik, Sweden	1926	1935	38	
Ole P. Stender	1892	Bornholm, Denmark	1937	1937	44	Danish Schoolship
George R. Hickey	1904	Rockland, Mass.	1937	1941	37	Mass. Naut. School
Alden G. Graham	1897	Portland, Ore.	1937	1941	44	LL.B., Stanford
Norris J. Chadbourne	1908	Waterboro, Me.	1939	1942	34	
Arthur Jensen, Jr.	1917	Huntington, N. Y.	1944	1944	27	
Richard N. LePage	1924	Mt. Clemens, Mich.	1944	1950	26	Kings Point
Russell E. McDow	1924	Lynchburg, Va.	1944	1951	27	Kings Point
Talbert K. Tonnensen	1924	Elizabeth, N. J.	1942	1950	26	Kings Point
Maxim Prenovich	1920	Lyndora, Pa.	1945#	1951	31	Kings Point
Erik Tallbe	1918	Vasteras, Sweden	1947	1951	33	
John J. Cannon	1924	Brooklyn, N. Y.	1948	1951	27	
Kenneth C. Torrens	1923	Cambridge, N. Y.	1949	1955	32	Kings Point
Alfred Boerum	1926	Norwalk, Conn.	1946	1955	29	Kings Point
Leonard Blanchart	1927	Worcester, Mass.	1947	1956	28	
Adrian W. Schodle	1920	Philadelphia, Pa.	1942#	1956	36	Kings Point
Raymond H. Ballard	1923	Ludlow, Mass	1945	1956	32	Kings Point
Arthur S. Jefferson	1924	New York City	1946	1957	32	N.Y. State; LL.B., Duke
James L. De Arce	1917	Honolulu, Hawaii	1944#	1957	39	

 # Service not continuous

APPENDIX H

ESSENTIAL TRADE ROUTES, 1957

No.	From	To	Subsidized Lines	1955 Trade Mil. Tons	1955 Trade Mil. $
1.	Atlantic	South America, East Coast	Moore-McCormack	3.6	817
2.	"	" West "	Grace	4.2	785
3.	"	Mexico, East Coast		.3	197
4.	"	Caribbean	Grace, Moore-McCormack	10.9	1,517
5.	No. Atl.	U.K. & Eire	U.S. Lines	7.6	942
6.	"	Scandinavia & Baltic	Moore-McCormack	4.8	501
7.	"	German North Sea Ports	U.S. Lines	4.9	449
8.	"	Belgium & Netherlands	" "	12.1	1,036
9.	"	Atl. France & No. Spain	" "	1.5	328
10.	"	Mediterranean, Black Sea &c	Am. Export, Am. Pres.	11.9	1,132
11.	So. Atl.	U.K., Eire, Continent no. of Port.	U.S. Lines	1.4	159
12.	Atlantic	Far East	" , Am. Pres., Lykes	5.5	958
13.	So. Atl; Gulf	Mediterranean, Black Sea &c	Lykes	3.0	374
14.	a. Atl; b. Gulf	West Africa	a. Farrell; b. Delta	2.4	399
15. A.	Atlantic	South & East Africa	Farrell, Moore-McCormack	1.4	395
15. B.	Gulf	" "	Lykes	.5	88
16.	Atl., Gulf	Australasia	U.S. Lines	.8	342
17.	" " , Pac.	Indonesia & Malaya	Am. Mail, Am. Pres., Lykes	.7	510
18.	Atl. Gulf	India-Persian Gulf, &c	Am. Export, Am. Pres.	2.6	698
19.	Gulf	Caribbean	Lykes	10.1	665
20.	"	South America, East Coast	Mississippi (Delta)	.9	233
21.	"	U.K., Eire, North Europe	Lykes, Bloomfield	6.8	759
22.	"	Far East	Lykes	3.3	322
23.	Pacific	Caribbean	Grace, Moore-McCormack	.2	57
24.	"	South America, East Coast	Moore-McCormack	.1	90
25.	"	West Coast So. Am., Cent. Am., Mex.	Grace	1.3	266
26. A	"	U.K. & Eire		.4	105
26. B	"	Havre-Hamburg Range		1.3	261
27.	"	Australasia	Oceanic	.3	66
28.	"	Indonesia, Malaya, India &c	Am. Mail, Am. President	.4	131
29.	California	Far East	" " Pacific Far East, Pacific Transport	2.9	545
30.	Wash., Oregon	" "	Am. Mail	2.4	195
31.	Gulf	South America, West Coast	Gulf & So. America	1.2	222
32.	Great Lakes	Western Europe		.3	125
33.	"	Caribbean		.01	3

Adapted from Maritime Administration, *United States Foreign Trade Routes*, 1957, *passim*, which also indicates the unsubsidized lines serving some of the routes. Early in 1959, Trade Route 30 was absorbed in Trade Route 29, and Grace was given an operating-differential subsidy on Route 33.

Notes

Information given to the author orally by members of Farrell Lines staff has not been noted here, as the references would be too numerous to include.

CHAPTER I

1. John G. B. Hutchins, *The American Maritime Industry and Public Policy 1789–1914*, pp. 152–55. This is by far the best general analysis and account of American shipping before World War I.
2. Robert G. Albion, *Square-Riggers on Schedule: The New York Sailing Packets to England, France, and the Cotton Ports, passim.*
3. Robert G. Albion, *The Rise of New York Port, 1815–1860,* Chaps. XV–XVII; Carl C. Cutler, *Greyhounds of the Sea, passim;* David B. Tyler, *Steam Conquers the Atlantic,* Chaps. IX–XV.
4. W. S. Lindsay, *History of Merchant Shipping and Ancient Commerce,* Vol. III; quoted in W. L. Marvin, *The American Merchant Marine,* p. 267, along with several similar British statements; R. H. Thornton, *British Shipping,* p. 25.
5. *Commerce and Navigation of the United States, passim;* summarized in *United States Merchant Marine Statistics,* 1925, pp. 13, 60–61; United States Bureau of Census, *Historical Statistics of the United States, 1789–1945,* pp. 207–08, 215–17.
6. John G. B. Hutchins, *op. cit.,* p. 534.
7. *Ibid.,* pp. 431, 453, 464, 485, 520.
8. *Ibid.,* p. 537.
9. *Commerce and Navigation of the United States,* 1858, pp. 178, 284, 414, 520; Union of South Africa, *Quarterly Abstract of Union Statistics,* July 1921, pp. 49–60.
10. See Chapter III.
11. J. B. Condliffe, *The Commerce of Nations,* Chaps. X–XII.
12. Compiled from record of shipping movements in *Journal of Commerce* (New York) and *New York Maritime Register.*
13. Marischal Murray, *Union-Castle Chronicle, 1853–1953, passim.*
14. *Ibid.,* p. 301.
15. House Committee on Merchant Marine and Fisheries, *Proceedings . . . in the Investigation of Shipping Combinations, 1913,* Joshua W. Alexander, chairman (hereafter cited as Alexander Hearings). Testimony of Joseph T. Lilly, p. 453.
16. See Chapter II.
17. For a general description and analysis of the conference system see Daniel Marx, *International Shipping Cartels: A Study of Industrial Self-Regulation by Shipping Conferences, passim.*
18. Alexander Hearings, testimony

of William E. Halm, Houston Line, p. 284.

19. *Federal Reporter,* Vol. 149, pp. 9, 33–36; Vol. 166, pp. 251–54; *United States Reports,* Vol. 243, pp. 66–89.

20. 39 Stat. 728, Sec. 14.

21. Alexander Hearings, pp. 243 ff., 270, 283, 313, 429.

22. *Ibid.,* pp. 243–45.

23. *Ibid.,* p. 243.

24. Advertisements in *Journal of Commerce* (New York), *passim;* also *New York Maritime Register,* Weekly Compendium, 1912, *passim.*

25. Full text in Alexander Hearings, pp. 278–88.

26. *Ibid.,* testimony of William E. Halm, Houston Line, p. 273.

27. *Ibid.,* Huebner Summary, IV, p.

93. This final volume was also produced separately as *Report on Steamship Agreements and Affiliations in the American Foreign and Domestic Trade; Prepared by S. S. Huebner, including the Recommendations of the Committee* (63rd Congress, 2nd Session, *House Document,* 805).

28. Paul M. Zeis, *American Shipping Policy,* p. 76.

29. Alexander Hearings, Huebner Summary, IV, p. 417.

30. *Ibid.,* Vol. I, pp. 95, 109.

31. See Chapter V.

32. *Commercial Relations of the United States,* 1907, Vol. I, pp. 704–06, 721; 1909, p. 963.

33. *Statesman's Year-book,* 1914, *passim.*

CHAPTER II

34. *New York Times,* July 1914, *passim,* advertisement of Pacific Steam Navigation Company.

35. Compiled from various editions of *Trade and Navigation of the United Kingdom,* (Foreign) *Commerce and Navigation of United States, Statistical Abstract of the United States,* and, for South African gold exports, *Official Year Book of the Union of South Africa* (hereafter cited as *Official Year Book*).

36. Summary of figures presented in Appendix A. The major aspects and commodities of the trade between the United States and Africa South of Sahara have been presented by Farrell Lines in two attractive 28-page brochures: *African Markets,* 1948, and *African Resources,* 1949.

37. *Official Year Book, passim.*

38. *Ibid.,* No. 2, 1917, p. 581; No. 20, 1939, p. 990 and *passim;*

David Shrand, *Financial and Statistical Digest of South Africa,* p. 130.

39. *Official Year Book, passim.*

40. United States Department of Commerce, *Commerce Reports,* Vol. 27-1, 1924, p. 319.

41. See Chapters IX and X.

42. See Chapter III.

43. Compiled from lists of importers and exporters, Farrell Lines Johannesburg office.

44. *Commerce Reports,* Vol. 27-3, 1924, p. 280, article by F. A. Christopher.

45. See Appendix B.

46. *Commerce and Navigation of the United States,* 1925 and *passim.* For the distribution of South African diamond exports, see *Official Year Book,* No. 8, 1924, p. 627 and *passim.*

47. United States Maritime Commission, *Post-War Outlook for United States Shipping in the*

South and East Africa Trade Area, Appendix Table 5, giving annual tonnage of principal commodities imported.

48. *Official Year Book,* No. 2, 1918, Annual Table p. 581.

49. See especially Erich W. Zimmermann, *World Resources and Industries, passim.*

50. See Chapter IX.

51. *New York Herald Tribune,* June 22, 1958, Sec. XII, p. 3; *South African Scope,* June 1958, p. 7; Dillon, Read & Company, prospectus, *American-South African Investment Company, Limited,* Sept. 17, 1958, p. 25; Union of South Africa, *State of the Union,* 1957, p. 114.

52. A. W. Wells, *Southern Africa, Today and Yesterday,* p. 397.

53. A. Gordon-Brown, ed., *Year Book and Guide to Southern Africa,* 1956, p. 221. Table of annual exports in *Official Year Book,* No. 2, 1918, p. 578; *British and South African Export Gazette,* Sept. 1917, p. 653.

54. *Ibid.,* May 1917, p. 348.

55. *Commerce Reports,* Vol. 17-2, 1914, pp. 353–62; Vol. 26-4, 1923, pp. 798, 815; A. Gordon-Brown, *op. cit.,* pp. 221, 618; *Official Year Book, passim.*

56. See Chapter XIV.

57. *Commerce Reports,* Vol. 26-1, 1923, pp. 506–07; Vol. 27-2, 1924, pp. 650–51.

58. George Auerbach, "Instant Coffee's Boon to Africa," *New York Times,* Nov. 17, 1957, Sec. III, p. 1; H. E. Jacob, *Coffee: The Epic of a Commodity, passim.*

59. A. W. Knapp, *Cocoa and Chocolate,* pp. 18–19, 42; Ernst Mai, *Die Kakao Kultur an der Gold Kuste,* p. 14.

60. See Chapters XI and XII.

61. *New York Times,* June 25, 1952.

62. *Farrell Lines News,* Oct. 1955, p. 1.

63. *Commerce and Navigation of the United States,* 1930, pp. 759–61, 769–71.

64. See Chapter III.

65. Sir Reginald Coupland, *The Exploitation of East Africa,* pp. 77, 320; C. T. Brady, Jr., *Commerce and Conquest in East Africa, with particular reference to the Salem Trade with Zanzibar, passim;* P. E. Northway, "Salem and the Zanzibar-East African Trade, 1825–1845," *Essex Institute Historical Collections,* April 1954; R. G. Albion, *Ibid.,* April 1959.

66. See Chapters I and XIV.

67. Adapted from manifest published in *Journal of Commerce* (New York), Oct. 11, 1913.

68. *British and South African Export Gazette,* Jan. 1914, p. 113 and *passim;* quoted in *Commerce Reports,* Vol. 21-3, 1918, pp. 859–66.

69. Compiled from tables in Appendices B and C. These totals are to be regarded as relative rather than absolute because annual totals less than $100,000 were not recorded in the tables.

70. *Commerce Reports,* Vol. 25-2, 1922, p. 214, quoting *The Times* (London), May 25, 1922.

71. *Commerce Reports,* Vol. 17-2, 1914, p. 1792.

72. *Ibid.,* Vol. 25-2, 1922, p. 224.

73. *Ibid.,* Vol. 20-1, 1917, p. 267.

74. *Commerce and Navigation of the United States,* 1913, 1927, 1937; *Commerce Reports,* Vol. 17-2, 1914, p. 1292; see also table of annual automobile exports, Appendix B.

75. E. M. Searle to author, March 19, 1958; *South African Scope,* Jan. 1959, p. 6.

76. *Commerce Reports,* Vol. 17-1, 1914, p. 199.
77. *Commerce and Navigation of the United States, passim.* For the background of South Africa's economic fluctuations, see M. H. de Kock, *Economic Development of South Africa;* J. C. Duplessis, *Economic Fluctuations in South Africa, 1910–1949;* and George Marais, *Dis-*

equilibrium in the South African Balance of Payments between 1925 and 1952, University of Wisconsin Ph.D. thesis, 1956.
78. *Commerce Reports,* Vol. 26-3, 1923, p. 671; Vol. 27-2, 1924, p. 305; Vol. 28-3, 1925, p. 328.
79. *Commerce Reports,* Vol. 24-1, 1921, p. 391.
80. W. Clifford Shields, *Some Current Africana,* 1957, pp. 6–8.

CHAPTER III

81. United States Hydrographic Office, H. O. No. 117, *Table of Distances Between Ports,* 1943.
82. For a detailed chronology of South Africa, see A. Gordon-Brown, ed., *Year Book and Guide to Southern Africa,* 1956, pp. 9 ff.
83. *Ports of South Africa: Harbour Reference Book,* 1956, pp. 91, 102, 115, 131; Theodore Hunter and Jarvis Patten, *Port Charges . . . in the Ports of the World,* 1884, pp. 172–73 and *passim;* Peter Scott, "Some Functional Aspects of Cape Town," *Economic Geography,* Oct. 1954.
84. *Official Year Book,* 1950, pp. 523–28. There was a detailed "Harbours" section in each issue of this valuable compendium; there is less detail in its successor, *State of the Union: Economic, Financial, and Statistical Year Book for the Union of South Africa;* see also "Railways and Ports of Southern Africa: A Review of the Present Position of Transport," *Dock and Harbour Authority,* March 1953.
85. James Duffy, *Shipwreck and Empire, being an Account of the Portuguese Maritime Disasters in a Century of Decline,* pp.

26 ff.; Genesta Hamilton, *In the Wake of Da Gama,* pp. 75–92.
86. George Carter, *A Narrative of the Loss of the "Grosvenor";* Hanson W. Baldwin, *Sea Fights and Shipwrecks,* Chap. 3, "The Birken'ead Drill"; Marischal Murray, *Union-Castle Chronicle,* pp. 279–80.
87. Theodore Hunter and Jarvis Patten, *op cit.,* p. 757; J. J. Redgrave, *Port Elizabeth in Bygone Days,* Chap. XI, "Some Tragic Wrecks and Floods."
88. See Chapter II.
89. Marischal Murray, *op. cit.,* p. 269; Theodore Hunter and Jarvis Patten, *op. cit.,* p. 288.
90. United States Hydrographic Office, H. O. No. 156, *Sailing Directions, South and East Africa,* 1936, p. 108.
91. *British and South African Export Gazette,* Aug. 1918, p. 553.
92. Marischal Murray, *op. cit.,* p. 275.
93. *Ports of South Africa,* 1956, pp. 87–89, with detailed map.
94. *Official Year Book,* 1950, pp. 523–28.
95. *Ports of South Africa,* 1956, pp. 93, 103, 113, 133.
96. James Duffy, *op. cit.,* pp. 43, 85, 139–40 and *passim.*
97. Great Britain, Parliament, Ac-

counts and papers, 1875, Vol. 83, *Delagoa Bay: Correspondence respecting the Claims of Her Majesty's Government,* pp. 3, 10, 249 and *passim;* Sir Edward Herstlet, *The Map of Africa by Treaty,* Vol. III, pp. 191–98; Sir Reginald Coupland, *East Africa and Its Invaders,* p. 206.

98. H. F. Varian, *Some African Milestones,* 1952, pp. 34–35.

99. *Official Year Book,* No. 10, 1929, p. 581; No. 2, 1918, p. 597; No.6, 1922, p. 734 and *passim; Commerce Reports,* Vol. 25-2, 1922, p. 658; Vol. 25-3, 1922, p. 431.

100. For an analysis of this port by two geographers, see W. A. Hance and I. S. van Dongen, "Lourenco Marques in Delagoa Bay," *Economic Geography,* July 1957. This and some other articles to be noted later have been prepared in connection with a Columbia University research project on the ports of Central Africa for the Office of Naval Research. Each article includes valuable bibliographical references.

101. H. C. Brookfield, "New Railroad and Port Developments in East and Central Africa," *Economic Geography,* Jan. 1955.

102. I. S. van Dongen, "Nacala: Newest Mozambique Gateway to Interior Africa," *Tijdscrift voor Economische en Sociale Geografie,* July–Aug. 1957, pp. 65–73.

103. H. F. Varian, *op. cit.,* pp. 10–11.

104. For a thorough analysis of the port and its hinterland connections see W. A. Hance and I. S. van Dongen, "Beira, Mozambique Gateway to Central Africa," *Annals of the Association of American Geographers,* Dec. 1957, pp. 307–35.

105. K. G. Sorensen, "Reconstruction of a Sea Wall at Beira," *Dock and Harbour Authority,* Sept. 1956.

106. W. A. Hance and I. S. van Dongen, "Beira, Mozambique Gateway to Central Africa," *loc. cit.,* p. 309.

107. *Ibid.,* p. 321.

108. *Ibid.,* p. 316.

109. John T. Rennie & Sons, Ms. Record, *American South African Ships on Cape Town-Beira Range,* 1938.

110. Farrell Lines, *Executive Committee Minutes,* Feb. 2, 1949; Marine Division, *Vessel Itineraries.*

111. Richard H. Browne to author, Jan. 24, 1958.

112. "Port Capacity and Shipping Turnaround in West Africa," *Economic and Statistical Review,* (United Africa Company), No. 19, March 1957, p. 3.

113. Farrell Lines, *Executive Committee Minutes,* Feb. 2, April 12, 1949.

114. Farrell Lines, *Annual Report,* 1949; *Directors' Minutes,* March 4, 1952.

115. Captain C. W. Schmidt to Farrel Lines, Oct. 6, 1952.

116. W. A. Hance and I. S. van Dongen, "Beira, Mozambique Gateway to Central Africa," *loc. cit.,* p. 323.

117. *Ibid.,* p. 314.

118. W. A. Hance and I. S. van Dongen, "The Port of Lobito and the Benguela Railway," *Geographical Review,* Oct. 1956, p. 487.

119. *Ibid.*

120. I. S. van Dongen, *The British*

East Africa Traffic Complex, University of Chicago Department of Geography Research Report 178.

121. See Chapter II.

122. J. A. Hunter and D. P. Mannix, *Tales of the African Frontier,* p. 171. Chap. IX, "R. O. Preston and the 'Lunatic Line,' " pp. 171–94, is one of the best accounts of this achievement.

123. *Ibid.,* p. 173.

124. S. E. W. Sundquist to author, June 20, 1957.

125. "The Port of Dar-es-Salaam: Completion of New Ocean Terminal," *Dock and Harbour Authority,* Nov. 1956.

126. *Farrell Lines News,* Jan. 1956.

CHAPTER IV

127. *New York Times, Journal of Commerce* (New York), *New York Maritime Register, passim.*

128. *Ibid.;* Robert G. Albion and J. B. Pope, *Sea Lanes in Wartime,* pp. 232–33.

129. John Barrett, Director General of Pan-American Union, quoted in *New York Maritime Register,* Aug. 12, 1914, p. 10.

130. See Chapter I.

131. Act of Aug. 24, 1912, 37 Stat. 562; Act of Aug. 18, 1914, 38 Stat. 698.

132. United States Department of Commerce, *Merchant Marine Statistics,* 1925, p. 36; United States Department of the Census, *Historical Statistics of the United States, 1789–1945,* p. 209.

133. Told by Clifford N. Carver to author.

134. Joan Bentinck-Smith, *The Forcing Period: A Study of the American Merchant Marine, 1914–1917,* Radcliffe Ph.D. thesis, 1958, prepared under supervision of author.

135. Adapted from Union of South Africa, *Quarterly Abstract of Union Statistics,* Jan. 1921, July 1921. For details of particular commodities during the period, see Appendix B.

136. Adapted from *Commerce and Navigation of the United States, 1913–19.*

137. See Chapter XII.

138. *New York Maritime Register,* July–Oct. 1914, *passim;* similar information in *Lloyd's List.* See also Marischal Murray, *Ships and South Africa,* Chap. XI.

139. *Commerce Reports, passim.*

140. Union of South Africa, *Quarterly Abstract of Union Statistics,* Jan. 1921, pp. 56–63; July 1921, pp. 49–60.

141. *Ibid.*

142. Robert G. Albion and J. B. Pope, *op cit.,* p. 224.

143. Marischal Murray, *Ships and South Africa,* Chaps. XI–XII; *Union-Castle Chronicle,* Chaps. XIX–XX.

144. *Commerce Reports,* Vol. 17-4, 1914, p. 796; *New York Maritime Register, passim.*

145. *British and South African Export Gazette,* Sept. 1916, p. 619.

146. *Commerce Reports,* Vol. 20-1, 1917, p. 1037.

147. See Chapter I.

148. *Commerce Reports,* Vol. 17-4, 1914, pp. 358–62, 796; Vol. 18-2, 1915, p. 537.

149. *Ibid.,* Vol. 18-2, 1915, p. 670; *New York Maritime Register,*

passim; *Boston Herald,* May 27, 28, 1915.

150. *New York Maritime Register, passim.*

151. *Commerce Reports,* Vol. 18-3, 1915, p. 746.

152. *British and South African Export Gazette,* Dec. 1915, p. 896.

153. See Appendix B.

154. *British and South African Export Gazette,* April 1916, p. 340; July 1916, p. 485.

155. *Commerce Reports,* Vol. 19-1, 1916, p. 395.

156. *Ibid.*

157. *Ibid.,* p. 725.

158. *British and South African Export Gazette,* Dec. 1915, p. 895.

159. *British and South African Export Gazette,* Sept. 1916, p. 615 (quoted in *Commerce Reports,* Vol. 20-2, 1917, p. 627); Aug. 1917, p. 560; Sept. 1917, p. 653; Oct. 1917, p. 787; July 1918, p. 482; *Official Year Book,* No. 2, 1918, pp. 595, 602.

160. C. E. Fayle, *Seaborne Trade,* Vol. III, p. 93.

161. *Ibid.,* p. 465; Robert G. Albion and J. B. Pope, *op. cit.,* Chaps. IX, X.

162. C. E. Fayle, *op. cit.,* Vol. III, p. 470. This account, in the British Official History, is the most complete and useful analysis of the situation. Some of the same material, less conveniently expressed, is in Sir Arthur Salter's *Allied Shipping Control.*

163. C. E. Fayle, *op. cit.,* Vol. III, p. 270.

164. *Ibid.,* pp. 122n., 125.

165. *Ibid.,* p. 122; Marischal Murray, *Union-Castle Chronicle,* pp. 164, 173.

166. *Commerce Reports,* Vol. 20-3, 1917, p. 883.

167. C. E. Fayle, *op. cit.,* Vol. III, p. 122n.

168. *Commerce Reports,* Vol. 20-4, 1917, p. 469; see also Vol. 20-3, 1917, p. 994; quoting *Cape Times,* July 27, 1917.

169. *Commerce Reports,* Vol. 21-1, 1918, p. 995, quoting *South African Government Gazette,* Jan. 18, 1918.

170. *New York Maritime Register,* Weekly Compendium, *passim;* F. C. Bowen, "Sailing Ships in the First Great War," *Sea Breezes,* Aug. 1946, pp. 146–50; "Sailing Traders to South African Ports," *ibid.,* Sept. 1946, pp. 197–202.

171. *British and South African Export Gazette,* Aug. 1918, p. 544. These figures do not indicate the considerable amount of Canadian products.

172. *Ibid.,* May 1918, p. 339.

173. *Official Year Book,* No. 20, 1939, p. 901.

174. *British and South African Export Gazette,* March 1917, p. 227; Sept. 1918, p. 619.

175. *Shipping Illustrated,* Oct. 23, 1915, p. 81.

176. The story is best told in Roy Alexander, *The Cruise of the Raider Wolf.*

177. *Shipping Illustrated,* March 31, 1917, p. 298.

178. Roy Alexander, *op. cit.,* p. 108.

179. Marischal Murray, *Ships and South Africa,* pp. 118–19.

180. *Ibid., passim; British and South African Export Gazette,* March 1916, p. 279; Oct. 1918, p. 681.

181. *New York Maritime Register,* April 17, 1917.

182. *Ibid.,* May 29, 1918, p. 11.

183. *British and South African Export Gazette,* June 1918, pp. 417, 479.

184. *Commerce Reports,* Supplement, 1919, Sec. 66a, pp. 7–8.

185. *Ibid.*, p. 28.
186. 39 Stat. 728.
187. W. C. Mattox, *Building the Emergency Fleet,* Chap. I; D H. Smith and P. V. Betters, *The United States Shipping Board,* pp. 8–9.
188. Shipping Act, 1916, preamble.
189. See Chapter VIII.
190. On the question of wood or steel, see W. C. Mattox, *op. cit.,* Chap. II; Edward N. Hurley, *The New American Merchant Marine,* pp. 27–31, and his *The Bridge to France,* pp. 27–28, 52–57. Detailed statistics and general account in F. G. Fassett, ed., *The Shipbuilding Business of the United States,* I, pp. 53–54, 78–87.
191. P. M. Zeis, *American Shipping Policy,* p. 107.
192. The correspondence between the Emergency Fleet Corporation and the Ames yard, one of better west coast yards, preserved at the National Archives, gives frequent illustrations of these practices.
193. Compiled from *Merchant Vessels of the United States, passim.* A complete list of the products of each yard is in the 1934 issue, pp. 1030–87; final list in the 1939 issue; intervening years show individual attrition by shipwreck, transfer to foreign registry, inactive lay-up, and scrapping or abandonment. See also American Bureau of Shipping, *Record, passim.*
194. *Ibid.*
195. United States Shipping Board, *Second Annual Report,* 1918, p. 53; full details in Shipping Board files, National Archives.
196. Told to the author by Sir Arthur Salter.

CHAPTER V

197. Merchant Marine Act, 1920, 41 Stat. 988, Sec. 7.
198. *Ibid.*
199. House Committee on Merchant Marine and Fisheries, *Hearings on Double and Triple Tracking on Subsidized Trade Routes,* March 13 and 14, 1956 (hereafter cited as Hearings on Double Tracking), statement of James A. Farrell, Jr., p. 123.
200. This situation is vigorously discussed, in detail, in *The Use and Disposition of Ships and Shipyards at the end of World War II, a Report prepared for the United States Navy Department and the United States Maritime Commission,* by the Graduate School of Business Administration, Harvard University, June 1945 (hereafter cited as Harvard Report), pp. 262–64.
201. *New York Maritime Register,* Jan. 22, 1919, p. 10.
202. Shipping Board, *Fourth Annual Report,* 1920, p. 54.
203. For lists of the managing operators, see Shipping Board, *Annual Reports:* Fourth, 1920, p. 257; Fifth, 1921, p. 259; Sixth, 1922, p. 249, etc.
204. Alexander Hearings, Huebner Summary, IV, p. 103; see also Chapter I.
205. *New York Maritime Register,* Jan. 22, 1919, p. 10.
206. *Ibid.*, Feb. 19, 1919, p. 22; Shipping Board, *Fourth Annual Report,* 1919, p. 55.

207. *Marine News,* Dec. 1919, p. 105.

208. *Journal of Commerce* (New York), March 30, 1919.

209. Shipping Board, *Fifth Annual Report,* 1921, p. 188.

210. *New York Maritime Register,* April 16, 1919, p. 23 and *passim.*

211. Shipping Board, *Fourth Annual Report,* 1920, pp. 33, 128, 242; *New York Maritime Register, passim.*

212. Shipping Board, *Sixth Annual Report,* 1922, p. 129.

213. Compiled from *New York Maritime Register,* Weekly Compendium, 1918–19, *passim.*

214. Adapted from figures in Shipping Board, *Sixth Annual Report,* 1922, p. 55. See also p. 126 of this report.

215. Shipping Board, *Fifth Annual Report,* 1921, p. 163.

216. Maritime Administration figures, in American Merchant Marine Institute *Bulletin,* 1956, *passim.*

217. *Commerce Reports,* Vol. 24-2, 1921, p. 1634.

218. *Ibid.,* Vol. 25-1, 1922, pp. 526, 771; Vol. 26-3, 1923, p. 109; compare *Journal of Commerce* (New York), Jan. 30, 1926, the day of the first Farrell sailing.

219. *Commerce Reports,* Vol. 26-4, 1923, p. 669.

220. *Commerce and Navigation of the United States,* 1920, 1922, *passim.*

221. *Commerce Reports,* Vol. 25-1, 1922, p. 355 and *passim.*

222. *New York Times,* April 1, 1922; *Journal of Commerce* (New York), April 3, 4, 1922.

223. National Archives, Shipping Board MSS., Mallory to Emergency Fleet Corporation.

224. Senate Special Committee, *Hearings in Investigation of Air Mail and Ocean Mail Contracts,* 1933–34 (hereafter cited as Black Hearings).

225. Shipping Board, *Eighth Annual Report,* 1924, p. 80; see also *Ninth Annual Report,* 1925, p. 141.

226. See Appendix A.

227. Shipping Board, *Ninth Annual Report,* 1925, p. 22; also Black Hearings, p. 931; *New York Commercial,* Aug. 28, 1924; C. C. Cutler, "Clifford Day Mallory," *American Neptune,* July 1941, pp. 205–08.

228. Shipping Board, *Ninth Annual Report,* 1925, pp. 18–22, 141, 186–89.

229. National Archives, Shipping Board MSS., Memorandum, A. H. Bull & Company to Emergency Fleet Corporation.

230. Shipping Board, *Sixth Annual Report,* 1922, pp. 251–53.

231. Shipping Board, *Fifth Annual Report,* 1921, pp. 310–11.

232. Shipping Board, *Seventh Annual Report,* 1923, p. 9.

233. See Chapters VI and X.

234. Shipping Board, *Eighth Annual Report,* 1924, pp. 46–47.

235. *Ibid.,* p. 143; *Ninth Annual Report,* 1925, p. 208; *Tenth Annual Report,* 1926, p. 129.

236. Shipping Board, *Ninth Annual Report,* 1925, p. 16–17; *Tenth Annual Report,* 1926, pp. 18, 92; *Eleventh Annual Report,* 1927, p. 108; *Twelfth Annual Report,* 1928, pp. 26, 109; *Thirteenth Annual Report,* 1929, pp. 88, 116; *Fourteenth Annual Report,* 1930, pp. 17, 103; *Fifteenth Annual Report,* 1931, pp. 4, 37, 103; *Sixteenth Annual Report,* 1932, p. 93;

Seventeenth Annual Report, 1933, p. 69.

237. *New York Times,* Oct. 7, 9, 1925.

238. American Shipmasters' Association, *List of Persons who have Applied for Certificates,* 1879, p. 14.

239. National Archives: Enrolment and Registry Certificates: New Haven, Enrolment 1, July 5, 1870 (the last pre-Farrell document); New Haven, Enrolment 38, May 16, 1872; New York, Temporary Enrolment 211, June 28, 1872; New Haven Enrolment 15, Oct. 31, 1872; New York Enrolment 14, Oct. 13, 1873; New Haven Permanent Registry 13, May 15, 1874; New York Temporary Registry 72, Sept. 21, 1874; New York Temporary Enrolment 130, Nov. 11, 1874; New Haven Permanent Registry 5, April 13, 1875; Boston Temporary Enrolment 118, June 3, 1875; New York Temporary Registry 428, April 12, 1876.

240. *New York Maritime Register,* Sept. 12, 1877, p. 38; Dec. 25, 1877, p. 35; Jan. 23, 1878, p. 36; April 3, 1878, p. 30; May 1, 1878, p. 37; Consular endorsement on New York Temporary Registry 428, April 8, 1878; New Orleans Permanent Register 27, March 28, 1878.

241. *Baltimore Sun,* April 14, 1929.

242. Atlantic Mutual Insurance Company, *Disaster Books,* Vol. 129, pp. 295, 299; Vol. 130, pp. 65, 76.

243. The best brief sketch of Farrell's career is by Rose C. Feld in the *New York Times,* Jan. 1, 1928, Sec. IX; see also *Ibid.,* March 29, 1943.

244. Charles M. Muchnic to Secretary of Commerce William C. Redfield, Feb. 19, 1912, quoted in Alexander Hearings, p. 211.

245. United States Steel Corporation, *Annual Report,* 1910, p. 56; 1911, p. 21; 1914, p. 28; *Fairplay,* Dec. 8, 1910, p. 789; Dec. 15, 1910, p. 825; Dec. 29, 1910, p. 885; American Bureau of Shipping, *Register,* 1915; *Lloyd's Register,* 1911–15, *passim.*

246. *Transcript of record: In the District Court of the United States for the District of New Jersey: United States of America vs. United States Steel Corporation and others,* No. 6214, 1913 (hereafter cited as the United States versus United States Steel), X, p. 3837.

247. The United States versus United States Steel, p. 3805.

248. Alexander Hearings, testimony of John J. Ryan, pp. 493–96.

249. The United States versus United States Steel, pp. 3805–07.

250. *Ibid.,* p. 3805.

251. *Ibid.,* p. 3807.

252. *Ibid.,* pp. 3811, 3819; Alexander Hearings, pp. 461–63.

253. The United States versus United States Steel, p. 3812.

254. United States Steel Corporation, *Annual Report,* 1918, p. 31; 1919, p. 28; 1920, p. 29; 1921, p. 26; *Marine Register,* Oct. 31, 1917. Lists of ships from the two yards are in *Merchant Vessels of the United States,* 1934, pp. 1041, 1048; also in American Bureau of Shipping, *Record, passim.*

255. *Journal of Commerce* (New York), Nov. 22, 1923.

256. *New York Commercial,* Jan. 23, 1923.

257. For full details of the Argonaut ships, see Appendix D.

258. See Chapter VIII.

259. Alexander Hearings, pp. 447–54 for scope of activities.

260. See Chapter VII.

261. These various holdings are analyzed in detail in the Black Hearings.

262. Felix Riesenberg, Sr., *Log of the Sea,* p. 283.

263. Joseph Conrad to James A. Farrell, Sr., June 2, 1923.

264. The actual purchase price was slightly less because of the substitution of two ships with slightly lower tonnage. The purchase price was given as $777,901.50 in the line's mail contract brief of 1934, but as $778,901.80 in Shipping Board, *Tenth Annual Report,* 1926, p. 92.

265. *Journal of Commerce,* (New York), Dec. 23, 1925. The details of the purchase and organ-ization are best covered in the testimony in the Black Hearings, in the corporate minutes of the new line, and in the local newspapers.

266. *New York Times,* Dec. 10, 1950.

267. Shipping Board, *Tenth Annual Report,* 1926, p. 9; *Marine Journal,* Jan. 9, 1926, p. 17.

268. *Marine Journal,* Dec. 19, 1925, p. 9.

269. *Ibid.,* Dec. 26, 1925, p. 9.

270. *New York Times,* May 30, June 6, 7, 1928; Shipping Board, *Twelfth Annual Report,* 1928, p. 27; *Thirteenth Annual Report,* 1929, p. 116.

271. Shipping Board, *Fourth Annual Report,* 1920, p. 257; *New York Herald Tribune,* June 14, 1953.

272. See Chapter XII for details of West African Service.

CHAPTER VI

273. *Journal of Commerce* (New York), Feb. 1, 1926; *Cape Times* (Cape Town), Feb. 9, 1926. A list of line sailings in the Shipping Board MSS. in the National Archives, however, gives the sailing date as Jan. 31.

274. For the individual payments, see Black Hearings, pp. 920–21.

275. *Ibid.,* pp. 949–50.

276. Farrell Lines, *Directors' Minutes,* March 7, 1955.

277. For full statistical data on all the line's ships, see Appendix D.

278. Individual yard lists in *Merchant Vessels of the United States,* 1934, pp. 1030–87.

279. John T. Rennie & Sons, *op. cit.,* Vol. I; American South African Line, *Directors' Minutes,* April 1, 1940.

280. National Archives, Shipping Board MSS.; individual ship records.

281. Senate Commerce Committee, *Hearings on the United States Shipping Board and Emergency Fleet Corporation,* 1918, Vol. 1, p. 130; American Bureau of Shipping *Record,* 1954, p. 1642.

282. L. A. Renehan in *Farrell Lines News,* Oct. 1955; *Lloyd's List,* April 10, 17, 24, May 15, 1929; Atlantic Mutual Insurance Company, *Disaster Books,* Vol. 313, p. 237.

283. Black Hearings, pp. 924–26; Atlantic Mutual Insurance Company, *loc. cit.*

284. National Archives, Shipping Board MSS., Line memo, 1927.
285. Shipping Board, *Fifth Annual Report,* 1921, p. 46.
286. *Ibid.,* p. 45.
287. See Chapters I and II.
288. *Journal of Commerce* (New York), Oct. 8, 1926.
289. See Chapter I.
290. Shipping Board, *Tenth Annual Report,* 1926, p. 7.
291. 45 Stat. 689.
292. *Ibid.,* Sec. 203.
293. *Ibid.,* Sec. 11 (a).
294. *Ibid.,* Sec. 407, 409.
295. H. L. Seward, Ms., *American South African Line Survey,* Oct. 2, 1943, table.

296. *New York Times,* Nov. 23, 1928.
297. See Appendix D for full details of ships and fleets.
298. Frank O. Braynard, *Famous American Ships,* pp. 171–74.
299. *New York Maritime Register,* Weekly Compendium, *passim.*
300. Marischal Murray, *Ships and South Africa,* pp. 127–28; also *New York Times,* April 30, 1926.
301. *Farrell Lines News,* July 1953, p. 5.
302. *New York Maritime Register,* Weekly Compendium, *passim.*
303. H. L. Seward, *loc. cit.*
304. See Appendix B.

CHAPTER VII

305. See Appendix B for export tables, based on *Commerce and Navigation of the United States.*
306. *Commerce Reports,* Vol. 17-3, 1914, p. 183; 19–2, 1916, p. 387; 20–1, 1917, pp. 262, 1037.
307. *New York Maritime Register,* Weekly Compendium, *passim.* See also Chapter III.
308. John T. Rennie & Sons, Ms. Record, *American South African Ships on Cape Town-Beira Range,* 1938.
309. *New York Maritime Register, passim.*
310. United States Shipping Board Bureau, Docket No. 120; Seas Shipping Company vs. American South African Line et al: *Complainant's Brief,* Dec. 30, 1935, pp. 29–30; *Decisions of the United States Shipping Board Bureau,* 1918–38 (hereafter cited as USSBB), pp. 572–73.
311. *New York Maritime Register, passim.*

312. American South African Line, Memo to Maritime Commission, 1942, on number of sailings from different ports.
313. H. L. Seward, Ms., *American South African Line Survey,* Oct. 2, 1943.
314. See Chapters X and XII.
315. H. L. Seward, *op. cit.*
316. See Chapter V.
317. Black Hearings, pp. 910–12; American South African Line, *Directors' Minutes, passim.*
318. Black Hearings, p. 960.
319. *New York Maritime Register,* Weekly Compendium, *passim.*
320. USSBB Docket 120, *Brief for Defendants,* Dec. 30, 1935, pp. 12–13.
321. *New York Times, Journal of Commerce* (New York), April 18, 1936.
322. See Chapter XIII.
323. See Chapter I.
324. USSBB, *Report,* Vol. I, p. 575.
325. Agreement 3578, approved Oct. 22, 1934, reproduced in USSBB Docket 120, *Complaint of Seas*

Shipping Company, Oct. 8, 1935, pp. 6–9.

326. *Ibid.,* pp. 10–13; see also Chapter I.

327. USSBB Docket 120, *Brief 'for Defendants,* Dec. 30, 1935, p. 5.

328. *Ibid.,* Agreement 3578 B.

329. See Chapter I.

330. USSBB Docket 120, *Complaint,* Oct. 8, 1935, p. 17, for actual detailed cut rates.

331. *Ibid.,* pp. 30–36, reproducing correspondence.

332. *New York Times,* Dec. 3, 4, 1935.

333. USSBB, Vol. I, p. 568.

334. L. C. Kendall, Ms. Memorandum, *The South African Rate War.*

335. *New York Times,* Aug. 5, 1936.

336. The most detailed account of the rate war and subsequent subsidy negotiations is to be found in United States Maritime Commission, No. S–1, reproduced in Hearings on Double Tracking, pp. 19–26.

337. *Our Ships,* by the Editors of *Fortune,* pp. 126–36, reproducing "H. R. 8555" and other articles from Maritime edition of *Fortune,* 1938. This gives one of the best accounts of the steps leading to the 1936 Act.

338. 72nd Congress, 2nd Session, Senate Resolution 349.

339. Black Hearings, *passim.*

340. *Ibid.,* pp. 907–66.

341. *Ibid.,* p. 964.

342. *Ibid.,* p. 955.

343. *Ibid.,* p. 952.

344. For the various Farrell maritime holdings on June 8, 1933 and Sept. 21, 1934, see National Archives, General Controller, United States Shipping Board Bureau, *Briefs on Foreign Ocean Mail Hearings.*

345. See *Brief of American South African Line, Inc., in Opposition to the Cancellation or Modification of Contract for Mail Service, F. O. M. 6,* 1934.

346. 49 Stat. 1485, Sec. 1101–1246.

347. See Chapter XIII.

348. Estimated totals based on Maritime Administration, *Operating-Differential Subsidies,* 1956, p. 19, with subsequent minor adjustments.

349. Farrell Lines, *Directors' Minutes,* May 3, 1949.

350. Maritime Administration, *Operating-Differential Subsidies,* 1956, p. 10.

351. See Appendix H.

352. *New York Times,* June 3, 1937; see also Nov. 12, 1936, Feb. 3, 1937.

353. *Ibid.,* April 19, 1936.

354. Merchant Marine Act of 1936, Sec. 605 (c).

355. Senate Commerce Committee, *Hearings on S2582,* (74th Congress, 1st Session), pp. 512–48; *Congressional Record,* Vol. 80, July 19, 1936, p. 10076; Hearings on Double Tracking, *Legislative History of Section 605 (c),* pp. 26–29.

356. United States Maritime Commission, *In the Matter of Application for Operating-Differential Subsidy, Memorandum on Behalf of Seas Shipping Company,* 1938, pp. 6, 8.

357. *Ibid., Brief for American South African Line,* May 4, 1938, p. 4.

358. *Ibid, Exceptions of American South African Line to Proposed Report,* June 1, 1938, pp. 8–9.

359. Hearings on Double Tracking, p. 22.

360. American South African Line, *Brief,* p. 18.

361. Hearings on Double Tracking, p. 25.

362. *Ibid.,* pp. 26–29.
363. James A. Farrell, Jr., to Admiral Emory S. Land, Sept. 19, 1938.
364. Congressional Information Bureau, Letter No. E-339, Sept. 30, 1938; also E-344, Oct. 11, 1938.
365. Senate Commerce Committee, *Merchant Marine Study and Investigation, Final Report* (81st Congress, 2nd Session, Senate Report 2494), p. 269.
366. House Merchant Marine and Fisheries Committee, *Hearings, Amending the Merchant Ma-*

rine Act, 1936, 1949, pp. 152–53, giving detailed annual figures for each line.
367. American South African Line, *Directors' Minutes,* Feb. 27, March 9, 1937; Shipping Board, *Seventh Annual Report,* 1923, pp. 98 and *passim.*
368. Hearings on Double Tracking, p. 32.
369. See Chapters X and XIV.
370. House Merchant Marine and Fisheries Committee, *Hearings, Amending the Merchant Marine Act, 1936, loc. cit.*

CHAPTER VIII

371. F. C. Lane, *Ships for Victory: A History of Shipbuilding Under the United States Maritime Commission in World War II,* pp. 21–32; F. G. Fassett, ed., *The Shipbuilding Business of the United States,* I, pp. 57–60, 89–101; E. S. Land, *Winning the War with Ships, passim.*
372. Maritime Commission, *Economic Survey of the American Merchant Marine,* 1937, pp. 39–42; Maritime Commission, *Annual Report,* 1939, p. 4.
373. American South African Line, *Directors' Minutes,* Aug. 17, 1939; *Lloyd's Register, passim.*
374. American South African Line, *Directors' Minutes,* April 1, 1940; Great Britain, Admiralty, *Merchant Vessels Lost or Damaged by Enemy Action during the Second World War, passim.*
375. American South African Line, *Directors' Minutes,* Aug. 16, Sept. 11, 1940; *Lloyd's Register,* 1941–53, *passim;* Great Britain, Admiralty, *op. cit.*
376. See Chapter IX.
377. *New York Times,* June 29,

1941; for further descriptions of the ship, see also March 10, Dec. 21, with photograph.
378. Agreement, Maritime Commission and American South African Line, March 16, 1942, re. Contract MCc 2496.
379. F. C. Lane, *op. cit.,* p. 33.
380. *New York Times,* Nov. 1, 1942.
381. F. C. Lane, *op. cit.,* p. 28; *Lloyd's Register, passim.* For the dimensions of the Farrell "Wests," C-2's and C-3's, see Appendix D; for Liberty ship statistics see E. S. Land, "The 'Wheel Horse' of World War II," United States Naval Institute *Proceedings,* Aug. 1958.
382. F. C. Lane, *op. cit.,* p. 4.
383. *Ibid.,* p. 8.
384. See Chapters IX and X.
385. American South African Line, *Application for Operational Subsidy,* Sept. 7, 1944; *New York Times,* March 25, 1945; Senate Committee on Commerce, *Hearings on Sale of Certain Government-Owned Vessels,* Sept. 14–Oct. 14, 1945, p. 19.

386. Farrell Lines, *Annual Report,* 1948.
387. James A. Farrell, Jr., statement, Application for Subsidy on Route 14, Sept. 1946.
388. Construction Differential Subsidy Agreement, Contract No. MCc-38569, March 6, 1945.
389. *New York Times,* Feb. 3, March 17, 1946.
390. Farrell Lines, *Annual Report,* 1948, giving "date purchased" for each ship of the fleet. Also, American Bureau of Shipping *Record,* 1948 and *passim,* giving full list of vessels built by each American yard.
391. Harvard Report, p. iii.
392. John G. B. Hutchins, "The American Shipping Industry since 1914," *Business Historical Review,* Vol. 28, June 1954, p. 119. See also his "United States Merchant Marine Policy and Surplus Ships," *Journal of Political Economy,* Vol. 59, 1951, p. 117.
393. Harvard Report, p. 1.
394. *Ibid.,* pp. 1–3.
395. 60 Stat. 41, Sec. 3–5.
396. See Chapters XI and XII.
397. C. C. Lewis, *West African Trade Route: Report Prepared for the Executive Committee,* Feb. 15, 1946, Exhibit B-2.
398. American South African Line, *Application to Purchase War-Built Vessels,* 1946.
399. See Chapter XIII.
400. Maritime Commission to American South African Line, Aug. 29, 1947; Farrell Lines to Maritime Commission, July 26, 1948; Farrell Lines, *Directors' Minutes, passim.*
401. *New York Times,* June 24, July 30, Sept. 1, 1949.
402. Committee of American Steamship Lines, *Tonnage of Member Lines,* 1955; the lists in most of the other sources are in gross rather than deadweight tons.

CHAPTER IX

403. See Chapter IV.
404. See Appendices B and C.
405. See Appendix A.
406. See Appendix B.
407. See Chapter IV.
408. See Chapter II.
409. John T. Rennie & Sons, Ms. Record, *American South African Line Ships on the Cape Town-Beira Range,* 1938.
410. See Appendix B.
411. See Chapter II for wartime developments in these and other commodities.
412. John T. Rennie & Sons, *loc. cit.*
413. M. H. de Kock, Governor of South African Reserve Bank, to author, July 29, 1958. See also Chapters II and X.
414. John T. Rennie & Sons, *loc. cit.*
415. See Chapter IV.
416. American South African Line, *Application for Operating-Differential Subsidy,* March 3, 1940, p. 14; American South African Line, *Directors' Minutes,* Jan. 5, 1940.
417. John T. Rennie & Sons, *loc. cit.* See also shipping advertisements in *Journal of Commerce* (New York), etc.
418. See Chapter VIII.
419. American South African Line, *Directors' Minutes,* March 31, Dec. 26, 1941; *New York Times,* March 2, 1941.
420. American South African Line

memorandum to Maritime Commission, 1942.

421. Chronological list of sinkings of United States ships in *Maritime Exchange Bulletin*, Aug. 1948.

422. Robert G. Albion and J. B. Pope, *Sea Lanes in Wartime*, p. 293.

423. *Farrell Lines News*, Oct. 1953, with reproduced picture.

424. H. L. Seward, Ms., *American South African Line Survey*, Oct. 2, 1943, p. 9.

425. See Chapter VIII.

426. Farrell Lines, *Quarterly Report of Executive Committee*, Oct. 8, 1946; *Tabulation of Vessels, Operated by Charterers and/or Agents of United States Maritime Commission*, various issues.

427. Report of John J. Monahan's trip to Washington, March 17, 1942.

428. *Norfolk Virginian-Pilot*, April 12, 1942; *Norfolk Ledger and Dispatch*, same date. The account of the sinking in Felix Riesenberg, Jr.'s, *Sea War*, pp. 74–75, is definitely inadequate.

429. *Farrell Lines News*, July, Oct. 1957; Jan., March 1958.

430. *Ibid.*, July 1957, p. 5; Jan. 1958, p. 4.

431. *Ibid.*, Jan. 1958, p. 8.

432. *Ibid.*, May 1958, p. 4

433. John T. Rennie & Sons, *loc. cit.*

434. *Farrell Lines News*, Jan. 1953, p. 4; Jan. 1955, p. 8; Oct. 1955, p. 5.

435. Farrell Lines, Marine Division, *Vessel Itineraries, African Sun*, Voyage 3.

436. S. E. Morison, *History of United States Naval Operations in World War II*, Vol. I, p. 179.

437. *Ibid.*

438. *Ibid.*, p. 188.

439. *Farrell Lines News*, April 1953, p. 5.

440. S. E. Morison, *op. cit.*, Vol. I, pp. 356–57.

441. House Merchant Marine and Fisheries Committee, *Hearings, Amending Merchant Marine Act, 1936*, 1949, pp. 152–53, giving detailed annual figures for each subsidized line.

442. Committee of American Steamship Lines, *Financial Analysis and Report of Companies Holding Differential Subsidy Contracts*, 1952, p. 5.

443. House Merchant Marine and Fisheries Committee, *Hearings, Amending Merchant Marine Act, 1936, loc. cit.*

444. E. S. Land, War Shipping Administration, *Report*, April 15, 1944.

445. Maritime Commission, *Special Report Prepared for Hon. George Weichel, Chairman, Merchant Marine and Fisheries Committee*, Feb. 16, 1948.

446. See Chapter VIII.

CHAPTER X

447. R. H. Thornton, *British Shipping*, pp. 93–94.

448. See Chapter VII.

449. George C. Wright, "Family Ship Team Shares Its Success," *New York Times*, Dec. 10, 1950, Sec. V, p. 7. See also "Shipping Men," *Fortune*, March 1949, pp. 100, 130.

450. See Farrell Lines *Directory*, in its annual editions, for lists of directors and officials; changes

Notes

in status are indicated in *Directors' Minutes.*

451. American South African Line, *Directors' Minutes,* Jan. 9, 1945.

452. See Chapters V and XII.

453. *Farrell Lines News,* Feb. 1957, p. 1; July 1957, p. 1.

454. *New York Times,* Dec. 19, 1956, ff.

455. See Chapter XIV.

456. Stevenson, Jordan & Harrison, Inc., Survey Reports: *Outward Cargo Booking and Documentation Procedures,* Nov. 1948; *Solicitation and Other Traffic Department Procedures,* May 1949; *Organization Charts and Job Descriptions,* May 1949; *Report on Organization and Procedures,* Aug. 1955.

457. For a detailed account of the organization and workings of a steamship line, see C. E. McDowell and H. M. Gibbs, *Ocean Transportation,* Chaps. 7–12; M. S. Rosenthal, *Techniques of International Trade.* For the British setup, see R. H. Thornton, *op. cit.,* Chaps. 9, 11.

458. Farrell Lines, *Summary of Shoreside Employee Benefit Plans,* Feb. 1958, *passim.*

459. The whole pier situation is reviewed in the New York City-Farrell Lines *Indentures* of March 4, 1958, based on Board of Estimates Resolutions of Jan. 23, 1958 (Calendar No. 12, 13). Further pier details and illustrations in "Farrell Lines—An Efficient Terminal Operation Concentrated at a Single Big Pier," *Via Port of New York,* March 1954, pp. 1–4.

460. Memorandum, F. C. Matthews to author, June 30, 1958; Farrell Lines, *Vessel Operating Year 1955. Statements, Voyage Results,*

461. Farrell Lines, *Annual Report,* 1948.

462. *Ibid.*

463. Farrell Lines, *Vessel Operating Statements, Voyage Results, Year 1955.*

464. *South African Investors' Guide,* 1954.

465. John T. Rennie & Sons, *The House of Rennie: One Hundred Years of Shipping, passim;* Marischal Murray, *Ships and South Africa, passim.*

466. See Chapter XII for further details.

467. This whole episode is reviewed in detail, including quotations of such correspondence, in James A. Farrell, Jr., to the chairman of the Maritime Commission, March 7, 1947.

468. *Farrell Lines News,* Oct. 1953, p. 1.

469. A full list of all agents is in the annual Farrell Lines *Directory,* while pictures and brief notices of them appear from time to time in the *Farrell Lines News.*

470. See Chapter XII.

471. Farrell Lines notices of appointment as master.

472. See Chapter V.

473. See Chapters IX and XII.

474. See Appendix G for individual data.

475. Farrell Lines, *Annual Report,* 1948.

476. Remarks of James A. Farrell, Jr., to the graduating class of the Maine Maritime Academy, Castine, Maine, July 31, 1954.

477. Senate Commerce Committee, *Interim Report: Waterfront Investigation: New York-New Jersey,* July 27, 1953 (83rd Con-

gress, 1st Session, Senate Report No. 653), *passim.*

478. The most comprehensive history of the maritime labor movement is J. P. Goldberg, *The Maritime Story: A Study in Labor-Management Relations.* The best account of shipboard functions and status is *Earnings and Employment of Seamen on U.S. Flag Ships,* (U.S. Bureau of Labor Statistics, Bulletin No. 1238, Nov. 1958).

479. Senate Commerce Committee, *loc. cit.*

480. *New York Maritime Register,* Weekly Compendium, *passim.* See also Chapter VII.

481. National Maritime Union, *op. cit.,* p. 59, picture showing list of "ships out."

482. Farrell Lines, *Annual Report,* 1948.

483. See comparative tables in House Merchant Marine and Fisheries Committee, *Hearings on Labor-Management Problems of the American Merchant Marine,* June 20–July 20, 1955,

pp. 946–51; *Earnings and Employment of Seamen, passim.*

484. Remarks of James A. Farrell, Jr., to the graduating class of the Maine Maritime Academy, Castine, Maine, July 31, 1954.

485. National Archives, Shipping Board MSS., Memorandum, A. H. Bull & Company to Emergency Fleet Corporation, 1926; Farrell Lines, *Vessel Operating Statements, Voyage Results, Year 1955, African Planet,* Voyage 32.

486. House Merchant Marine and Fisheries Committee, *op. cit.,* pp. 1, 2, and *passim.*

487. For increase in longshoremen's and seamen's wages, 1937–54, see *ibid.,* p. 934.

488. "Shipping Men," *Fortune,* March 1949, p. 99.

489. Ivy Lee and T. J. Ross, *Memorandum on Public Relations for the Government-Aided American Shipping Lines,* p. 12.

490. CASL Files, Minutes Sept. 15, 1952 Dinner at University Club.

CHAPTER XI

491. *Commerce Reports,* Supplement 1920, 70a, p. 9.

492. Captain C. W. Schmidt to Farrell Lines, from *African Grove,* Jan. 17, 1950.

493. On West African ports in general see F. J. Pedler, *Economic Geography of West Africa;* B. E. Thomas, "Railways and Ports in French West Africa," *Economic Geography,* Jan. 1957; and W. A. Hance, *African Economic Development,* Chapter IV.

494. United States Hydrographic Office, H. O. No. 117, *Table of Distances between Ports.*

495. Theodore Hunter and Jarvis Patten, *Port Charges . . . in the Ports of the World,* 1884, p. 362.

496. H. R. Jarrett, "The Port and Town of Freetown," *Geography,* April 1955; "The Port of Freetown, Sierre Leone," *Dock and Harbour Authority,* July 1953.

497. *Commercial Relations of the United States,* 1908, Vol. II, p. 814.

498. George Wauchope, Ms., *Proposed West African Service,* July 1946.

499. Wayne C. Taylor, *Firestone Operations in Liberia* (Na-

tional Planning Association, United States Business Performance Abroad, Case Study No. 5), *pasim.*

500. See especially *Dock and Harbour Authority,* July 1951, pp. 69–74.

501. See Chapter XII.

502. Captain C. W. Schmidt to Farrell Lines, Feb. 1950.

503. Farrell Lines, Monrovia Resident Manager's Report, Feb. 10, 1948.

504. Captain C. W. Schmidt to Farrell Lines, Feb. 1950.

505. J. L. Tournier, "The Port of Abidjan: Development of Harbour Facilities in French West Africa," *Dock and Harbour Authority,* March 1958.

506. Maritime Commission, Official Transcript of Hearing, *Application for subsidy on Trade Route 14, Sept. 4, 1946;* Testimony of Captain George Wauchope, pp. 66–67.

507. "Port Capacity and Shipping Turnaround in West Africa," *Economic and Statistical Review* (United Africa Company), No. 19, March 1957, p. 3.

508. Captain C. W. Schmidt to Farrell Lines, Jan. 17, 1950.

509. This Nigerian trade and shipping is particularly well described in *Merchant Adventure,* the story of John Holt & Company.

510. W. A. Hance and I. S. van Dongen, "Matadi, Focus of Belgian African Transport," *Annals of the Association of American Geographers,* March 1958.

511. Adapted from Belgian Congo, Secrétariat Général, Section Statistique, *Bulletin Mensuel du Commerce Exterieur,* Vol. VI, Dec. 1955, pp. 287–94; Vol. VII, Feb. 1956, pp. 185–88, as tabulated in W. A. Hance and I. S. van Dongen, "Matadi," p. 49.

512. See Appendices A and C.

513. W. A. Hance and I. S. van Dongen, "The Port of Lobito and the Benguela Railway," *Geographical Review,* Oct. 1956; I. S. van Dongen, "Angola," *Focus,* Oct. 1957. See also Chapter III.

CHAPTER XII

514. See Chapter V.

515. See Chapter II.

516. *Sea Breezes,* Sept. 1948, pp. 150–68.

517. Tabulated from fleet lists in *Lloyd's Register,* 1949–50, Vol. II, pp. 59, 190.

518. 31st Congress, 1st Session, *House Report No. 438;* also published separately together with "An Appendix added by the American Colonization Society."

519. *Commercial Relations of the* *United States,* 1907, Pt. I, p. 704.

520. Alexander Hearings, Huebner Summary, IV, pp. 97–99.

521. *Commerce Reports,* Supplement, 1920, 70a, p. 15.

522. See Chapter V for details of Shipping Board's service and sales.

523. *Marine Review,* Nov. 1919, p. 516.

524. Black Hearings, p. 1384.

525. For full list of Barber agents, see George Wauchope, Ms.,

Proposed West African Service,
p. 26.

526. See Chapter VI.

527. Black Hearings, p. 1425.

528. Shipping Board, *Seventeenth Annual Report,* 1933, p. 71.

529. Harvard Report, p. 60.

530. George Wauchope, *op. cit.,* p. 6.

531. American West African Line Financial Statements for 1936 and 1937, quoted in C. C. Lewis, *West African Trade Route: Report Prepared for the Executive Committee,* Feb. 15, 1946, Exhibit C.

532. See Chapter VI.

533. *Official Transcript: Before the United States Maritime Commission, In the Matter of: The application for financial aid in the operation of a service between United States Atlantic and Gulf ports and West Coast of Africa, filed by American South African Line, Incorporated, and Mississippi Shipping Company, Incorporated, Washington, D.C., September 4, 1946* (hereafter cited as Official Transcript), pp. 15–16.

534. C. C. Lewis, *op. cit.*

535. See Chapter V.

536. Telegram, American South African Line to Maritime Commission, July 19, 1946.

537. Official Transcript, p. 103.

538. See Chapter VII.

539. Official Transcript, p. 12.

540. *Ibid.,* pp. 38–39.

541. *Ibid.,* p. 53.

542. *Ibid.,* pp. 105–18, 139.

543. *Ibid.,* p. 143.

544. *Ibid.,* p. 37.

545. *Ibid.,* p. 96.

546. See Chapter XIII.

547. See Chapter X for details of agency quest.

548. See Chapter VIII.

549. *Ibid.*

550. This whole section, unless otherwise indicated, is based upon two detailed reports of Maguire to Wauchope.

551. Farrell Lines Marine Division, *Voyage Itineraries.*

552. *New York Times,* Nov. 2, 1947.

553. Farrell Lines, *Quarterly Report of Executive Committee,* April 13, 1948.

554. Monrovia Resident Manager's Report, *passim.*

555. See Chapter XI.

556. Monrovia Resident Manager's Report, *passim.*

557. United States State Department, Executive Agreement Series, 411; Agreement of Dec. 3, 1943, between Liberia and the United States.

558. For details of dimensions and service of the various feeder craft, see Appendices D and E.

559. Monrovia Resident Manager's Report, *passim.*

560. See Chapter XI.

561. *Farrell Lines News,* Jan. 1953, p. 7, for typical list of feeder fleet officers; full data on feeder craft in Appendix E.

562. Farrell Lines, *Quarterly Report of Executive Committee,* Aug. 12, 1949.

563. Farrell Lines, *Annual Report,* 1949; Farrell Lines to Maritime Administration, July 28, 1950.

564. W. C. Shields to Barber Line, July 22, 1954.

565. Farrell Lines Monrovia memorandum, Jan. 1957.

566. Farrell Lines, *Executive Committee Minutes,* Sept. 20, 1950.

567. See Appendix A.

568. See Chapter XI.

569. Wauchope to Polpen, March 7, 1952.

CHAPTER XIII

570. See Chapter VIII for ship details.

571. American South African Line, *Quarterly Report of Executive Committee,* Jan. 2, 1946.

572. American South African Line, *Annual Report,* 1946.

573. American South African Line, *Quarterly Report of Executive Committee,* July 2, 1946; Oct. 8, 1946.

574. See Chapter IX.

575. Harvard Report, p. 3; see Chapter VIII.

576. 60 Stat. 4, Sec. 5b; Maritime Commission, *Bareboat Charter Agreement on War-built Dry-cargo Vessels,* Sept. 2, 1946; Maritime Commission, *Annual Report,* 1947, p. 1.

577. See Chapter VIII.

578. Farrell Lines, Marine Division, *Vessel Itineraries.*

579. Maritime Commission, Traffic Analysis Branch, *Farrell Lines Foreign Flag Competition encountered on Trade Route 15-A, 1947–1948,* May 3, 1950.

580. See Chapters I, VII, and IX.

581. Maritime Commission, Traffic Analysis Branch, *op. cit.* The Maritime Commission reported to Farrell what its foreign-flag competitors were carrying, but did not give figures for its American-flag competitors, Robin and Lykes.

582. *Ibid.,* appendices showing "Amount and Per Cent of Dry Cargo Commercial Lines Traffic"; "List of Freighter Type Vessels of Principal Foreign Flag Lines"; and "Sailing Frequencies and Itineraries Usually Followed."

583. "South Africa's Merchant Marine is Growing," *South African Exporter,* April 1958, p. 8.

584. "Shipping Men," *Fortune,* March 1949, p. 131; *New York Times,* June 28, 1946.

585. *Ibid.,* April 13, 1947; see also *Sea Breezes,* July 1950, pp. 50–52.

586. *New York Times,* Aug. 22, 1947. For a further development of these ideas, see *South African Stockholders' Manual,* 1954, p. 921.

587. See, for example, "Safmarine" advertisement, *Natal Mercury,* June 17, 1949.

588. Maritime Commission, Traffic Analysis Branch, *op cit.; South African Stockholders' Manual, loc. cit.*

589. Defendants' Brief, United States vs. States Marine Corporation.

590. *South African Exporter, op. cit.,* p. 9.

591. Harvard Report, pp. 33–34.

592. *Ibid.,* pp. 63–64.

593. *Annual Report of the Postmaster General,* 1891, pp. 1067–72; 1929, pp. 35–36; 1930, p. 142; 1931, p. 131; 1932, p. 23; 1933, p. 18. Shipping Board, Circular letter, April 28, 1923; Shipping Board and Maritime Commission, *Annual Reports, passim; Economic Survey of the American Merchant Marine,* 1937, pp. 15–16; Maritime Administration, *Review of Essential Foreign Trade Routes,* 1953, pp. 4–5, and later editions; see also Appendix H.

594. See, for example, disgruntled article from *Shipping Survey,* quoted in House Merchant Marine and Fisheries Committee, *Hearings on Proposed*

Amendments to the Merchant Marine Act of 1936, 1953, p. 441.

595. Maritime Commission to American South African Line, July 23, 1946.

596. See Chapter XII for subsidy grant to Farrell Lines for Route 14-1.

597. See Chapter VIII.

598. See Appendix A for annual overall totals.

599. See Appendix B for annual commodity totals.

600. Farrell Lines, *Traffic Summaries,* 1948.

601. See Appendix F for analysis of the *African Planet's* cargo and voyage statistics.

602. See Chapter IX.

603. United States Department of Commerce, *Investment in the Union of South Africa: Conditions and Outlook for United States Investors,* 1954, pp. 13–14.

604. M. H. de Kock, Governor of South African Reserve Bank, to author, July 29, 1958.

605. Farrell Lines, *Annual Report,* 1948.

606. Farrell Lines, *Directors' Minutes* and *Executive Committee Minutes, passim.*

607. Farrell Lines, Marine Division, *Voyage Itineraries.*

608. Farrell Lines, *Directors' Minutes,* Sept. 12, Oct. 10, Dec. 12, 1950, Jan. 12, 1951; *Annual Report,* 1950.

609. Farrell Lines, *Executive Committee Minutes,* June 30, 1950; *Directors' Minutes,* Oct. 7, 1952.

610. *New York Times,* Dec. 17, 1944; American South African Line, *Quarterly Report of the Executive Committee,* July 3, 1945.

611. *New York Times,* June 2, 1946.

612. Memorandum, Farrell Passenger Traffic Files.

613. Memorandum, South African Tourist Corporation to author, Oct. 17, 1958.

614. Farrell Lines, *Report of Sales Promotion Committee,* Jan. 4, 1956; *Directors' Minutes,* Jan. 10, 1956; David Sherrard, *Financial and Statistical Digest of South Africa,* 1955, pp. 110–15; Cunard-Union-Castle advertisement, *New York Times Magazine,* Feb. 26, 1956.

615. See Chapter VI.

616. See Chapter IV.

617. For further data on captains, see Chapter X and Appendix G.

618. Farrell Lines, *South and East African Services: Outward and Homeward Schedules,* No. 50, Dec. 20, 1957. See also Chapter III.

619. See Chapter XIV.

CHAPTER XIV

620. Luncheon remarks, transmitted by E. H. Louw to C. W. Schmidt, April 8, 1957.

621. M. H. de Kock, Governor of South African Reserve Bank, to author, July 29, 1958.

622. *New York Times,* April 18, 1926, Sec. II, p. 19.

623. *New York Times Magazine,* Jan. 13, 1957.

624. *Ibid.,* Nov. 18, 1956.

625. See Chapter I.

626. Consul Edwin S. Cunningham, Durban, *Commercial Relations of the United States,* 1907, Vol. I, p. 748.

627. Monrovia Resident Manager's Report, 1947.
628. See Chapter I.
629. See Chapter X.
630. *New York Times,* May 25, 1958; *South African Scope,* Nov. 1957, p. 1.
631. *South African Scope,* Nov. 1958, p. 1; *Ibid,* Jan. 1959, p. 5.
632. Dillon, Read & Company, prospectus: *$15,000,000 Union of South Africa Ten Year 5½ per cent External Loan Bonds,* Jan. 20, 1956.
633. See Chapter III.
634. United States Department of Commerce, *Investment in the Union of South Africa: Conditions and Outlook for the United States Investors,* 1954.
635. *Statistical Abstract of the United States,* 1957, p. 878.
636. *Ibid.*
637. See Chapters XI and XII.
638. *Statistical Abstract of the United States,* 1957, pp. 251–52.
639. *South African Scope,* July 1958, p. 7; *New York Herald Tribune,* June 22, 1958, Union of South Africa Section, p. 1; Dillon, Read & Company, prospectus: *American-South African Investment Company, Limited, 1,200,000 Common Shares,* Sept. 17, 1958; *$6,000,000 Federation of Rhodesia and Nyasaland External Loan Bonds,* June 1958.
640. See Chapter IV.
641. Marischal Murray, *Union-Castle Chronicle,* pp. 313–15; *Commerce Reports,* Vol. 28-2, 1925, pp. 470–71.
642. *British and South African Export Gazette,* Nov. 1925, p. 921.
643. *Commerce Reports,* 1936, pp. 822, 890.

644. See Chapter X.
645. *British and South African Export Gazette,* Sept. 1936.
646. *New York Times,* May 6, 1937.
647. See Chapter XIII.
648. *New York Times,* June 19, 1946.
649. *Commerce Reports,* Vol. 17-1, 1914, p. 333; 21-3, 1918, p. 889; *British and South African Export Gazette,* March 1914, p. 320; J. E. McFee, "Trade in South African Rock Lobster Expanding," *Mooremack News,* Spring 1958, p. 10; *South African Scope,* Nov. 1958, p. 12.
650. See Chapters II and VIII.
651. Maine, Public Law 260, 1941; *Revised Statutes,* 1957, Sec. 107; Massachusetts Public Law 598, 1941; *Annotated Laws of Massachusetts,* c. 150, p. 51.
652. 82nd Congress, S-1514; HR-4174, 4175, 4177; Farrell Lines to House Committee on Interstate and Foreign Commerce, June 19, 1951.
653. Senate Committee on Interstate and Foreign Commerce, *Hearings on Fisheries Legislation,* July 15–17, 1958, pp. 14, 34–58, 239.
654. *Ibid.,* p. 35, testimony of W. Clifford Shields.
655. *Portland Press-Herald,* March 6, 1958.
656. E. Winthrop Hall to author, April 8, 1958.
657. E. Winthrop Hall to Farrell Lines, 1957.
658. Farrell Lines, *Annual Report,* 1948; see Chapter XII.
659. Farrell Lines, *Executive Committee Minutes,* June 30, 1950.
660. *Budget of Fiscal Year,* 1955, 1956, passim; *Statistical Abstract of the United States,* passim; *World Almanac,* 1958, pp. 652, 751.
661. Wytze Gorter, *United States*

Shipping Policy (published for the Council of Foreign Relations), p. 198.

662. *Maritime Affairs*, March 1957; see also Clarence C. Morse, Maritime Administrator, in *Marine News*, Sept. 1957.

663. *Ibid.*

664. *New York Herald Tribune*, Feb. 23, March 25, April 26, 1957.

665. Farrell Lines, Meeting at the University Club, Nov. 25, 1957, Re: New Operating-Differential and Construction-Differential Subsidy Agreements. (Ms. Minutes).

666. James A. Farrell, Jr., Statement in behalf of application for Operating-Differential Subsidy on Trade Route 14A, Sept. 1946.

INDEX

Abidjan, 199, 206, 216, 224, 228, 236
Accra, 198, 208, 225
Africa, 15ff; *see* East Africa, South Africa, West Africa
African Comet, 141, 284, 285
African Crescent, 145, 248, 284
African Dawn, 142, 148, 165, 252, 256, 265, 270, 284
African Endeavor, 150–51, 253, 254ff, 274, 280, 284, 285
African Enterprise, 150–51, 254ff, 274, 280, 284, 285
African Glade, 107, 149, 226ff, 252, 284, 285
African Glen, 107, 149, 226, 284, 285
African Grove, 149, 174, 205, 228, 237, 284, 285
African Guide, 232ff, 284, 285
African Lightning, 145, 174, 252, 284
African Meteor, 141, 284, 285
African Moon, 145, 174, 248, 284, 285
African Patriot, 150, 230, 246, 253, 284, 285
African Pilgrim, 30, 150, 246, 253, 284, 285
African Pilot, 150, 246, 253, 284, 285
African Planet, I, 141, 284, 285
African Planet, II, 145, 248, 252, 257, 284, 286–87
African Rainbow, 145–46, 253, 284
African Star, I, 142, 165, 284, 285
African Star, II, 30, 145, 240, 272, 284
African Sun, 58, 142, 149, 165, 238, 240, 252, 256, 284
Agents and representatives, 8, 178ff, 226ff, 257, 287
Agricultural Machinery & Implements, 35, 71, 216, 248, 282
Air lines, competition, 254–55
American Export Lines 82, 88, 90, 110, 130, 132, 151, 288
American Mail Line, 131, 194, 288
American Merchant Marine Institute, 188, 192, 196
American President Lines, 131, 151, 288
American South African Line, origin of name, 88; sold to Farrells, 101ff; extension of service, 116ff; becomes Farrell Lines, 217; and *passim*
American West African Line, 83, 101, 103, 156, 220ff
Angola, 17, 22, 27, 182, 198ff, 215, 228, 235
Animals, transportation of, 30

Argonaut Line, 94, 119, 121, 126, 128, 140, 157, 159, 186, 257, 285
Arthur, E. C., 162
Atlantic, 77, 99, 119, 140, 284, 285
Automobiles, 31, 71, 86, 115, 126, 214, 216, 236, 247, 259, 282, 283, 286

Barber Steamship Co., 82, 101, 103, 220ff, 225, 235ff
Beira, 38, 48ff, 54, 86, 101, 118, 125, 156, 180, 209, 214, 216, 252, 258
Belgian Congo, 20, 22, 26ff, 37, 59, 154, 182, 211ff, 236, 267, 281, 283
Belgian Line, 215, 218, 229, 237
Black Committee, 112, 127ff, 192
Bloomfield Steamship Co., 131, 149, 246, 253, 288
Bucknall Line, 9, 94, 96; *and see* Ellerman & Bucknall
Bull, A. H. & Co., 62, 82, 88, 220
Bull, Ernest M., 102–03, 252
Bunkerage and fuel, 109, 118, 145
Byrne, J. T., Jr., 183

Cameroons, 199, 200, 210
Canary Islands, 197, 199, 220, 228
Cape of Good Hope, 15, 40
Cape Town, 8, 9, 38, 57, 66, 69, 86, 162, 180, 183, 249, 256, 271, 286–87; and *passim*
Cargo details, 9, 31, 109, 157, 248, 286
Cayzer, Irvine & Co., 9; *see* Clan Line
Challenger, 136, 141, 157, 165, 284, 285
Charles H. Cramp, 98, 119, 121, 135, 141, 146, 157, 160, 165, 284, 285
Chartering, 6, 94, 100, 136, 158, 160, 239ff, 247, 252ff
Chincha, 108, 118, 120, 140, 284, 285
Chrome, 21, 50, 52, 54, 109, 157, 267, 282, 287
City of New York, 108, 112, 136, 141, 150, 157, 161, 163ff, 188, 254, 256, 268, 271, 284, 285
Clan Line, 9, 51, 124, 241
Cloves, 25, 31, 60
Cocoa, 27, 208, 210, 220, 235, 283
Coffee, 26, 210, 214ff, 235, 258, 282, 283
Committee of American Steamship Lines, (CASL), 192ff
Conakry, 199, 201
Conference, U.S.A.-South Africa, 10, 12, 65, 85, 110, 117, 124ff, 157, 240, 278; West African, 210, 240

313

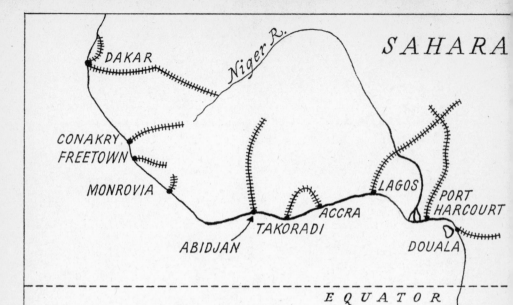

SAHARA

DAKAR

CONAKRY
FREETOWN

MONROVIA

ABIDJAN

TAKORADI

ACCRA

LAGOS

PORT
HARCOURT

DOUALA

Niger R.

EQUATOR

POINTE
NOIRE

MATAD

.Ascension

LUANDA

LOBITO

RIVAL RAIL ROUTES	Miles	Completed
From Johannesburg to		
Lourenco Marques	394	1894
Durban	482	1895
East London	665	1892
Port Elizabeth	712	1892
Cape Town	956	1892
From N'dola (Copperbelt) to		
Beira	1,446	1909
Lourenco Marques ("Limpopo")	1,449	1955
Lobito ("Benguela")	1,478	1931
Durban	1,938	1909
Port Elizabeth	2,064	1909
From Elisabethville (Katanga) to		
Lobito ("Benguela")	1,309	1931
Lourenco Marques ("Limpopo")	1,612	1955
Beira	1,619	1909
Port Francqui (Kaisai River)	1,932	1928
Durban	2,001	1909
Port Elizabeth	2,327	1909

WAL
B.

Principal Ports
and Railways
SOUTH OF SAHARA

MILES └─────┴─────┴─────┘
         100   300   500